The Hunt in Ancient Greece

THE HUNT IN ANCIENT GREECE

Judith M. Barringer

THE JOHNS HOPKINS UNIVERSITY PRESS
BALTIMORE AND LONDON

The Johns Hopkins University Press
2715 North Charles Street
Baltimore, Maryland 21218-4363
www.press.jhu.edu

LIBRARY OF CONGRESS CATALOGING-IN-PUBLICATION DATA
Barringer, Judith M., 1959–
The hunt in ancient Greece / Judith M. Barringer.
p.   cm.
Includes bibliographical references and index.
ISBN 0-8018-6656-1
1. Hunting—Greece—History—To 146 B.C.
2. Greece—Civilization—To 146 B.C.
I. Title.
SK203 .B37 2001
799.2938—dc21
00-011276
A catalog record for this book is available
from the British Library.

For Ino and Agave,
who taught me all they know about hunting,
and, most of all,
for Greg

CONTENTS

Tables are on pages 60–69 and 172–173

ACKNOWLEDGMENTS

This book has been a long time in coming and would have been a far lesser product were it not for the assistance of many people. Richard Garner discussed every stage of this project with me, asked probing questions, and read and commented on the manuscript numerous times. Unstinting in his friendship, his intellect, and his time, he often lit the way for me and helped me see what I could no longer see. Sarah Peirce read and thought carefully about several portions of this book; I have profited greatly from detailed and enjoyable discussions with her. Eve D'Ambra, Bettina Kreuzer, Susan Matheson, and Olga Palagia also read various parts of this book and kindly offered their reactions, suggestions for improvement, and references to relevant material. Anneliese Kossatz-Deissmann also provided assistance and references for chapter 3. Jerry Pollitt continues to set an example of intellectual exploration and excellence. I benefited from his comments on parts of this study and remain indebted to him not only for his wisdom but also for his encouragement and friendship. It is a pleasure to acknowledge the generosity of these friends and colleagues, who have certainly kept me on the right track and bettered this book, though they bear no responsibility for errors that might remain.

Alain Schnapp has been an enthusiastic supporter of this project and kindly sent me his book *Le Chasseur et la cité* as soon as it was published. Ann Steiner made available to me her unpublished book manuscript, from which I profited greatly. I owe a great debt to Diana Kleiner, John Oakley, and Alan Shapiro, who together with others already mentioned in these acknowledgments offered their support, counsel, and friendship over the years.

A Richardson-Goldsmith Fellowship at the Whitney Humanities Center, Yale University, in 1993–94 enabled me to get started on this project in earnest, and the Blegen Research Fellowship at Vassar College in 1998–99 speeded its conclusion and also funded a trip to Turkey to examine some of the monuments discussed in this text. I am also indebted to members of the library staff at Yale University, who have lent a hand at every turn.

Audiences at Boston University, Bryn Mawr College, Tufts University, State University of New York at Buffalo, University of Texas at Austin, Vassar College, the Whitney Humanities Center at Yale University, and at the annual APA/AIA meeting in 1998 in Washington, D.C., heard various parts of the manuscript as it progressed from its earliest stages on, and I thank all participants for their stimulating questions and discussion.

For providing photographs and permissions for this publication, I am grateful to the following individuals and institutions: Susanne Reim, Lindenau-Museum, Altenburg; Ioannis Touratsoglou, National Museum, Athens; Vera Slehoferova, Antikenmuseum Basel und Sammlung Ludwig; Kristine Gex-Morgenthaler, Archäologisches Seminar der Universität, Basel; Ilona Trabert, Antikensammlung, Staatliche Museen zu Berlin; Gerhard Joehrens, Deutsches Archäologisches Institut, Berlin; Cristiana Morigi Govi, Museo Civico Archeologico, Bologna; Christopher Atkins and Leah Ross, Museum of Fine Arts, Boston; Fitzwilliam Museum, Cambridge; Elizabeth Gombosi, Harvard University Art Museums, Cambridge; Emily S. Rosen, The Cleveland Museum of Art; Bodil Bundgaard Rasmussen, Nationalmuseet, Copenhagen; Jette Christiansen, Ny Carlsberg Glyptotek, Copenhagen; Torben Melander, Thorvaldsens Museum, Copenhagen; Marina Volonté, Museo Civico, Cremona; M. Cristina Guidotti, Soprintendenza Archeologica, Florence; Uta Wallenstein, Schlossmuseum, Gotha; Thomas Berg, Museum für Kunst und Gewerbe, Hamburg; Axel Filges, Deutsches Archäologisches Institut, Istanbul; Caroline Jorrand, Musée Archéologique Municipal, Laon; Peter Jan Bomhof, Rijksmuseum van Oudheden, Leiden; Ivor Kerslake, The British Museum, London; Jocelyne Timm, Sotheby's, London; Jacklyn Burns, The J. Paul Getty Museum, Malibu; V. Brinkmann, Staatliche Antikensammlungen, Munich; The Metropolitan Museum of Art, New York; Ashmolean Museum, Oxford; Bibliothèque nationale de France, Paris; Pierrick Jan and Michel Richard, Réunion des Musées Nationaux, Paris; Christian Le Roy, *Revue archéologique*, Presses universitaires de France, Paris; Brigitte Taillez, Musée du Louvre, Paris; Melody Ennis, Museum of Art, Rhode Island School of Design, Providence; Anna Maria Moretti, Soprintendenza Archeologica per l'Etruria Meridionale, Rome; Anna Sommella Mura, Sovraintendenza ai Beni Culturali, Rome; Edith Cicerchia and Francesco Riccardi, Monumenti Musei e Gallerie Pontificie, Rome; Giuseppe Andreassi, Soprintendenza Archeologica della Puglia, Taranto; Elisabeth Reicher and Alfred Bernhard-Walcher, Kunsthistorisches Museum, Vienna; and Irma Wehgartner, Martin von Wagner Museum, Universität, Würzburg. I owe a special thanks to the ever patient Hans Rupprecht Goette at the Deutsches Archäologisches Institut, Athens, who entertained many requests and questions and was always willing to help. Thanks also to Jan Jordan at the Agora Museum, Athens; J. Stroszeck at the Kerameikos Museum, Athens; and N. Prokopiou at the National Museum, Athens, who offered kind hospitality and a willingness to allow me to examine objects closely, and to the staff of The American School of Classical Studies in Athens under the directorship of James Muhly, which facilitated these visits.

Others have sustained me at a more fundamental, day-to-day level with their friendship and humor and deserve special recognition. I again cite Eve D'Ambra, Richard Garner, Bettina Kreuzer, and Sarah Peirce, and add Mary Albis, Robert Albis, Emily Anhalt, Mary Ann Carolan, Karen Hanson, Leslie Morris, Eric Orlin, Joanne Schneider, Paula Schwartz, and Deanna Shemek. Special heartfelt thanks go to Michéle Dominy, who gave so much and asked for so little, and to Beth Margolis, who liberated me so that I could finish this.

I wish to thank the excellent staff at the Johns Hopkins University Press. Brian MacDonald's thoughtful copyediting bettered the text in many ways, and Julie McCarthy provided careful editing and patient response to questions at the end stages. Maura Burnett offered encouragement and forbearance and kept me laughing throughout the last stages of this work.

I am enormously thankful for my cheerful and patient feline companions Ino and Agave, who have been right by my side (and on my desk) throughout the years as I worked on this book. My greatest debt (and one that I can never repay) is to my husband, Greg, who has read and commented upon the entire manuscript, shared my travels and dreams, and given me support, encouragement, and happiness beyond measure. I have learned the most important things from him.

NOTE ON ABBREVIATIONS

Abbreviations used for ancient authors are those set forth in S. Hornblower and A. Spawforth, eds., *The Oxford Classical Dictionary*, 3d ed. (Oxford, 1996), xxix–liv, and modern journal and book abbreviations generally follow the guidelines of the *American Journal of Archaeology* 104 (2000): 10–24. Exceptions to this format are the abbreviations *Para* for J. D. Beazley, *Paralipomena* (Oxford, 1971), and *Addenda²* for T. H. Carpenter, *Beazley Addenda²* (Oxford, 1989). All dates used in the discussion of the ancient world are B.C. unless noted otherwise.

The Hunt in Ancient Greece

INTRODUCTION

Hunting, once a necessity for survival in some distant past, had ceased to play this basic role in Greek life long before the archaic and classical periods, the time under consideration in this book. Nevertheless, the hunt had a significant place in archaic and classical Greece, both in cultural representations and in practice. Why did hunting survive in art, literature, and in actuality long past its utilitarian function? Clearly, some other factor is at work. One might point to the ubiquitous hunting images in Homeric poetry and the influence of such poetry on Greek society, but this offers only a partial answer. Although the Homeric poems liberally employ hunting similes to describe human battles, the comparison usually involves a lion attacking another animal, a motif surely borrowed from Near Eastern royal tradition, where images of animals attacking other animals adorn palaces and royal objects. Near Eastern images, particularly Assyrian and Achaemenid depictions of armed kings hunting animals (mostly lions) with bow and arrow from chariots, may have provided some models for human confrontations with lions on Greek Geometric pottery and seventh-century Protocorinthian pottery (which also includes other prey as well). And we see the influence of this Eastern royal hunt again in the fourth century on the Alexander Sarcophagus and at Vergina. But in the archaic and classical periods, images of hunting in Greek art, specifically Attic art, take their own form: instead of Eastern lions, we find boar, deer, and hare, animals native to Greece. Lion hunting virtually disappears from Greek art after the seventh century B.C. with the exception of Herakles' wrestling the Nemean lion, a motif itself borrowed from the Near East but not properly a hunt. In archaic and classical Greek images, hunters never hunt from chariots (as do their Near Eastern counterparts) but from horseback or, more commonly, on foot. There is no royal entourage, merely a group of men, attired and armed as Greeks.

What did hunting mean to the Greeks of the archaic and classical periods? The investigation of this question, particularly for Athenian society of the sixth, fifth, and fourth centuries B.C., is the subject of this book. What types of hunting are there, and what relationship exists between hunter and prey? Why do Greek art and literature depict hunting, and what messages or information do these images (both written and visual) convey? Who is the intended audience? Why is hunting so common in myth, and what do such myths mean? Why and where is hunting used as a rite of passage for young men? How and why does the hunt serve as a metaphor for other activities? The answers to these questions involve investigation of many types of evidence, including vase painting, sculpture, "high" literature, and inscriptions, and of the issues of social class, sexuality, gender, and culture. Consequently, the methodologies employed here are varied: semiotics, political theory, structural anthropology, and gender theory. Athenian material of the sixth through fourth century, both visual and written, is the focus of this project, but by necessity evidence from other regions and time periods, particularly postclassical written evidence, is used to amplify and illuminate it. This text restricts its purview to images of humans killing animals and does not address the numerous images of animals fighting or killing other animals.[1] Included here, however, are images of hunters themselves, the return from the hunt, and the presentation of spoils of the hunt. In addition to these literal images, metaphorical hunts—warfare and erotic pursuit—are also integral to this study.

Certain assumptions underlie this investigation. Greek art, particularly Greek vase painting, does not offer snapshots of real life or a faithful record of real events. This claim will come as no surprise to many of those working with vase painting, especially to my colleagues in the Parisian school, who have long recognized that Greek vase paintings and Greek art in general are cultural constructs, selective, manipulated images that employ their own language to reflect societal values and beliefs. But many classicists continue in the false belief that these representations are direct records of the "real" and fail to recognize that vase paintings are not plein-air paintings or documentary photographs, faithfully recording an event as it happened, nor are they slice-of-life depictions, capturing "a moment in the life of."[2] For example, Greek images of humans hunting animals are representations of valor in the face of danger: animals are sometimes enormous in comparison with the hunters, who are often few in number; their weapons, often spears, seem inconsequential next to the ferocity or swiftness of the prey. Yet some of these enormous animals are hares, animals that do not pose a threat to their human predators, or deer, fleet-footed but hardly fierce creatures. This distinction between actuality and representation is thus critical to understanding Greek art.

Another important methodological point concerns the difference between the point of manufacture of the art examined here, Athens, and the findspot of many of the items, beyond Attica. Athenian-manufactured vases compose the largest body of visual evidence in this cultural study, but most Attic vases were found in Etruria. So questions of artistic intent arise: were the images created with an Etruscan audience in mind? Can they be reliable indicators of Athenian thinking? We don't know the answer to the first question or whether their export resulted from a primary market or secondary market, but I believe that the answer to the second question is clear: the archaic and classical Attic artists who created the vases painted them with images familiar to an Athenian audience as attested by monumental art, which shares the same artistic language, and by written evidence. My argument rests on the premise that such paintings reflect Athenian cultural values and attitudes.

I realize that the export question and its impact on imagery are controversial points and that many issues arise, such as whether an Etruscan market drove the production of some kinds of images and not others, but we do not and presently cannot know the answer to such questions. We can only start from the source, the Athenian artist's hand, and move forward from there. On the other hand, I do not wish to suggest that findspot is irrelevant; on the contrary, it is often illuminating, particularly when Attic items are found in Attic contexts. But we know so little about the trade and transport of painted Athenian vases that it seems foolhardy and shortsighted to dismiss the ability of images on Attic vases found in Etruscan contexts to reflect Athenian culture. I think it safe to presume that special commissions were rare, so the body of Athenian vase painting, regardless of where it was found, can illuminate Athenian culture, particularly when evidence from monumental art or literature can confirm and shape the reading of the images.

Distinguishing between mythological and nonmythological hunting scenes also presents a methodological challenge. Three broad categories of hunt scenes in Attic vase painting can be recognized: those that are clearly mythological as indicated by a fantastic animal or a clearly identifiable mythological figure, those that may be mythological because of compositional similarities to the former, and those that are clearly not mythological (generic scenes). As an example, Calydonian boar hunt images are usually recognizable by the presence of inscriptions of the hunters' names, which are known from ancient literature; or of Atalanta; or of dogs attacking the boar from specific vantage points; or of a dead hunter beneath the boar (e.g., fig. 80). Any or all of these elements are enough to identify the scene as the Calydonian boar hunt. There are, however, boar hunt compositions with dogs attacking a boar but nothing else to suggest the Calydonian boar hunt. These ambiguous paintings fall in the second category of hunts: not clearly mythological but resembling those that are. I argue that the blurring of the line between mythological and generic is deliberate, designed to heroize the hunt in general, even when it is not mythological. In this study, I am less interested in distinguishing mythological from nonmythological than I am in arguing that the difficulty in doing so is intentional on the part of the artist.

Blurring the boundaries between myth and everyday life is one way to lend heroic luster to daily routine; repetition of nearly identical hunt compositions on two sides of a given vase is another.[3] The representations usually present a contrast between mythological and nonmythological or, more precisely, a comparison of the latter with the former.

In addition to teasing out the meanings of mythological and nonmythological depictions and looking at repeated images, there are other ways of reading and extracting information from vase paintings. One can compare the entire ensemble of images on any given vase, be they repeated or not, and read coherent visual programs, which work together to create complementary, but not analogous, meanings. Some scholars, particularly our Parisian colleagues, have done this with great success.[4]

But the most sophisticated and subtle of narrative techniques is visual simile and metaphor, the implicit comparison between two different types of scene on a given vase, sometimes on the same side, sometimes on opposing sides.[5] Such images are meant to be read as analogous commentaries on each other; for example, the hunt might be paired with a scene of

Herakles on the same vessel in order to create resonances between the two. Visual similes liken one scene or one activity to another; in visual metaphor, the two scenes merge so that one scene or activity *is* another. When the viewer sees a hunt scene in which hunters carry armor, the viewer conjures up a "system of associated commonplaces" for the idea of battle, and these associations inform the notion of hunting.[6] As Gloria Ferrari explains, metaphor can be interaction, "seeing one thing in terms of another," and the images represent ideas and not things.[7]

One can also extract meaning from the types of vase shapes that are ornamented with hunting scenes. Although scholars have occasionally noted the thematic correspondence of two different scenes on a single vase or the aptness of a given scene for a particular shape, only recently have they turned their full attention to the correlation between shape and scene. For example, Ingeborg Scheibler's examination of Attic belly amphorae and their ornament demonstrates that this shape was linked to rituals and cults related to the initiation of Athenian ephebes.[8] Likewise, Alan Shapiro recently argued that archaic Attic black-figure pelikai were associated with the craftsmen who produced olive oil and who made and decorated the Panathenaic amphorae to contain it; the oil served as prizes in the Panathenaic games.[9]

This book, particularly chapter 1, examines repeated images of hunting on the same vase; the correspondences between hunting and other types of scenes on a single vase; and the relationship between hunting paintings and the shapes they adorn to discern and enrich our understanding of hunting ideology in the archaic and classical periods. Thus far, I have spoken only of vases, but I also consider sculpted hunting depictions, specifically on tombs and *heroa*, where one sees repeated hunt images, mythological and nonmythological, which, like the vase paintings, work together with other scenes on the monument to convey meaning to the viewer.

This is not the first investigation of the hunt in ancient Greece, and it would have been impossible without the work of my predecessors in this area. Nineteenth-century scholars, such as Otto Manns, first began to organize and collect examples of hunting imagery in Greek writing, and numerous scholars in the twentieth century tackled various manifestations of the hunt in Greek tragedy and philosophy, particularly the metaphor of hunting in tragedy, and translated and offered commentary on ancient hunting handbooks, such as Xenophon's *Cynegeticus*. Konrad Schauenburg helpfully collected and discussed vase painting examples of hunting scenes in his small but indispensable 1969 publication, *Jagddarstellungen in der griechischen Vasenmalerei*. And J. K. Anderson's 1985 publication included both visual and written examples to describe Greek hunting practices. Some studies, such as Walter Burkert's *Homo Necans* (1983), posit a link between hunting and sacrifice and regard sacrifice as a guilty atonement for having killed, a view that has been convincingly challenged recently by Sarah Peirce in 1993.

And yet these studies do not address the question of the hunt's cultural importance, its meaning for the Greeks. In the 1970s Alain Schnapp stepped into the breach and, using more theoretical approaches, began pressing Attic vase painting for answers to just this question. His work was complemented by that of his colleague Pierre Vidal-Naquet, whose 1986 book, *The Black Hunter* (originally published as *Le Chasseur noir* in 1981), examined hunting in Greek myth and articulated a relationship between hunting and warfare in Athens based on a structuralist reading of the myth of Melanthos and Xanthos. Vidal-Naquet's work had a profound impact on Schnapp's interpretation of the Attic vase painting depictions of the hunt, and Schnapp's work culminated in the publication of *Le Chasseur et la cité: Chasse et érotique dans la Grèce ancienne* in 1997, which includes a catalog of hunting scenes in Greek vase painting. Schnapp examines some of the issues treated in the present study, such as the heroic nature of the hunt and the relationship between eros and hunting, but my methodology and concerns differ from his and consequently yield different results. Schnapp's focus is much broader than mine, encompassing the concept of the hunter (including Centaurs and satyrs), the ephebe, and "la cité grecque" from the eighth through fourth century. Whereas Schnapp is only occasionally concerned with political and social issues (other than *paideia*, education) and their impact on hunting imagery or on cultural ideas of the hunt,[10] these issues are central to my study and, in my view, the only means by which to explain much of the evidence. Contrary to Schnapp, I reject Vidal-Naquet's black hunter construct and substitute the real aristocratic, heroic warrior in its place.[11]

Jeanmaire and Brelich, followed by many others, view hunting—all types of hunting—as initiatory in character. Hunting exalts the adolescent male to adulthood, as is demonstrated by way of comparative anthropology and structuralist readings of mythological hunters. But hunting, I believe, is much more than that. An examination of the ancient evidence, paying careful attention to its historical context, reveals that hunting was, along with the *symposion*, athletics, and battle, a defining activity of the masculine aristocracy and that those social connotations pervade its many depictions in art and literature. Moreover, hunting is, by definition, a masculine activity in ancient Greece. Thus, using all types of evidence, both written and visual, high and low, I investigate the meaning and practice of the hunt in archaic and classical Athens through a sociohistorical lens.

The term *sport* has been applied to archaic and classical Greek hunting, but this word is misleading because hunting was not performed competitively as were Greek athletics or poetry. Yet hunting shares some of the qualities of athletic competition, such as mental concentration and physical fitness, and the danger and courage associated with hunting find athletic counterparts in boxing or the *pankration*. To be sure, hunting was a leisure activity, associated with the leisure class and not with necessity, but sport implies a competitive aspect, which is absent from Greek hunting, unless one views the hunter and his prey as competitors. The requisite qualities for hunting are also components of warfare, whose conduct underwent a fundamental change in the sixth century with the introduction of hoplite tactics. Written and visual evidence both attest to the Greek view that hunting, athletics, and warfare share many of the same skills, and that hunting and athletics were suitable training for warfare.

This trio of physical activities—hunting, warfare, and athletics—constitute defining occupations of the aristocracy of the archaic and early classical periods, and chapter 1 examines their interaction and appearance on Greek vases and in written texts. The hunt's connection to the elite class surely stems from its royal associations in the Near East, particularly in Assyria, but by the archaic period the royal connotations are muted, and instead the hunt is simply aristocratic and purely Greek. Sometimes on horseback but usually on foot, Greek hunters pursue boar and deer. Inspired by aristocratic concerns, Attic vase paintings use a variety of narrative strategies to create visual metaphors to express the idea that hunting is warfare and that both are heroic in nature. Moreover, the tempo of production of hunting images, I believe, directly relates to current political events in late-sixth- and early-fifth-century Athens as aristocrats endeavored to control the social agenda even as they were losing official political clout under the new democracy. Initiation rituals designed to prepare young

men for adulthood and warrior status included hunting in various locations in Greece. Because no concrete evidence attests to ritualized initiatory
hunting in Athens in the sixth and fifth centuries, the second half of chapter 1 explores how non-Athenian initiatory hunting can illuminate our
knowledge of Athenian ideas of masculinity and adulthood.

Masculinity and aristocracy also play a prominent role in chapter 2,
which examines another, metaphorical type of hunting, pederastic
courtship. Late archaic and early classical Attic vase paintings portray pederastic courtship scenes, many of which include animal gifts—often products of the hunt—from lover to beloved. These depictions, together with
written evidence, emphasize the hunt that takes place between lover and
beloved, often in a gymnasion setting. In contrast to previous scholarly interpretations, this chapter argues not only that the gift animals signify
desirous qualities of the courtship participants but that the roles of hunter
and prey are not exclusively assigned to lover and beloved respectively but
are interchangeable. And while role reversal is natural, even desirable, in
real-life erotic encounters, it is only permissible under certain conditions:
men can pursue men, women can pursue women, and men can pursue
women, but women should not pursue men. Such interpretations have a
dramatic impact on how we read images and how we understand Athenian sexuality and social roles. The chapter closes by considering how
hunting and pederasty are manifested in the symposion, yet another aristocratic masculine activity.

Thus far, hunting is presented as both real activity and as metaphor;
hunting is a metaphor for warfare, and erotic courtship is a metaphor for
hunting. Hunting and warfare and hunting and sex are closely connected
in real life. But Greek myth offers a stark contrast to the real world, because Greek myth is replete with hunters, both male and female, who
hunt but never fight in wars or who hunt but do not have sex. This apparent disparity between myth and real life is evaluated in chapter 3, which
concerns the theme of the hunt in Greek myth. Three examples—Aktaion, Kallisto, and Atalanta—demonstrate the variety and range of Greek
hunting myths. In each instance, role reversals befall hunters who violate
codes of behavior with the result that hunters become the prey, either to
actual or erotic hunters. One is struck by the oddity of an Atalanta or a
Kallisto because women do not hunt in real life, but myth reflects societal norms often by demonstrating their breach and the accompanying con-

sequences. For example, if one depended solely on Greek myth for our picture of Greek culture, most Greek wives would be Medea or Clytemnestra, Greek daughters Iphigeneia or Antigone, young men Achilles or Theseus, and so on. Myth is not a mirror but a prism; rather than reflecting real life directly, myth, like Greek art, manipulates and shuffles material to provide views of Greek culture. The interpreter must examine these images with their complex facets and reveal the cultural norms and beliefs beneath. Once again, gender is critical to understanding Greek hunting myths and the culture that shapes them.

By the end of the fifth century, hunting scenes virtually disappear from Attic vase painting, but hunters continue to appear on Attic funerary stelai. One must travel to Ionia or Lycia to see actual hunting scenes in the fourth century, where they adorn tombs and sarcophagi, or to Macedonia, where hunting appears in such places as the Vergina tomb paintings. Chapter 4 takes up the theme of hunting in funerary contexts first in Attica on stelai and white-ground lekythoi, and then, as a coda to the book, the scope of my study expands to survey hunting imagery in funerary art of East Greece and Lycia. The Attic images continue to employ many of the artistic motifs already observed in earlier chapters, but the artists of the Eastern depictions create hybrid images by combining Greek and Near Eastern features; traditional Near Eastern royal hunting imagery mixes with Greek heroic myths, particularly on Lycian heroa, to heroize local rulers. As with the Attic vase paintings of the actual hunt, various narrative strategies are deployed to create visual juxtapositions between real life and myth. While the hunt can heroize obliquely through metaphor and myth in the sixth and fifth centuries, fourth-century rulers, including Alexander the Great, explicitly and self-consciously heroize themselves by imitating or likening themselves to mythological hunters.

Hunting then is bound up with the aristocracy and its activities—warfare, athletics, symposion, and pederasty—but also exists in the world of myth, where hunters demonstrate the limits and norms of Greek society and sexuality. It is my hope that this work will serve as the stimulus for further discussion and exploration and will offer a new way of understanding Greek culture through its visual and written remains.

Chapter One
HUNTING, WARFARE, AND ARISTOCRATS

Passages of ancient literature demonstrate an association between hunting and warfare, and scholars have made passing mention of the connection in studies of Greek vases. But this relationship merits more attention because the analogy between the two activities expresses cultural values, particularly aristocratic values, in the written and visual record of the archaic and classical periods. Ironically, although Athens provides the greatest amount of evidence, both written and material, for the analogy between hunt and battle, we know little about hunting practices in Athens, particularly the use of hunting as initiation and preparation for military activities. Yet hunting ideologies and an association between hunting and battle, even the likening of the former to the latter, find visual expression on archaic and classical Attic vases. Some scholars claim that the hunting images reflect the change to democracy, the associated weakening of aristocratic power, and the relation of hunting to sport. Rather than reflecting a loss of Athenian aristocratic power, I argue, on the contrary, that the vase paintings reveal an aristocratic concern with social prerogatives that intensifies as a response to the waning of aristocratic political privilege.[1] Furthermore, these scenes provide evidence for the critical place that the hunt occupied in the construction of male gender in Athenian aristocratic culture, which embraced the heroic aspects of the hunt as part of its ideology of *arete* and emulation of Homeric ideals.[2]

Hunting was clearly part of male initiation in various parts of the Greek world, for example, in Sparta and on Crete, with the aim of training young men to participate in battle. Adolescent males would acquire the skills of

10

tracking, ambushing, and confronting animals, which would serve them in warfare, where the "game" was armed, usually more fierce, and fought back. By extrapolation from the evidence for other locations, some scholars claim that the hunt also constituted part of military training in Athens, institutionalized as the *ephebeia*. But our knowledge of the Athenian ephebeia is so meager before its first uncontested attestation in the fourth century that such a claim is difficult to sustain. Beyond the written evidence, however, lie material remains that substantiate a link between the hunt and military activity, if not actual training, in Athens well before the first mention of the ephebeia. A careful reading of both types of documentation reveals the perception and function of hunting in archaic and classical Athens.

Literary Evidence for the Nature of the Hunt

Nearly all of the handbooks and texts directly concerning hunting date from the fourth century (or later), almost a century after most visual sources, thus making it difficult to access archaic and classical Greek attitudes to the hunt. General remarks on hunting and types of hunting come from Xenophon (*Lac.* 4.7), who discusses the suitability of the hunt for both youths and adult men, referring to it as "the noblest activity."[3] In his hunting handbook for aristocrats, Xenophon (*Cyn.* 6.13) says that before hunting, the hunter should vow a share of spoils to Artemis Agrotera and Apollo (cf. Arr., *Cyn.* 22.1).

Numerous texts describe hunting as training for future citizens, as central to the community, and as preparation for warfare (e.g., Pl., *Leg.* 763b; Xen., *Cyn.* 12.7–8; and cf. Pl., *Soph.* 219d–e, 222c). The entire community benefits from training adolescents to hunt, which teaches them to be law-abiding, according to Xenophon (*Cyn.* 12.14, 13.11, 13.15). Plato points to hunting as central to the *polis* and warfare in his discussion of the origins of man in *Protagoras* (322b): in an earlier era men lacked the art of hunting "for they had not the art of politics, of which the art of war is a part" (trans. Guthrie); in other words, not only do hunting and battle go hand in hand but hunting is a central part of the world of the polis. Aristotle (*Pol.* 1256b 23–26) declares hunting part of the art of warfare. Plato (*Resp.* 549A) ascribes hunting, along with gymnastics, to the lover of honor, and Xenophon's *Cynegeticus* (1.18, 12.1–5, 12.9) and his *Cyropaedia* (1.2.10–11) state that hunting is an essential form of education and training for warfare, providing the necessary discipline, endurance, and courage.[4] This attitude is scarcely surprising since warfare is described elsewhere as a hunt of a different nature (Pl., *Soph.* 222b–c; *Leg.* 823b; Isoc., *Panath.* 163).[5]

The worship of Artemis Agrotera also illustrates the association between hunting and warfare. Spartans make sacrifices to Artemis Agrotera before both activities (Xen., *Hell.* 4.2.20, and cf. *Lac.* 13.8), and the Athenians sacrifice to the goddess at an annual celebration of their victory at Marathon, replicating their invocation before the battle (Xen., *An.* 3.2.12).[6] Pausanias (1.19.6) locates the temple of Artemis Agrotera in Attica just beyond the Ilissos area in Athens and ascribes its location to the place where Artemis first hunted after her arrival from Delos.

Two passages in Xenophon's *Cyropaedia* draw an analogy between warfare and hunting: Xenophon compares a hound rushing at a boar to Cyrus rushing at the Assyrian army (1.4.20), and a boar charging Cyrus and his companions to brave warriors charging the enemy in battle (1.4.11).

Although the preceding references all derive from fourth-century writers, oblique references to the hunt's relationship to warfare already exist in fifth-century texts. Herodotos (1.36–43) relates the story of Croesus's son Atys and the prophecy of his death by an iron weapon, which is fulfilled by a misdirected spear during a boar hunt. Before the hunt, Croesus protests against his son's participation, but Atys prevails, arguing that a boar possesses no iron and therefore he is in no danger. In the exchange between father and son, Croesus's fear that an iron weapon will prove deadly in hunting and Atys's insistence that an iron weapon will not be used and his implicit understanding of the weapon as suited to warfare suggest a conflation of battle and hunt; Atys understands Croesus's fears as extending only to battle while the hunt, in fact, turns out to have the same dangers.[7] Herodotos (6.31) tells of a Persian maneuver on islands off the coast of Asia Minor in 493 in which the Persian army linked hands and swept across the island, serving as a human dragnet to capture or hunt the native peoples.[8] Plato (*Men.* 240b–c; *Leg.* 698d) describes the same strategy for the Persian conquest of Eretria in 490.[9] A direct reference to the association of warfare and hunting appears in Aischylos's *Agamemnon* 694–95, which refers to the Achaeans setting off for the Trojan War as hunters (κυναγοὶ).

The use of the hunt as initiation to hoplite status is well documented for some areas of Greece. By "initiation," I mean a maturation procedure not necessarily ritualized in a formal public presentation (though this is sometimes the case as on Crete or at Brauron)—whose completion is socially acknowledged in some way. Plutarch (*Lyc.* 28) and the scholiast to Plato's *Leges* (633b) describe the Spartan *krypteia*,[10] a training method for young warriors. Equipped with only daggers and the bare essentials, the Spartan youths lived away from the city for a period of time, during which they were expected to hunt and kill helots, the native enslaved population, at night.[11] In addition to this use of the hunt as initiation, passages from ancient writers attest that hunting was generally extremely important to Spartan hoplite society:[12] Plutarch (*Lyc.* 12.2–3) records that hunters had to provide spoils of their hunt at the communal hoplite meals or at one's home,[13] Xenophon (*Lac.* 6.3–4) tells us that hunting dogs were freely shared,[14] and Libanius (*Orat.* 5.23) reports that Spartan boys could not participate in the banquet in honor of Artemis without having first hunted.[15] Plato (*Leg.* 823b), as well as modern scholars, have remarked on the similarity between stealing and hunting in Sparta.[16] Thus, the ritual cheese stealing from the altar of Artemis Orthia in archaic and classical Sparta, which involved fighting between those who were trying to steal the cheeses and those trying to protect them in honor of the goddess of the hunt (Xen., *Lac.* 2.9), can be understood as a form of hunting. This ceremony occurred just as young men were about to become warriors (Pl., *Leg.* 633a–b).[17]

Ephoros (as quoted in Strabo 10.483–84) describes a practice on Crete that is similar to the Spartan krypteia. Although Ephoros wrote in the mid-fourth century, he apparently relates a Cretan custom of long standing. Cretan boys lived outside the city for two months, where they learned to hunt animals and were introduced to sex by their adult lovers. When the Cretan youth returned to the city, he was awarded three gifts: military weapons that marked his exaltation to warrior status; an ox for sacrifice to Zeus, the mark of an initiate's ability to host public meals and enter into the religious life of the community;[18] and a drinking cup that entitled him to participate in the adult drinking parties.[19] The new initiate then took an oath to observe the laws, customs, and allegiances of the city. The wild location of the Spartan and Cretan rites is well suited to these youths, who are untamed adolescents when they begin the process but, by learning the skills of citizens, by hunting and by sexual encounter, become civilized adults. It is worth noting here that the Cretan practice involved the ab-

duction of the adolescent by the adult lover with the complicity of family
and friends and that the Spartan educational system undoubtedly included
pederasty.[20]

Athenaeus (1.18) attests to the connection between hunting and entry
into adult male society in Macedonia, where from at least the archaic period one could not recline at dinner until one had speared a boar without
a hunting net.

Such firm documentation is lacking for Athens, the focus of this study,
although that has not prevented some scholars from postulating an initiatory hunt in Athens; we return to this subject later in this chapter.

Ancient authors made distinctions between types of hunting. Plato (*Leg.*
823b–824c) distinguishes two categories; he disapproves of nets, snares,
night trapping, and poaching and applauds the chase on horseback or on
foot with dogs. According to this line of thinking, physical confrontation
with the animal, a meeting with danger, is an essential part of the good
hunt.[21] Xenophon (*Cyr.* 1.6.27–40) combines the ideas of hunt as appropriate training for warfare and the distinction between types of hunting as
enunciated by Plato. In a dialogue with his father, Cyrus learns that the
stealthy hunting he acquired as a youth was appropriate training for warfare and that the noble hunting prepared him for dealing with allies. But
such tricks (αἱ μηχαναί) should be practiced on small game (*Cyr.*
1.6.39–40) rather than on warriors. Noteworthy is Cyrus's father's inclusion
of the art of deception in his description of training for wrestling (*Cyr.*
1.6.32).

Although the foregoing are fourth-century texts, such distinctions can
also be detected in earlier poetry and drama. Pindar (*Nem.* 3.43–52) offers
Achilles, the supreme warrior, as a heroic model for hunting: he killed
deer by chasing them down, rather than by using hounds or nets. Euripides' *Herakles* (151–203) of c. 416 or 414 debates the relative virtues of archer
and hoplite and the military value of the hunt.[22] Lycus insults the mem-
ory of Herakles with the claim that Herakles hunted with nets, rather than
using his bare hands, or hunted with a bow rather than a spear. Amphi-
tryon responds by defending the use of the bow.

In sum, written texts of the fifth and fourth centuries demonstrate a
strong association between the activities and attained skills of hunting and
their direct applicability to warfare, although the evidence for Athens is
thin indeed. Moreover, the evidence presents hunting as central to social

cohesion and as part of the fabric of the polis. Just as several of the written sources—passages from Plato and Xenophon, for example—are aimed at an aristocratic audience,[23] issues of social class figure prominently in vase painting depictions of the hunt.

Visual Evidence for the Hunt and Its Relationship to Battle

Unlike the written evidence concerning the cultural significance of the hunt, the material record in archaic and classical Athens, especially Attic vase painting, provides ample evidence expressing ideologies of the hunt and an association between hunting and battle. Because Attic hunting images have been enumerated and sorted according to type, and their development has been traced elsewhere,[24] their treatment here is limited to a presentation of standard compositions and anomalies. This chapter concerns itself with nonmythological paintings of boar and deer hunts;[25] mythological images, such as the Calydonian boar hunt,[26] are treated in chapter 3. And hare hunting, neither dangerous nor associated with warfare, is considered in conjunction with pederastic vase paintings, to which it is related, discussed in chapter 2.

Approximately 121 examples of nonmythological boar (50) and deer hunts (71) exist on Attic vases (see tables 1 and 2 at the end of this chapter), which is the largest corpus of hunting depictions in Greek vase painting dating from c. 600–425. Most date from the second half of the sixth century,[27] but it is noteworthy that there are two peak periods of production of such Attic scenes: c. 560–550 and c. 520–470. Admittedly, we should allow a margin of error of fifteen years because of the impossibility of accurate dates for the vases. This jump in production is more pronounced for deer hunting images than for boar hunts (though paintings of the Calydonian boar hunt are also most numerous in c. 560–550). The iconography for each type of scene is remarkably static until c. 520, when a series of marked changes, including the infiltration of martial weapons into some hunting scenes, begins, and then intensifies after 510.

Scholars explain the changes in hunting depictions at the end of the sixth century and beginning of the fifth as reflecting a devaluation of hunt to sport because of the association of hunting with the aristocracy, and the unpopularity of everything aristocratic after the advent of democracy in Athens. Although they mention that the majority of vase paintings of the hunt occur in the second half of the sixth century, they do not, however, note the increases in production in the two periods noted here. Yet the increasing numbers of hunt scenes between 520 and 470 and the dominance of cups after 510 can both be explained by the aristocracy's loss of political power during this turbulent time. A consideration of the images accompanying hunting on any given vase and the shapes of the hunting vases also enhances this reading of the images. As we shall see, the aristocracy exploited the ideologies of hunting, hunting as analogous to warfare, and hunting as a heroic activity in an effort to assert and maintain social control even as its own political power was waning.

An Attic black-figure amphora lid of c. 550 (London, British Museum B147; fig. 1) carrying scenes of boar and deer hunting depicts the typical composition of each type of hunt before c. 520.[28] Two boar hunters on foot converge on their prey with spears, while on the other portion of the lid, four mounted hunters, one wielding a spear, approach a fallen doe pierced with several spears. Two of the deer hunters wear chitons but all the other hunters are nude; one of the boar hunters sports a beard while the rest appear to be beardless. The viewer is invited to compare, juxtaposed side by side, the dangerous hunt of the boar, fought down in the dirt, with the fleeting speed and thunder of the mounted hunt. The perception of the boar's ferocity is attested elsewhere by the use of boars as shield devices in paintings of hoplite battles.[29]

Typical of hunting depictions is the symmetrical placement of hunters around a centrally placed animal; both are collective hunts, although a few images of solitary hunters on foot (e.g., New York, Metropolitan Museum of Art 74.51.1371 of c. 540) or on horseback (e.g., London, British Museum 1891.8–6.84) also occur.[30] Unlike the deer hunters, the boar hunters are only occasionally mounted, as on a Siana cup of c. 560 in Hamburg (Museum für Kunst und Gewerbe 1908.255; fig. 2).[31] The boar stands, whereas the hunted deer is usually wounded and stumbling or already downed. Spears are the usual weapons, as in the boar hunt on an Attic black-figure amphora of c. 575–550 by the Goltyr Painter (Rome, Museo del Palazzo dei Conservatori 119–39; fig. 3) and in the deer hunt on an Attic black-figure kylix of c. 550–530, now in Naples (Museo Archeologico Nazionale H2500 [81132]).[32] The hunters are often nude but can also wear short chitons; when legible, boar hunters are often bearded. Once in a while, a hunter wears a Scythian cap or a pilos (felt cap). During the two peak periods of production, c. 560–550 and c. 520–470, cups are particu-

FIGURE 1. Attic black-figure amphora lid attributed to Group E, c. 550 B.C. London, British Museum B147. Photo courtesy of the British Museum. © The British Museum.

larly prevalent for the boar hunt paintings.[33] Stags and does seem to be hunted in about equal numbers in Attic black- and red-figure, and sometimes both are hunted together in the same scene (e.g., Oxford, Ashmolean Museum 1889.1013).[34]

Occasionally, a Centaur substitutes for the human deer hunter as on a cup by the Centaur Painter now in Würzburg (Martin von Wagner Museum der Universität 405) from the end of the sixth century.[35] On the obverse, a hunter wearing a *chlamys* (cloak) and carrying a club pursues a stag on foot; on the reverse, a Centaur with a stone pursues a doe. One also sees the standard deer hunt combined with its inversion on another cup by the Centaur Painter of c. 540 in London (British Museum

FIGURE 2. Attic black-figure Siana cup by the C Painter, c. 560 B.C. Hamburg, Museum für Kunst und Gewerbe 1908.255. Photo courtesy of the Museum für Kunst und Gewerbe, Hamburg.

1891.8–6.84), where a hunter hunts a deer on one side, and a panther pursues a hunter on the other.[36] The Centaur Painter shows a predilection for deer hunting scenes, which appear on four of his cups, and he also paints hunters pursuing Centaurs.[37]

A series of important changes in vase paintings of the hunt that begin c. 520 and are most common after 510 signals a change in perception of this activity. Although the cup is always a common shape for hunting vase paintings, other shapes are employed in the earlier period. But beginning c. 520 and particularly after 510, cups and other drinking vessels are nearly the only shapes on which hunting imagery occurs, especially for Attic red-figure ware.

Formerly a collective enterprise, the boar hunt largely becomes a solitary activity after c. 500, though this is only occasionally so for deer hunts, and after c. 520 most hunts, of boar and deer alike, are conducted on foot (e.g., Attic black-figure lekythos of c. 500–475 painted in the Manner of the Athena Painter, Oxford, Ashmolean Museum 1889.1013).[38] On a white-ground oinochoe of c. 500 in the Bibliothèque nationale (Cabinet des Médailles 274; fig. 4), a lone bearded hunter, dressed in a short tunic with a chlamys slung over his left arm, spears an oncoming boar against a backdrop of a tree with sprawling branches.[39] The use of landscape is notable as

FIGURE 3. Attic black-figure amphora by the Goltyr Painter, c. 575–550 B.C. Rome, Museo del Palazzo dei Conservatori 119–39. Photo courtesy of the Archivio Fotografico dei Musei Capitolini, Rome.

it becomes an increasingly common element in hunt imagery in the early fifth century, perhaps emphasizing the wild location of the hunt as opposed to the civilized spaces of the city. The image on an Attic black-figure lekythos of c. 510–500 in a private Swiss collection crackles with tension as hunter and hunted confront each other (fig. 5):[40] a crouching bearded hunter with a chlamys draped over his left arm, who carries a spear and wears a short tunic and boots, approaches a boar; a dog accompanies the man, and a tree separates the hunter and his quarry. Crouched low, the hunter is at the same spatial level as the boar, underscoring the shifting roles of hunter and hunted. Is the hunter here the boar or the man?

More significant for this study is a change of weaponry. The spears and tridents of old are replaced or supplemented by new weapons, such as rocks and unsheathed swords, as on an Attic red-figure cup of c. 510–500 by the Ambrosios Painter (Rome, Museo Nazionale Etrusco di Villa Giulia 50535; figs. 6–7)[41] and an Attic red-figure hydria of c. 500 by the Charpentier Painter (Rome, Museo Gregoriano Etrusco Vaticano 16548).[42] An Attic black-figure lidded amphora of c. 500 in Altenburg (Lindenau-Museum 207; figs. 8–9) is ornamented with a solitary boar hunter on each side.[43] On the obverse, a beardless male wearing a short tunic with a sheathed sword at his waist aims two spears at the forehead of a facing boar while a hunting dog rips at the boar's torso. The hunter wears a pilos and a chlamys draped

FIGURE 4. Attic black-figure white-ground oinochoe Near the Athena Painter,
c. 500 B.C. Paris, Bibliothèque nationale, Cabinet des Médailles 274. Photo
courtesy of the Bibliothèque nationale de France.

FIGURE 5. Attic black-figure lekythos by the Athena Painter, c. 510–500 B.C. Swiss
private collection. Reproduced with permission from A. Schnapp, "Images et
programmes: Les Figurations archaïques de la chasse au sanglier," *RA* (1979): 213,
fig. 13.

across his bent left arm as if it were a shield. On the reverse, a bearded
hunter wearing a short tunic, pilos, and sheathed sword raises a rock in his
right hand and holds a spear in his left. Like the hunter on the obverse, he
wears his chlamys slung over his left arm as if it were a shield. The boar
here has been struck by one spear and is threatened by a hunting dog. The
repetition of nearly the same scene invites the viewer of the Altenburg amphora to compare and contrast each side of the amphora.[44] An unbearded
hunter, perhaps indicating a younger hunter, uses only spears against his
foe, while a bearded, possibly older, hunter takes down his opponent with
spears and a rock.[45] Similarly, the exterior images on a later Attic red-figure
cup of c. 450 (Paris, Musée du Louvre G637; fig. 10) are also clearly analogous but with variation in the positioning of the figures and the

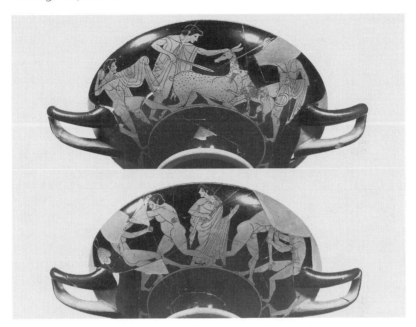

FIGURES 6–7. Attic red-figure cup by the Ambrosios Painter, c. 510–500 B.C.
Rome, Museo Nazionale Etrusco di Villa Giulia 50535. Photos courtesy
of the Soprintendenza Archeologica per l'Etruria Meridionale, Rome.

weapons.[46] A solitary, beardless hunter wearing a short tunic and chlamys
confronts a boar on either side of the cup, but on one side the hunter holds
a club in his left hand and a rock in his right, whereas on the reverse, a
sword substitutes for the rock, and a long-handled club replaces the shorter
club of the obverse.

Spears are the standard weapons against boar and deer on Attic vases in
the sixth century but beginning c. 520 and more commonly in the first half
of the fifth century, weapons uncongenial to hunting but standard in warfare are occasionally used against boar and deer, such as the shield, helmet, and greaves, together with the drawn sword noted already,[47] thus creating visual metaphors that convey the idea that hunting is warfare. Only
Calydonian boar hunt scenes show the use of bows and arrows in Attic
hunts before c. 530, but thereafter these weapons become more common
in generic boar hunt depictions.[48] Two mounted hoplites, complete with
helmets and cuirasses, spear a fallen deer on an Attic black-figure lekythos
of c. 490 in Athens (National Museum 14858).[49] A deer hunt ornaments

FIGURES 8–9. Attic black-figure lidded amphora by the Edinburgh Painter, c. 500
B.C. Altenburg, Lindenau-Museum 207. Photos courtesy of the Lindenau-
Museum.

both sides of the exterior of an Attic red-figure cup of c. 510 (Paris, Musée
du Louvre G22; figs. 11–12) and presents mirror compositions of hunters
furnished with hoplite equipment.[50] Two beardless hunters pursue a doe
on the reverse; one is nude save for a chlamys on his outstretched left arm,
worn as if it were a shield, while his companion carries an actual shield.
The first holds a sword in his right hand and wears a baldric across his
shoulder. The other is entirely nude save for greaves and raises a spear in his
right hand. On the obverse, two hunters flank a doe; the hunter on the left
is beardless and nearly nude but wears a baldric across his shoulder and a
petasos (broad-brimmed hat), and holds a rock in his raised right hand. A
feline skin rather than a chlamys hangs from his outstretched left arm. His
counterpart on the right, also unbearded and almost nude, charges at the
doe with a poised spear, an animal skin on his extended left arm, and a

FIGURE 10. Attic red-figure cup Related to the Sotades Painter, c. 450 B.C. Paris, Musée du Louvre G637. Photo by M. Chuzeville and C. Larrieu, courtesy of the Musée du Louvre.

helmet on his head. This infusion of hoplite weaponry into hunting scenes expresses a cultural understanding of battle and hunt as analogous activities, both the proving ground of men.[51]

Another aspect of this scene, the chlamys extended and held as if it were a shield, first makes an appearance in a few hunting compositions dated c. 550–530 but then becomes very common for hunters c. 510 and thereafter. In addition to its use on the Altenburg amphora (figs. 8–9) and the Louvre cup (figs. 11–12), it also appears on many other vessels, such as the predella of an Attic black-figure hydria of c. 520–515 by the Antimenes Painter (Leiden, Rijksmuseum van Oudheden II 167 [PC 63]; figs. 13–14),[52] and in Naples on another Attic black-figure hydria of c. 530–510 (Naples, Museo Archeologico Nazionale H2777 [81173]).[53] The juxtaposition of Calydonian boar hunters wearing chlamydes held as if they were shields

FIGURES 11–12. Attic red-figure cup in the Manner of the Epeleios Painter, c. 510
B.C. Paris, Musée du Louvre G22. Photos by M. Chuzeville and C. Larrieu,
courtesy of the Musée du Louvre.

FIGURES 13–14. *(opposite)* Attic black-figure hydria by the Antimenes Painter,
c. 520–515 B.C. Leiden, Rijksmuseum van Oudheden I1167 [PC63]. Photos courtesy
of the Rijksmuseum van Oudheden.

FIGURE 15. Attic black-figure cup, c. 550–530 B.C. Rome, Museo Nazionale Etrusco di Villa Giulia 74981. Photo courtesy of the Soprintendenza Archeologica per l'Etruria Meridionale, Rome.

with hunters carrying actual shields on an Attic black-figure cup of c. 550–530 (Rome, Museo Nazionale Etrusco di Villa Giulia 74981; fig. 15) emphasizes the similarity of the two objects.[54] This unusual arrangement of the chlamys is particular to hunters, especially nonmythological hunters, and is only occasionally seen in mythological hunting scenes as on the aforementioned cup.[55] Another exception is the figure of Theseus on an Attic red-figure cup by Douris (London, British Museum E48), which depicts the various adventures of Theseus.[56] As Theseus attacks the Krommyonian sow (recognizable by her swollen teats), he lunges forward with a chlamys held on his outstretched left arm although one cannot tell if his hand grips the chlamys because that portion of the cup is missing. Another mythological exception may be the boar hunter on an Attic red-figure cup of c. 490 by the Antiphon Painter (Baltimore, Walters Art Gallery 48.2115):[57] some scholars have identified this solitary hunter as Theseus, Meleager, or Herakles, although there is no inscription, and the boar is not clearly recognizable as a sow.[58] In the latter case, the ambiguity in the identification of the figure may be intentional, designed to blur the distinction between mere mortal and hero.[59]

The same idea of hunting likened to warfare is illustrated on an Attic black-figure amphora of c. 520 (Munich, Staatliche Antikensammlungen 1386; figs.16–17), where the boar hunter on our right carries what appears to be a shield on his right arm and wears a cuirass.[60] This scene also demonstrates the heroization of nonmythological hunters by means of a compositional device. The dogs attacking the boar in this hunt recall the typical Calydonian boar hunt composition, although nothing else about this painting does. This mythological quotation is an instance of the blurring of the boundaries separating myth and generic scene discussed earlier. Moreover, a hoplite battle on the reverse complements the boar hunt on the obverse, inviting the viewer to compare and contrast the two scenes. We can note that the shield of the central hoplite is ornamented with an animal pelt, perhaps that of a hare. The amphora thus likens these hunters to both heroes and hoplite warriors.

Changes in poses and attire of hunters also take place c. 520. Although hunters occasionally sported Scythian caps prior to c. 520, Eastern dress becomes more common for boar and deer hunters thereafter. A cup of c. 440 now in Paris (Musée du Louvre G623; fig. 18) features the same boar hunt composition on both obverse and reverse.[61] In each case, the solitary hunter to the left stands before a horse and holds the reins in his left hand. Each hunter wears a spotted chiton, Scythian cap, and Scythian boots. Eastern attire figures prominently in the deer hunt on a cup by the Bonn Painter of c. 500–480 (Basel, Antikenmuseum und Sammlung Ludwig BS438; fig. 19).[62] Two other examples of deer hunters wearing Eastern attire can be added: an Attic red-figure amphora by the Kleophrades Painter of c. 500 (the neck, where some deer hunters wear Persian caps, and lid of the amphora are black-figure; Munich, Staatliche Antikensammlungen 2305 [J.411]; figs. 20–21);[63] and an Attic red-figure cup of c. 505, on which a panther accompanies two Scythians and a hoplite in pursuit of a stag (Berlin, Antikensammlung F2324; fig. 63).[64]

Moreover, after c. 520 deer and boar hunters wear attire or appear in poses that have heroic or ephebic connotations, which underscore the heroic nature of the hunt. Fifth-century hunters frequently adopt poses associated with the sculpted Tyrannicides group of 477/6 by Kritios and Nesiotes, known only from later copies: lunging with arms held overhead

FIGURES 16–17. Attic black-figure amphora by the Balançoire Painter, c. 520 B.C. Munich, Staatliche Antikensammlungen 1386. Photos courtesy of the Staatliche Antikensammlungen und Glyptothek München.

FIGURE 18. Attic red-figure cup Near the Painter of London E105, c. 440 B.C. Paris, Musée du Louvre G623. Photo by M. Chuzeville and C. Larrieu, courtesy of the Musée du Louvre.

FIGURE 19. Attic red-figure cup by the Bonn Painter, c. 500–480 B.C. Basel, Antikenmuseum und Sammlung Ludwig BS438. Photo courtesy of the Antikenmuseum Basel und Sammlung Ludwig.

or extended straight out with a chlamys hanging from it (though not grasped in the hand).[65] The statue group provided a prototype used for depictions of heroes in fifth-century sculpture and vase painting;[66] these stances became associated with youthful heroism (in spite of the fact that one of the Tyrannicides is bearded), especially with Theseus,[67] the paradigmatic ephebe, who participated in the Calydonian boar hunt. On the reverse of an Attic red-figure cup of c. 470 in Copenhagen (Nationalmuseet 6327; figs. 22–23),[68] a hunter approaches each side of a centrally placed boar. The hunter on our left, who lunges toward the boar, is nude save for a petasos slung around his neck and a chlamys. He holds an unsheathed sword in his right hand, and the empty sheath hangs at his left side. On the right, another hunter wears similar attire except that he sports a pilos on his head. The figure lunges forward on his right leg and raises his sword above his head. Both figures' poses recall those of the sculptural group of the Tyrannicides. On this cup, the hunters wearing petasoi and carrying swords on the left of both scenes recall contemporary images of Theseus. Both hunters are unbearded and use their chlamydes extended on one

FIGURES 20–21. Attic red-figure amphora by the Kleophrades Painter, c. 500 B.C. Munich, Staatliche Antikensamm- lungen 2305 [J.411]. Photos courtesy of the Staatliche Antikensammlungen und Glyptothek München.

arm as if they were shields, an iconographical device occasionally em- ployed for Theseus. Are the hunters Theseus? One cannot say because there is no identifying inscription or definitive marker of Theseus. Like the Calydonian boar hunt quotation on the black-figure amphora in Munich (Staatliche Antikensammlungen 1386; figs. 16–17), this ambiguity in de-

FIGURES 22–23. Attic red-figure cup by the Dokimasia Painter, c. 470 B.C. Copenhagen, Nationalmuseet 6327. Photos courtesy of the Department of Classical and Near Eastern Antiquities, National Museum, Copenhagen.

termining whether the hunters are mythological is deliberate, designed to associate nonmythological hunters with heroes.

The chlamys, noted in serveral hunt scenes, serves as another visual marker for the ephebe because it was the ceremonial dress for ephebes (at least in the fourth century; Philostr., VS 2.550), aristocratic young men aged eighteen to twenty engaged in military training. The association of chlamys and ephebe is especially pronounced for the Calydonian boar hunt, which has initiatory associations. Furthermore, the aristocratic hunters wear the chlamys held out as if it were a shield, and this practice is peculiar to hunters in generic hunting scenes and occasionally to heroic hunters, such as Theseus or Herakles. The viewer of such images reads the deer and boar hunters as aristocratic hunters, who are likened to hoplite warriors and heroes.

These changes in deer and boar hunt vases—reduction in number of hunters, the move to hunting on foot, the changes in weapons, the adoption of heroic poses, the use of chlamydes worn as if they were shields, and the move to drinking ware—require an explanation. Some scholars reason that the transition from collective hunt, sometimes mounted, to solitary hunt on foot was due to a shift in government in Athens from aristocracy to democracy. According to this line of thought, the mounted hunt was no longer commonly depicted after the change because of the horse's association with the aristocracy (cf. Xen., *Eq. Mag.* 1.11–12, *Ages.* 9.6; Arist., *Pol.* 1289b33–39, 1321a7–11; Isoc. 16.33 [horse racing]; Pind., *Pyth.* 1.90–91, 2.56–57, 5.1–7, 103–7, frag. 129).[69] Another view holds that the vase painting changes are due to a new perception of the hunt itself: collective pursuits were abandoned because the hunt was no longer regulated by the state but had become mere sport. Solitary, heroic hunts now celebrated the prowess of an individual;[70] the mounted hunters of boars or deer (the compositions are interchangeable) "illustrano un modo di vita legato all'equitazione e agli esercizi sportivi degli efebi."[71] Both explanations focus on whether the hunt is mounted or not and on how many hunters participate but leave other issues unexamined, such as the peak periods of production, the shape of the vases, and other compositional changes.

The Visual Context for Hunting Imagery

The kinds of images that accompany hunting on the same vase can further our understanding of the iconology of hunting depictions. Often the juxtaposition of hunt scenes with other themes on the same vase, particularly in the period c. 520–480, contributes to the heroic, aristocratic character of the hunting depictions themselves. Sometimes the connections between scenes on a vase are more obvious than on others. But even when using stock repertoire, vase painters or designers choose one image and not another to decorate their vases, and we must ask ourselves what compels this particular choice. The underlying assumption in this study is that such choices are largely culturally determined:[72] a painter chooses a particular set of images for a given shape because it forms a coherent whole in his mind, whether that whole be iconographical, decorative, or iconological. Moreover, it may be the case that the less inventive the painter, the more automatic and culturally determined the choice. One might object that there are vases whose images seem to betray no relationship whatsoever to one another; undoubtedly, there may be a few, although I would argue that even if there is no iconographical or iconological connection (at least that we can grasp), there may still be a decorative one.

Recurring patterns of juxtaposed images on many vases would indicate a coherence of images on a given vase. A careful examination of the artistic contexts of which hunting forms a part enables us to understand how hunting depictions relate to the whole program of a given vase or set of vases and reveals underlying cultural attitudes about the hunt, of which we can only catch furtive glimpses from a more superficial study. The hunts are often paired with battle images; chariot scenes,[73] including warriors' departures; *palaistra* activities; scenes of revelry; depictions of Herakles' adventures; and Dionysos banqueting. The viewer is invited to view all images on a given vase, drawing comparisons and contrasts, which are fostered sometimes by simple juxtaposition and sometimes by symmetrical compositions. The visual context of hunting imagery on Attic vases reveals a complex network of themes concerning military prowess, hunting, valor, and heroization that highlight the aristocratic aspect of the hunt and its ability to exalt the quotidian male to heroic status.

It may come as a surprise to learn that the boar hunt paintings, for example, are notable for the paucity in the variety of accompanying scenes. Other types of hunting scenes are the commonest complement. Hare hunts occasionally appear on the same vessel with the boar hunt, such as the Siana cup in Hamburg (Museum für Kunst und Gewerbe 1908.255; fig. 2),[74] and other vases combine the deer hunt and boar hunt: London

(British Museum B147; fig. 1); an Attic black-figure lekythos of c. 510 in Munich (Staatliche Antikensammmlungen 1966);[75] and the Copenhagen cup of c. 470 (Nationalmuseet 6327; figs. 22–23). The first of these, the London amphora, bears other scenes, including a chariot depiction, that combine with the hunting images to give an array of aristocratic adult male activities, specifically hunting and warfare. The birth of Athena as full-grown warrior on one side of the body of the vase is paired with a warrior in a chariot on the other, where shields, helmets, and spears emphasize the martial aspects of the scene. Animal friezes fill both the predella of the main amphora panels and the exterior ring of the lid, visually linking together the two portions of the vase, lid and body. Interestingly, beneath Zeus's throne is a scene of homosexual courtship, also one of the key activities of the adolescent and adult Athenian male, and a horse protome, certainly an aristocratic marker, constitutes the back of Zeus's throne.[76] Taken together, the images on the London amphora display a range of male activities—hunting, warfare, pederasty—central to the life of the aristocratic Athenian male in the late sixth century.

Chariots, battles, and warriors' departures are combined with boar or deer hunts elsewhere, as on an Attic black-figure hydria of c. 520–515 by the Antimenes Painter, now in London (British Museum B304; figs. 24–25).[77] The central panel of the hydria depicts two youths and a bearded man harnessing horses to a chariot while another youth steps up to the chariot. Nothing about this depiction suggests either myth or warfare save the chariot, which has been interpreted as signifying an epic scene.[78] A boar hunt fills the predella, and the shoulder bears an image of hoplite combat. In the former, mounted hunters wielding spears attack a central boar, and male figures wearing only chlamydes draped over their outstretched arms run behind the mounted hunters. One of the mounted hunters wears a Scythian cap. On the shoulder two armed hoplites approach a third who has fallen to his knee; a spear from the nearer of the two advancing figures has pierced him. All three are armed with cuirass, helmet, shield, and spear, and two of the three have sheathed swords at their waists. To the right of the fallen hoplite, a quadriga is driven over the outstretched body of a fallen male; another armed hoplite runs behind the chariot, and a Scythian archer appears at the far right of the image. The shoulder and predella images form compositional complements of each

FIGURES 24–25. Attic black-figure hydria by the Antimenes Painter, c. 520–515 B.C. London, British Museum B304. Photos courtesy of the British Museum. © The British Museum.

other. Hoplite warriors spear a human victim on the shoulder, while hunters spear an animal victim on the predella.

The use of the boar hunt as a visual simile to battle is especially appropriate because conquest of this fierce animal involved a dangerous physical confrontation. The chariot passing over the wounded or dead warrior is another compositional quotation from Calydonian boar hunt paintings, where the boar moves above a dead or wounded hunter. Again, we may understand this battle image as one that merges myth with generic scene. When read as a whole, the hydria shows hunting and warfare with chariot harnessing sandwiched between. Because of the lack of weapons, the chariot activity should signify an athletic event rather than a battle. The chariot may signal epic overtones or, more accurately, heroic overtones, thus adding even more heroic luster to the hunters, who are visually compared with hoplites and athletes. The hydria can be envisioned then as a thematic unity, combining three aristocratic male events: warfare, athletics, and hunting.[79]

FIGURES 26–27. Miniature Attic black-figure cup, c. 550–530 B.C. Cambridge, Mass., Arthur M. Sackler Museum 1925.30.131. Photos courtesy of the Arthur M. Sackler Museum, Harvard University Art Museums, Bequest of Joseph C. Hoppin. © President and Fellows of Harvard College, Harvard University.

The combination of hoplite battle, warrior's departure, and a hunt, this time a deer hunt, occurs on an Attic red-figure volute krater of c. 450 by the Niobid Painter (Paris, Musée du Louvre G343).[80] A deer hunt on the neck of one side of the krater is combined with hoplite battle on the body, while the reverse bears a warrior's departure on the body and the departure of Triptolemos on the neck.

Athletics are also occasionally paired with the boar hunt and constitute the most common theme to be combined with the deer hunt. A miniature Attic black-figure kylix of c. 550–530 (Cambridge, Arthur M. Sackler Museum 1925.30.131; figs. 26–27) juxtaposes boar hunting with boxing,[81] thus yielding two types of athletic activity on the same vessel. What is striking about this cup is the use of the same compositional scheme for the boar hunt on one side and boxing on the reverse. In the hunt scene, two hunters converge on a centrally placed boar; on the reverse, two males flank a central pair of boxers, and in both instances hunters and onlookers adopt precisely the same pose and the same accoutrements, chlamys held on outstretched arm and a spear. While the spear may be appropriate for hunters, and we have observed that the chlamys is identified with hunters, the onlookers of a boxing match would scarcely need the same attire and weapons. One can surmise that the artist intended the two scenes and the two activities to be compared.[82] The viewer reads the visual simile thus: hunting is like fighting or fighting is like hunting.

Hunting and athletics are combined elsewhere as well, as on the Villa Giulia cup of c. 500 (50535; figs. 6–7). The exterior is decorated with a deer hunt on the obverse, a palaistra scene on the reverse, while a youth, presumably an *eromenos*, holds a hare on the interior tondo.[83] As was the case with the black-figure examples discussed already, we see either a combination of aristocratic male activities—hunting, athletics, and pederasty, all three of which involve *agon*—or an analogy between the deer hunt and athletic contest.[84] An Attic red-figure amphora of c. 500 by the Kleophrades Painter (Munich, Staatliche Antikensammlungen 2305 [J.411]; figs. 20–21) also pairs deer hunting with athletics on the lip and belly of one side respectively, while the reverse of the vase combines a chariot scene on the lip with a warrior's departure on the belly.[85] Athletics formed part of the training of warriors, as did hunting. The juxtaposition on the obverse is of two physical confrontations that are good preparation and even analogues for warfare, while a warrior departs on the reverse. Note that a hunting dog stands alongside the hoplite warrior so that the warrior also appears as a hunter; once again the two activities are linked.[86] The chariots lend heroic overtones to the warriors and, by extension, to the hunters and athletes.

Mythological themes, particularly Herakles' labors, also frequently accompany hunting depictions. The Antimenes Painter and His Circle of c. 520–510 are responsible for a series of painted hydriae that pair predella

FIGURE 28. Attic black-figure hydria
by the Antimenes Painter, c. 515
B.C. Copenhagen, Thorvaldsens
Museum H554. Photo courtesy of
the Thorvaldsens Museum.

deer hunts and a boar hunt
with various scenes on the
body and shoulder,[87] often a
youth mounting a quadriga
or simply a frontal quadriga,
but also Dionysos reclining on a *kline* surrounded by his entourage, fountainhouse scenes, Herakles fighting various adversaries, warriors' departures, and hoplite battles; the scenes are primarily heroic or martial, some
of which are visual similes.[88]

The Antimenes Painter and His Circle are particularly adept at creating visual similes on their hydriae, which invest generic hunt scenes with
greater meaning, particularly when hunts are paired with Heraklean adventures. For example, Herakles wrestles with the Nemean lion on the
shoulder of a hydria in Copenhagen (Thorvaldsens Museum H554; fig.
28), a frontal quadriga with flanking hoplites occupies the central panel,
and a deer hunt fills the predella.[89] Both the hoplites and the deer hunters
use spears, underscoring the association of warfare and hunting, whose
heroism is exemplified by Herakles, who can even hunt the Nemean lion
without weapons. Thus, we are meant to read the hunt as if it were battle
and Herakles as either a model for the warrior or hunter, perhaps even as
heroic analogue for the quotidian aristocratic warrior-hunter. The simile
would suggest that hunting is like battle, and the hunter or warrior is like
Herakles fighting an opponent. The same kind of interpretation applies to
another hydria of c. 510 (Ex-Küsnacht, Hirschmann Collection G9),[90]
whose shoulder is painted with Herakles fighting Kyknos, while a deer
hunt fills the predella and a frontal chariot with hoplites occupies the central panel. Another hydria of c. 530–510 by the Alkmene Painter (London,

FIGURE 29. Attic black-figure hydria by the Lysippides Painter, c. 525–500 B.C. Paris, Musée du Louvre F294. Photo by M. Chuzeville and C. Larrieu, courtesy of the Musée du Louvre.

British Museum B301),[91] part of the Antimenes Painter's Circle, joins deer hunting with depictions of Herakles, his wrestling the Nemean lion and Herakles banqueting. The heroic conflict with the lion and the hero enjoying the fruits of his labors seem to offer heroic analogues with the everyday hunter, who also performs a heroic feat.

This pairing of Herakles' labors with hunting also occurs on vases by painters outside the Antimenes Painter's Circle, such as a hydria of c. 525–500 by the Lysippides Painter (Paris, Musée du Louvre F294; fig. 29).[92] Felled by three spears, a centrally placed doe stumbles as two hunters approach from either side on the predella. Herakles' transportation to Olympos with Athena and other deities appears on the body, and a frontal chariot is painted on the shoulder. If we understand the hunters as likened to Herakles, then by this brave deed the hunter, like the hero, may also attain immortal status.

Two hydriae from the Antimenes Painter corpus pair deer hunts with fountainhouse scenes. On the Antimenes Painter's name vase in Leiden (Rijksmuseum van Oudheden II 167 [PC63]; figs. 13–14), two youths shower beneath panther head spouts within a fountainhouse in the cen-

FIGURE 30. Attic black-figure
hydria by the Antimenes Painter,
c. 515 B.C. Rome, Museo
Gregoriano Etrusco Vaticano
426. Photo courtesy of the
Direzione Generale,
Monumenti Musei e Gallerie
Pontifiche, Rome.

tral panel, and pairs of nude
youths interact on either ex-
terior side of the fountainhouse. Aryballoi and chlamydes, suggestive of
the world of the palaistra and ephebe, hang on the trees outside the fountainhouse, and one of the youths empties an aryballos into his left hand.
A warrior's departure on the hydria's shoulder is enhanced by the presence
of Hermes, indicated by his caduceus, winged boots, and petasos. The appearance of Hermes, escort of the dead to the Underworld, may suggest
that the warrior prepares to meet his death on the battlefield. At the bottom of the vase is a deer hunt: two mounted hunters with spears poised attack a central doe, and at the margins of the composition are two male figures on foot wearing only chlamydes over their extended arms as if the
garments were shields. Again, the images can be read as a collection of
aristocratic male activities: aristocratic youths destined to become warriors
and hunters.

The other hydria with a fountainhouse–deer hunt combination, however, is more puzzling (Rome, Museo Gregoriano Etrusco Vaticano 426;
fig. 30).[93] Women gather around a fountainhouse, where they fetch water
in hydriae like the vessel on which they are painted. Beneath them is a
deer hunt scene precisely like that on the Leiden hydria, and on the shoulder we see actual hoplite combat, where hoplites spear each other much as
the hunters do their prey. Fountainhouse scenes are, of course, appropriate
for hydriae, and we should not be surprised to see them on these water vessels. The conglomeration of images on the hydria in Leiden suggests the

world of the Athenian male but only two of the three paintings on the Vatican hydria do so, and not only are these activities of the aristocratic male but they are visual analogues or similes: combat against an animal adversary, combat against a human adversary (a pairing that also occurs on the British Museum hydria [B304], figs. 24–25). The Athenian viewer, who understood combat and hunting as analogous activities, would have read the images on this vase in this fashion. If we view the Vatican hydria as a thematically unified whole, then perhaps we should see the vase as a contrast between male and female activities unless, as has been suggested, the women at the fountainhouse are engaged in a religious ritual, the Hydrophoria, which occurred on the last day of Anthesteria.[94]

To sum up, the hunt series of Antimenes Painter hydriae combines deer hunts with subjects that are clearly part of the world of the aristocratic Athenian male,[95] and the hunt's placement in conjunction with the heroic is designed not only to link the generic hunt to the heroic realm but to liken the former to the latter. It is difficult, however, to posit an association between the hunt and some themes, such as the women at the fountainhouse.

The juxtaposition of Dionysos and hunting on the Antimenes Painter hydriae is intriguing. But the association of Dionysos and hunting on the same vase is not restricted to this painter and his circle. Returning hunters approach Dionysos on several vases; deer hunting is paired with satyrs and maenads on an Attic black-figure amphora by the Painter of Vatican 342 of c. 510–500 in Basel (Antikenmuseum und Sammlung Ludwig BS 495);[96] and deer hunting is combined with drinking youths on Attic red-figure cups of c. 510 now in Würzburg (Martin von Wagner Museum der Universität 473), Paris (Musée du Louvre G21), and New York (Metropolitan Museum of Art, Gallatin 41.162.129).[97] We consider the combination of hunt with Dionysiac scene later in this chapter.

Finally, we should note the pairing of deer hunting with Peleus's abduction of Thetis on a hydria of c. 520–500 now in Rome (Museo Nazionale Etrusco di Villa Giulia, Cerveteri, Monte Abatone T610).[98] Such a juxtaposition may at first be puzzling but a greater consideration of the mythological theme demonstrates yet another visual simile. The unmarried female was regarded as a wild animal, in need of the taming and domestication that marriage can bring. This is certainly the case for Thetis, whose animal qualities are made manifest by her transformation into various wild creatures in an effort to escape Peleus's grasp. Vase paintings demonstrate this through a visual metaphor in which Thetis is shown in female form but animals surround her: she is both female and animal. It is also noteworthy that the deer being hunted is a doe. When read together, both images depict a wild animal being hunted: one is a sexual pursuit, the other a potentially deadly pursuit, and both test a young man's fitness for adulthood.

Thus, many deer and boar hunt images appear in close physical proximity with paintings of activities definitive of the Athenian aristocratic male, athletics and battle, or with mythological scenes that celebrate the hero Herakles, a model for athletic prowess and bravery in the face of deadly conflict. In some cases, a clear analogy or simile is intended between the hunt and accompanying scene; elsewhere, they are simply complementary. Both juxtaposition and symmetrical compositions are used to express these ideas. When read together, the combination of hunt and heroic deed suggests the heroic nature of the hunt and its ability to exalt the quotidian male to heroic status; the combination of hunt and other aristocratic activities, such as battle, underscores the aristocratic nature of the hunt. One might argue that because many of the deer hunt–heroic theme combinations appear on hydriae associated with one painter and his circle, such a combination may have been a standard fill pattern for the workshop and has no special significance. But because we have many other depictions of deer hunts juxtaposed to heroic themes outside of this set of vases, we should consider reading the deer hunts together with heroic themes as a meaningful juxtaposition. Moreover, as argued earlier, the "random decorative choice" explanation is largely untenable.

Hunting, Warfare, and the Aristocrat

The archaic and early classical Attic vase paintings, together with the written evidence, admittedly of a later date, suggest that the hunt had heroic connotations and close links to warfare[99] and, in Athens and elsewhere, indicated a man's fitness for participation in civic and military life. The use of hunting and battle scenes on the same vases, beginning in the mid-sixth century and continuing into the fifth century, suggests that the viewer of such depictions would have understood a close association of these two activities in which males could demonstrate courage or valor. By the end of the sixth century, the two types of imagery, hunt and battle, begin to fuse as martial elements occasionally spring up in hunting scenes: hunters wear helmets and greaves and carry shields; swords become primary weapons; spears play a secondary role; even chlamydes are poised on a bent or outstretched arm, recalling images of shields; and in some instances, such armor manqué is visually paired with a shield. In these cases, a visual metaphor for the hunt as battle is achieved, and the ideas of hunt and battle become one—that is, hunting is warfare. The poses of several fifth-century painted hunters mimic those of the civic heroes who were (falsely) credited with overthrowing the tyranny, the Tyrannicides. Hunting depictions are paired with heroic mythological scenes or battle depictions, which conjure up associations in the viewer's mind. Hunting and fighting are activities of brave adult men, and they can be done heroically; in other words, heroes hunt and fight, and so do real men. The latter are like heroes when they face extraordinary danger unflinchingly and successfully.[100] Taken as a whole, the weapons, poses, and accompanying images heroize hunting and hunters and demonstrate that, for the Greeks, hunting is battle.

What is lacking in this equation is the visual evidence for the inverse analogy: that battle is like hunting or that battle is hunting.[101] There are no extant battle scenes marked with hunting peculiarities unless we count hoplite shield devices of boar and other animals, although a fallen warrior and a fallen, hunted animal appear in a similar fashion on opposite sides of the same Attic red-figure cup signed by Douris (Boston, Museum of Fine Arts 00.338).[102] Although this book concerns the archaic and classical periods, it should be mentioned that Homeric epic repeatedly draws analogues between hunting and battle, using hunting metaphors, particularly lion hunting, to describe battle situations between Achaeans and Trojans.[103] And the episode of Dolon's capture in *Iliad* 10, which concerns a night raid, ambush, and warriors disguised as animals, offers a literary example of battle likened to hunting.[104] The Homeric epics played a prominent role in Athenian sixth-century culture, and the poems' hunting images—and their aristocratic flavor—certainly may have influenced the popularity and ideology of vase paintings of both heroic and heroizing hunts.[105]

Finally, we must address the striking issue of the dates when hunting scenes are most numerous in Attic vase painting and when marked compositional changes occur that liken hunting to battle and heroize the hunters. As noted earlier, scholars have pointed to the transition from tyranny and aristocratic power to democracy at the end of the sixth century to explain the diminution of scenes of collective hunting and hunting on horseback. But if aristocratic pursuits and activities are eschewed by democratic Athens, how does one explain the continued appearance of monumental marble *kouroi*, symbols of the aristocracy, as votives and funerary markers until c. 480, nearly thirty years after the Kleisthenic reforms? Perhaps the kouroi would have persisted even longer had there been no Persian invasion. This examination of the hunting scenes and their contexts not only supports the claim that hunting depictions are clearly associated with aristocrats but extends it considerably and leads to different conclusions.

The subject matter of hunting itself commonly had aristocratic connotations and in both visual and written texts, hunting became closely connected with, and even identical to, hoplite battle. Both hunting and warfare were especially associated with the aristocracy or small property owner,[106] who commanded economic, religious, and much political power until the advent of the Kleisthenic reforms in 508.[107] This class was able to live by the labor of others and consequently spent its time engaged in warfare[108] and those pursuits prescribed by Isocrates (*Areopag.* 45) a century later: horsemanship, athletics, hunting, and philosophy.[109] By its very definition, the hoplite class provided its own armor and therefore had to possess a fair amount of money or land, although this category of men increasingly widened over the sixth century.[110] The shape that becomes dominant in the late sixth and early fifth centuries for hunting paintings is the cup, followed by other symposion ware, and the symposion was an aristocratic activity.[111] The vase painting iconography from c. 520–470 likens the hunter, engaged in an aristocratic leisure pursuit to the noble hoplite warrior, who embodies aristocratic virtue.[112] The palaistra imagery that accompanies hunting is linked with both the aristocrat and battle: athletics and hunting were part of the education of youths in some locations,[113] and the gymnasion provided the training ground for military activity (Plut., *Mor.* 639d–e refers to Greek athletics as "imitation and preparation for war" [cf. Pl., *Prt.* 326b–c; Xen., *Mem.* 3.12.1–4]).[114] In fact, it has been suggested that the surge of athletics in the sixth century is attributable to the growth of hoplite warfare and the concurrent need for trained bodies.[115] The association of hunting with the aristocracy also explains the juxtaposition of hunting with heroic activities, particularly those of Herakles, who reflected the aspirations of the aristocratic class (Boardman's argument of Herakles as tool of the tyranny notwithstanding). In other words, the iconography and visual context of the Attic hunting depictions should be understood as references to aristocratic ideals.

The number of Attic hunt depictions and their accompanying scenes, both of which possessed aristocratic connotations, increases c. 520–470. This phenomenon can be understood if the paintings are considered in their historical context. This was a period of profound political and social change for Athens, which experienced radical transformations that ultimately resulted in the overthrow of tyranny, the advent of democracy, and the loss of *official* aristocratic political power. But, in actuality, the aristocracy did not lose much political power. The aristocracy stepped into the void after Hippias's ouster in 510 but soon became divided by faction (Hdt. 5.66). The Kleisthenic reforms actually benefited the political power of the Alkmeonid family by taking power away from other aristocratic families.[116] And although the reforms broadened the powers of the *demos*, aristocrats did not wither away and die but continued to exert a degree of political power (e.g., in the Areopagos),[117] which was finally sharply truncated by the Ephialtic reforms of 462.[118] Although aristocrats may not have held official political power under the democracy, most of the chief leaders of the young Athenian democracy, such as Kimon (ostracized in 461), were aristocratic,[119] and clearly aristocratic social values were still held in high esteem.[120]

Even during the rule of Peisistratos and his sons, when aristocrats were often in opposition to the Athenian tyranny,[121] the aristocracy maintained a level of social control and leadership embodied in the concept of *kaloskagathos*, exemplified in such activities as the symposion (e.g., Thgn. 983–88; Pind., *Nem.* 9.49–52) and pederasty. Artistic and literary production, such as archaic kouroi, reliefs, and the poetry of Pindar and Bacchylides, whose subjects and patrons were the *agathoi*,[122] also attest to this aristocratic ideology.[123] Even as their power ebbed and flowed under the tyrants in the sixth century and gradually declined under the democracy, the agathoi continued to maintain social leadership and enjoy leisure pursuits, including hunting.[124]

When viewed against this background, the Attic vase paintings of hunting with their subject matter, shape, and martial and heroic associations, which reach a peak of production as the polis undergoes the transition to democracy, reveal what is otherwise unknown from written documents:

the aristocratic reaction to the social and political changes at the end of the sixth century. Rather than diminishing in numbers in response to the advent of democracy as has been posited, hunting imagery intensifies in Attic pottery as aristocrats struggled to maintain their leadership role and set the tone in artistic and social practices as their political power was officially truncated.[125] Instead of indicating an aversion to aristocratic pastimes and ideology, the hunting vases underscore and emphasize them. As the political and power base widened to include the demos, the cultural associations of the hunt and other aristocratic activities, such as battle and athletics, remained wedded to the aristocratic ideal expressed by the term kaloskagathos and seems to have served even as a social model for the democracy.[126] Hunting depictions that combine Eastern and Greek hunters (e.g., figs. 18–21, 63) were perhaps envisioned as occurring in Eastern lands, particularly when palm trees appear alongside Eastern-attired hunters, but such images were nonetheless created by Athenian artists and reflect Athenian concerns; the royal, and therefore exclusive, connotation of the Eastern hunt may have appealed to Athenian aristocratic sensibilities.[127]

In addition to the concentration of images c. 520–470, hunting imagery in Attic vase paintings experienced a boom period at an earlier time, c. 560–550. Perhaps this surge resulted from a similar sociopolitical cause. Peisistratos, tyrant of Athens, first came to power c. 560, and the vase paintings of the hunt may be an aristocratic response to this new form of government, which sharply curtailed aristocratic political power. Such an interpretation assumes that aristocrats had some control of ceramic production, either directly in the manufacturing stage or as patrons of ceramics—that is, the law of supply and demand.[128] Even if Michael Vickers and David Gill are correct in arguing that ceramic vases were cheap imitations of gold and silver vessels used by aristocrats,[129] they also acknowledge that metal vessels had the great disadvantage of marring the taste of liquids.[130] It seems likely that silver and gold plate were reserved for special occasions and that the terracotta hunt vases were probably used most of the time or at least simultaneously with plate at the aristocratic symposion, that quintessential symbol of Athenian aristocratic males, and by nonelites wishing to imitate and appropriate the customs and ideology of the propertied class.

Hunt, the Ephebe, and Battle

Written evidence attests that the hunt was used as a rite of passage in
Sparta and on Crete to prepare young men to become soldiers—hunting
skills were applicable to warfare—and to exalt adolescent males to adulthood status. Whereas hunting was definitely a part of these other rites, no
written documentation attests to the hunt's use as preparation for the military in Athens. However, Attic vase painting of the late sixth and early fifth
centuries invites visual comparisons of hunting and battle, suggesting a
strong association of the two activities, and fourth-century written texts are
unequivocal in connecting them. But an association and an analogy between hunting and battle are not the same things as an initiation ritual to
adult status. Using the cases of Sparta and Crete and combining them with
myth, Pierre Vidal-Naquet argues that hunting was part of ephebic training
in Athens,[131] although he acknowledges that this practice is attested in
myth rather than in actuality[132]—an important, and I think, critical, distinction. Certainly the archaic and early classical vase paintings of hunting have a paramilitary character, equating hunting with hoplite warfare,
but whether such paintings can be adduced as evidence of an early
ephebeia in Athens is harder to say. In order to challenge Vidal-Naquet's
claim in light of the conclusions drawn earlier in this chapter, we should
define the limits of what can be known about the hunt and military training in fifth-century Athens.

The date of the inception of the Athenian ephebeia will never be
known for certain from the extant evidence. An ephebeia was institutionalized in Athens by the fourth century. Whether it existed as a formally or-
ganized program earlier cannot be verified, but scholars have pointed to
passages of fifth-century literature that mention Athenian activities much
like those that were definitely part of the fourth-century (and later)
ephebeia and to the fourth-century ephebic oath, whose language includes
archaizing forms, which suggest that it is older.[133] From the activities and
the archaizing aspects of the oath, some scholars have advocated an
ephebeia, however loosely comprised, in fifth-century Athens.

Our knowledge of the Athenian ephebeia comes primarily from fourth-
century inscriptions, the *Athenaion Politeia* 42, and literary references of
the fourth-century and later. According to the *Athenaion Politeia*, when
citizens were registered with the deme at age eighteen, these new citizens

were called ephebes.[134] The ephebes were supervised by adult men and served guard duty for one year at Piraeus, Mounichia, and Akte, where they were instructed in the use of the bow, javelin, and catapult while wearing armor. At the beginning of the second year, the ephebes gave a demonstration of their skills in warfare before a meeting of the *ekklesia* in the theater and in turn, received a shield and spear from the city. They spent the second year patrolling the countryside. During this two-year period, the ephebes wore a military cloak and were exempt from all civic duties; they could not prosecute or be prosecuted in the lawcourts (save for inheritances) or adopt a hereditary priesthood. At the end of the two-year period, the ephebes joined the citizen body.

The earliest inscription that clearly refers to an institutionalized ephebeia dates in the mid-330s and is one of a number of texts that record the oath or activities of Athenian ephebes.[135] The inscriptions tell us that ephebes served guard duty at Eleusis and Phyle, and participated in games at religious festivals.[136] Wilamowitz proposed that the ephebeia mentioned in these late-fourth-century texts is a new institution,[137] but other scholars maintain that some form of the ephebeia existed already in the fifth century. Reinmuth suggests a date of inception just after the Persian Wars[138] and some go so far as to see the ephebeia or some form of it going back to the sixth century. According to this line of reasoning, Lykourgos made adjustments to an already existing institution in c. 336/5 and made the ephebeia full-time service for all Athenian citizens. Thus, the *Athenaion Politeia* was written after modifications were made.[139] Reinmuth sees the early fourth-century ephebeia as a military organization of eighteen- to twenty-year-olds, who served part-time during a two-year period of service; when Lykourgos made the service continuous, its nature changed from a military to an educational institution.[140]

The ephebic inscriptions (admittedly of the fourth century and later) provide evidence that the annual class of ephebes was between 450 and 500 youths; thus, the entire two-year class numbered around 1,000.[141] Estimates of the number of ephebes who participated in a hypothetical pre-336/5 ephebeia may be overly speculative and matters little for our purposes.[142] After all, whether all aristocrats or only a few participated, the symbolic value of the few for the whole would have been evident.

In addition to the *Athenian Politeia*, preserved texts of the ephebic oath on a fourth- century B.C. stele from Acharnai (now in the École française d'Athènes) and in passages of Pollux (8.105–6) of the second century A.D. and Stobaeus (*Flor.* 43, 48) of the early fifth century A.D. yield more detailed information regarding the duties of ephebes, at least in the fourth century B.C.[143] According to the oath, which was sworn in the sanctuary of Aglauros in Athens, the ephebes promised to behave properly in hoplite battle, to defend public and religious institutions, to help expand the territory, and to obey the laws. The oath was witnessed by a series of deities and by the boundaries of the territory: πυροί, κριθαί, ἄμπελοι, ἐλᾶαι, συκαῖ—that is, the agricultural products of the land—and the ephebes made a sacrifice to Artemis Agrotera.[144] The oath has also been invoked as evidence of a pre-fourth-century B.C. ephebeia. Scholars have noted the archaic quality of its language,[145] and P. Siewert claims to see traces of the ephebic oath in fifth-century B.C. literature, including the works of Thucydides, Aischylos, and Sophocles, although he distinguishes the ephebic oath as a civil oath from an oath connected with military duties.[146]

Scholars have also adduced passages of fifth century B.C. literature to argue for an ephebeia preceding the fourth century. For example, if, as some claim, Aischylos's *Seven against Thebes* (10–16) refers to ephebes like those of the *Athenaion Politeia*, then the earliest literary reference to the ephebeia can be dated at 467.[147] Passages of Thucydides (2.13.7, 4.67.2, 8.92.2), Xenophon (*Vect.* 4.47.52), and Aischines (1.49, 2.167–68) also mention frontier duty performed by youths known as *peripoloi*, whom scholars identify as ephebes,[148] and Thucydides (1.105.4) talks about *neotatoi*, who engage in activities that are characteristic of the later ephebeia.[149] The fourth-century Aischines claims to have served as peripolos for a period of two years. The service as peripolos, literally "one who circles the city," coincides with the activities of the ephebic peripolos of the fourth century, who were normally stationed in the frontier.[150] We know that Aischines was born c. 390, so Aischines' two-year period beginning at age eighteen in c. 372/1 was far earlier than the first ephebic inscriptions.[151] J. Lofberg also cites passages of Demosthenes and Lykourgos that indicate that some form of the ephebeia existed prior to the late fourth century.[152]

These efforts at trying to locate the ephebeia earlier than the fourth century have not been limited to written texts. The painting on a black-figure vase in the Hermitage has been read as the swearing of the ephebic oath; because the vase is black-figure, it must date before c. 430, hence the ephebeia must exist by this date.[153] Reinmuth even claims that the equestrian figures on the Parthenon frieze of c. 442–438 wearing petasoi and chlamydes are ephebes.[154]

If there was an ephebeia prior to the fourth century and it already possessed fourth-century ephebic traits, we would expect that ephebes patrolled border areas, wore chlamydes, and were youths between eighteen and twenty years old. But did they hunt as part of their training as did youths in Sparta and on Crete? Pierre Vidal-Naquet tries to draw connections between Athenian ephebes and hunting in the fifth century based on analogies with the Spartan and Cretan rites of passage and on a reading of the myth of Melanthos, the aitiological myth of the Apatouria, a key festival for Athenian ephebes.[155]

The myth of Melanthos and Xanthos, who fought in the border territory between Boeotia and Attica, is recounted by Hellanicus (*FGrH* 4 frag. 125 = schol. Pl., *Symp.* 208D), Ephoros (*FGrH* 70 frag. 22 in Harp., Ἀπατούρια), Conon (*FGrH* 26 frag. 39 = Phot., *Bibl.* 186), Polyaenus 1.19, Plato (*Ti.* 21b and scholiast ad loc.), and the scholia at Aristophanes, *Acharnenses* 146e and *Pax* 890.[156] A dispute broke out between Boeotia and Attica over a border territory, and to settle the disagreement, a duel was arranged between the Athenian king Thymoites of Attica and Xanthos (the "White One") of Boeotia. But Thymoites stepped down, and Melanthos ("the Black One") was promised the kingship should he win. In the duel, Melanthos diverted Xanthos by claiming that there was a figure standing behind him wearing a black goatskin; Xanthos turned round to look and Melanthos took the opportunity to kill him. Thus, Melanthos won the kingship of Athens by means of a trick. Some sources omit Thymoites, and some accounts relate that the figure wearing the black goatskin was Dionysos Melanaigis.[157] Ancient authors saw this myth as an aition for the Athenian Apatouria, a festival in honor of Athena Phratria and Zeus Phratrios, at which youths aged sixteen years old dedicated a lock of their hair to Artemis on the third day of the festival in a rite called the *koureion*.[158] According to this reasoning, the *apate* (trick) of the victor is commemorated by this festival.[159] Theseus, with his tests on his journey from Troezen to Athens, has also been nominated as the mythical model for this rite.[160]

The boys who enrolled in the phratry at the Apatouria were eligible for ephebic service two years later after their registration with the deme at age eighteen. Using the Spartan and Cretan rites of passage combined with the texts of Plato and Xenophon that discuss appropriate and inappropriate methods of hunting, Vidal-Naquet and others posit a model of Athenian ephebic behavior, including hunting, which is in opposition to that of the Athenian hoplite and is initiatory.[161] While the hoplite hunts at day in a collective hunt for large game using spears, the ephebe hunts alone at night for small game using snares and nets. For the former, the emphasis is on collective action and dangerous, life-threatening confrontations with animals, a model for the battlefield, whereas ephebic hunts stress individual action and conquest by means of ambush and trickery, the opposite of hoplite tactics.[162] Vidal-Naquet finds a prototype for the Athenian ephebe in the myth of Melanthos's trickery; he notes the similarities of the border location of the Attic-Boeotian dispute and the border patrols mentioned in fifth-century texts and in the fourth-century ephebic oaths;[163] and the use of the color black in the myth, which recalls the black chlamydes worn by the fourth-century ephebes on ceremonial occasions.[164] According to this argument, Vidal-Naquet speculates that fifth-century Athenian ephebes, eighteen- to twenty-year-old males, were "black hunters," who found their prototype in Melanthos. They "hunted" their prey at night, using trickery and stealth like their mythological model. Vidal-Naquet further offers the mythological Melanion as an exemplar of the black hunter.[165] Melanion was a chaste hunter devoted to Artemis, who eventually married Atalanta and fathered Parthenopaios, and was among the hunters of the Calydonian boar.[166]

Such a neat explanation is very appealing, although no Athenian written record supports the entirety of this formula. In the Hellenistic period ephebes may have marched in armor to the temple of Artemis Agrotera (*IG* II² 1058, 8), that deity of warfare and hunting, but the paucity of hard evidence remains problematic in postulating a fifth-century ephebeia. While Plato (*Leg.* 822d–824a) and Athenaeus (18a) praise the type of hunting that Vidal-Naquet links to the mature hoplite and condemn that associated with the immature ephebe, these authors do not frame their comments in terms opposing ephebe and hoplite; rather, Plato simply addresses his recommendations about hunting to young people.

According to Vidal-Naquet, the black hunter model expresses cultural values regarding hunting and warfare, both in Athens and elsewhere. If we consult Attic vase painting, we find that paintings of the hunt, especially the boar and deer hunt, certainly possess martial elements, including the use of hoplite equipment in the hunt for large game; according to Vidal-

Naquet's model, these would be mature, hoplite hunters, who hunt fierce opponents, rather than small prey. Attic vase painting offers striking similarities between hunters of large game and warriors and the required valor for both activities, but seems not to emphasize age difference with regard to types of hunting.

For example, if beards are used as an index of maturity, the vase painting record is ambiguous because both beardless and bearded hunters participate in deer and boar hunting, although beardlessness is prevalent for all types of hunters in Attic red-figure. We might also consider the black chlamydes worn by fourth-century ephebes, which, according to Vidal-Naquet, correspond to the black goatskin worn by Melanthos's attendant. As noted earlier, many of the hunters on vase paintings of the end of the sixth century and into the fifth century sport chlamydes, frequently on otherwise nude bodies, and wear them draped over outstretched arms as if the fabric were a shield. On one red-figure cup of c. 510 (Paris, Louvre G22; figs. 11–12), paired deer hunters make clear the visual analogy between the chlamys and shield. Admittedly, one cannot tell the intended color of the chlamydes on Attic vases so the analogy to the black chlamydes of fourth-century ephebes cannot be proved. But rather than being associated with immature hunting, which, according to the black hunter model, would mean hare hunting, chlamydes are most frequently worn by boar and deer hunters.

In fact, the chlamys, even when associated with ephebes, seems to have heroic connotations. Pierre Roussel claims that the traditional black chlamys of the ephebe was worn to commemorate the return of Theseus to Athens after killing the Minotaur.[167] Because Theseus forgot to change his sail from black to white to signal a successful venture, his father committed suicide and thus Theseus ascended to the kingship of Athens (Plut., *Thes.* 17, 22).[168] Theseus was considered the ephebe par excellence among fifth-century Athenians, the hero of the Athenian democracy. The link between Theseus and the Athenian ephebes is underscored by the fact that the Apatouria, at which boys were enrolled in the phratry, was followed by the Oschophoria, an Athenian festival that commemorated Theseus's return.[169] We might also consider the heroic connotations attached to the hunting scenes with hunters posed as if they were tyrant slayers, proudly brandishing hoplite weapons and outstretched chlamydes as they dispatch large game. Because these are beardless males wearing chlamydes who perform adult, hoplite hunting, either beardlessness is not an index of age, or young men can act as mature hunters, thus vitiating Vidal-Naquet's argument.

Although initiation rites in Sparta and Crete employ the hunt as preparation for warfare, no such activity is attested for Athens, where the ephebeia, only evidenced for certain in the fourth century, serves to prepare young men for battle. It has been argued that hunting is part of the Athenian ephebe's service on the basis of analogy with these other regions of Greece and the myth of Melanthos, the mythical ancestor of the Athenian ephebe, whose tricky behavior in fighting a human opponent corresponds to the immature hunting deplored by Plato and Athenaeus. But, although Athenian vase painting demonstrates a clear simile and even metaphor for hunting and warfare, and associates both with the aristocracy, there is no visual evidence that hunting was part of initiation in Athens in preparation for military service. Moreover, vase paintings do not clearly display polar opposites of types of hunting corresponding to age groups but rather suggests a continuum along which one can mark necessary levels of courage or speed with no obvious link to age.

Dionysos's connection with the myth of Melanthos is somewhat puzzling because this deity has no association with the Apatouria.[170] His inclusion in the myth may be a late addition to an earlier core, but several Athenian festivals involving ephebes who honor Dionysos may help explain Dionysos's role in the myth of the Athenian ephebe's prototype. This is particularly true for the City Dionysia, whose tragedies often concerned ephebes and employed hunting imagery.

Ephebes and Tragedy

In this final section, we explore the relationship of hunting themes in tragedy to their social and religious context in an effort to discern more clearly why Dionysos is an appropriate subject to accompany hunting in vase painting. Dionysos or Dionysiac subject matter may appear together with hunting scenes simply because the vessels that it decorates are drinking vessels. But considering the existing links between aristocratic ephebes and hunting, hunting and warfare, and ephebes and Dionysos, it seems worth exploring possible further associations of Dionysos, ephebes, and hunting.

Two Athenian festivals honoring Dionysos involve the participation of ephebes. The Oschophoria was believed to have been founded by Theseus and honored his return from Crete via Phaleron (Plut., *Thes.* 23). Ancient texts say that the festival's procession was led by two aristocratic ephebes dressed as females, carrying vine branches or *oschoi*[171] to honor Dionysos and the vintage.[172] The procession passed from a sanctuary of Dionysos in Athens to the temple of Athena Skiras in Phaleron. The ephebes also seem to have played a major role in the City Dionysia.[173] Second-century B.C. inscriptions (*IG* II² 1028, *IG* II² 1008) attest to the ephebes' participation in the procession of the statue of Dionysos Eleuthereus from its temple at Eleutherai to Athens just before the City Dionysia.[174] Ephebes conducted a sacrifice following the procession, which took place at the precinct of Dionysos.[175] Isocrates (*De pace* 82) mentions that war orphans, probably ephebes,[176] were brought onstage during the Athenian Dionysia, and Aischines reports in c. 330 B.C. that this event was something that used to occur in the past. We know from the *Athenaion Politeia* that ephebes "performed" in the theater after their ephebic service.

Greek tragedy is also replete with the language and themes of the hunt, a topic on which much has already been written; this section will simply offer a few observations and examples then return to the central theme of hunting.[177] In play after play, hunting language is a key motif. It is logical for it to occur as frequently as it does in Euripides' *Bacchae* because the play concerns hunting: Pentheus's attendants capture their prey, Dionysos (434: τήνδ' ἄγραν ἠγρευκότες), and Agave describes Pentheus's death as blessed hunting (1171: μακάριον θήραν) and successful hunting (1183: εὐτυχής γ' ἅδ' ἄγρα). But tragedy also uses hunting in a metaphorical sense. Most instances involve nets and snares, but occasionally characters chase down their prey. Unlike the hunt's didactic use in preparation for warfare as described in written texts or the hunt's equivalence to battle as articulated in vase painting, tragedy focuses on the hunt, often of human prey, in contexts expressive of betrayal and entrapment, often of the unwitting.[178] Aischylos's *Oresteia* is a case in point, using hunting language to describe Clytemnestra's betrayal and slaughter of Agamemnon and Cassandra,[179] Orestes' quest for revenge,[180] and Orestes' pursuit by the Erinyes.[181] For example, Cassandra is caught in nets of doom in *Agamemnon* (1048: μορσίμων ἀγρευμάτων), the dead Agamemnon lies in a spider's web in *Agamemnon* (1516: κεῖσαι δ' ἀράχνης ἐν ὑφάσματι), nets ensnare Agamemnon in *Choephoroi* (493: πέδαις ἀχαλκεύτοισι), and Clytemnestra claims that Agamemnon escapes them like a fawn in *Eumenides* (111–12:

ἐκ μέσων ἀρκυστάτων). Elsewhere, we can observe the same phenomenon, both in literal and metaphorical hunts: in Euripides' *Bacchae*, for example, Pentheus captures Dionysos in nets (451–52: ἐν ἄρκυσιν γὰρ ὂν οὐκ ἔστιν οὕτως ὠκὺς ὥστε μ᾽ ἐκφυγεῖν); Pentheus is caught in a net (848: ἀνὴρ ἐς βόλον καθίσταται); and the Bacchae are urged to capture Pentheus, hunter of Bacchae, with a noose or snare (1020–21: ἴθ᾽, ὦ βάκχε, θηραγρευτᾷ βακχᾶν γελῶντι προσώπῳ περίβαλε βρόχον).[182] Similarly, Hippolytos is dragged to his death, literally entangled in the reins of his horses, in Euripides' *Hippolytos* (1236: ἡνίαισιν ἐμπλακεὶς). This quality of deception, of ignoble sportsmanship, of reliance on cleverness or a ruse rather than on physical prowess and courage, is inherent to the immature hunt as described in the fourth-century texts, such as Plato and Athenaeus; as noted, however, the chase is also one mode of hunting in tragic plays.

Young men or young ephebes are frequently tested in tragedy, which is often expressed as hunting, both actual and metaphorical. Neoptolemos's moral testing is a central part of Sophocles' *Philoctetes*, in which Neoptolemos tries to deceive Philoctetes (55:λόγοισιν ἐκκλέψεις); later Philoctetes refers to himself as having been hunted by Odysseus (1007: μ᾽ ἐθηράσω), blaming his conquest on craftiness.[183] Orestes is likewise tried in the *Oresteia* when he proves his manhood by hunting and killing his mother Clytemnestra, and then becomes the prey as the Furies track him down.[184] Euripides' *Bacchae* includes the hunt for Pentheus, a young man who inverts the rules of conduct for adult males not only by dressing as a woman (like an initiate at the Oschophoria) but by stalking the maenads like a hunter from the safety of the treetops. And, of course, the quintessential example of hunting in tragedy is Hippolytos, the devoted follower of Artemis, who hunts with the goddess (*Hipp.* 17–18, 1128–29), hunts with words (956–57), and is himself hunted (54–55). Here, Phaedra also expresses a desire to hunt (215–16). Hippolytos refuses to attain maturation by leaving the world of chaste hunting and accepting his sexuality and the duties of marriage, and unwed maidens will honor Hippolytos on their wedding day by cutting their hair and dedicating it to him (1424–25).[185]

Because so many of these plays deal with ephebic themes and because the ephebes themselves displayed their prowess before the ekklesia in the theater of Dionysos after which they received a shield and spear from the city (*Ath. Pol.* 42.4), scholars have seen links between the actual Athenian ephebes and their dramatic counterparts. For example, the production of the *Philoctetes* would have been preceded by a parade of military orphans in military dress, and the play itself underscores the tensions between the war orphan Neoptolemos's civic duty and his perception of what constitutes appropriate behavior; according to Goldhill, the play deals with the ambiguities of the divided loyalties of the ephebe.[186] The presentation of the shields and spears to the ephebes recalls the Cretan and Spartan rites of passage. The aristocratic nature of tragedy's protagonists is also noteworthy, even though the audience would have comprised many classes: do these plays speak to young men, offering negative paradigms of behavior through hunting images, terms that would be familiar to the audience?

Vidal-Naquet reads the plays as expressions of the transition from ephebic (black hunter) to hoplite status.[187] Considering the complexity of using the term *black hunter* to refer to young men in fifth-century Athens, it may be best to describe these plays as exploring the maturation of young men and using the hunt to portray this process. The emphasis on testing young men by hunting might offer some support for the argument that initiatory hunting took place in fifth-century Athens—at the very least on stage. But it is important to note that in the case of Pentheus, Hippolytos, and Orestes, the hunter is not exalted to some new level of maturity but instead ends up as the hunted (we might recall those vases mentioned earlier on which such an inversion occurs). It is, of course, the negative example that creates the tragedy.

The chain of associations grows even more complex when we consider the exercises performed by the ephebes in the Athenian theater after their ephebic duty. Rhodes designates them as military formations and maneuvers;[188] thus aristocratic youths would have engaged in military practices in the Theater of Dionysos, where plays about ephebes who hunt were performed. John Winkler, however, argues that the ephebes themselves composed the chorus in tragic productions, hence the display of maneuvers before the ekklesia.[189] He points to various literary citations as references to the ephebes' marching, which is performed as tragic marching in front of the ekklesia. For example, Athenaeus (14.629b–c) says that men prepared themselves to move in heavy armor and to move as hoplites by singing, which is the origin of pyrrhic and all such dances. Aristoxenos, as attested in Athenaeus (631c), points out that the ancients performed the *pyrrhike* before entering the theater. Winkler goes on to conclude that the black billy goat sacrificed on the first day of the City Dionysia at the Marathonian Tetrapolis (*IG* II² 1358b17–18) is symbolic of the goatskin of Dionysos Melanaigis in the Melanthos myth, which is the aitiological myth of the Apatouria at which ephebes registered in their phratries. By extension, Winkler argues, the black goat also signifies the ephebes or *tragoidoi* (the billy goats), whose voices changed because of puberty; these youths may also behave like goats with their randy sexuality.[190]

If Winkler is right, the relationship between Dionysos and ephebes grows more complex: ephebes, the "descendants" of Melanthos, who was aided by Dionysos, were critical players in Athenian tragedy at the City Dionysia, whose themes often center around ephebes initiated into adulthood or ephebes who hunt or are hunted. And the choruses of ephebes would have displayed military maneuvers to the public after which they received hoplite armor, in essence, ushering them into adulthood.

Having now laid out this intricate web (or net) of associations, let us return to vase painting and recall that several of the vases cited earlier juxtapose images of Dionysos with hunting (though not in a dramatic context). Furthermore, a series of drinking cups by the Leafless Group of c. 500–480 are ornamented with images of Dionysos or satyrs or both on the exterior, and a solitary hunter holding a club runs in the interior tondo.[191] A cup in Madrid (Museo Arqueológico Nacional 10907 [L.103]) has a hunter (beardless) with club on the interior, and the identical exterior sides show maenads and satyrs with donkeys.[192] Other paintings display elements of Dionysiac iconography in hunting images. Another solitary hunter decorates the tondo of an Attic red-figure cup in Munich (Staatliche Antikensammlungen 2639), and here the beardless figure sports a petasos, a spear, and, in place of the usual chlamys, a panther skin on his outstretched left arm;[193] the panther skin is, of course, a common attribute of Dionysiac followers, particularly maenads, and of the god himself.[194] Thus the god of wine and the theater and his entourage are paired with images of hunters, visual expressions of the youthful characters tested in tragic plays and perhaps of the actual ephebes of fifth-century Athens. Hunters, as we have seen, are associated with aristocrats, who would have both composed the ephebic class and eventually drunk from these cups at the symposion.

In addition to these juxtapositions of hunting and the Dionysiac sphere, two paintings by the Amasis Painter portray nude beardless youths, presumably ephebes, carrying small game, such as hares and foxes, to the god Dionysos. Here we do not see hunting per se but the return from the hunt, a theme that appears with increasing frequency on late archaic and early classical vases, and the animals may be understood as provisions for the banquet or symposion. Moreover, unlike the other hunting and Dionysiac paintings discussed thus far, the "hunt" scene now occupies the same visual space as the image of Dionysos. For example, on the obverse of an amphora of c. 550–530 in Munich (Staatliche Antikensammlungen 8763),[195] two youths stand on either side of a centrally placed Dionysos. From left to right, we see a youth carrying a wineskin; a youth holding a sprig of ivy raised in his left hand and a pole to which a hare and fox are tied in his right; Dionysos crowned with ivy and holding a kantharos and an ivy sprig, an amphora at his feet; a youth pouring wine from an oinochoe into Dionysos's kantharos; and a youth holding a pole with fox and hare. The reverse displays four horsemen with spears together with a running dog. Similarly, four youths flank Dionysos on another Amasis Painter amphora of the same date (Geneva, Musée d'Art et d'Histoire I4),[196] but here all the nude youths carry ivy branches; the figure at the far left carries a hare hung from a pole over his left shoulder, and the adjacent figure, who is next to the god, holds a wineskin. The departure of a warrior adorns the reverse; again, we should think of hunting in conjunction with warfare. But the prey offered as a gift is featured here rather than the hunt itself.

This chapter has examined the use of the hunt as a rite of passage to adulthood, as preparing aristocratic youths for warfare, and civic and social responsibility. Although literary evidence for the hunt as a maturation ritual and as preparation for military service in Athens is lacking, Attic vases demonstrate a close association of hunting and warfare, even borrowing imagery from both areas to create visual metaphors. Athenian civic festivals in honor of Dionysos included ephebes, who are featured in tragic plays filled with hunting imagery, and Attic vases also attest to a connection between Dionysos and hunters.

Another aspect of the hunt, the prey that is captured, is also of importance in a youth's maturation process because the spoils of the hunt were offered as love gifts to youths, *eromenoi*, by their adult male lovers, *erastai*. This leads us to the world of aristocratic pederasty, which ushers a young man into sexual maturity. As will be demonstrated in chapter 2, such activities occur at the symposion and in the gymnasion; in both locales youths exercise their bodies or minds under the supervision of adult males and attain a complete physical and intellectual education in preparation for the rigors of adulthood.

Table 1: Nonmythological Boar Hunts
A. Attic Black-Figure

Vase	Date	Shape	Artist
1. Paris, Musée du Louvre C12249 (*ABV* 31, 4, *Para* 16)	580	Column krater	KY Painter
2. Hamburg, Museum für Kunst und Gewerbe 1908.255 (*ABV* 56, 102, *Para* 23, *Addenda²* 15), fig. 2	560	Cup	C Painter
3. Copenhagen, Nationalmuseet 959 (62, *ABV* 56, 103, *Addenda²* 15)	560	Cup	C Painter
4. Rome, Museo del Palazzo dei Conservatori 119–39 (*ABV* 96, 21, *Para* 37, *Addenda²* 26), fig. 3	575–550	Amphora	Goltyr Painter
5. New York, Metropolitan Museum of Art and Tarquinia, Museo Nazionale Tarquiniense (*ABV* 227, 13), cf. **no. 52**	550	Frag. Siana cup	BMN Painter
6. London, British Musem B147 (*ABV* 135, 44, *Para* 55, *Addenda²* 36), fig. 1, **cf. no. 53**	550	Amphora lid	Group E
7. Basel, Cahn Coll. HC843 (Schnapp 1997, 488 no. 106), **cf. no. 68**	550	Frag. Cup	?
8. Bochum, Ruhr Universität, Kunstsammlungen (Schnapp 1997, 504 no. 261)	550	Cup	?
9. German priv. coll. (Schnapp 1997, 506 no. 278)—may be myth	550	Droop cup	?
10. Baltimore, Walters Art Gallery 48.41 (Schnapp 1997, 506 no. 276)	550–540	Cup	?
11. Zurich, Mildenberg Coll. (Kozloff 1981, 119–21 no. 100)	550–540	Lip cup	?
12. Cambridge, Arthur M. Sackler 1925.30.131 (Schnapp 1997, 493 no. 150), figs. 26–27	550–530	Cup	?
13. Heidelberg, Ruprecht-Karl-Universität, Archäologisches Institut S13 (Schnapp 1997, 492 no. 139)	550–525	Frag. band cup	?
14. Rhodes, Archaeological Museum (*ABV* 89, 2)	550–525	Frag. neck amphora	Painter of Rouen 531
15. Naples, Museo Archeologico Nazionale H2777 (inv. 81173, *ABV* 276, 3)	530–510	Hydria	Antimenes Paint
16. London, British Museum B304 (*ABV* 266, 4, *Para* 117, *Addenda²* 69), figs. 24–25	520–515	Hydria	Antimenes Paint
17. Munich, Staatliche Antikensammlungen 1386 (*ABV* 306, 39; *Addenda²* 81), figs. 16–17	520	Amphora	Balançoire Paint
18. Rome, Museo Gregoriano Etrusco Vaticano 17807 (332, Albizzati 4, 1925 118 no. 332, Tav. 36)	520–510	Cup frags.	?
19. Munich, Staatliche Antikensammlungen 1966 (J121, Schnapp 1997, 506 no. 275), **cf. no. 91**	510	Kyathos	?
20. St. Petersburg, State Hermitage Museum B162 (St. 85, *Para* 130, *Addenda²* 78)	510	Amphora	Princeton Painte
21. Basel, Antikenmuseum und Sammlung Ludwig BS 495 (*Para* 187; *Addenda²* 111), **cf. no. 92**	510–500	Amphora	Painter of Vatica 342
22. New York, market (Schnapp 1997, 492 no. 141)	End of 6th c.	Band cup	?
23. Paris, Bibliothèque nationale, Cabinet des Médailles 274 (*ABV* 530, 69; *Addenda²* 132), fig. 4	500	Oinochoe	Near the Athena Painter
24. Altenburg, Lindenau-Museum 207 (*Para* 217; *Addenda²* 120), figs. 8–9	500	Lidded amphora	Edinburgh Paint

Mounted	Beards	Attire	Hunters	Weapons	Other Scenes
No	Not extant	Chitons	4	Spears	Horsemen, animals
Yes	0	Chitons	2	Spears	Horsemen, dog chasing hare, deer
Yes	0	Nude	2	Spears	Horsemen, dogs, panthers
No	Yes	Chitons	4	Spears	Animals, komos
Yes	Yes	Nude	5	Spears, trident	Boar hunt, swan
No	1 of 2	Nude	2	Spear	Deer hunt
Yes	At least 2	Chitons	3 extant	Spears	Deer hunt
Yes	?	?	?	?	?
2 of 4	No	Two females in peploi, males wear chitons	?	Spears, dogs	Hoplites?
4 of 5	?	Chitons, Scythian caps	6	Spears, bows and arrows	Mounted boar hunt
No	?	Nude	1	Spear	Hunter/boar on opposite sides
No	1 of 2	Nude chlamydes as shields, one pilos	4	Spears	Boxers
Yes	Not extant	Nude	1 extant	Not extant	Not extant
No	Yes	Chitons	2 extant	Spears	Not extant
3 of 5	?	Chitons, nude, chlamydes as shields	5	Spears	Herakles vs. Kyknos, chariot scene
2 of 4	No	Nude, chlamydes as shields, Scythian cap	4	Spears, sheathed sword	Chariot harnessing scene, hoplite battle
No	1 of 2	Chitons, one pilos	2	Shield or chlamys as shield, dogs	Hoplite battle
Yes	?	Nude	At least 2	?	Boar hunt
No	0	Nude, chlamys as shield	2	Spears, sheathed sword, dogs	Deer hunt
2 of 3	?	Chlamys as shield	3	Spears, dogs	Mounted boar hunt, departure of warrior
Yes	0	Chitons	4	Spears	Satyrs and maenads; deer hunt; Herakles, Athena, et al.
Yes	?	?	?	?	?
No	1	Chiton, chlamys, boots	1	Spear	0
No	0	Chiton, chlamys as shield, pilos	1	Spear, dog	Boar hunt with bearded hunter using spear and stone

Table 1 (continued)

A. Attic Black-Figure (continued)

Vase	Date	Shape	Artist
25. Paris, market (Schnapp 1997, 506 no. 281)	500	Oinochoe	?
26. Swiss priv. coll. (*Para* 262; *Addenda*² 131), fig. 5	510–500	Lekythos	Athena Painter
27. Winchester, College Museum 47 (*ABV* 587, 2)	490	Lekythos	Beldam Painter
28. Palermo, Banco di Sicilia 396 (Giudice et al. 1, 1992 foldout XVI no. 6)	c. 480–450	Skyphos	Láncut Group

B. Attic Red-Figure

Vase	Date	Shape	Artist
29. Rome, Museo Gregoriano Etrusco Vaticano 16548 (*ARV*² 179, 3; *Addenda*² 185)	500	Hydria	Charpentier Painter
30. Adria, Museo Civico B93/B71/B609 (*ARV*² 414, 33)	c. 500–450	Skyphos frag.	Dokimasia Painter
31. Baltimore, Walters Art Gallery 48.2115 (*ARV*² 336, 16; *Addenda*² 218)	490	Cup	Antiphon Painter
32. Basel, Cahn Coll. HC56 (*ARV*² 325, 73bis), **cf. no. 112**	490	Cup frag.	Onesimos
33. Aberdeen, University 743 (*ARV*² 336, 17)	480	Cup	Antiphon Painter
34. Adria, Museo Civico B590 (*ARV*² 411, 3)	475	Frag. cup	Manner of the Briseis Painter
35. Columbia, University of Missouri, Museum of Art and Archaeology 66.2 (*Para* 432; *Addenda*² 306)	475–450	Cup	Curtius Painter
36. Copenhagen, Nationalmuseet 6327 (*ARV*² 413, 16, *Addenda*² 233), figs. 22–23, **cf. no. 115**	470	Cup	Dokimasia Painter
37. London, British Museum E789 (*ARV*² 764, 9)	470–450	Frag. rhyton	Sotades Painter
38. New York, Metropolitan Museum of Art 41.162.9 (*ARV*² 882, 39; *Addenda*² 301)	460	Cup	Penthesilea Painter
39. Vienna, Kunsthistorisches Museum 781 (Schnapp 1997, 522 no. 438)	450–425	Pelike	Makron
40. Paris, Musée du Louvre G623 (*ARV*² 1294; *Addenda*² 359), fig. 18	440	Cup	Near Painter of London E105
41. Paris, Musée du Louvre G637 (*ARV*² 770, 5; *Addenda*² 287), fig. 10	450	Cup	Related to the Sotades Painter
42. Ex-Castle Ashby (Schnapp 1997, 522 no. 435)	450–440	Cup	Curtius Painter
43. Naples, Museo Archeologico Nazionale 81671 (H3251, Schnapp, 1997 523 no. 448), **cf. no. 118**	440	Volute krater	?
44. Paris, Bibliothèque nationale, Cabinet des Médailles 853 (*ARV*² 776, 2)	440–430	Askos	Group of Bonn Askos
45. Bonn, Akademisches Kunstmuseum 90 (*ARV*² 776, 1; *Addenda*² 288)	440–430	Askos	Group of Bonn Askos
46. Aberdeen, University, Marischal College 698 (Schnapp 1997, 522 no. 439)	450–400	Miniature krater	?
47. Philadelphia, University Museum L64.191 (1889-162, Schnapp 1997, 525 no. 463)	425–400	Askos	?
48. Olynthos 361 + 476 (Schnapp 1997, 521 no. 423)	400–390	Krater frags.	?
49. Ferrara, Museo Archeologico Nazionale di Spina VP T. 136 (Arias 1963, 7, pl. 13)	c. 400–390	Volute krater	?

Mounted	Beards	Attire	Hunters	Weapons	Other Scenes
Yes	?	?	At least 1	Spears, dog	0
No	1	Chlamys as shield, petasos, boots	1	Spear, sheathed sword, dog	0
?	?	?	?	?	0
Yes	?	?	1	Spear	Leopard(?) vs. boar
No	0	Nude, chlamys as shield, pilos	1	Unsheathed sword, spear, rocks?	0
?	0	Petasos, chlamys	1 extant	Stone	?
No	0	Nude, chlamys	1	Spears, sheathed sword	?
No?	?	Chlamys held as shield	1 extant	Spear?	Deer hunt, discus thrower
?	?	?	1	?	?
No	0	Chlamys as shield, pilos	1 extant	Spears	Not extant
No	0	Chlamydes, petasoi	4	Swords, dog	Courtship scene?
No	0	Nude, chlamydes as shields, petasos, pilos	2	Swords	Deer hunt
No	1	Nude, chlamys as shield	1 extant	Stone, club	Birth of Pandora
No	1	Chlamys, petasos	1	Sword, club	Athletes
No	0	Nude, chlamys as shield	1	Spears	Draped man at goalpost
No, but holding horse	0	Chiton, Scythian cap, boots	1	Spear	Boar hunt
No	0	Chiton, chlamys, petasos, boots	1	Sword, spear, pike?	Boar hunt with club and rock
No	0	Chlamys	1	Spear	Boar hunt
2 of 5	?	Scythian dress	At least 6	Rocks, axes, spears	Pan, deer hunt
No	1	Chlamys as shield, pilos	1	Spear	0
No	1	Chlamys as shield, pilos	1	Spear	0
No	0	Pilos, boots	1	Spear?	?
No	0	Pilos, chlamys as shield	1	Club	0
No	No	Chlamys	3 extant	Spears, rocks	?
No	1	Chlamydes, boots, pilos	5	Spears, axe, lagobolon, sword	Dionysos, maenads, satyrs; Ilioupersis; Centauromachy

Table 2: Nonmythological Deer Hunts
A. Attic Black-Figure

Vase	Date	Shape	Artist
50. Brussels, Musées Royaux d'Art et d'Histoire A 715 (*ABV* 103, 109; *Addenda²* 27)	575–550	Tyrrhenian amphora	Tyrrhenian Group
51. Brussels, J. L. Theodor Collection (Heesen 1996, 130–31 no. 30)	c. 550	Band cup	?
52. New York, Metropolitan Museum of Art and Tarquinia, Museo Nazionale Tarquiniense (*ABV* 227, 13), **cf. no. 5**	550	Frag. Siana cup	BMN Painter
53. London, British Museum B147 (*ABV* 135, 44; *Para* 55, *Addenda²* 36), fig. 1, **cf. no. 6**	550	Amphora lid	Group E
54. Rome, Museo Gregoriano Etrusco Vaticano Astarita 497 (Schnapp 1997, 485 no. 79)	550–540	Lip cup	?
55. Naples, Museo Archeologico Nazionale H2500, inv. 81132 (*ABV* 252, 1)	550–530	Band cup	Painter of Louvre E7
56. Moscow, University 81 (Schnapp 1997, 488, no. 102)	550–525	Cup	?
57. Thasos (Schnapp 1997, 489 no. 110)	550–525	Band cup	?
58. St. Petersburg, State Hermitage Museum B2362 (216, *ABV* 252; *Para* 88; *Addenda²* 65)	550–530	Skyphos	Manner of Elbows C
59. Orvieto, Museo Civico, Collection Faina 69 (*ABV* 140, 4; *Addenda²* 38)	550–525	Hydria	Painter of the Vatica Mourner
60. Thera, Necropolis (Schnapp 1997, 488 no. 109)	550–530	Band cup	?
61. Orvieto, Museo Civico, Collection Faina 722 (Schnapp 1997, 487 no. 95)	550–530	Cup	?
62. New York, Metropolitan Museum of Art 74.51.1371 (CP 2012, *ABV* 189, 5; *Addenda²* 52)	540	Cup	Centaur Painter
63. London, British Museum 1891.8–6.84 (*ABV* 190, 19; *Addenda²* 52)	540	Band cup	Centaur Painter
64. Würzburg, Martin von Wagner Museum der Universität 405 (H1644, *ABV* 190, 18)	540	Band cup	Centaur Painter
65. Utrecht I.A. 245 (Schnapp 1997, 498 no. 200)	540	Band cup	Centaur Painter
66. Basel, market (*Para* 61, 2bis)	540	Lip cup	Exekias as potter
67. Basel, market (*Para* 102, 44)	540–530	Cup	Class of the Top B Stemlesses
68. Basel, Cahn Coll. HC843 (Schnapp 1997, 488 no. 106), **cf. no. 7**	550	Cup	?
69. Berlin, Antikensammlung F1806 (*ABV* 223, 65; *Addenda²* 58)	530	Cup	Painter N
70. Rome, Museo Nazionale Etrusco di Villa Giulia 7847A (Schnapp 1997, 489 no. 112)	530	Frag. eye cup	?
71. Wellesley, College Art Museum 1961-5 (Schnapp 1997, 491 no. 134)	530	Hydria	?
72. Rhodes, Archaeological Museum 12206 (Schnapp 1997, 489 no. 114)	530–520	Cup	?
73. London, British Museum 1843.11-3.73 (B301, *ABV* 282, 2; *Para* 124, *Addenda²* 74)	530–510	Hydria	Alkmene Painter
74. London, British Museum 1843.11-3.71 (B319, *Para* 124; *Addenda²* 73)	530–510	Hydria	Related to Antime Painter
75. Taranto, Museo Archeologico Nazionale I.G. 4486 (Schnapp 1997, 489 no. 113)	525–500	Cup	?
76. Orvieto, Opera del Duomo 1006 (Schnapp 1997, 491 no. 136)	525–500	Amphora	?
77. Paris, Musée du Louvre F294 (*ABV* 256, 18; *Addenda²* 66), fig. 29	525–500	Hydria	Lysippides Painte
78. Havana, Museo Nacional 140 (*ABV* 518, 5; *Addenda²* 129)	c. 525–475	Alabastron	Theseus Painter
79. Leiden, Rijksmuseum van Oudheden II 167 (PC 63, *ABV* 266; 1, *Para* 117; *Addenda²* 69), figs. 13–14	520–515	Hydria	Antimenes Painte

Mounted	Beards	Attire	Weapons	Other Scenes
No	2 of 2	Nude	Spears	Satyrs and maenads, running warriors, animals
Yes	No	Chitons	Spears	Deer hunt
Yes	?	?	Spears	Boar hunt, swan
Yes	0	Chitons	Spears	Boar hunt
?	?	?	Club	?
Yes	?	Chitons	Spears	Same
Yes	?	Chitons	Spear	Deer hunt
Yes	?	?	?	?
No	0	Chiton	Spears	Deer hunt
Yes	?	?	Spears	Hoplite battle, chariot harnessing
Yes	?	Chitons	Spears	?
No	?	Chlamys as shield, nude	Rocks, lagobolon	Deer hunt
No	Yes	Nude	Spear, sheathed sword	Deer
Yes	?	Chitons, chlamys as shield	Spear	Panther hunting hunter
No	Not extant	Chlamys as shield	Spear	Centaur hunting deer
1 of 2	Yes	Chiton, nude	Shield, lagobolon	Five dancing women
No	Yes?	Scythian dress and cap	Bow and arrow	Deer
Yes	?	Chiton	Spear?	Same
Yes	At least 1	Chitons	Spears	Boar hunt
No	?	Nude?	Spears	Plowing, hunter with lagobolon, animals, Siren
Yes	Not extant	Nude	Spears	Horsemen, perhaps deer
Yes	?	?	?	?
Yes	0	?	Spears?	Deer hunt (same scene)
2 of 4	3 of 4	Nude	Spears?	Herakles vs. Nemean lion, Herakles banqueting
Yes	?	?	?	Herakles vs. Nemean lion, Herakles' entry to Olympia
Yes	?	?	?	?
Yes	?	?	?	Birth of Athena; hoplite battle; Apollo, Leto, Artemis
Yes	0	Chitons, chlamydes	Spears	Herakles' entry to Olympos, frontal chariot
4 of 5	?	Chiton	Spears	Prothesis
2 of 4	2 of 4	Chlamydes as shields, nude	Spears	Men at fountainhouse, warrior's departure

Table 2 (continued)

A. Attic Black-Figure

Vase	Date	Shape	Artist
80. Rome, Museo Gregoriano Etrusco Vaticano 426 (*ABV* 266, 2, *Para* 117, *Addenda²* 69), fig. 30	520–515	Hydria	Antimenes Painter
81. Munich, Staatliche Antikensammlungen 1694 (*ABV* 266, 5)	520–515	Hydria	Antimenes Painter
82. Formerly London, market, Sotheby's (once Basel, Bloch, *Para* 120; *Addenda²* 70)	520–510	Hydria	Antimenes Painter
83. Rome, Museo Nazionale Etrusco di Villa Giulia (Cerveteri, Monte Abatone T610, Schnapp 1997, 492 no. 147)	520–500	Hydria	?
84. Princeton, University Art Museum y171 (*ABV* 260, 34)	510	Hydria	Manner of Lysippide Painter
85. Los Angeles, County Museum of Art 50.8.5 (A5933.50-11, *ABV* 277, 6; *Addenda²* 72)	510	Hydria	Manner of Antimenes Painter
86. Copenhagen, Thorvaldsens Museum H554 (*ABV* 267, 20; *Addenda²* 69), fig. 28	510	Hydria	Antimenes Painter
87. Norwich, Castle Mus. 72.20 (*ABV* 268, 23)	510	Hydria	Circle of Antimenes Painter
88. Ex-Küsnacht, Hirschmann Coll. G9 (*Para* 119; *Addenda²* 69)	510	Hydria	Circle of Antimenes Painter
89. Geneva, Baron Edmond de Rothschild (*ABV* 268, 30; *Para* 118)	510	Hydria	Antimenes Painter
90. Würzburg, Martin von Wagner Museum der Universität L307 (*ABV* 276, 4)	510	Hydria	Antimenes Painter
91. Munich, Staatliche Antikensammlungen 1966 (J121, Schnapp 1997, 506 no. 275), **cf. no. 19**	510	Kyathos	?
92. Basel, Antikenmuseum und Sammlung Ludwig BS495 (*Para* 187; *Addenda²* 111), **cf. no. 21**	510–500	Amphora	Painter of Vatican 342
93. Rome, Museo Nazionale Etrusco di Villa Giulia 50543 (Schnapp 1997, 489 no.115)	515–505	Cup	?
94. Fiesole, A. Costantini (Schnapp 1997, 492 no. 148)	End of 6th c.	Hydria	?
95. Los Angeles, priv. coll. (Schnapp 1997, 493 no. 149)	End of 6th c.	Hydria	?
96. Munich, Staatliche Antikensammlungen 2305 (J.411, *ABV* 182, 4; *Para* 340, *Addenda²* 186), figs. 20–21	500	Amphora	Kleophrades Painter
97. Oxford, Ashmolean Museum 1889.1013 (Schnapp 1997, 487 no. 99)	500–475	Lekythos	Manner of Athena Painter
98. London, Victoria & Albert Museum 831–1884 (Schnapp 1997, 487 no. 96)	500	Bowl	?
99. Athens, National Museum 14858 (Schnapp 1997, 492 no. 145)	490	Lekythos	Beldam Painter
100. Würzburg, Martin von Wagner Museum der Universität 319 (HA 61, *ABV* 293, 10; *Addenda²* 76)	490	Hydria	Psiax
101. Athens, National Museum 17711 (Schnapp 1997, 492 no. 146)	480	Lekythos	Haimon Painter
102. Bologna, Museo Civico Archeologico P.149 (M600, Schnapp 1997, 500 no. 222)	480–470	Plate	Haimon Painter

Mounted	Beards	Attire	Weapons	Other Scenes
Yes	?	Nude	Spears?	Women at fountainhouse, hoplite battle
Yes	0	Chitons	Spears	Chariot harnessing, warrior's departure
3 of 4	?	?	Spears?	Warrior in chariot; 3 riders, warrior, woman
No	0	Nude, chlamydes as shields	Spears	Peleus abducting Thetis
Yes	At least 2 of 5	Chlamys as shield, chitons, chlamydes, petasos	Spears	Herakles' entry to Olympos, warriors' leavetaking
Yes	?	Nude?	Spears	Hoplite in chariot, departure of warriors?
Yes	0	Nude	Spears?	Frontal chariot with hoplites, Herakles vs. Nemean lion
2 of 4	?	Chitons, chlamydes as shields	Spears	Herakles vs. lion, panther & animals
2 of 4	?	Chlamydes as shields	Spears	Frontal chariot. Herakles vs. Kyknos with hoplites
Yes	?	?	Spears	Dionysos banqueting, youth between 2 quadrigas
5 of 6	0	Nude	Spears, sheathed daggers	Warrior mounting chariot, chariot & youth with horse
1 of 2	1 of 2	Chlamys as shield on one, chiton and Scythian cap on one	Spears	Boar hunt
Yes	0	Chitons	Spears	Satyrs and maenads, boar hunt; Herakles, Athena, et al.
Yes	?	Chlamydes, chitons	Spears	Deer hunt, male with kantharos
No	2 of 2	Chlamydes as shields	Spears	Lyre player with 2 men
Yes	?	?	?	?
Yes	0	Chlamydes, 2 with Scythian caps	Spears	Boxers under supervision; warrior's departure; chariot, horsemen, youths; chariot race
No	0	Chlamys as shield	Spears, sheathed dagger	0
No	0	Chlamys as shield, nude	Rock	?
Yes	?	Chitons	Spears, helmets, cuirasses(?)	0
Yes	?	Chitons	Spears	Scythian archer, Adrastos's departure; rider (N.B. goalposts in hunt)
Yes	2 of 2	Chitons, chlamydes	Spears	0
No	0	Scythian dress and caps	Bows and arrows	Dancing females, male flutist

Table 2 (continued)
B. Attic Red-Figure

Vase	Date	Shape	Artist
103. Basel, Antikenmuseum und Sammlung Ludwig BS438 (*ARV*[2] 351, 8; *Addenda*[2] 221), fig. 19	500–480	Cup	Bonn Painter
104. Paris, Musée du Louvre G22 (*ARV*[2] 151, 52; *Addenda*[2] 180), figs. 11–12	510	Cup	Manner of Epeleios Painter
105. Museo Nazionale Etrusco di Villa Giulia 50535 (*ARV*[2] 174, 15; *Addenda*[2] 184), figs. 6–7	510–500	Cup	Ambrosios Painter
106. New York, Metropolitan Museum of Art 41.162.129 (*ARV*[2] 92, 66)	510	Cup	Euergides Painter
107. Würzburg, Martin von Wagner Museum der Universität 473 (*ARV*[2] 92, 65; *Addenda*[2] 171)	510–500	Cup	Euergides Painter
108. Berlin, Antikensammlung F2324 (*ARV*[2] 126, 26; *Addenda*[2] 176)	505	Skyphos	Nikosthenes Painter
109. Paris, Musée du Louvre G21 (*ARV*[2] 92, 68; *Addenda*[2] 171)	500	Cup	Euergides Painter
110. Rome, Ex-Spagna (*ARV*[2] 92, 67)	500	Cup	Euergides Painter
111. Baltimore, Ex-Robinson (Schnapp 1997, 520 no. 415)	Beginning of 5th c.	Lekythos	
112. Basel, Cahn Coll. HC56 (*ARV*[2] 325, 73bis), **cf. no. 32**	490	Cup frag.	Onesimos
113. Berlin, Antikensammlung V.I. 3311 (Schnapp 1997, 519 no. 404)	490–470	Omphalos phiale	?
114. Florence, Museo Archeologico Etrusco 73131 (*ARV*[2] 120, 5; *Addenda*[2] 175)	490–480	Cup	Apollodoros
115. Copenhagen, Nationalmuseet 6327 (*ARV*[2] 413, 16; *Addenda*[2] 233), figs. 22–23, **cf. no. 36**	470	Cup	Dokimasia Painter
116. Paris, Musée du Louvre G343 (*ARV*[2] 600, 17; *Addenda*[2] 266)	450	Volute krater	Niobid Painter
117. Basel, Antikenmuseum und Sammlung Ludwig Kä 404 (*ARV*[2] 1067, 2bis; *Para* 447, *Addenda*[2] 325)	450–440	Bell krater	Barclay Painter
118. Naples, Museo Archeologico Nazionale 81671 (H3251, Schnapp 1997, 523 no. 448), **cf. no. 43**	440	Volute krater	?
119. Paris, Musée du Louvre C11803 + C11810 (*ARV*[2] 828, 32; *Addenda*[2] 294)	450–425	Cup frags.	Stieglitz Painter
120. Bedford, Woburn Abbey (*ARV*[2] 1426, 33)	c. 400–300	Bell krater	Telos Painter
121. Malibu, J. Paul Getty Museum 87.AE.93 (Burn 1991)	c. 390–380	Dinoid volute krater	Meleager Painter

Mounted	Beards	Attire	Weapons	Other Scenes
2 of 4	0	Nude, 3 with Scythian caps, 1 with Scythian jumpsuit	Spears, bows and arrows	Athletes exercising under supervision
No	0	Nude, chlamydes and animal skins as shields, petasos	Spears, drawn daggers, shield, helmet, rock	Deer hunt
No	0	Chlamys, chlamys held as shield	Rock, dagger, spear, dog	Boxers and wrestlers, youth holding hare and leaning on stick
No	0	Nude	Panther	Athletes, komast
No	0	Nude with chlamys as shield	Panther	Komos, youth with chlamys as shield and stick
No	0	Scythian dress, chiton	Shield, helmet, cuirass; bows and arrows; panther	Chariot, Gorgoneion
No	0	Nude	Panther	Horse trainer, komast
?	?	?	?	Nude youth, panther hunting deer
No	0	Petasos, chlamys?	Spear	0
No?	?	Chlamys held as shield	Spear	Boar hunt, discus thrower
Yes	?	Nude?	Spears	0
No	Not extant	Chlamys	Spear, sheathed dagger	Warrior arming, deer hunt
No	0	Chiton, chlamys, chlamys as shield, petasoi	Daggers	Boar hunt
No	0	Chitons, chlamydes, chlamydes as shields, petasoi, sandals	Spears, clubs	Hoplite battle, warrior's departure, Triptolemos
No	0	Chitons, chlamydes, piloi, sandals on 1; female hunter has animal skin, boots, chiton	Spears, dagger; female hunter has bow and arrow	Boar hunt
2 of 5	?	Scythian dress	Rocks, axes, spears	Pan, deer hunt
No	No	Chlamys, chiton	Swords	Woman with stephanos, woman holding sash, male
No	No	Chlamys, animal skin	Swords, spear	Nike, youths
No	No	Chlamys	Sword	Hare hunt, bull slaughter, griffin fight; symposion; Adonis(?); Dionysos, maenads satyrs

Chapter Two
EROS AND THE HUNT

This chapter addresses a different kind of hunting and one that is expressed in the form of a written and visual metaphor: pederastic courtship. The subject of Greek homosexuality is ground well trodden by modern scholars, who have discussed numerous aspects of this topic, particularly pederasty,[1] including its origins;[2] whether it was socially acceptable; how widespread it was in Greece;[3] its aristocratic patina;[4] its links to military service, to the palaistra, and to the symposion;[5] legislation concerning such conduct;[6] its educational aspects;[7] its psychological motivations; its use as initiation;[8] and the relationship of such mortal behavior to divine prototypes.[9] This study limits its ambit to a discussion and reexamination of the visual and written evidence for pederasty.

Attic vase painting scenes of pederastic courtship in which the older erastes courts a younger eromenos usually depict the couple standing opposite one another; such images differ compositionally from traditional paintings of amorous pursuit, which typically show the aggressor physically chasing or grappling with his quarry, akin to the physically energetic boar and deer hunts discussed in chapter 1. Though they are compositionally dissimilar, the Attic pederastic courtship paintings are also expressions of hunting. So in this chapter, we invert the relationship described in chapter 1, where hunt depictions are visual metaphors for warfare; here, the pederastic courtship scenes are visual metaphors for hunting. And just as the hunting depictions in chapter 1 borrow warfare imagery to express the metaphor between hunt and battle, pederastic courtship vase paintings borrow iconography from hunting scenes to create the metaphor of courtship as hunting. Animal gifts, most commonly hares and cocks, but also deer and felines underscore the metaphor.[10] Presumably, animal gifts were given to help persuade the eromenos to favor the erastes.[11] The presentation of animal gifts signifies the amorous negotiation between aristocratic erastes and eromenos, which is part of the economy of aristocratic society. The animals themselves are imbued with qualities and associations championed by aristocrats and expressive of aristocratic ideals of masculinity, such as swiftness, intelligence, and military valor.

In this chapter I argue that, homosexual courtship, like hunting and warfare, was an important element of the ideology of late archaic and early classical Athenian masculinity and was also inextricably bound up with the social politics of the aristocracy. Pederasty formed part of coming-of-age rituals for adolescent males and marked sexual and social maturation, if not an actual initiation, in many parts of Greece, and pederasty was widely practiced in late archaic and classical Athens.[12] Participation in pederastic courtship was critical to a sense of belonging and acceptance in the world of aristocratic males (cf. Pl., *Symp.* 178c), and the gift exchange between erastes and eromenos revolved around issues of power, control, and social status.[13] Using the metaphor of hunting to describe pederastic encounters, scholars argue that the metaphorical hunter is always the erastes and the hunted the eromenos;[14] the former is empowered and the latter is not. The relationship, however, is actually more complex and ambiguous, involving a vacillating exchange of power between the older erastes, who holds social status, and the eromenos, who, by virtue of the desire that he inspires in the erastes, possesses power.

Pederastic relationships not only benefited the social networking of aristocrats and offered them status, but this amorous hunting and agonistic behavior served the military as well. Literary texts attest to the encouragement of pederasty in the military, a practice that would ensure the noblest fighting effort because no man would wish to appear cowardly to his lover. This practice, however, is not made explicit in visual texts, perhaps because the vases are predominantly Attic, and the combination of pederasty and the military is not attested in writing for Attica. But a sensitive reading of the Attic vases yields clues that may help fill the lacuna in the written documents and further contributes to our picture of the intersection and interrelationship of hunting, warfare, and pederasty.

Furthermore, as was the case with the actual hunting paintings, the chronology of the Attic pederastic paintings coincides with contemporary political changes. The use of animal gifts in pederastic courtship scenes first begins in the Peisistratid period, the time of the very first pederastic scenes in Attic vase painting, not, I believe, because of the influence of Homeric poetry, as Koch-Harnack argues,[15] but because of an aristocratic effort to dominate the social discourse in political circumstances that were not officially governed by aristocratic interests. Aristocrats wished to hold onto power during the tyranny and the democratic government in Athens. Even though their official political power was truncated, aristocratic concerns dominated cultural and social norms in Athens in the late archaic and early classical periods, and pederastic courtship paintings, like the actual hunting images themselves, reflect this trend.

Together with hunting and warfare, pederasty claimed a central place in the ideology of aristocratic masculinity in Athens, and one of its primary settings was the symposion. Scholars argue that the hunt and symposion have no meaningful contact, that the former refers to the world of the youth, whereas the latter pertains to the world of men; the symposion lies at the heart of civic life, while the hunt exists at its periphery.[16] Here, I argue that the two are related, not polar opposites, but distinct points along a continuum of a man's life—for youths grow into men and adult hunters, and warriors are destined to recline on couches, drink, engage in intellectual discourse, and court young men.

The Vases

More numerous than hunting itself in Attic vase painting of the late sixth and early fifth centuries are pederastic courtship images.[17] Representations of homosexual or pederastic courtship scenes (both with animal gifts and without) in Attic vase painting have already been collected and classified by several scholars.[18] Such scenes consist of an older, aristocratic male, who fondles, embraces, or pursues his younger prey.[19] Beazley carefully distinguished three types of pederasty scenes in Attic vase painting: the alpha type, with the erastes and eromenos facing each other, the erastes placing one hand on the chin of the eromenos and the other on the eromenos's penis—the up-and-down hand position; the beta type, in which the youth holds a cock given to him by the erastes; and the gamma type, where the figures are actually sexually interlocked.[20] Although intercrural intercourse occasionally appears,[21] it is not common in vase painting.[22]

FIGURE 31. Attic black-figure cup by the Sokles Painter, c. 550–530 B.C. Swiss private collection. Reproduced by permission from K. Schauenburg, "Erastes und Eromenos auf einer Schale des Sokles," *AA* (1965): 854 Abb. 3.

Most significant and intriguing for this study are pederastic scenes that include the presentation of animal gifts to the beloved, which are usually held in the arms or out to the recipient. The animals are often captured prey, including hares, deer, and felines,[23] and occasionally birds, though the most common animal gift is the cock. Although dead foxes appear in pederastic courtship scenes, they are never exchanged as love gifts,[24] and while live felines are carried in the same fashion as other animal gifts and surely were intended as such, they are never actually portrayed being handed over as gifts.[25] Not every pederastic courtship painting includes animals but many do; we limit our examination of pederastic scenes to those in which game or other animals appear.

Strikingly similar to the production of hunting images discussed in chapter 1, the manufacture of Attic black-and red-figure vase paintings of pederastic courtship (with animal gifts and without) begins c. 560, flourishes c. 525–500, then fades out c. 470; far fewer red-figure than black-figure examples exist.[26] Most of the pederastic scenes occur on drinking cups, but also on skyphoi and amphorae, vessels connected with the aristocratic symposion.[27] Oil containers and pyxides are also occasionally adorned with such representations; Sutton speculates that these were intended as love gifts whose decoration was meant to be persuasive.[28]

Most images depict a courting couple with the two protagonists and at least one animal, such as the Attic black-figure cup tondo of c. 550–530 in a Swiss private collection, on which a nude male, identified as the erastes by his beard, his larger size, and his aggressive gestures, stands opposite a nude, unbearded eromenos according to Beazley's alpha scheme (fig. 31).[29]

FIGURES 32–33. Attic red-figure cup by Makron, c. 490–480 B.C. Munich, Staatliche Antikensammlungen 2655. Photos courtesy of the Staatliche Antikensammlungen und Glyptothek München.

A dead hare and dead fox hang from the surrounding "walls." The compositions of Attic red-figure pederastic courtship scenes are similar to Attic black-figure types, but both erastai and eromenoi are now sometimes beardless (e.g., a cup by Makron of c. 490–480 in Munich, Staatliche Antikensammlungen 2655; figs. 32–33).[30]

FIGURE 34. Attic black-figure amphora by the Painter of Cambridge 47, c. 550 B.C. Munich, Staatliche Antikensammlungen 1468. Photo courtesy of the Staatliche Antikensammlungen und Glyptothek München.

The courtship compositions can expand to include many courting couples or contract to a solitary figure, whose mode of depiction indicates that he is either an erastes or eromenos.[31] An Attic black-figure amphora of c. 550 in Munich (Staatliche Antikensammlungen 1468; fig. 34) is an example of the former:[32] the courting couple, together with two dancing onlookers, appears on the belly of the obverse (note that one of the cavorting onlookers has a deer slung over his left shoulder). An Attic black-figure amphora in London of c. 540–530 (British Museum 1865.11–18.39 [W39]; fig. 35) provides another typical example of an expanded scene.[33] On the obverse, seven nude males compose three distinct groups. At the left, a bearded male with an erect phallus touches the chin of a beardless youth with his left hand; the youth holds a small stag in his arms as he moves away from the first figure. Just to the left of center, two males engage in intercrural copulation: the taller, presumably older, figure bends his knees slightly to place his penis between the thighs of a shorter, beardless youth, who holds a wreath in his raised right hand. The older man embraces the

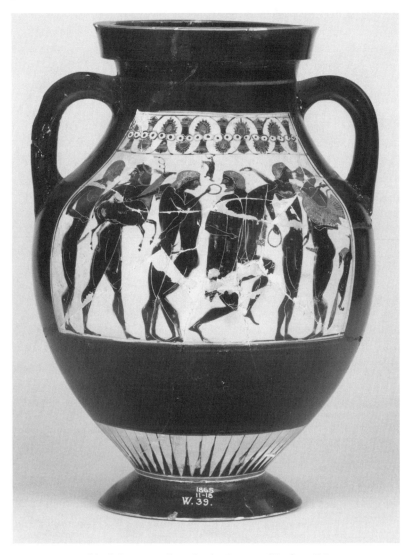

FIGURE 35. Attic black-figure amphora by the Painter of Berlin 1686, c. 540–530
B.C. London, British Museum 1865.11–18.39 [W39]. Photo courtesy of the British
Museum. © The British Museum.

torso of the younger. Beyond them to the right, a bearded, mantled figure
dances and looks back toward them. At the far right, another courting couple appears (here, the figures are nearly equal in height); the bearded
erastes holds a cock on his left arm and reaches down toward the genitals

FIGURE 36. Attic red-figure cup tondo by the Brygos Painter, c. 490 B.C. Athens, National Museum 1357. Photo courtesy of the National Museum and the Archaeological Receipts Fund, Athens.

FIGURE 37. Attic red-figure cup tondo by Douris, c. 490 B.C. New York, ex-Hirschmann Collection G64. Photo courtesy of Sotheby's, London.

of the beardless eromenos with his right. The eromenos carries a wreath in his lowered right hand. A small hare dangles from the "background" in the center of the representation, and a fox hangs from an imaginary "wall" at the right. The reverse bears much the same composition with a few small variations.

The reclining erastes with a hare on the tondo of an Attic red-figure cup by the Brygos Painter of c. 490 in Athens (National Museum 1357; fig. 36) demonstrates a contracted scene, reduced to a single figure and the love gift.[34] This cup is, however, extraordinary because of its inscription, written in retrograde, ΟΠΑΙΔΟΝΚΑΛΛΙΣΤΕ, which may quote Theognis's exhortation (2.1365) to an eromenos.[35] Vase painters also might represent a solitary eromenos as on the tondo of an Attic red-figure cup signed by Douris of c. 490 in New York (ex-Hirschmann Collection G64; fig. 37).[36]

Various stages of the pederastic courtship appear in vase painting, ranging from the first tentative approaches of the erastes to actual copulation. A red-figure amphora of c. 490 in Rome (Museo Nazionale Etrusco di Villa Giulia 50462; fig. 38) shows a bearded draped man leaning on a walking stick, who extends a hare, held by the front and back paws, to a draped, beardless, smaller eromenos.[37] The interior of a cup of c. 490 in Tarquinia

FIGURE 38. Attic red-figure
amphora by the Matsch
Painter, c. 490 B.C. Rome,
Museo Nazionale Etrusco
di Villa Giulia 50462.
Photo courtesy of the
Soprintendenza Archeo-
logica per l'Etruria
Meridionale, Rome.

(Museo Nazionale Tarquin-
iense 701; fig. 39) depicts a
later stage in courtship: the
bearded, larger male, partially draped about the waist
and hips, sits on a stool.[38] A
nude, beardless, smaller eromenos holding a hare by the
ears leans on the erastes' lap and gazes up at him. Here the gift exchange
has already taken place, the figures have disrobed, and the object of desire
is fully exposed to the viewer both on and off the vase. On a cup of c. 480
by Makron in Munich (Staatliche Antikensammlungen 2655; figs. 32–33),[39]
three courting couples adorn each side of the exterior, and the images on
the obverse reveal three different stages of courtship. Reading from right
to left, one sees the first encounter and offer of a gift (flowers), next the
eromenos reaching for a gift (hare), and finally the full display of the
eromenos's nude body while the erastes, who holds a cock, gazes at his
beloved. In the case of the Tarquinia and Munich cups, the viewer of these
nude eromenoi was undoubtedly an aristocratic male as the cups are symposion ware.[40]

The Attic pederastic scenes sometimes include bejeweled nude
women, surely *hetairai* (courtesans), who receive gifts from men, as on an
Attic black-figure cup-skyphos of c. 550 by the Amasis Painter from Rhodes

FIGURE 39. Attic red-figure cup tondo by the Cage Painter, c. 490 B.C. Tarquinia, Museo Nazionale Tarquiniense 701. Photo courtesy of the Soprintendenza Archeologica per l'Etruria Meridionale, Rome.

(Paris, Musée du Louvre A479 [MNB 1746], figs. 40–41).[41] Nude erastai offer a stag, a cock, a swan or heron, a small panther, and a hare to their eromenoi, who are also nude; the youths carry spears, an allusion to the hunt or battle, and two hold aryballoi, references to the palaistra. Additionally, a man stands before a nude woman on each side of the vase; in one instance, he offers her a hen. The women carry blossoms and necklaces or garlands. Aside from their white skin color, the women's physiques are entirely masculine, undifferentiated from that of the males around them.[42]

Other courtship compositions expand not only in the number of participants but also in their iconography: they borrow elements from "return from the hunt" scenes and incorporate them into the courtship composition. An Attic black-figure lekythos of c. 570–560 from the Athenian Kerameikos (6159; figs. 42–44), the earliest extant example of pederastic courtship in Greek vase painting,[43] demonstrates this appropriation. At the center of the image stands a bearded nude male, who holds a cock in his right hand and extends his left hand downward toward the genitals of the beardless, almost nude youth standing opposite him (and here the figures are the same size). The two figures form the core of the courtship composition, which expands here to include two additional male figures on ei-

FIGURES 40–41. Attic
black-figure cup by the
Amasis Painter, c. 550
B.C. Paris, Musée du
Louvre A479 [MNB
1746]. Photos by M.
Chuzeville and C.
Larrieu, courtesy of
the Musée du Louvre.

ther side of the central scene, who approach the courting couple; all wear
a garment except the figure directly to our right of the erastes. This nude figure holds a dead hare slung from a pole over his left shoulder (another
hare hangs from the background), and the combination of male figure
with game on a pole is a standard motif in images of returning (successful) hunters.[44] For instance, a solitary hunter and his dog appear on the
tondo of an Attic black-figure plate by the Tleson Painter of c. 550–540 in
London (British Museum 1867.5–8.946 [B421]; fig. 45), and the hunter
holds a dead hare and dead fox on a pole.[45]

Variants on the return from the hunt motif include hunters laden with
game approaching Dionysos or an anonymous banqueter. The latter is
visible on an Attic black-figure lekythos of c. 500 B.C. in Laon (Musée
Archéologique Municipal 37.892; figs. 46–47), where a hunter wearing a
petasos, chiton, and chlamys, and carrying a pole with a dead fox and dead

FIGURES 42–44. Attic black-figure lekythos by the C Painter, c. 570–560 B.C. Athens, Kerameikos Museum 6159. Photos courtesy of the Deutsches Archäologisches Institut, Athens, negative numbers KER 2890, KER 6159.

FIGURE 45. Attic black-
figure plate by the Tleson
Painter, c. 550–540 B.C.
London, British Museum
1867.5–8. 946 [B421]. Photo
courtesy of the British
Museum. © The British
Museum.

hare, is joined by a male
attendant, a hunting dog,
and a draped female holding a plemochoe.[46] The figures approach a reclining banqueter; a table piled high with victuals appears before the kline,
and a seated female and two nude male youths appear beyond it. The
youth nearest the banqueter holds an oinochoe with which to serve wine.
Likewise, the same type of composition appears in Attic red-figure, as on
the amphora of c. 490 in Munich (Staatliche Antikensammlungen 2303
[J479]), where a hunter carrying game, his dog, and a female approach a
banqueter.[47] The reverse of this amphora displays Dionysos, a satyr, and
maenad, and, when read together with the obverse, suggests a sympotic
occasion. Returning hunters sometimes approach Dionysos himself, perhaps to bring provisions for a banquet; this motif occurs several times on
amphorae by the Amasis Painter (see chapter 1).[48]

    In the case of the Kerameikos lekythos (figs. 42–44), the courtship com-
position incorporates the hunter, pole, and dead game from the returning
hunters imagery, perhaps to suggest a forthcoming banquet or to com-
pound the metaphor of courtship as hunting by offering an example of a
successful hunter to the metaphorical, amorous hunter. This is the only
example in which the three elements—hunter, pole, and dead game—in-
trude on the courtship imagery. But other courtship paintings include
dead game, either adorning the walls, as on the cup in a Swiss private collection (fig. 31) and the London amphora (British Museum 1865.11–18.39
[W39]; fig 35), or offered as courtship gifts, such as the dead hare on the
Attic black-figure cup by the Amasis Painter in Paris (Musée du Louvre

FIGURES 46–47. Attic black-figure lekythos by the Edinburgh Painter, c. 500 B.C. Laon, Musée Archéologique Municipal 37.892. Photos courtesy of the Musée Archéologique Municipal du Laon.

A479, figs. 40–41).[49] One also sees courtship scenes in which there are no animal gifts or hunters but a hunting dog is present, for example, the Attic black-figure tripod pyxis of c. 550 in Munich (Staatliche Antikensammlungen 2290a),[50] and cup of c. 540 in Bochum (Ruhr Universität, Kunstsammlungen, Funcke Collection 68).[51] Another way that hunting imagery directly intrudes into these courtship images is the inclusion of dogs chasing hares, sometimes around the courting erastes and eromenos in the tondo of a cup, such as the Attic black-figure example of c. 550–525 in the Musée du Louvre (F85bis; fig. 48).[52] On the tondo of an Attic red-figure cup of the last quarter of the sixth century in Gotha (Schlossmuseum AVa 48; fig. 49), a dog jumps up toward a caged hare while an erastes embraces his eromenos in his cloak.[53]

But in most pederastic courtship scenes, particularly in Attic red-figure, the animal gifts offered to the eromenos are alive, as indicated by the animal's flailing legs or tensed body. The proffered animals are most commonly cocks and hares, but one also sees leopards and deer, usually stags,

FIGURE 48. Attic black-figure cup, c. 550–525 B.C. Paris, Musée du Louvre F85bis. Photo by M. Chuzeville and C. Larrieu, courtesy of the Musée du Louvre.

and an occasional bird. For example, two erastai, one holding a live hare, the other a cock, woo an eromenos on the interior of an Attic black-figure plate of c. 520 in Leiden (Rijksmuseum van Oudheden RO II 89);[54] an erastes dangles an animated hare in front of an eromenos on an Attic red-figure stamnos of c. 490 in Vienna (Kunsthistorisches Museum 3729);[55] and on the exterior of an Attic red-figure cup of c. 490–480 (Munich, Staatliche Antikensammlungen 2655; figs. 32–33), six erastai present blossoms, a crown, a cock, and a hare to their eromenoi. A stag and leopard, as well as a cock, dead hare, and a bird are offered to eromenoi on the Amasis Painter cup in Paris mentioned earlier (Musée du Louvre A479 [MNB 1746], figs. 40–41). These courtship scenes with live animals do not seem to have the same direct relationship to the returning hunter iconography, especially in the case of cocks, which are not wild animals (though they can be very difficult to catch!), but we should note that hunting dogs are often included in these scenes; see, for example, a cup in Bologna of c. 540–530 (Museo Civico Archeologico PU 189);[56] a cup in Providence of c. 550–525 (Museum of Art, Rhode Island School of Design 13.1479 [C183]);[57] and one in Rome of c. 550 (Museo Gregoriano Etrusco Vaticano 352).[58]

FIGURE 49. Attic red-figure cup tondo, the Gotha Cup, last quarter of the sixth century B.C. Gotha, Schlossmuseum AVa 48. Photo courtesy of the Schlossmuseum.

In addition to elements of the hunt, several pederastic courtship vase paintings include references to the palaistra, one of the loci of pederastic activity.[59] An example is the scene on a cup tondo from the 470s by the Brygos Painter in Oxford (Ashmolean Museum 1967.304; fig. 50), which depicts a crouching, bearded erastes whose thighs enfold a standing, beardless eromenos, who is much smaller.[60] The erastes fondles the eromenos's genitals and has a prominent erection.[61] Neither carries small game, but the eromenos carries a hunting net, and a strigil and staff appear in the background.

The palaistra is one of several iconographic markers in the Attic pederastic scenes that indicate the importance of pederastic activities to the visual construction of Athenian aristocratic society. This setting underscores the agonistic nature of gift giving and courtship, which were designed to enhance the status of both erastai and eromenoi. We have also noted that a majority of the pederastic depictions occur on drinking paraphernalia affiliated with the symposion, an aristocratic institution. *Kalos* inscriptions addressed to beautiful aristocratic youths, the walking sticks on which the erastai lean, and the mantles casually thrown over the shoulders of erastai have also been cited as aristocratic markers.[62]

Courtship as Metaphorical Hunting

Why do the pederastic courtship paintings include dead animals, hunters with dead game, hunting dogs, and live game? I propose that the icono-

FIGURE 50. Attic red-figure cup tondo by the Brygos Painter, c. 470s B.C. Oxford, Ashmolean Museum 1967.304. Photo courtesy of the Ashmolean Museum.

graphical borrowing from the hunting scenes is not just one of form but also of meaning; that is, the courtship images borrow hunting motifs to express the metaphorical hunt that takes place between erastes and eromenos—just as the hunter hunts his prey, so the erastes pursues the eromenos.

The notion that courtship is a metaphorical hunt finds ample support from the ancient written tradition that describes amatory activity or desire in terms of hunting. For example, Ibycus (287) speaks of Eros hurling the poet into the nets of the Cyprian (Aphrodite).[63] Plato takes up this image repeatedly, comparing wolves attacking lambs to erastai pursuing eromenoi (Phdr. 241d), and likening hunters and their prey to lovers and the objects of their affection (Lysis 206a).[64] Xenophon (*Mem.* 1.2.24) claims that Alcibiades was hunted by desirous women, a play on the same idea to express the reversal of usual gender roles. Such images often describe the capture as aided by nets or snares (Ibyc. 287; *Anth. Pal.* 12.142, 146), a type of hunting already familiar to us from tragedy, but examples exist in lyric, Plato,

Xenophon, and epigrams in the *Palatine Anthology* (12.92), as well.[65] In some instances, the roles of pursuer and pursued, hunter and hunted, are reversed, and the usual aggressor is hunted down by desire or love. For example, Sophocles describes a woman, usually the recipient of another's passion, who is struck with physical desire, as being caught in nets (frag. 932: ἐν τοῖσιν αὐτοῖς δικτύοις ἁλίσκεται πρὸς τοῦ παρόντος ἱμέρου νικωμένη).[66] She possesses the desire rather than being the object of another's. A fragment by the lyric poet Ibycus written in the last third of the sixth century has the lover as hunted quarry: "Eros will yet again eye me tenderly from beneath dark brows and cast me . . . into the hopeless net of the Cyprian goddess Aphrodite" (frag. 2). This is also the first attestation of another hunting metaphor, "the lover hunted down by the eyes of the beloved."[67] The gaze shared by erastes and eromenos on the vases may also express this idea.[68] Desire is not the aggressor but the quarry according to Ariphron (*apud* Ath. 15.701f–702b, 4–5), who notes that men hunt desire using Aphrodite's secret nets (frag. 813: πόθων οὓς κρυφίοις Ἀφροδίτας ἕρκεσιν θηρεύομεν). The net metaphor may be somewhat puzzling considering Plato's disapproval of nets for the hunting of actual animals (*Leg.* 823b–824b); he claims their suitability for youths and not for adult men, but we have also noted in chapter 1 that Plato's dictum may not be applicable at all times. Ironically, despite the net's association with amorous capture, its inventor is said to be Hippolytos (Oppian, *Cyn.* 2.25), the chaste devotee of the goddess Artemis, who refused to grow up and marry.

Not only can the lover or beloved be the hunter, but so can Eros himself as literary texts such as Plato's *Symposium* (203d) describe. The same motif occurs in Attic red-figure vase painting, where Eros pursues and sometimes copulates with young eromenoi, as on the tondo of an Attic red-figure cup by Douris of c. 470–460 from Nola but now in Berlin (Antikensammlung F2305).[69] Eros sometimes holds, or is accompanied by, a cock, deer, or hare;[70] presumably the animals serve as Eros's courtship gifts for a beloved, or the juxtaposition of Eros and these animals indicates an amorous theme in a multivalent way.[71] Also noteworthy is the fifth-century development in vase painting of Eros and sometimes Aphrodite equipped with arrows with which they target their quarry. For example, Eros first appears as archer on an Attic red-figure lekythos of c. 490 by the Brygos Painter (Fort Worth, Kimbell Art Museum AP84.16),[72] and Eros sets a trap on the tondo of an early-fourth-century Attic red-figure cup by the Diomed Painter.[73] A century later, Xenophon (*Mem*.1.3.13) writes that οἱ Ἔρωτες are called archers since οἱ καλοὶ can wound from afar.

In addition to the general view of desire or amorous pursuit as hunting, written texts explicitly liken the pursuit of an eromenos by an erastes to hunting (the Cretan rite of passage in which an adult erastes hunts and has sex with his adolescent eromenos is the real-life equivalent of the written and visual metaphor).[74] Aischines (1.195) speaks of erastai as "hunters of young men, who are easily caught."[75] Borrowing a Homeric simile, Theognis (1278c–d) and Plato (*Chrm.* 155d–e) liken the erastes to a lion and the eromenos to a fawn, and the latter simile can also be found in epigrams in the *Palatine Anthology* (12.142, 146). Plato (*Soph.* 222d–e) describes how erastai are said to hunt their eromenoi by using gifts as weapons, and Aristophanes (*Plut.* 155–56) describes hunting dogs and horses, the quintessential aristocratic symbol, as pederastic courtship gifts. Plato (*Soph.* 223a–b) also refers to sophists as hunters whose prey is those they educate. This analogy between sophists and erastai may suggest that pederasty is part of aristocratic education (cf. also Pl., *Lysis* 206a–b, *Prt.* 309a). Alcibiades recounts his attempts to win Socrates in Plato's *Symposium* (217c–d), which result in Alcibiades adopting the role of the pursuer; by inviting Socrates to dine with him, Alcibiades acted as a lover laying his snares for his beloved (ὥσπερ ἐραστὴς παιδικοῖς ἐπιβουλεύων).

Vase paintings of pederastic courtship also include hunting elements. This inclusion of the world of the hunt in such courtship scenes makes literal the metaphorical relationship of courtship to hunting, which is evidenced elsewhere in Greek literature. For example, an erastes embraces an eromenos while a dog chases a hare on the border of a cup tondo (Paris, Musée du Louvre F85bis; fig. 48). By means of juxtaposition, the viewer is invited to compare these two hunts, one in progress, the other a success for the hunter. But the placement of the predatory dog next to the unbearded and smaller eromenos, and the fleeing hare next to the crouching erastes raises the question: who is the hunter and who is the hunted? Has the erastes been captured by the eromenos's beauty or is the eromenos the victim of the erastes' predation? A seated erastes enfolds an eromenos in his arms and the eromenos holds a hare by the ears in his outstretched hand on the cup tondo in Tarquinia (Museo Nazionale Tarquiniense 701; fig. 39): the prey has been captured as indicated by the struggling hare. Because the erastes grasps the eromenos, it is easy to read the image as follows: just as the hare is captured, so is the eromenos. But the hare is held by the eromenos, prompting a more ambiguous reading: perhaps the hare signifies the erastes, who has been captured by desire. Both of these visual examples offer complex images to the viewer involving ambiguity as to who constitutes the hunter and who the prey, and in each instance I have identified the animals with the human participants. An examination of the animal gifts that appear in the pederastic courtship images and their possible relationship to their human companions helps us to disentangle this web of meanings.

The Animal Gifts

The animals most commonly chosen for love gifts—cocks, hares, deer, and small felines—are critical to an understanding of the negotiation: they are not mere props but contribute to the metaphor of courtship as hunting.[76] Scholars sometimes note the animals' connection to the aristocratic practice of hunting or posit vague associations of the animals with the captured eromenos but have failed to address the questions of why particular animals and not others are selected and how the animals specifically relate to the amorous encounter. I contend that the choice of animal is not random because only certain animals are given as gifts and that this choice is particular to the context of courtship. Not only do elements of hunting iconography infiltrate the pederastic courtship paintings to create a metaphor for courtship as hunting, but the animals that are offered as gifts may be metaphorical expressions of the characteristics of the eromenos (or the erastes?).[77] The relationship between animal and eromenos is explicit in two epigrams in the *Palatine Anthology* (12.142, 146) that liken the beloved to a fawn, and it is likely that the visual images also intend to draw parallels between the two types of game. As we shall see, virility, combativeness, courage, and cunning are all associated with the animals given in pederastic courtship paintings, and such qualities were certainly admirable in the soldier and arguably so in the lover or beloved.[78] Just as the walking stick signals "aristocrat," and the strigil alludes to the palaistra and its athletic and aristocratic connotations, the animal gifts convey information about the giver or receiver.[79] Although much of the written evidence attesting to the nature and attributes of the animals used as courtship gifts is later than the vases under discussion, it still merits consideration because it is the only available written evidence.

Aristophanes is the first to enumerate animal gifts in pederastic relationships, naming quail, coot, the goose, and cock (*Av.* 707), as well as
horses and hunting dogs (*Plut.*155–56), the latter two noteworthy for their
aristocratic associations. But Attic vase painting offers no examples of
equine, quail, coot, or goose gifts. Instead, cocks are the commonest gift
from erastes to eromenos with hares a strong second; birds (usually swans),
stags, does, and small felines often described as leopards, cheetahs, or panthers occasionally appear.[80] Hunting dogs often turn up but whether they
are intended as gifts or not is unclear.[81] Although cocks were not hunted
at all and leopards were not hunted in Greece (the hunting of large felines
was part of Near Eastern traditions), these animals are as central to understanding the metaphorical hunting scenes as the hares and stags used as
love gifts, and so they must be considered here.

Foxes and hares appear dead in the pederastic courtship scenes, but
cocks, felines, and deer are always alive,[82] and hares are often alive as on
an Attic black-figure neck amphora of c. 550–530 by the Affecter (London,
British Museum 1836.2–24.46 [B153]; fig. 51), where a live hare with legs
pawing the air is held under the chin.[83] Another example is the Tarquinia
cup (Museo Nazionale Tarquiniense 701, fig. 39),[84] where the eromenos
holds the struggling hare by the ears and leans into the lap of a seated,
bearded erastes. The hare is sometimes even in motion as on an Attic red-
figure cup tondo of c. 490–480 by Makron in Berlin (Antikensammlung
F2291; fig. 52).[85] A living stag accompanies the courting pair on an Attic
black-figure amphora in Providence (Museum of Art, Rhode Island
School of Design 13.1479 [C183]; fig. 53).[86]

Cocks, though neither wild nor hunted, are the commonest animal gift
in Attic pederastic vase paintings.[87] Known for its combative spirit,[88] the cock
possessed associations with the military and the aristocracy; this is not a surprising combination as we learned in chapter 1. As reported by Philo (*Quod
omnis Probus liber* 132–4), the fifth-century B.C. tragic poet Ion (frag. 53N)
speaks of the cock's unstoppable courage in combat: οὐδ᾽ ὅ γε σῶμα τυπεὶς
διφυεῖς τε κόρας ἐπιλάθεται ἀλκᾶς, ἀλλ᾽ ὀλιγοδρανέων φθογγάζεται·
θάνατον δ᾽ ὅ γε δουλοσύνας προβέβουλεν. According to Aelian (*VH* 2.28),
the Athenians, inspired by the sight of a cockfight on their way to Salamis,
decisively defeated the Persians—this is the aition for annual cockfights in
the theater in Athens. However, because the age of this custom cannot be
determined, whether or not it took place in the archaic and classical peri-

FIGURE 51. Attic black-figure amphora by the Affecter, c. 550–530 B.C. London, British Museum 1836.2–24.46 [B153]. Photo courtesy of the British Museum. © The British Museum.

FIGURE 52. Attic red-figure cup tondo by Makron, c. 490–480 B.C. Berlin, Antikensammlung F2291. Courtesy Antikensammlung, Staatliche Museen zu Berlin, Preussischer Kulturbesitz.

ods is not known.[89] Plutarch also attests to the connection between cocks and warfare, in this case, in Spartan military practice; if a Spartan general had overcome an enemy by force of arms, he sacrificed a cock or, if he had used deception or persuasion, an ox (*Marc.* 22); and if the Spartans were victorious, they routinely sacrificed a single cock as a thank offering to the gods (*Agesilaus* 33). Moreover, the crests worn on hoplite helmets may have been intended to evoke cocks' combs.[90] Pausanias also reports that the helmet of the chryselephantine Athena by Pheidias on the Elean Acropolis was adorned by a cock, a bird that easily goes to fight (6.26.3: οὗτοι προχειρότατα ἔχουσιν ἐς μάχας οἱ ἀλεκτρυόνες). Not only did cocks have associations with the military but also with the aristocracy: cock fighting was an aristocratic activity beginning with its introduction from Persia to Greece in the sixth century, and it retained an aristocratic patina even after the Persian Wars when it was enjoyed by nonaristocrats.[91]

Further attestation of the cock's competitive and combative nature comes from the visual record. Cocks perch atop columns that flank Athena on sixth- and fifth-century Panathenaic amphorae awarded to athletic victors,[92] and opposed cocks accompany battle scenes in Attic vase painting,[93] creating a visual parallel between the two types of combat. Cocks also adorn warriors' shields on Corinthian and Attic vases,[94] and Hoffmann notes that fighting cocks on vases often have the names of Homeric heroes inscribed beside them.[95] Cocks appear in gymnasia settings on vases, a combination that alludes to the virile nature of the youth's physical education and its purpose as preparation for warfare.[96] The op-

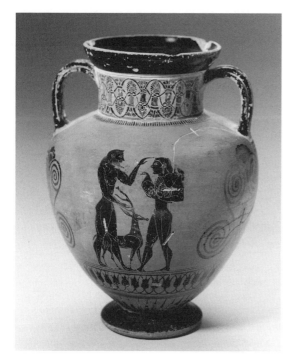

FIGURE 53. Attic black-figure amphora by the Painter of Louvre F51, c. 550–510 B.C. Providence, Museum of Art, Rhode Island School of Design 13.1479 [C183]. Gift of Mrs. Gustav Radeke. Photo courtesy of Erik Gould for the Museum of Art, Rhode Island School of Design.

posed cocks on both sides of an East Greek silver alabastron of the sixth century formerly in the Metropolitan Museum of Art in New York (66.11.27) also illustrate this combative spirit: opposed cocks appear in the top frieze; in the frieze below, lions attack bulls; beneath this frieze is a scene of hoplite battle, and stags and does fill the bottom figural frieze.[97] By means of juxtaposition, fighting cocks are visually likened here to a violent animal confrontation and fighting warriors. Similarly, opposed cocks appear below Herakles wrestling the Nemean lion,[98] Herakles and Cerberus,[99] and warriors carrying their dead comrades on the interior of three Laconian cups, respectively, of c. 560–550 by the Hunt Painter.[100]

The cock's reputation for virile masculinity and combative spirit has sexual associations as well.[101] On an Attic white-ground lekythos of the late fifth century in Limassol, a winged Eros, holding an aryballos and an alabastron, and with a wreath dangling from his left forearm, hovers over two fighting cocks.[102] Eros, combat, and the palaistra are combined in this image. A phallos bird adorns an Attic red-figure skyphos in Boston (Museum of Fine Arts 08.31c; fig. 54) of the early fifth century,[103] presenting the

FIGURE 54. Attic red-figure skyphos, early fifth century B.C. Boston, Museum of Fine Arts 08.31c. Gift of Fiske Warren and E. P. Warren. Photo courtesy of the Museum of Fine Arts, Boston. Reproduced with permission. © 1999 Museum of Fine Arts, Boston. All rights reserved.

actual assimilation of cock (bird) and phallos.[104] Elsewhere, a satyr rides a phallos bird in the midst of cavorting satyrs on an Attic red-figure cup of c. 490 in Brussels (Musées Royaux d'Art et d'Histoire A723),[105] and the phallos bird also serves as a shield device in some vase paintings.[106] A vertical reading of an Attic black-figure lekythos of c. 500 in Boston (Museum of Fine Arts 08.291; figs. 55–57) demonstrates the likening of cockfight to erotic struggle, since a cockfight takes place directly below a scene of pederastic courtship.[107] And Koch-Harnack offers the same kind of interpretation for the figures on an Attic black-figure cup in Boston (Museum of Fine Arts 63.4), where several pederastic pairs squat opposite each other and hold cocks as if they are about to release them.[108] Perhaps the choice of the cock in pederastic courtship scenes signifies not only the courtship itself but also the fighting spirit that the eromenos ideally possessed; the eromenos was expected to resist his erastes, and an easy conquest was considered dishonorable to the eromenos.[109] As Dover notes, the disdain for easily caught prey derives from the world of aristocratic hunting: because hunting is not necessary for survival, easily attainable prey is considered unworthy of the effort.[110] Alternately, the cock's salacious nature, amply attested in literature[111] and alluded to by the painted phallos bird, may signify the erastes' desire or perhaps was intended as an example and inspiration to the eromenos.

Hares, the second most common animal gift and the prey of hunters, are fast (Hom., *Il.* 17.676; Hes., *Sc.* 302–4; Ael., *NA* 13.14),[112] difficult to catch, highly sexual, and cunning. Hares are reputed to be among the most fertile animals, able to conceive repeatedly while pregnant (Hdt. 3.108; Xen., *Cyn.* 5.13; Arist., *Hist. an.* 5.9.542b30–31; Plin., *HN* 8.81.219, 10.83.179, 10.83.182; Plut., *Mor.* 829b; Ael., *NA* 2.12), and hunters dedicate newborn hares to Artemis (Xen., *Cyn.* 5.14). The hare is cunning and able to trick huntsmen (Plut., *Mor.* 971d; Ael., *NA* 6.47), but timid (Arist., *Hist. an.* 1.1.488b15; Plin., *HN* 11.70.183).[113] Both the hare and the fox fear dogs (Ael., *NA* 5.24), and using skill and cunning to achieve their aims, foxes exhaust and capture hares (Ael., *NA* 8.11).[114] It is noteworthy that when Pan, a god associated with sexuality among other things, is born, Hermes wraps him in hare skins and takes him to Mount Olympos, where the gods are charmed by the newborn (*Hymn. Hom. Pan.* 41–46). Perhaps most tellingly, Xenophon says, "Thus the sight [of the hare] is so pleasing that there is no one who would not forget about whomever [or whatever] he loved once he saw the hare being tracked, found, pursued, and caught" (*Cyn.* 5.33: οὕτω δὲ ἐπίχαρί ἐστι τὸ θέαμα, ὥστε οὐδεὶς ὅστις οὐκ ἂν ἰδὼν ἰχνευόμενον, εὑρισκόμενον, μεταθεόμενον, ἁλισκόμενον ἐπιλάθοιτ᾽ ἂν εἴ του ἐρῴη). The mere sight of the hare being hunted and captured replaces desire for something or someone. As will be demonstrated, vase painting makes this analogy between hare and eromenos explicit.

Hare hunting was the special province of ephebes, who used nets and *lagobola* (staffs for hurling at hares) to snare and then kill their swift prey. Plutarch (*Cim.* 16) relates that one day in Sparta, while the youths and boys were exercising inside the colonnade, a hare appeared, and the boys, still naked, ran out and chased it. This anecdote underscores the naturalness and appropriateness of boys chasing hares and implicitly likens it to a form of exercise,[115] which involved the display of youthful male bodies to older mature men, an exhibition of "prey" for the amorous hunter. Attic vase painting also presents hare hunting, in twenty-two black-figure, nine red-figure, and four white-ground examples. Like the boar and deer hunts discussed in chapter 1, hare hunts are most prevalent on Attic vases in the

FIGURES 55–57. Attic black-figure lekythos by the Painter of Boston 08.291, c. 500 B.C. Boston, Museum of Fine Arts 08.291. Gift of E. P. Fiske Warren. Photo courtesy of the Museum of Fine Arts, Boston. Reproduced with permission. © 2000 Museum of Fine Arts, Boston. All rights reserved.

second half of the sixth century, with cups (symposion ware) and lekythoi the dominant shapes.[116] Beardless nude males, often solitary but as many as three in number, wield lagobola and, together with hunting dogs, chase hares into nets.[117] An Attic black-figure kylix of c. 525 from Rhodes (London, British Museum B386; fig. 58) provides a typical example.[118] On the obverse, a solitary hunter wearing only a chlamys follows a large dog, which pursues an enormous hare into a net. The reverse depicts much the same scene except that a standing onlooker has replaced the hunter. Several examples exhibit dogs chasing hares but no hunters, such as the Attic cup in Hamburg (Museum für Kunst und Gewerbe 1908.255; fig. 2), on which hare hunting on the lip accompanies boar hunting on the body,

and the Boston lekythos (Museum of Fine Arts o8.291; figs. 55–57), on which two dogs chase a hare into a net.[119] The presence, however, of nets or a throwing stick alludes to a human agent, and these therefore still constitute scenes of humans hunting hares. Like the boar and deer hunters, hare hunters occasionally carry military weapons (e.g., sheathed sword on a cup in Naples, Museo Archeologico Nazionale Stg. 200 of c. 520;[120] spears on vases of c. 500 in Vienna, Kunsthistorisches Museum 194 [figs. 59–60],[121] and of c. 500–475 in Athens, National Museum 1973 [CC.964])[122] or wear chlamydes held as if they were shields,[123] which begin to appear at the end of the sixth century.[124] In this instance, the metaphor of hunting as warfare is hardly credible because the hare is a harmless opponent, but its swiftness and cunning present challenges to the future hoplite. Perhaps the hare used as a shield device on an Attic black-figure amphora of c. 520 in Munich (Staatliche Antikensammlungen 1386; figs. 16–17) alludes to these qualities of the hoplite holding the shield.

The appearance of hare hunting on white-ground lekythoi deserves further consideration. White-ground lekythoi are commonly associated with funerary use, and the connection between hare hunting and the funerary realm is evident on an Attic white-ground lekythos of c. 450 by the Thanatos Painter (London, British Museum D60; figs. 61–62), on which two hunters chase a hare scrambling around a tomb.[125] The lunging hunter with chlamys on the left, like the heroic boar and deer hunters, recalls the Tyrannicides sculptural group. For the moment, we might speculate that the lekythoi with hare hunts are intended for males who died while still

FIGURE 58. Attic black-figure cup, c. 525 B.C. London, British Museum B386.
Photo courtesy of the British Museum. © The British Museum.

ephebes. Pederastic courtship depictions also appear on a Clazomenian
sarcophagus of c. 510 (Berlin, Antikensammlung 30030) using the same
compositional types as the Attic vases.[126] But let us leave aside the funerary
associations until chapter 4, which is devoted solely to this issue.

Deer (ἐλάφοι) or fawns (νεβροί) are also occasionally offered as gifts in
pederastic images, where they are remarkably small and usually held in
the figures' arms as if they were small dogs (e.g., London, British Museum
1865.11–18.39 [W39]; fig. 35), but they also stand on the groundline, as on
the Providence amphora (Museum of Art, Rhode Island School of Design
13.1479 [C183]; fig. 53), and in one instance, as we have seen, a doe is slung
over a human shoulder (fig. 34). Like boar, deer are hunted by heroes,
such as Herakles and Theseus, and by mortal hunters but do not possess the
fierce reputation of the boar (note that boar are never offered as gifts in
pederastic scenes). We have also seen that eromenoi are likened to captured fawns in literature. But deer can also be hunters: they easily attract
snakes and eat them, according to Plutarch (*Mor.* 976d) and Aelian (*NA*
8.6). The deer is reputed to be content with its lot and does not yearn for
more than it has (Ael., *NA* 6.13) and, like the hare, is intelligent but timid
(Arist., *Hist. An.* 1.1.488b15).

FIGURES 59–60. Attic black-figure lekythos, c. 500 B.C. Vienna, Kunsthistorisches Museum 194. Photos courtesy of the Kunsthistorisches Museum.

Small felines, called leopard or panther (πάρδαλις, πάνθηρ, πάρδος, or λεόπαρδος) by ancient authors, also served as courtship gifts. Their appearance in vase painting varies: they are sometimes spotted like the modern leopard, sometimes solid black like the modern panther, and nearly always remarkably small.[127] They are usually held (e.g., Paris, Musée du Louvre A479 ([MNB 1746]; figs. 40–41), but also stand on the groundline (e.g., Boulogne, Musée Communal 134).[128] Aristotle(?) (*Pr.* 13.4 [907b]) says that of living creatures only the leopard (ἡ πάρδαλις) has a pleasant smell, and even other animals enjoy the odor. Both Theophrastus (*Caus. Pl.* 6.5.2) and Aelian (*NA* 5.40, 8.6) echo this information and add that the leopard uses his extraordinary scent as a lure to capture its prey; hidden in the thickets, the leopard would spring out and attack fawns and gazelles that came near.[129] Plutarch (*Mor.* 976d) reports that the panther's scent is

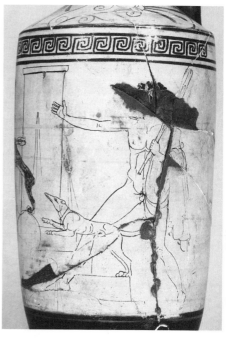

FIGURES 61–62. Attic white-ground lekythos by the Thanatos Painter, c. 450 B.C. London, British Museum D60. Photos courtesy of the British Museum. © The British Museum.

especially attractive to the ape (ὁ πίθηκος), who is captured by the panther. Much later c. 1275–1340, Manuel Philes (*De animalium proprietate* 37) recounts the same method of hunting; lists the prey captured by the leopard or panther (Philes uses both πάρδαλις and πάνθηρ), including wild goats, fawns, wild boar, hares, and roes; and then likens this form of hunting to a charm used to drag wretched youth pleasantly to the destructive fire of love. Again, the analogy of hunting and eros is clear. Ancient authors also celebrate the female panther for her extraordinary courage (Arist. *Hist. an.* 9.1.608a33; Plin., *HN* 11.110; Ael., *NA* 4.49).

I have suggested that the leopard signifies characteristics of the erastes or eromenos so we may conjecture that the predatory leopard offered as a gift in the courtship scenes alludes to the attractive scent of the eromenos or the duplicitous tactics of the erastes or the courage of either eromenos or erastes.[130] The panther, however, not only lures others but itself can be lured by the odor of wine, according to Oppian (*Cyn.* 4.320–53), so that the hunter can become the enticed prey.[131] If the panther of the pederastic courtship paintings represents the eromenos or the erastes, we might imagine him being lured by the wine of the symposion, which was one arena for pederastic courtship. An even closer identification of panther and eromenos or erastes is suggested by the inscription on an engraved agate gem of the first century B.C. in Leiden (Royal Coin Cabinet 1948).[132] Two males engaged in anal sex lie on a bed. Inscribed above them is: Πάρδαλα, πεῖνε, τρύφα, περιλάμβανε, θανεῖν σε δεῖ. ὁ γὰρ χρόνος ὀλίγος. Αχαιέ, ζήσαις (Leopard—drink, live luxuriously, embrace! You must die, for there is little time. May you live, Greek!). The inscription addresses the viewer, whom one may deduce is male because of the subject matter on the gem (and not from the vocative form in the inscription). Here, the leopard and the lover or beloved are one and the same.

While leopards are occasionally hunted in Attic black-figure vase painting, one also pursues a human hunter.[133] Elsewhere, several Attic red-figure cups attest to leopards assisting hunters in bringing down deer.[134] Leopards leap on the back of does and bite their flanks while a youth runs nearby on a cup of c. 510 in New York (Metropolitan Museum of Art 41.162.129) ; a cup of c. 510–500 in Würzburg (Martin von Wagner Museum der Universität 473); and another of c. 500 in Paris (Musée du Louvre G21).[135] The youth holds no weapons, although his arm is extended with a chlamys held as a shield. On a cup of c. 505 in Berlin (Antikensammlung F2324; fig. 63), two Scythians and an armed hoplite move in for the kill.[136] Like the boar and deer hunters of chapter 1, these hunters are likened to warriors. Surely, the leopards (and Scythians) allude to Eastern hunting practices (both as prey and as assistants in human hunting) with their noble, hence aristocratic, connotations.

In sum, the various animal gifts presented by the erastes to the eromenos in Attic vase painting possess qualities associated with the giver and receiver; erastai should be virile and fight for their eromenoi, whereas eromenoi should be attractive and difficult to catch.

Reading the Vases

Having examined the elements drawn from hunting iconography in the pederastic courtship scenes, the written attestations for courtship as hunting, and the animal gifts that contribute to the visual metaphor, we may read the pederastic courtship paintings as metaphors for hunting. The

FIGURE 63. Attic red-figure cup by the Nikosthenes Painter, c. 505 B.C. Berlin, Antikensammlung F2324. Photo courtesy of the Antikensammlung, Staatliche Museen zu Berlin, Preussischer Kulturbesitz.

roles of erastes and eromenos are likened to those of hunter and hunted. Xenophon (*Cyn.* 5.33) suggests that the sight of a hare being caught can make one forget one's beloved, that the hare hunt can replace or substitute for the erotic. Other texts describe the eromenos in terms of a captured fawn. Most tellingly, an erastes reclines on the tondo of an Attic red-figure cup of c. 490 in Athens (National Museum 1357; fig. 36) and strokes a hare while singing O ΠΑΙΔΟΝ ΚΑΛΛΙΣΤΕ; as Lissarrague succinctly states, "Touching the animal is a substitute for touching the beloved."[137]

But one can go beyond the claim that the eromenos is like the captured prey in terms of action to say that the eromenos is like the captured prey in character. Hares are swift, difficult to catch, and cunning; deer are timid; panthers or leopards hunt by means of their attractive scent, which is likened to sexual allure. Honor was accorded the eromenos who displayed the virtue of being difficult to catch (which implies swiftness and cunning) and who was nonaggressive in his sexual behavior (i.e., timid). Such a reading becomes more persuasive if we also consider depictions of cocks in pederastic contexts.

The Attic black-figure lekythos of c. 550 in Boston (Museum of Fine Arts o8.291; figs. 55–57) exhibits three aspects of the life of the ephebe: courtship, riding, and hare hunting, the world of kalokagathia.[138] Like the Attic black-figure cup in Paris (Musée du Louvre F85bis, fig. 48), the Boston lekythos also employs the motif of dog chasing hare on the bottom frieze as visual commentary on the top frieze, which is filled with a depiction of homosexual courtship; that is, the dog chases the hare just as the erastes pursues his quarry. The courting couple accords with Beazley's alpha composition while hunting dogs stand nearby. At the left of the central pair are two males carrying athletic paraphernalia and a spear, and another male holding a cock. Following the eromenos is a male holding a struggling hare (signifying the resistant eromenos?) and a nude male holding another rooster. Elements of warfare and the palaistra combine with hunting and courtship imagery. A band of horsemen parades around the middle frieze, a subject that together with pederasty is emblematic of aristocratic interests. When read vertically, the central courtship scene of the lekythos aligns with a scene of opposed roosters in the bottom frieze, as if to suggest that the courtship is a type of combat, like a cockfight. What associations would the ancient Greek viewer have brought to this vase? Cocks are virile, brave, combative, and have erotic connotations. The successful erastes will need these qualities to win his beloved. Pederastic courtship is visually equated with hunting and contest, and the cock's pluckiness is paired with the dogs' energetic pursuit of the hare and the erastes' pursuit of the eromenos.

The analogy between eromenos and wild animal that is captured by the erastes has a heterosexual counterpart in the pursuit and abduction of young females in sixth- and fifth-century literature and vase painting.[139] *Parthenoi*, such as Thetis, Oreithyia, and the Leukippidai, are regarded as wild animals in need of taming by a man, by marriage.[140] But in these cases, unlike the pederastic courtship paintings, the prey, the female, is literally chased, hunted down, and caught, as the hunter does with mature game, which often involves resistance, an important element for the eromenos in pederastic relationships. The myth of Peleus and Thetis is exemplary.[141] The mortal Peleus accosts the goddess Thetis, who attempts to elude his grasp by metamorphosing into a variety of forms, including wild animals, before resuming her "normal" shape and submitting to marriage with him, her first sexual experience. This event is depicted on the inte-

FIGURE 64. Attic red-figure cup by Peithinos, c. 500 B.C. Berlin, Antikensammlung 2279. Photo courtesy of the Antikensammlung, Staatliche Museen zu Berlin, Preussischer Kulturbesitz.

rior of an Attic red-figure cup from Vulci by Peithinos of c. 500, now in Berlin (Antikensammlung 2279).[142] The exterior of this cup offers contrasting images of homosexual and heterosexual courting, the former occurring in a gymnasion, as indicated by athletic paraphernalia—sponges, strigils, aryballoi—on the "walls" (fig. 64).[143] When read together, the exterior scenes and the interior tondo offer a panoply of courtship images: mortal and immortal, homosexual and heterosexual. Also notable are the hunting dog and lion skin painted near the figures underneath the handles: their presence suggests a gloss on the scene, that amorous courtship is a kind of hunting. Elsewhere, we can observe pursuit and not actual capture, such as Boreas pursuing Oreithyia,[144] or in a reversal of usual gender roles, Eos pursuing Kephalos.[145] Perhaps in every instance we are meant to understand the pursued as a wild animal captured by a lover. While the quarry's resistance is clearly manifested in the case of Thetis, it can be inferred in the other two scenes from our knowledge of courtship protocol.

I wish to argue, however, that the analogy in vase painting is not always or simply, as scholars have observed, between the eromenos and the prey and the erastes and hunter. Rather, the roles can be transposed, and the lover can be hunted down by the eyes of the beloved or by Eros or desire,[146] a reversal of roles already observed in ancient literature. If we look at the pederastic courtship vase paintings with this interchangeability of hunter

FIGURE 65. Attic red-figure cup tondo by the Ancona Painter, c. 460 B.C. Laon, Musée Archéologique Municipal 37.1056. Photo courtesy of the Musée Archéologique Municipal du Laon.

and hunted in mind (and, as we shall see in chapter 3, interchangeability of these roles constitutes a cardinal aspect of hunting myths), our reading of vase painting images expands and deepens.

An example of the ambiguity between hunter and hunted occurs in the scene on an Attic red-figure cup tondo of the late sixth century in Gotha (Schlossmuseum AVa 48; fig. 49). An erastes embraces an eromenos, and a hunting dog next to the erastes leaps toward a caged hare on the wall behind, offering a gloss on the scene: the eromenos, like the wild hare, has been caught.[147] The eromenos holds a lyre, and an aryballos, sponge, and strigil at the right indicate the placement of the scene in the palaistra, the locus of much aristocratic pederastic activity.[148] Is the analogy here between hare and eromenos, who has been captured by his erastes, or between hare and erastes, who has been captured and captivated by love and desire? Perhaps the ambiguity is intentional.[149] A bearded erastes grasps a hare by the ears in front of a beardless eromenos on an Attic red-figure cup tondo of c. 460 in Laon (Musée Archéologique Municipal 37.1056; fig. 65).[150] The bearded erastes is still partially clothed and holds the hare, but the eromenos is already nude and, in fact, gestures toward the erastes, a variation of the usual pederastic courtship composition in Attic red-figure, where the erastes appears partially or completely nude and still holds the animal gift but a mantle envelopes the eromenos.[151] Rather than reading this as the eromenos equated with the hare, we might understand the hare as identified with the erastes. Of course, the hare is not a gift for the erastes because that contradicts all we know about these pederastic exchanges, but we should understand both the erastes and the hare as captured prey. In this case, the power belongs to the fully displayed eromenos, who has become the hunter. Desire for the eromenos has captured the erastes, whose eyes are transfixed on the eromenos's genitals. Implements of the palaistra and the aristocratic walking stick indicate the location of the action and the designated viewer: an aristocratic male.

Early lyric poetry also attests to the interchangeability of pursuer and pursued. In a fragmentary poem of Sappho (frag. 1), Aphrodite asks Sappho, "Whom am I to persuade this time to lead you back to her love? . . . If she runs away, soon she shall pursue; if she does not accept gifts, why, she shall give them instead."[152] In this same-sex relationship (now female), not only does Eros or desire pursue the lover as was the case in other Greek literature but pursuer and pursued can exchange roles, and the beloved can take on the role of pursuer.

Using this model of the interchangeability of power and pursuit, other readings of Attic pederastic paintings are available to the attentive viewer. On several Attic red-figure cups, an eromenos wearing a *stephanos* (crown) receives an animal gift from an erastes, or wreaths are held by the eromenos (e.g., fig. 35). The wreaths and stephanos suggest that the eromenos is a victor and the hare (representing the erastes?) is his prize. Or perhaps the hare indicates an even more complicated reading: the eromenos has won (hence the crown) by inspiring desire in his erastes, who has awarded him the animal as a gift, which in turn signifies the capture of the eromenos.[153] An Attic black-figure alabastron of c. 500 attributed to the Diosphos Painter from the small heroon of Iphigeneia at Brauron alludes to the victorious eromenos.[154] On the reverse, a hunting dog leaps up in front of an enshrouded eromenos, above whose head hovers a winged Eros holding a crown. The inscriptions ΚΑΛΟΣ and Ο ΚΑΛΟΣ appear in the background. Perhaps Eros awards the crown to the eromenos because he is the object of someone's affections or because he is victorious; he has conquered the erastes, who appears on the obverse, wearing only a himation draped around his upper arms and leaning on a walking stick held in his right hand. The erastes carries a hare by the ears in his left hand while a cock (only the crest and the rear feathers survive) is visible at his feet. ΚΑΛΟΣ and ΚΑΛΟΣ ΗΟ ΠΑ[ΙΣ] are inscribed in the field. The hare and eromenos are one and the same because both have been captured. The dog that leaps up toward the eromenos may be construed as ei-

FIGURE 66. Attic red-figure amphora by the Kleophrades Painter, c. 500 B.C. Leiden, Rijksmuseum van Oudheden PC80 [18 H 35]. Photo courtesy of the Rijksmuseum van Oudheden.

ther bringing his prey, the eromenos, to bay or simply accompanying the hunter, who, in fact, may be the eromenos.

The idea of the victorious eromenos is again represented by a solitary, crowned eromenos holding a hare on an Attic red-figure amphora of c. 500 by the Kleophrades Painter in Leiden (Rijksmuseum van Oudheden PC80 [18 H 35]; fig. 66).[155] On the interior of the cup in the Louvre (F85bis; fig. 48), which depicts a pederastic couple embracing and a dog pursuing a hare, the eromenos brandishes a hunting club or lagobolon. Perhaps we are meant to read this as the older man being conquered by desire, hunted by Eros, who is embodied in his beloved. The tondo of another cup, this one of c. 490 by Douris (New York, ex-Hirschmann Collection G64;

fig.37),[156] displays a beardless, partially nude eromenos sitting alone: he holds a staff in his left hand and a hare rests on his lap. The hare apparently has been removed from an open cage that hangs from the background "wall," and a basket hangs above it. One might read the depiction in a conventional manner—that the hare and the eromenos are alike, a reading that assumes that the seated figure is the eromenos. But if this is a beardless erastes, which becomes a more common visual phenomenon in the fifth century, then perhaps the hare should be viewed as a substitute for the eromenos. Another possible reading sees the hare as signifying the erastes, and perhaps the erastes has been released from the prison (the hare's cage) of his sexual desire by its fulfillment.

Ancient authors report that hares are the prey of foxes, but in the occasional instance when foxes appear in Attic pederastic paintings, they are dead, suggesting that the traditional predator has been conquered.[157] The contemplative eromenos who gazes at a dead fox on the fragment of an Attic red-figure cup by Douris in Munich (Staatliche Antikensammlungen 8710; fig. 67; supra n. 49) may regard the conquest of his erastes, represented by the fox. We might infer the same kind of interpretation for an Attic white-ground lekythos of c. 470 (Cambridge, Arthur M. Sackler Museum 1925.30.51; fig. 68) on which a beardless youth, wearing only a chlamys, carries a pole laden with a dead hare and a dead fox across his left shoulder; that is, the composition fits the "returning hunter" motif.[158] Alongside the youth is a ΚΑΛΟΣ inscription. The lack of petasos, boots, weapons, horse, or other figures sets this "hunter" apart from other hunters. Possibly we see an eromenos, signaled by his appearance and the inscription, portrayed as hunter together with the prey that he has caught, and the animals may represent erastai, not literally but metaphorically. In the case of the Attic black-figure cup in the Swiss private collection (fig. 31), the presence of both dead hare and dead fox, together with the animation of both the eromenos and erastes, suggest that the relationship is more equal than one might have thought and that the attraction is mutual.

This complicated set of possibilities is designed to illustrate that the animal gift exchange between erastes and eromenos is not clear-cut, that the animal may not always "equal" the eromenos, that a fluidity exists in the roles of hunted and hunter, and that the vase paintings offer insights into actual human behavior. Such flexibility in roles of pursuer and pursued directly contrasts with sexual protocol in heterosexual relationships, at least

FIGURE 67. Attic red-figure cup tondo fragment by Douris, c. 480 B.C. Munich, Staatliche Antikensammlungen 8710. Photo courtesy of the Staatliche Antiken-sammlungen und Glyptothek München.

in the mortal realm, where sexually aggressive, predatory women are simply nonexistent or are punished,[159] or women who inspire intense sexual desire (such as Helen) in men are viewed as dangerous, at the very least, and as a bane (Pandora). An exception occurs with goddesses, who may pursue mortal males, but mortal protocols do not apply to them.

The transfer of animal gifts in pederastic courtship paintings thus conveys important information about power relations between the participants and characteristics possessed by the erastes and eromenos. As was the case in the literary treatments of courtship as hunting, vase painting allows for the vacillation of power between hunter and hunted so long as both are male.[160] If we follow the "courtship as hunt" metaphor, then the trapped animals are metaphors for the trapped erastes or eromenos, and the painter

FIGURE 68. Attic white-ground lekythos, c. 470 B.C. Cambridge, Mass., Arthur M.
Sackler Museum 1925.30.51. Photo courtesy of the Arthur M. Sackler Museum,
Harvard University Art Museums, Bequest of Joseph C. Hoppin. © President and
Fellows of Harvard College, Harvard University.

sometimes expressly indicates the metaphor, using his composition to draw the parallel.

As was the case with the actual hunting depictions discussed in chapter 1, looking at the entirety of a given vase can advance our understanding of the courtship scenes. The absence of actual hunting scenes on the same vases with courtship scenes, which are metaphorical hunts, is remarkable. Instead, images of heterosexual courtship, abduction, symposion activities, and heroic adventures appear. Mythological scenes complement the pederastic courtship adorning the Attic red-figure cup of c. 480 attributed to Makron in Berlin (Antikensammlung F2291, fig. 52).[161] The courtship representation is on the interior while the exterior bears the judgment of Paris on one side and Paris leading Helen away on the other. When read together, the three images are a commentary on beauty and love, both hetero- and homosexual: Paris selects the most beautiful of the three female deities; he leads away the most beautiful of mortal women; and an erastes contemplates the beauty of an eromenos, a different kind of love, on the interior. Perhaps we should understand the eromenos as likened to Helen; this is not such a radical idea, and, in fact, other scholars have read the eromenos as similar to a woman.[162] In this light, the Attic black-figure cup by the Amasis Painter in the Louvre (A479 [MNB 1746], figs. 40–41) should be reconsidered: women and boys alike are targets of sexual advances by the erastes. If the eromenoi and women are similar (and are similarly portrayed), and the women are hetairai, are the eromenoi *pornoi* (prostitutes) or aristocratic youths? Koch-Harnack argues that pornoi did not receive animal gifts so we may conclude that the young males on the Amasis Painter cup are not pornoi.[163] Moreover, Schnapp argues that the leopards or panthers given as gifts here signify the hetairai but we have already seen that the term πάρδαλα can be applied to males, and such felines appear in other pederastic images.[164]

Paired with heroic images, pederastic courtship scenes can be read as metaphorical expressions for heroic, and thus aristocratic, behavior. For example, pederastic courtship is juxtaposed with Herakles and the Amazons on an amphora from Vulci attributed to Group E (Rome, Museo Gregoriano Etrusco Vaticano 352) of the mid-sixth century.[165] The viewer reads the two scenes as analogues: just as Herakles, the hero, fights and sexually conquers female resistors, so the heroic erastes "does battle" with the eromenos to win his sexual favors.

Finally, the paintings on an Attic black-figure cup by the Centaur Painter in London (British Museum 1891.8–6.84) offer a summation of the complex relationship of courtship as hunting and pursuer as animal.[166] The deer hunt on one side of the exterior was discussed in chapter 1. When considered together with the panther hunting a boy on the opposite side of the cup, one might view the panther as an erastes pursuing an eromenos so that metaphorical, amorous hunting is likened to actual hunting on the two sides of the vessel.[167]

Pederasty, Hunting, and Masculinity

The metaphor of courtship, particularly pederastic courtship, as hunting contributes to the modern understanding of ancient Greek perceptions of hunting—what it is, who may or may not hunt, and what constitutes suitable prey. Pederastic courtship can be expressed in hunting terms with erastes and eromenos playing interchangeable roles of predator and prey. Same-sex relationships, as evidenced in vase painting and literature, allow interchangeability of roles, but heterosexual relationships demand that the male be the hunter. We may learn even more if we regard homosexual courtship in the context of Athenian constructions of masculinity. Kenneth J. Dover has argued that the social acceptance of pederasty was certainly widespread in Athens and elsewhere by the end of the seventh century.[168] Pederasty persisted in Athens through the fourth century, as attested in visual and written sources. Young men were admired, both in poetry, such as the lyric poems of the sixth-century Anakreon, and in inscriptions on late-sixth-century Attic vases, where various youths are praised as *kalos*, beautiful. Such an inscription occurs on the interior of a cup of c. 490–480 by Makron in Munich (Staatliche Antikensammlungen 2655; figs. 32–33),[169] where erastes and eromenos face each other: the inscription reads "Hippodamas kalos." But David Cohen points to laws against hubris designed to check the sexual exploitation of free boys in the fifth and fourth centuries.[170] If pederasty was so widely accepted, what was the purpose of the laws?

The answer lies in the dichotomy between the ideal and the reality of homosexuality in ancient Athens, which was intimately bound up with issues of honor and shame.[171] Separating the ideal from the reality is made difficult by the varying kinds of evidence available to us. Plato's ideal of a young eromenos chastely admired by an adult erastes was merely an ideal to judge by later written texts, which sometimes portray the eromenos not as a young adolescent but considerably older; that is, the reality suggests not only pederasty but also adult homosexuality.[172] If so, Attic vases seem to reflect the ideal for they nearly always depict a beardless, physically diminutive eromenos and a larger, sometimes bearded erastes—that is, pederasty, not adult homosexuality. This is to be expected since vases are not snapshots of reality but selective reflections of cultural values (just as we know that men did not conduct warfare in the nude as vase painting might lead one to believe). The rarity of sexual intercourse, intercrural or anal, between males on Attic vase painting seems to suggest that fondling was permissible and accepted but actual intercourse was frowned upon;[173] that is, the vases reflect a Platonic ideal of pederasty but the reality was surely different, as attested by the need for legislation and by poetic and visual sources.[174]

Pederasty was practiced not only in Athens but also in other Greek states, such as Sparta, Crete, and Thebes, where it was associated with the military.[175] Pederasty constituted part of the educational system in Sparta (cf. Xen., *Lac.* 2.12) and of hunting maturation rituals on Crete,[176] activities that were clearly preparatory for the military.[177] Ancient authors, such as Plutarch (*Lyc.* 17.1) and Aelian (*VH* 3.9), admittedly much later than the vases under discussion, speak of ritualized pederasty in the course of military training from the age of twelve on.[178] One aspect of the Spartan marriage custom also reveals the importance of pederasty for young men and sexual attraction between males: when Spartan men married, their brides were to come to them on their wedding night dressed up as men with shaved hair and false beards so as to have maximum sexual appeal for their grooms (Plut., *Lyc.* 15.3).[179]

The same phenomenon of pederasty as part of the maturation process leading to adult military status exists elsewhere; Plutarch (*Mor.* 761b) reports that in Thebes erastai presented their eromenoi with armor when they came of age, a custom that recalls the ephebic exhibition after border patrol service in Athens and the post-hunting rituals for young men on Crete (see chapter 1). Athenaeus (565, 609) reports that the Eleans held beauty competitions for boys and that the victor received armor as a prize.[180]

Thus far, we see pederasty as preparatory for the military but not included as part of military activities among adults. Yet clear evidence from Thebes and elsewhere documents that homosexuality existed and was sometimes even encouraged in the military (though it could also have a divisive effect).[181] Xenophon (*Symp.* 8.34–35) notes that the Eleans placed erastai and eromenoi side by side in battle and discusses the disposition of eromenoi and erastai in the Spartan army. One might argue that Xenophon's testimony is too late to have any relevance to the Greek vases of the late archaic and early classical periods, and, in fact, there is no definitive evidence for pederasty in Sparta before the late fifth century.[182] But it was during the Lelantine War in the archaic period that Plutarch (*Mor.* 760e–761b) locates the origin of homosexuality in the Chalcidian army. In addition to the chronological discrepancy between written and visual sources, one might also object that this evidence is for locales other than Athens (the vast majority of written evidence for pederasty and homosexuality refers to Dorian sites, such as Sparta, its colony Thera, and so on), where pederasty was part of initiation to manhood.[183] Moreover, the practice of homosexuality in the military would not seem to accord with the Athenian pederastic model, which specifies an older, adult erastes, and a younger, still immature eromenos, because of the adult age of all military participants.[184] It is true that the evidence for homosexuality in the military in Athens is very meager.[185] Plato (*Symp.* 178e–179a) proposes an army or city composed of lovers and παιδικά, which suggests that such a thing did not presently exist—at least in Athens.

Yet written texts intimate that pederasty occurred in the Athenian military though there is no bald statement to this effect. At least some erastai wished to impress eromenoi by performing bravely in battle as indicated by *IG* I² 920 from late-sixth-century Attica: "Here a man in love with a boy swore an oath to join in strife and woeful war. I am sacred to Gnathios of Eroiadai, who perished in battle[?]."[186] Plato (*Resp.* 468b–c) echoes this sentiment: "But the man who distinguishes himself and wins the prize of valor shall be crowned first by his comrades-in-arms and then in turn by the youths and the boys . . . if anyone be in love with another, whether man or woman, he would be all the more eager to win the hero's reward."[187] And again in Plato (*Sym.* 179a): "For a man in love would surely choose to have all the rest of the host rather than his favorite see him forsaking his station or flinging away his arms."[188]

Furthermore, Athenian gymnasion training aimed to produce good warriors, and the gymnasion was a primary locus of pederastic activity.[189] It seems plausible that homosexual activity did not simply cease when an Athenian ephebe attained the age of maturity and donned his hoplite armor. As at Elis, beauty contests, *euandriai*, took place at Athens, and here

FIGURE 69. Attic red-figure pelike by the Geras Painter, c. 480 B.C. Rome, Museo Nazionale Etrusco di Villa Giulia 50457. Photo courtesy of the Soprintendenza Archeologica per l'Etruria Meridionale, Rome.

it possessed a military character.[190] Winners of the euandria held at the Panathenaia received an ox (*IG* II² 2311) and shields (*Ath. Pol.* 60.3); the euandria at the Athenian Theseia was closely linked to military euploia as indicated by second-century B.C. inscriptions (*IG* II² 956, *IG* II² 958).[191] So although we have no definitive attestation to the practice of pederasty in the Athenian military, strong hints exist in the written record.

Attic vase painting, however, possibly offers illumination on this point. Cocks were offered as courtship gifts in pederastic scenes in Attic vase painting, and we have already examined the cock's associations with warfare and the erotic realm, and also the metaphor of cockfighting for pederastic courtship. But two pederastic scenes are even more explicit in their mingling military and erotic imagery in that they substitute armor for the more common animal gifts. On an Attic red-figure pelike by the Geras Painter in Rome (Museo Nazionale Etrusco di Villa Giulia 50457; fig. 69), an erastes on the obverse presents a helmet to an eromenos on the reverse.[192] The in-

FIGURE 70. Attic red-figure cup tondo by the Berlin Painter, c. 490 B.C. Cambridge, Fitzwilliam Museum 16.1937. Photo courtesy of the Fitzwilliam Museum.

terior of an Attic red-figure kylix of the same date by the Berlin Painter in Cambridge (Fitzwilliam Museum 16.1937; fig. 70) depicts a solitary erastes with a bloom in his left hand and a helmet in his right.[193] These two images not only suggest the interchangeability of armor and animals as gifts in this context but also an association between warfare and pederasty,[194] and, by extension, warfare, pederasty, and hunting; such antagonism and contest are simply other forms of combat.[195]

Power and status were central components of the aristocratic practice of pederasty. Written evidence attests that gift giving was agonistic in that lover vied with lover for the attention of an adolescent by offering more and more sumptuous gifts, which would have been publicly noted.[196] Scholars have rightly argued that the erastes sought to gain honor by his actions;[197] the conquest of an especially attractive eromenos was considered a coup for the erastes.[198] Dishonor was accorded the eromenos if he submitted too easily but being pursued by many suitors was clearly a badge of honor (e.g., Pl., *Symp.* 182a–184e).[199] In other words, honor is gained at another's expense.[200] Cartledge sees pederasty as greasing the wheels of society to mediate conflicts and create alliances,[201] and it seems safe to say that pederasty was a form of socialization for aristocratic Athenian males.[202] Stewart argues that Athenian homoeroticism even had a political dimension as a result of the celebrated actions of the lovers, Harmodios and Aristogeiton, who were credited (falsely) with freeing Athens from tyranny.[203]

Homoeroticism may have had a political component, as Stewart claims, but it certainly had a social one. As was the case for the actual hunting scenes discussed in chapter 1, the pederastic courtship images have the same theme—hunting—only expressed in a metaphorical fashion. What is more, the chronological range of the pederastic vase paintings corresponds with that of the actual hunting scenes. The vase paintings of pederastic courtship with its agonistic component, animal gifts, and allusions to the palaistra, which occur largely on symposion ware, were not only produced for aristocratic tastes, but, as was the case for the hunting scenes of chapter 1, the tempo of production stepped up as aristocrats struggled to maintain control of the social discourse. As was posited for the actual hunting paintings, the pederastic images may have inspired nonelites either to imitate or to accept the behavior (both symposion and pederasty).[204]

Noble and Ignoble Hunting

Thus far, I have argued that contrary to scholarly opinion, the relationship between eromenos and erastes is not a bilateral, polar one with a clear opposition between the hunted and hunter respectively. Instead, those roles are fluid and can shift back and forth both in literary and visual images where the animal gifts express the idea of pederastic courtship as a form of hunting for either erastes or eromenos. In these instances, the prey is ambiguous; it can be either the erastes or the eromenos. Literary images of pederasty used nets or snares to express the notion of amorous pursuit as hunt from at least as early as c. 530, but this type of hunting is discordant with Plato's dictum against entrapment (*Leg.* 823b–824b). How do we reconcile this seeming difference between Plato's account of appropriate and inappropriate hunting and the actual, metaphorical amorous hunting of fifth-century aristocratic Athenian men, which is visually expressed in vase painting? Three possible explanations can account for the paradox: either Plato relates a fourth-century view of hunting behavior that was not applicable a century or so earlier (and may be peculiar to Plato even in his own time); or the negative connotations of hunting by entrapment were applicable in the fifth century but did not apply to pederastic courtship, perhaps because it was only metaphorical hunting; or that Plato's view prevailed in the late archaic and early classical period and pederastic hunting was considered ignoble.

As for the first possibility, it is difficult to determine whether Plato's negative view of hunting by entrapment prevailed in the time of our vases. As stated earlier, his idealized view of pederasty, one that involved no base physical contact, was surely not a reflection of actual behavior but an ideal; certainly, the vase paintings are not scrupulous records of real life either and are instead, selective constructs of a culture's ideas about itself. If Plato's valuations of hunting are not applicable to late archaic and classical Athens, then Vidal-Naquet's black hunter, discussed in chapter 1, evaporates.

The third possibility seems the least likely to be true given the prevalence of pederastic themes in vase painting and poetry. Purists or conservatives may have objected to this amorous hunting but the visual and written images of pederasty spoke to a sizable audience, and we can safely assume that that audience was approving, or pederastic themes in art and poetry would have died out quickly.

As for the second possible explanation, the idea that Plato's negative view of hunting by entrapment existed in the late archaic and early classical periods but was not applicable to pederastic hunting, is more compelling. Because Plato's writings and the vase paintings are nearly a century apart, we must rely on other evidence to help bridge the temporal gap and provide insight into the fifth-century view of hunting. That source is, of course, Athenian tragedy, where hunting with nets, the most commonly mentioned hunting technique, also has negative connotations (see chapter 1). Is it justifiable to read literary descriptions of pederastic courtship that use entrapment images differently?[205] To be sure, the mixture of actual (rather than metaphorical) hunt and amorous activity or desire in tragedy is uniformly disastrous, and the same can be said of myth in general. One thinks of Hippolytos and Phaedra, Atalanta and Meleager, Aktaion and Artemis, Orion and Artemis, Adonis and Aphrodite.[206] At the heart of the problem is the question of whether it is plausible to "transfer" the cultural readings of society that are derived from tragedy (and myth in general) to real life. I believe that the answer to this last question is yes, provided that it is always understood that myth in its tragic form or otherwise always reflects societal attitudes but often exaggerates them, refracts them, and distorts them to make its point.

If visual and literary imagery reflects societal attitudes, then the paintings of pederastic courtship reveal that viewers of these images found pederasty acceptable and regarded it as metaphorical hunting, with the animal gifts serving as analogues to the participants. Literary texts describe such metaphorical hunting as involving entrapment or ensnaring.[207] Although negative connotations attached to this form of hunting in Plato's time and perhaps earlier, there is no evidence that pederastic courtship shared these negative associations. On the contrary, there is a mythological counterpart that not only effaces all negative connotations of this particular mode of metaphorical hunting but also offers a model for the erastes and eromenos. The mythological prototype is, of course, Zeus's abduction of Ganymede, the boy so famously portrayed carrying a cock.[208]

Mythological Pederasty and the Aristocratic Symposion

Theognis (1345–50), writing in the sixth century, contemporary with our vases, offers Ganymede and Zeus as a prototype for an actual pederastic relationship, and the comparison between actual pederastic relationships and that of Zeus and Ganymede exists in later poetry, such as the *Palatine Anthology* (12.133).[209] One might also think of Poseidon and Pelops (Pind., *Ol.* 1) but neither Zeus's nor Poseidon's aggression was acceptable behavior for the real-life erastai, although admittedly gods were given a moral license that mortals could only dream of.[210]

Attic vase paintings of Zeus abducting or pursuing Ganymede appear mostly on drinking cups of the late archaic and early classical period,[211] and the greatest number of such paintings coincides with the time when the number of generic homosexual courtship depictions dwindles.[212] Fifth-century written texts, however, do not evidence this diminution of interest in nonmythological pederastic themes; rather, homosexuality, specifically pederasty, is common in the works of Phrynichus, Aischylos, and Pindar,[213] texts that are contemporary with the Attic vase paintings of Zeus and Ganymede. An Attic red-figure kantharos of c. 490–480 by the Brygos Painter in Boston (Museum of Fine Arts 95.36; fig. 71) exemplifies the Zeus and Ganymede depictions.[214] Zeus pursues Ganymede on the obverse while the reverse is ornamented with a man's (probably Zeus's) pursuit of a female in a sanctuary of Artemis, as indicated by the altar and palm tree.[215] Another example of Zeus pursuing Ganymede occurs on the obverse of an Attic red-figure neck amphora of c. 480–470 by the Briseis

FIGURE 71. Attic red-figure kantharos by the Brygos Painter, c. 490–480 B.C. Boston, Museum of Fine Arts 95.36. Catharine Page Perkins Fund. Photo courtesy of the Museum of Fine Arts, Boston. Reproduced with permission. © 1999 Museum of Fine Arts, Boston. All rights reserved.

Painter in Cambridge (Fitzwilliam Museum 37.23);[216] the reverse of this amphora presents an old, balding man, perhaps gazing wistfully at the pursuits of his past expressed in mythological form. Note that in these images, Ganymede is actually pursued, not yet caught. Elsewhere, Ganymede is in Zeus's arms, such as the terracotta sculptural group from Olympia of c. 470 (Olympia Museum T2; fig. 72) and on an Attic red-figure cup tondo of c. 460–450 by the Splanchnopt Painter in Ferrara (Museo Archeologico Nazionale di Spina 9351 [T212 B VP]).[217] Ganymede holds a cock in both of these examples, perhaps a metaphor for his own capture or symbolic of the erotic-combative virility of both Zeus and Ganymede. With the exception of the images of Zeus pursuing Ganymede, the other Zeus-Ganymede depictions (those where Zeus has

FIGURE 72. Terracotta group of Zeus and Ganymede, c. 470 B.C. Olympia, Museum T2. Photo courtesy of the Deutsches Archäologisches Institut, Athens, negative number Ol. 3365.

caught Ganymede) have compositional and thematic similarities with the pederastic courting scenes discussed earlier, such as the inclusion of the cock as gift for Ganymede or gymnasion apparatus, the differentiation in appearance of erastes and eromenos, and the use of frontal nudity to display the eromenos's, here Ganymede's, extraordinary beauty to the viewer.[218] Such a display invites the admiring appraisal of the spectator, who was most likely a male symposiast in light of the prevalence of Zeus-Ganymede depictions and other pederastic imagery on symposion ware. Pederasty was not only viewed on vases used at the symposion but was an integral component of the symposion.

After Ganymede's abduction, he was taken to Mount Olympos, where he served as cupbearer to the gods (Hom., *Il.* 20.232–35; *Hymn. Hom. Ven.* 202–6; Paus. 5.24.5). Poseidon fell in love with Pelops, who also served wine to the gods (Pind., *Ol.*1.42–45; Philostr., *Imag.* 1.17). Traditional cupbearers and attendants at late archaic and early classical symposia, both in Athens and elsewhere, were often adolescent boys as evidenced in literature,[219] vase painting (figs. 46–47),[220] and sculpted reliefs.[221] These boys served not only wine but also sexual pleasure to the adult males, as suggested by Laconian vases of the sixth century and early classical Attic red-figure vases, on which youths recline on couches with adult males and Erotes hover overhead.[222] Moreover, pederastic scenes and symposion images are combined on the same fifth- century Attic drinking cups,[223] inviting the viewer to read the two images as an ensemble of related activities. In addition to the sex appeal and butler service provided by Ganymede, adolescent boys in the real-life symposia also engaged in intellectual discussions; youths were expected to ask questions, which would lead to fruitful philosophical and intellectual exchanges, so the symposion was a form of education for young men.[224] Bremmer also notes that the many fragments of archaic poetry that are clearly associated with the symposion and didactic in nature are addressed to boys.[225] Elegies from the time of Theognis that concern martial courage were performed at symposia to offer models of good warriors to the listeners,[226] and such military sympotic poetry was performed in the sixth century as well.[227] Furthermore, Attic red-figure vase paintings of boys playing or holding lyres at the symposion suggest that adolescent boys performed at the symposion, and such performances would have included didactic songs about heroes, according to Bremmer.[228] Moreover, we know that the Apatouria, the Athenian festival at which pre-ephebes were enrolled in their phratries, included a song contest for the initiates.[229]

Anakreontic vases also demonstrate the link between lyric poetry, symposion, and sexuality, perhaps pederasty. Named for the Ionian poet Anakreon, who immigrated to Athens c. 522 and wrote of wine, song, and boys, Anakreontic vases constitute a subset of Attic black-figure drinking cups of c. 510–460 ornamented with symposion scenes, some of which may depict the poet himself as indicated by inscription.[230] Erotic indicators are usually absent from these vases save for a few such as the Bomford Cup of c. 520 in the Ashmolean Museum (1974.344), where the foot of the vase is fashioned into a penis and testicles. In the tondo, symposiasts recline on klinai and one of the symposiasts threatens a young male attendant with a sandal. Grapevines circling the edge of the tondo hang above the heads of the drinkers, and a lyre is affixed to the "background." As Shapiro notes, the Bomford vase may have been a special commission,[231] and perhaps this is true of the others of this special shape.

As was the case with the homosexual courtship paintings and the actual hunting depictions, many of the images of Zeus's abduction of Ganymede occur on drinking cups and other symposion ware (a few appear on oil containers, presumably used in the gymnasion, which is also appropriate),[232] objects designed for the use of aristocrats.[233] Sexual imagery is well suited to drinking cups, and erotic themes become popular in symposion depictions beginning c. 530.[234] Thus, the vases—their decoration and shape—offer evidence of both sexual and social education, the world of hunting (both literal and metaphorical) and of adult intellectual discourse at the symposion.

One important aspect of the symposion was eating, specifically eating meat, which was provided by hunters. In chapter 1, we noted that Spartan hunters had to provide spoils of their hunt at communal meals (Plut., *Lyc.* 12.2–3). Earlier in this chapter, we cited the numerous vase paintings that depict the return from the hunt with dead game, mostly hares and foxes and sometimes birds, tied to poles slung over the shoulders of hunters. Sometimes, hunters with game approach symposiasts but the vase paintings never portray the game being eaten;[235] elsewhere, returning hunters approach Dionysos, presumably the embodiment of wine drinking, the central sympotic activity.[236]

This chapter has tried to demonstrate and argue that hunting, courtship, conquest, and warfare were inextricably linked in the minds of classical Athenians. Depictions of hunting in vase painting are visual metaphors for battle, pederastic courtship images are metaphors for hunting, and both types of depictions were important to the Athenian aristocratic ideology of the late archaic and early classical period. Chapters 1 and 2 demonstrate the interconnections between hunting, sexual courtship, gymnasion, symposion, and battle and that this nexus of activities constitutes the core occupations for Athenian aristocrats and for the construction of aristocratic Athenian male identity in the archaic and classical periods (cf. Isoc., *Areopagiticus* 45).[237] As was the case for the actual hunting scenes, the tempo of production of pederastic courtship scenes increased in the final years of the sixth century as aristocrats vied to maintain control of the social agenda and politics, then died out in the 470s because nonelites adopted the aristocratic ideal.[238]

Scholars frequently cite Jean-Pierre Vernant for his observation that warfare is to a man what marriage is to a woman,[239] and we examined the analogy between the eromenos and female virgin in this chapter. Although both women and boys are pursued, only the male can become the hunter in heterosexual relationships (as we have seen, same-sex relationships permit the interchangeability of roles). When the mortal female tries to reverse the roles, as when Clytemnestra tries to catch Agamemnon in her nets, or when Phaedra pursues the reluctant Hippolytos, disaster and chaos result. But we have seen that the fluidity of roles of hunter and hunted in pederastic relationships is normal—indeed, is even required of males, at least aristocratic males. For the young males, the object of the erastai, will one day take their place next to the adult males on couches or in gymnasia, where they too will educate and initiate their young prey and where they will be preyed upon by Eros and the "eyes of their beloved."

Chapter Three
HUNTING AND MYTH

Two kinds of hunting myths survive from the Greek world: those about heroic hunters and those about the followers of Artemis. Among the former, we can cite the hunting exploits of Herakles and Theseus while the latter includes the myths of Kallisto and Hippolytos among others.[1] Heroic hunting myths commonly explore issues of valor and the male transition to adulthood and offer positive paradigms for human behavior. Myths about the followers of Artemis, by contrast, describe the closed world of young male and female hunters, who absent themselves from society and abstain from sex (e.g, Ar., *Lys.* 781–96).[2] This pattern sounds strikingly close to the hunting rites of passage already noted in Sparta and on Crete in which a young man leaves civilized society to hunt for a period of time. In the Cretan rite of passage, initiatory sex and hunting combine in a socially sanctioned way. But myths about hunting explore the results that arise from a violation of, or threat to, the hunters' sexual chastity, usually involuntarily as in the case of Kallisto or Hippolytos, but sometimes voluntarily as in the case of Atalanta.

Straddling these two categories of myth is the Calydonian boar hunt, the most acclaimed hunting myth in antiquity, which celebrated the heroic exploit of numerous heroes. Because the myth also includes one of the followers of Artemis, Atalanta (and sometimes also Melanion), and some versions of the myth relate a love affair between Atalanta and Meleager, this myth also explores the relationship between hunting and the erotic realm.

In both the Calydonian boar hunt and the myths of individual hunters,

125

scholars explain the disaster that arises as the result of the violation of a boundary between the realms of Aphrodite and Artemis.[3] Although Artemis punishes each violator for engaging in sexual activity, it would be fallacious to interpret the myths, as scholars have done,[4] as simply indicating an interdiction against mingling hunting with sex. On the contrary, as shown in chapter 2, in the real world sex and hunting were closely connected and often thought of as synonymous activities. The hunt supplies a metaphor for eroticism or amorous pursuit, and the two realms—hunting and sex—are also joined in real chronological life passages, such as the Attic *arkteia* or the Cretan rite cited earlier. It is true that in the mythical world, Artemis does not want her followers to engage in sex, and disobeying the goddess has terrible consequences. But such a reading is incomplete: the point of the myths is that one should be a follower only for a time in one's life but not for a lifetime; one should not devote oneself to a life of chastity with Artemis as do Atalanta, Kallisto, or Hippolytos. Such myths offer negative paradigms of what one should not do, but the negative behavior is not the intrusion of sexuality but rather the sustained commitment to Artemis and virginity, the absence of sexuality, and finally the disobedience that creates the negative image. To be sure, there is a time for Artemis and a time for Aphrodite in the life of a young person—and these periods often overlap. These ideas are expressed in myth by the disaster that befalls the hunter who tries to enforce a strict separation of eros and hunting, adhering to a diet of sexual abstinence.[5]

This observation has been made by others, but the contribution of this chapter is to demonstrate and detail, particularly in the visual record, that the consequence of the immoderate mythological hunter who loses self-control is to suffer a role reversal: one is not oneself but its opposite (and one can observe role reversal in rites of transition, such as transvestism).[6] For example, when the hunter, Meleager, becomes so enamored of his prey, Atalanta, that he is no longer a hunter or erastes but becomes the hunted and is trapped by love, then the hunter becomes the hunted both in love and in hunting or combat, a situation that recalls the erastes of chapter 2, who becomes helpless before his eromenos. As for the chaste hunter dedicated to Artemis whose chastity is disrupted, it is not the confusion of the realms of Artemis and Aphrodite but the fact that the hunter has become prey to love or to a lover-hunter (and this reversal of roles is sometimes signified by the hunter's transformation into a wild animal) that seals his or her doom. And so, for example, the chaste hunter Hippolytos, who becomes entangled in the consequences of his stepmother's desire for him, and her subsequent accusation after being spurned, takes on the role of parthenos[7] and, like an animal, is caught in the netlike reins of his horses and killed. Through her refusal to marry, the parthenos and hunter Atalanta denies her femininity, even outstripping other ephebes at being an ephebe (though ephebes must also marry). Thus, it is not a question of polarities between hunting and eros but of interlocking realms and shifting social roles, the struggle for power and self-control. The reversal of roles, not the obfuscation of boundaries, is key. Rather than exemplifying the firmness of boundaries and the punishment allotted to transgressors, the myths point to the malleability of social roles and the societal limits placed on them.

Role reversal in the literal hunt by definition constitutes a tragedy because the hunter is threatened or killed by his prey.[8] But role reversal in real and mythological erotic pursuits has different outcomes depending on the sex of the pursuer. Male pursuing male, as in pederastic relationships, is permissible and so is male pursuing female, even a male pursuing a goddess in some instances, such as Peleus's quest for Thetis. Female pursuing female is also tolerable as documented by Sappho (e.g., frag. 1). But female pursuing male, such as Phaedra and Hippolytos, Akastos's wife and Peleus, or even Jocasta and Oedipus, can lead only to disaster because hunters should not be female. Hunting with or without sex or erotic pursuit is acceptable but sexual pursuit always implies a hunt, and, for this reason, females who sexually pursue or hunt bring about disaster.

In each instance, we shall examine the written and visual sources for the myth before interpreting them. Because the mythological material has received exhaustive documentation in the recent *Lexicon Iconographicum Mythologiae Classicae*, this discussion explores in depth only three examples of myth that richly illustrate loss of control, role reversal, and appropriate and inappropriate gender roles in ancient Greek society.

Heroic Hunters: Herakles and Theseus

The hunting exploits of Herakles and Theseus, part of the heroes' well-known cycles of labors, were amply exploited in both the written and visual tradition. Herakles, for example, hunts the Nemean lion, the Erymanthian boar, and the Keryneian hind. But although Theseus takes on the Krommyonian sow and the Minotaur, and captures the Marathon bull, most of his opponents are brigands, not wild animals. And we also know that Theseus's labors are a late invention of the mid-sixth century, modeled, as Plutarch (*Thes.* 6) says, on the labors of Herakles.[9] Aspects of these heroic hunting labors differentiate this kind of hunting from the type that has been treated in this book. The animals are all fantastic creatures, possessed of some extraordinary traits that make their conquest particularly challenging, even to such heroes as Herakles and Theseus. But remarkably, the three animal combatants of Herakles just cited are aberrant and exaggerated versions of the everyday animals—lion, boar, and deer—that define heroic behavior and heroic hunting for the real-life Greek male. Moreover, the hunting exploits of Herakles and Theseus differ in another way from the hunting myths we treat in the remainder of this chapter. Rather than being full-blown narratives with a prelude, the main action, and aftermath, these labors are simple actions, easily summed up by the sentence: Herakles or Theseus fought and killed the fantastic creature X. The conquest in and of itself is emphasized so as to fit into the long catalog of superhuman deeds that distinguish Herakles and Theseus from mere mortals. Unlike Meleager, for example, their lives are not defined by a single narrative but by the accumulation of heroic accomplishments. Consequently, although this type of hunting labor offers a heroic model, the labors, having so little narrative complexity, do not provide material to illuminate the social and cultural issues under examination here. More developed hunting narratives, however, deviate from this heroic ideal.

Hunting and Transgression: Aktaion

Aktaion and Kallisto represent the different varieties that the hunting transgression myth can take. In the former instance, Aktaion exemplifies myths concerning hubris toward the goddess, either by challenging Artemis's skills or authority, or by an attempt at sexual conquest.[10] Kallisto, on the other hand, offers the example of a chaste devotee of Artemis (others include Melanion and Hippolytos) who refuses to accept her sexuality. She is eventually accosted by a god and suffers for it; similarly, the other followers of Artemis experience threats to their virginity. Both categories of myth represent transgressions against the norms, either of relations between humans and gods or the norms of human society, and both types address the relationship between hunting and sexuality. Aktaion's exces-

sive sexual desire causes him to exceed boundaries, whereas Kallisto's refusal to engage in sex marks her own form of excess. In both cases, the
hunters experience a role reversal: they are transformed into hunted animals, and both pay with their lives.

Transgression, metamorphosis, and death at the hands of Artemis stalk
the hunter Aktaion of Boeotia.[11] A fragment of Hesiod's *Catalogus
mulierem* (217A M-W) provides the earliest surviving account.[12] Of this
myth, the only consistent elements are Artemis's anger and Aktaion's death
as a victim of his own hunting dogs. Aktaion's actions are variously reported but each variant involves hubris. The hunter Aktaion, who was
trained by Chiron (Apollod. 3.4.4), either wished to marry Semele (Hes.
217A M-W; Stesichoros as told in Paus. 9.2.3; Aischylos's fragmentary *Toxotides*)[13] and thus angered Zeus (Acusilaos as recounted in Apollod. 3.4.4);
or boasted of greater hunting prowess than Artemis (Eur., *Bacch.* 337–42;
Diod. Sic. 4.81.4–5); or was a voyeur to the nude, bathing Artemis (Cal-
lim., *Hymn* 5.107–16; Apollod. 3.4.4; Ov., *Met.* 3.155–90, *Tr.* 2.105–6; Paus.
9.2.3, Hyg., *Fab.* 181), sometimes with the added element of Aktaion's de-
siring the goddess (Hyg., *Fab.* 180, where Aktaion is referred to as a "pas-
tor" or "shepherd"). In each instance, we have a case of a common topos in
Greek myth, hubris against the goddess or against Zeus. A passage of
Diodorus Siculus (4.81.4) mentions the boast as one possibility but adds
an erotic element: he writes that Aktaion set up spoils of the hunt as dedications to Artemis, then tried to marry her.

In any case, Artemis was angered and she transformed Aktaion into a
stag, whereupon his own hunting dogs devoured him on Mount
Cithaeron (Hes. 217A M-W; Apollod. 3.4.4; Ov., *Met.* 3.194–252; Hyg., *Fab.*
180, 181). As recounted by Pausanias (9.2.3), Stesichoros adds that Artemis
covered Aktaion in deerskins to inspire his dogs to attack him.[14] Mount
Cithaeron is familiar for its associations with the events of Euripides' *Bacchae*, and, in fact, various elements of this myth recall that of Pentheus:
the hubris toward a god; the setting on Mount Cithaeron; and the death
by being ripped apart alive by maddened creatures, behaving as if they
were wild (but which are domesticated in their normal state). Semele,
sometimes Aktaion's object of desire, is Dionysos's mother and Aktaion's
aunt because Semele's sister, Autonoe, is Aktaion's mother; Dionysos or-
chestrates Pentheus's doom at the hands of the wild maenads, and Artemis
brings on Aktaion's terrible fate.[15] These cousins, Pentheus and Aktaion,

seem peculiarly prone to the phenomenon of turning from predator to prey.

The dates of the extant written sources suggest that the Semele version is the oldest variant of the myth, the boast a later addition, and the titillating variant of a voyeuristic Aktaion gazing upon the bathing goddess a Hellenistic development. Certainly the only relevant element to our thematic and chronological concerns would seem to be Aktaion's form of punishment. But this standard view of the development of the myth has recently been challenged with implications for this study.[16] Lamar Ronald Lacy argues that both the boast and the bath were early parts of the myth, briefly alluded to by Euripides and Callimachus,[17] and that Apollodoros, who also relates the bath story, relies heavily on fifth-century tragedians, whom we know treated the tale of Aktaion's punishment in plays now lost to us. According to Lacy, the bath story may be as early as the fifth century and the boast even earlier; moreover, Diodorus's account, read together with an Apulian vase, suggests that the elements of the boast and Aktaion's desire to marry Artemis perhaps belonged to a single myth.[18] In sum, Lacy claims that the Apulian krater (and other South Italian vases as well) allude to a now lost tale, known to Callimachus and Diodorus, in which Aktaion was a friendly hunting companion of Artemis, hunted a deer, and offered the spoils to the goddess. He then felt desire for Artemis when he saw her bathing, leading him to want to marry the goddess, which resulted in his metamorphosis and death. We can add to this interpretation that the spoils of the hunt offered by Aktaion to Artemis imply amorous desire on Aktaion's part, and not simply hunting prowess or a thank offering,[19] for these are the gifts offered by the erastes to his eromenos and, as we shall see, by Meleager to Atalanta. In any case, Lacy's reconstruction offers a classical version of the myth that incorporates sexual transgression or hubris toward Artemis on the part of a hunter, falling into the pattern familiar from other myths that describe interactions between hunters and Artemis.

Visual images of Aktaion nearly always include a male figure being attacked by dogs while Artemis stands nearby. Almost all the archaic and classical Greek and South Italian objects are vases: twenty Attic, one Boeotian, and fifteen South Italian examples.[20] Lekythoi and kraters dominate the Attic shapes with five examples of the former and six of the latter (three bell kraters, two volute kraters, and one kalyx krater). Names are occasionally inscribed, and additional figures sometimes appear. Aktaion also

makes an appearance on three coins, a bronze relief, a metope from Seli-
nus, six Melian reliefs, an Italiote terracotta, as part of a large-scale statuary
group, and in a wall painting in the Lesche of the Knidians at Delphi, no
longer surviving but known from Pausanias's description (10.30.5). The
vases have often been discussed in terms of their relationship to literature,
especially Aischylos's *Toxotides*, with scholars perceiving varying degrees
of influence of the tragedy on the vase paintings.[21] The vases have also
been scrutinized with an eye to which version of the Aktaion myth is portrayed or alluded to in the painting.[22]

Typical of the Attic black-figure vases is a black-figure white-ground
lekythos of the end of the sixth century painted in the Manner of the Emporion Painter (Athens, National Museum A488 [CC.883]; fig. 73).[23] The
centrally placed figure is easily identified as Aktaion because this nude,
bearded male is attacked by eight dogs, who bite at his legs, back, and
shoulders. A standing female, wearing a long, sleeved chiton, flanks either
side of Aktaion, and these females gesture with their arms outstretched toward the hapless hunter. One of these females must be Artemis; the other
is perhaps a devotee of the goddess. Similar compositions occur on a cup
of c. 550 from Bomarzo, now lost,[24] a white-ground alabastron of c. 470
from Eretria (Athens, National Museum A12767),[25] and three lekythoi, also
from the end of the sixth century: a black-figure lekythos from Attica
(Athens, National Museum A489 [CC.882]),[26] another white-ground
lekythos in a private collection in London,[27] and a Six's technique lekythos
from the Athenian Acropolis (Athens, Agora Museum P1024).[28] Variants in
the composition include the number, placement, and color of the dogs
and the gestures of the females. Only one female is present on the Six's
technique lekythos, and Aktaion wields an unsheathed sword to defend
himself on the alabastron. Otherwise, Aktaion never wears the hunting attire we have observed elsewhere—chlamys, petasos, or boots.

In his central placement and the treatment of the dogs, the Attic black-
figure representations of Aktaion resemble the standard Attic black-figure
composition of the Calydonian boar hunt, where the centrally placed prey
is attacked by dogs who jump on and around him (see chapter 1 and infra).
In both types of scenes, figures flank the attack but, of course, those in the
Calydonian boar hunt actively participate in the killing, whereas Artemis
and her companion are passive observers (though admittedly, Artemis ex-
horts the dogs to kill). One might expect the composition to resemble deer

FIGURE 73. Attic black-figure white-ground lekythos in the Manner of the Emporion Painter, end of the sixth century B.C. Athens, National Museum A488 [CC.883]. Photo courtesy of the Deutsches Archäologisches Institut, Athens, negative number NM3014.

hunting scenes more closely because Aktaion, according to many versions of the myth, is supposed to be transformed to a stag. However, vase paintings of the deer hunt generally do not show dogs attacking deer. Moreover, in spite of its early mention in literature, the metamorphosis of Aktaion does not appear in art until the second to third quarter of the fifth century, precisely the time when the number of nonmythological deer hunt vase paintings dwindles in Attica.

Attic red-figure vases exhibit more variety in their compositions, which focus on a later moment in the story when Aktaion is already down on the ground, and they also tend to reduce figures extraneous to the tale. The best-known Attic red-figure example of this myth is surely the Pan Painter's bell krater of c. 470–460 in Boston (Museum of Fine Arts 10.185; fig. 74).[29] At the left, Artemis draws her bow, aiming its arrow at the fallen Aktaion to the right. Aktaion kneels, supporting his upper body with his left hand while his right extends directly upward in a theatrical gesture. He wears a

FIGURE 74. Attic red-figure bell krater by the Pan Painter, c. 470–460 B.C. Boston, Museum of Fine Arts 10.185. James Fund and by Special Contribution, 1910. Photo courtesy of the Museum of Fine Arts, Boston. Reproduced with permission. © 1999 Museum of Fine Arts, Boston. All rights reserved.

hunter's chlamys draped round his shoulders, a sheathed sword, and patterned boots, and four small dogs resembling terriers attack him. Similar depictions are visible on an amphora of c. 490–480 attributed to the Eucharides Painter in Hamburg (Museum für Kunst und Gewerbe 1966.34) on which the inscriptions ΑΡΤΕΜΙΣ and ΑΚΤΑΟΝ (written in retrograde) appear, and on a pelike of c. 480 from Vulci by the Geras Painter in Paris (Musée du Louvre G224; fig. 75).[30] Although the Pan Painter's mannerist style is absent, Artemis stands at the left in both depictions, holding a quiver, while Aktaion struggles on his knees against the dogs. In both cases, Aktaion wears a deerskin round his shoulders, evoking Stesichoros's claim that Artemis clad Aktaion in deerskins, thus enticing his dogs, and on the

FIGURE 75. Attic red-figure pelike by the Geras Painter, c. 480 B.C. Paris, Musée du Louvre G224. Photo courtesy of the Réunion des musées nationaux. © Photo RMN.

Hamburg example, the doe's head is visible above Aktaion's own. It has even been suggested that the doeskin represents a theatrical costume and that at least the Hamburg vase may have been inspired by contemporary theatrical productions.[31] On the Paris pelike, Aktaion raises a cudgel or lagobolon and grabs one dog by the waist; the Hamburg Aktaion behaves less aggressively. The Pan Painter is also credited with another image of the death of Aktaion, the fragments of a volute krater of c. 470–460 in Athens (National Museum, Acropolis 760), unusual for showing Aktaion fully clothed in deerskin suit complete with deer-head hat, rather than simply having horns or a deerskin thrown about his neck.[32] Artemis now appears to Aktaion's left, and dogs attack the hapless hunter.[33]

Fragments of an Attic red-figure plate and pyxis are worthy of note because of their findspot, Brauron, which was sacred to Artemis and Iphigeneia. Of the former, found in the small heroon of Iphigeneia and dating c. 440, only a small portion remains, showing the lower half of Aktaion and three dogs.[34] The remains of the pyxis, which were found near the heroon and date c. 425–400, preserve more.[35] The entire figure of Aktaion survives: he kneels and fends off dogs with his club. Fronds of a palm tree allude to Artemis, who may very well have been present beyond the tree when the vase was intact.[36] Both of these objects were dedications to Artemis, and, as such, the myth of Aktaion is fitting decoration for them. The choice of this myth seems strange when one considers that the dedicant was likely to be female (though males also made dedications at Brauron), especially in the case of the pyxis, but one might argue that anything having to do with Artemis, particularly her power and the dangers of crossing her, might be suitable as a dedication at Brauron.

Several depictions of Aktaion's death include Lyssa, the personification of madness,[37] a signal that the painting depends on Greek tragedy, which frequently includes Lyssa. For example, Lyssa, Artemis, and Zeus witness the death of Aktaion on an Attic red-figure bell krater of c. 440 by the Lykaon Painter (Boston, Museum of Fine Arts 00.346; fig. 76).[38] Lyssa wears a short tunic, boots, and an animal skin, and a small dog's head emerges from her own head. As others have noted, the presence of Zeus may refer to the version of the myth that attributes Aktaion's punishment to his amorous interest in Semele.[39] In addition to the names of the figures, an additional inscription above Aktaion has excited some speculation about further indication of theatrical influence. While some suggest that the in-

FIGURE 76. Attic red-figure bell krater by the Lykaon Painter, c. 440 B.C. Boston, Museum of Fine Arts 00.346. Henry Lillie Pierce Fund, 1900. Photo courtesy of the Museum of Fine Arts, Boston. Reproduced with permission. © 1999 Museum of Fine Arts, Boston. All rights reserved.

scription is a kalos name, though "kalos" is omitted,[40] others think that the label refers to the actor Euaion, son of Aischylos, and his portrayal of Aktaion in a theatrical production, presumably the *Toxotides* of Aischylos.[41] The presence of Lyssa has also prompted scholars to see Aischylean influence on this painting.[42] While Lyssa may be a reflection of a tragic production, one must also question why she was included in the play in the first place. Presumably, she indicates Artemis's fury or the fury of the dogs, emphasized by the dog's head atop her own, but perhaps Lyssa also alludes to Aktaion's own madness—his loss of self-control or hubristic action that led to his death.

Unlike the Attic black-figure shapes, the Attic red-figure examples also offer the opportunity for a second image on the vase and in each case, the artist seems to have chosen an apt scene to juxtapose with the death of Aktaion. The reverse of the Louvre pelike (fig. 75) bears a depiction of Zeus and Ganymede, and the other side of the Boston Pan Painter bell krater (fig. 74) shows Pan pursuing a shepherd. On both sides of each vase, one observes two types of hunting: the hunter being hunted by his own dogs on each vase juxtaposed to sexual pursuits. And if we accept an early date for Aktaion's desire for Artemis, then the scenes of his death include an erotic motivation, which pairs nicely with the reverses of the Louvre pelike (fig. 75) and the Boston bell krater (fig. 74).[43] The reverse of the volute krater fragments by the Pan Painter depict Dionysos fighting a Giant. Here we have two images of hubris: the Giants challenge the gods and Aktaion offends Artemis; both are punished. In both scenes, dogs attack the transgressors, Aktaion in his deer-head hat and the helmeted Giant. The Eucharides Painter amphora in Hamburg is adorned with depictions of the death of Aktaion and the death of Argos. If we understand Aktaion's crime to have been his desire for Semele,[44] then the two sides of the amphora depict the aftermath of Zeus's love affairs. If, on the other hand, the Eucharides Painter has Aktaion's desire for Artemis in mind, then he presents the viewer with two examples of love "affairs" involving a mortal and a deity that result in the mortal's transformation into an animal.

South Italian vase paintings of the death of Aktaion all include a centrally placed standing figure of Aktaion, who fends off dogs with an upraised sword or club, much like the Attic black-figure vases just described.[45] In most instances, Artemis and at least one other figure accompany the hunter, usually flanking him, and horns, presumably those of a stag, appear on Aktaion's head. Pan is among the attendant figures on several vases, and we might recall the presence of Pan on the reverse of the Pan Painter bell krater. The frequently included grottoes may reproduce stage sets and therefore point to a theatrical influence on the vase.[46] The South Italian corpus also includes some puzzling paintings that show Aktaion but are not the violent images of his death that we have come to expect. In two cases, Aktaion is clearly identifiable by his stag horns. Figures also sit idly in two registers, perhaps representing the cast of a play,[47] on an Apulian situla of 340 (Bloomington, Indiana University Art Museum 70.97): Aktaion flanked by friendly dogs, Artemis, and an elderly woman, perhaps a nurse, in the bottom register; Apollo, Pan, and a nude youth above (another Pan or a satyr?).[48]

A final ceramic example should be mentioned: the funeral of Aktaion is painted on a Boeotian pyxis of c. 470 (Athens, National Museum 3554).[49] Autonoe and her sisters, Kadmos, and an old messenger stand around the shrouded body of Aktaion. This singular scene catches one's attention not only for its subject but also for its fabric: this is a Boeotian vase that depicts a peculiarly Boeotian myth. Also noteworthy are six Melian reliefs, all dating between c. 475 and 450, which depict the death of Aktaion,[50] and, among the Attic shapes, the prevalence of white-ground lekythoi, best known for their funerary associations. We return to these funerary objects in chapter 4.

That the hunter Aktaion offends Artemis or Zeus, either through excessive pride or by his sexual desire for Artemis or Semele, receives emphasis from the presence of Lyssa, madness, on several of the vases, as Aktaion struggles with the consequences of his own madness or loss of self-control, and the madness of his dogs. Like the erastes who loses his self-possession and finds himself in the role of the hunted, Aktaion the hunter finds himself transformed, quite literally, into prey for his own hunting dogs. In this case, the inappropriate behavior is not the mixture of hunting and sex or that a hunter "has desired a female,"[51] but that he has desired the *wrong female* (Semele or Artemis) or has committed another type of hubris by boasting of his superior hunting abilities.

Hunting and Transgression: Kallisto

The mythological huntress Kallisto was a chaste follower of Artemis,[52] and the sole myth concerning Kallisto is her seduction by Zeus and the birth of her child, a tale similar to that of Io and other amours of Zeus. Like Atalanta and other devotees of Artemis, the sexually perverse Kallisto refuses sexuality altogether, although her misanthropy is nowhere as marked as that of Atalanta, nor does she share Atalanta's androgyny. Kallisto and her family play a prominent role in Arcadian legend.[53] Kallisto's father, Lykaon, was said to have founded the cult of Zeus Lykaios, one of the key religious cults in Arcadia,[54] which included athletic games as part of the rite.[55] In light of the discussion of hunting and warfare in chapter 1, it is noteworthy that Arcadian warriors carried the skins of wolves and bears instead of shields (Paus. 4.11.3). The Arcadians viewed Kallisto's son, Arkas, as their eponymous hero. Kallisto's sexual abstinence is the key to her downfall and her metamorphosis from human to animal. But unlike sexual transgressors, such as Atalanta or Aktaion, whose transformation or death signifies mere punishment, the ursine Kallisto, although she is killed, persists as a symbol of the transformation from virgin to mother, a change perhaps expressed in actual cult ritual at Brauron.

The literary evidence for Kallisto has been thoroughly examined[56] and requires only a brief review here. A fragment of Hesiod (163 M-W) provides the earliest known attestation for the myth of Kallisto,[57] although an earlier version has been posited.[58] There are additional references in Euripides' *Helen* (375–81) and in fragments of Eumelos, Asios, Pherecydes, Araithos of Tegea, Epimenides, Callimachus, and in Pausanias and Hyginus. We know that Aischylos wrote a Καλλιστώ but nothing of the plot remains. Apollonius Rhodius and Ovid give fuller accounts. The basic pattern of the Kallisto story includes the following elements. Kallisto, the daughter of Lykaon (though her father is sometimes named as Nykteus or Keteus),[59] was a chaste Arcadian devotee of Artemis (Hes. 163 M-W).[60] Zeus (sometimes in the guise of another, either Artemis, Apollo, or a lion)[61] seduced Kallisto, and she conceived a child. She was transformed into a bear, then gave birth to a son Arkas (from *arktos* or bear),[62] or to two sons, Arkas and Pan (Epimenides, *FGrH* 457 F9; cf. Aisch. frag. 65b–c Mette).[63] Kallisto was killed by Artemis or was about to be killed by her son, then was catasterized by Zeus.[64]

Explanations vary as to the motivation for Kallisto's transformation. Usually, it is said that Artemis discovered Kallisto's pregnancy while they were bathing and, in anger, the virgin goddess transformed the pregnant girl into a bear (Hes. 163 M-W). Other authors include Hera as a motivation for Kallisto's transformation. Apollodoros (3.8.2) explains that Zeus brought about Kallisto's transformation so as to avoid Hera's taking notice of his infidelity, whereas Pausanias (8.3.6) and Hyginus (*Fab.* 177) write that Hera detected Zeus's infidelity and changed Kallisto to a bear.[65] After his birth, Arkas was rescued either by Hermes acting on Zeus's behalf or by Zeus himself.[66]

Kallisto's fate is also explained in various ways. Artemis killed Kallisto either at Hera's bidding (Apollod. 3.8.2; Paus. 8.3.6) or because of Artemis's anger at Kallisto's failure to remain chaste (Apollod. 3.8.2). Zeus then transformed her into a star. But Hesiod (163 M-W) provides a very different explanation of Kallisto's fate in two variants. Long after giving birth, Kallisto entered the forbidden precinct of Zeus and was pursued by Arkas and the

Arcadians, who wished to kill her for violating the rule prohibiting entry into the sanctuary;[67] or Arkas, not knowing that Kallisto is his mother, chased her to the Lykaon abaton or precinct *in an effort to marry her* (my emphasis).[68] Zeus rescued Kallisto or Kallisto and Arkas, and placed her or them among the stars.[69] The erotic connotations of the Hesiodic account are striking: Arkas behaves as an ardent lover, taking on the role of Zeus.

Kallisto seldom appears in extant art. Written sources document sculptural dedications of Kallisto and her son Arkas in major sanctuaries. Pausanias (1.25.1) reports that Deinomenes (active c. 400 B.C.) made statues of Kallisto and Io, which were located on the Athenian Acropolis,[70] and the periegete, like modern scholars, notes the similarities of the two mythological figures: both lovers of Zeus, both metamorphosed.[71] Kallisto also made two appearances at Delphi. Pausanias (10.31.1) tells us that she, like Aktaion, was included in the now lost painting of the Underworld by Polygnotos in the Lesche of the Knidians;[72] and that the Arcadians dedicated a bronze statue of Kallisto made by Pausanias of Apollonia together with statues of Arkas, Arkas's sons, Apollo, and Nike (Paus. 10.9.5–6).[73] The Delphi sculptural dedications expressed thanks for an Arcadian victory over the Lacedaimonians, who attacked Tegea in 369; hence the sculptural group should be dated shortly thereafter. Only the base of this sculptural group survives on which are recorded the dedication, the sculptors' names, and those of the figures.[74]

Not only did the Arcadians include Kallisto and Arkas in their victory dedication at Delphi, but the pair also appears on two bronze Arcadian coins. One was issued by Orchomenos, the other by Methydrion, and both date c. 370–360.[75] The two reverses resemble each other: Kallisto, notably still in human form, falls backs, having been pierced by an arrow. To her left is a baby, presumably Arkas. The Orchomenos obverse has a kneeling figure of Artemis drawing her bow,[76] while that of the Methydrion coin bears a head of Zeus, Kallisto's seducer and Arkas's father.[77]

Aside from the aforementioned works, only four Apulian vases and perhaps two Attic vases are all that remain of depictions of Kallisto from the Greek world. Although the coins and the dedication at Delphi may, as Ian McPhee suggests, have been inspired by the establishment of the new Arcadian League in 370, the few vase paintings seem to reflect a different motivation. Since so few depictions of Kallisto exist on which to formulate any interpretation, we consider the South Italian examples, which also have the advantage of being clearly identifiable depictions of Kallisto. The four fragmentary Apulian vases bear similar compositions. The two better surviving pieces, a kalyx krater of c. 360 in the Museo Civico, Cremona (Dordoni Coll. 43; fig. 77), which possesses identifying inscriptions, and a chous in the J. Paul Getty Museum (72.AE.128; fig. 78) of c. 380–370, provide an index to identify the two remaining, very small, fragments, one in Boston (Museum of Fine Arts 13.206) and the other in an American private collection.[78] On the Cremona kalyx krater, Kallisto (ΚΑΛΛΙΣΤΩ) sits on a fawn skin; her chiton has slipped from her right breast, and she holds her mantle out with her left hand while a spear balances in her right hand (fig. 77). No indications of her metamorphosis occur in spite of the fact that Arkas (ΑΡΚΑΣ) is already born and carried by Hermes (ΕΡΜΑΣ). A tree stands above and beyond Hermes on another groundline, and a hunting dog rests in the background above Kallisto. At the right of Kallisto are Lyssa, Artemis, and Apollo, all identified by name. Lyssa's presence is significant: although she appears in several depictions of Aktaion's death, her inclusion here is unique for depictions of Kallisto. Lyssa is a common figure in Greek tragedy and in vase paintings that rely on Greek tragedy, and we may surmise that the Cremona krater falls in this category, influenced perhaps by Aischylos's *Kallisto*.[79] Because Kallisto still maintains her human form, we cannot interpret Lyssa as somehow associated with the animal transformation. Instead, as was the case with the Aktaion paintings, Lyssa perhaps indicates Kallisto's madness—her refusal to accept her sexuality and the consequences of its breach by the god.[80]

The painting on the Getty chous is similar, although Kallisto does not hold a spear (fig. 78); the number of figures shrinks here to Kallisto (wearing tall hunting boots), Hermes, Arkas, and a hunter.[81] Most importantly, Kallisto is in the midst of her transformation on the Getty chous as evidenced by her long ears, shaggy hair, and the claws and hair on her right hand. Although fragmentary, the krater sherd in an American private collection offers a variant in that both Kallisto's breasts are bared. The head of a small figure, presumably Arkas, appears just beneath Kallisto's shaggy, clawed left hand as if the child were on her lap. Kallisto wears a mantle over her head from which sprout enormous animal ears. The upper portion of a pair of crossed spears appears at the right. The Boston fragment bears only the head and right hand of Kallisto, part of a tree, and a small portion of a draped figure at the left beyond the tree. Kallisto's ears are ursine, and

FIGURE 77. Apulian kalyx krater by the Judgment Painter, c. 360 B.C. Cremona, Dordoni Collection, Museo Civico "Ala Panzone" 43. Photo courtesy of the Museo Civico, Cremona.

FIGURE 78. Apulian chous Near the Black Fury Group, c. 380–370 B.C. Malibu, J. Paul Getty Museum 72.AE.128. Photo courtesy of the J. Paul Getty Museum.

her hirsute hand has claws. Trendall speculates that the formation of the Arcadian League in 371 might explain the appearance of this myth on four Apulian vases in the fourth century,[82] although one wonders why these Apulian vases would reflect events occurring in the distant Peloponnese.

Perhaps the theater served as inspiration for these vases, as McPhee suggests.[83]

One of the most striking features of the two better-preserved Apulian vases is Kallisto's bared breast. In both examples, the presence of Arkas explains the exposed right breast, a sign of nursing and maternal care. Trendall suggests that she is shown just having given birth to Arkas, but the exposed right breast also recalls Amazons, who are sometimes depicted in art with an exposed breast and who were reputed to have excised their right breasts.[84] Another female devotee of Artemis, Atalanta, frequently appears in art as an Amazon. This attire and its Amazonian associations signify sexual and social perversity, and we should understand Kallisto as another of these wild, untamed women who refuse marriage and civilized society. Like Atalanta, Kallisto eventually experiences sexual initiation, and her time with Artemis, who also oversees childbirth, comes to an end.

Kallisto has been named as one of the figures on two Attic vases as well. The painting on an Attic red-figure amphora by the Niobid Painter from Vulci of c. 470–460, now in the Baron Seillière Collection in Paris,[85] is commonly designated as Artemis attacking Niobe, although Schefold alone has read the figures as Artemis about to shoot an arrow at Kallisto.[86] More compelling are the fragments of a red-figure krateriskos of c. 440–420 in the Herbert Cahn Collection in Basel (inv. no. HC503; fig. 79), whose findspot is unknown.[87] A reconstruction of the fragments yields the following scene: a woman enveloped in a mantle gazes to the right at the striding figure of Artemis, identified by her quiver, chiton, tunic, and boots, who draws her bow, aiming her arrow to the right. Immediately to the goddess's right are the upper body and lower legs of a young nude male figure, who wears a wreath and carries a sash; he gazes back toward Artemis. On the next portion, a deer runs to the right; one then sees a laurel tree and the remains of a figure with the upper torso of a man and the head of a shaggy bear. The final, adjoining fragment is ornamented with a frontal female figure with the head of a bear; she raises her hands, and a deer runs to the right beyond her. Although the identifications of the figures are disputed, the enshrouded woman is usually identified as Leto or Hera,[88] the nude male to Artemis's right probably Apollo,[89] and the bear-headed male perhaps Arkas, Kallisto's son; the bear-headed female is surely Kallisto. The shape is one peculiar to sanctuaries of Artemis in Attica, particularly the sanctuary at Brauron,[90] and both Lilly Kahil and Erika

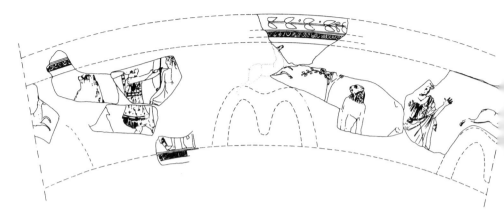

FIGURE 79. Reconstruction of Attic red-figure krateriskos fragments, c. 440–420 B.C. Basel, Cahn Collection HC503. Reproduced with permission from L. Kahil, "L'Artémis de Brauron: Rites et mystère," *AntK* 20 (1977): fig. C (drawing by I. Athanassiadou).

Simon connect this vase, like the other krateriskoi, with the arkteia.[91] In order to evaluate these claims, we must first understand something about the arkteia.

A detailed discussion of all aspects of the arkteia, a complex ritual about which there is little knowledge and much speculation,[92] would be out of place here. But some basic information about the cult and an abbreviated examination of the foundation legends of the arkteia may prove useful for this discussion of Kallisto, hunters, and Artemis, especially in light of the krateriskos fragments discussed earlier. Brauron was the chief site of the arkteia but the festival was celebrated elsewhere in Attica, including Mounichia and the Athenian Acropolis. Aristophanes (*Lys.* 641–67 with the scholia) provides the key information about the rites at Brauron:[93] young girls "acted the bear" at Brauron and wore saffron robes, *krokotoi*. What this phrase means and to whom it applied have been the source of much discussion. Ceramic evidence exists in the form of painted krateriskoi found at the various cult sites in Attica, and scholars interpret the paintings as depictions of the cult rituals of the arkteia.[94] The vessels are painted with girls, both nude and clothed, running and standing, some

holding torches, some holding garlands, many running with arms outstretched, some with arms pumping at their sides. The girls run near or
around an altar, and a palm tree is often included in the images. Thus, it
seems that footraces and dances for young girls were part of the arkteia. In
the few instances where mythological figures, such as Artemis, appear, the
depictions are thought to refer to some aspect of the cult legend.[95]

Kallisto has another connection with Brauron and, perhaps, the arkteia
through an association with Iphigeneia. According to Henrichs, the
Kallisto myth presents a variant of the myth of Iphigeneia and her sacrifice at Aulis, which was motivated by an offense against Artemis. The Attic
version of this myth describes the aition for the arkteia. According to the
account enunciated by Henrichs,[96] a bear was a key element in the foundation of the rites to Artemis at Brauron and Mounichia. According to one
version of the aitiological myth (of which there are variants), a bear sacred
to Artemis was killed,[97] sometimes by the brothers of a young girl in
vengeance for the death of their sister by the bear after the animal was pro-
voked by the girl's teasing. Artemis sent a plague so a girl was offered up
for sacrifice, or Attic girls had "to play the bear," which they did by insti-
tuting the arkteia, which included a goat sacrifice. In the case of the
maiden sacrifice, either Iphigeneia was sacrificed at Brauron (rather than
at Aulis as told in other traditions) or the girl was not killed at all but a bear
(or goat or deer) was substituted for her (e.g., schol. ad Ar., *Lys.* 645).[98] The
myths of Kallisto and Iphigeneia share several features: Kallisto is transformed into a bear, and a bear replaced Iphigeneia in a sacrifice to
Artemis.[99] Both Kallisto and Iphigeneia narrowly avoid death and are transported to another place. Significantly different from the Iphigeneia myth,
however, is Kallisto's death after her animal transformation.[100]

In any case, the bear is a key element in the myth of Kallisto and the
aitiological myth of the arkteia.[101] Because of what we know of the ritual, the
stages of a girl's life outlined in the *Lysistrata* passage, and the Suda's note
that no Athenian girl could be married without playing the bear for
Artemis, the arkteia has been interpreted as a rite of passage, designed to
promote girls to marriageable status.[102] Scholars point out that the saffron
robes (krokotoi) mentioned by Aristophanes (*Lys.* 641–47) as worn by girls
in the Brauronian arkteia may have provided a costume imitating a bear's
pelt in which the girls could "play the bear."[103] According to some schol-

ars, the prenuptial element is underscored by the girls' dressing up as bears, who were regarded by the ancient Greeks as paragons of motherly behavior,[104] and ancient myths suggest a link between the bear and female sexuality and childbearing.[105] If this is so, however, why do the girls shed their saffron robes, their pelts? It seems more likely that the girls dress as bears to imitate Iphigeneia, whose death was averted by a bear substitute, or possibly Kallisto, who is a mythological model for the change from adolescence to adult sexuality, a change that the arkteia is designed to effect for real girls.[106] Kallisto sheds her robes when she bathes, thus exposing her to the punishment of Artemis and transformation to a bear. Perhaps the *arktoi* at Brauron shed their robes, which do not signify bears' pelts but Kallisto's robes, and *then* become bears, that is, eligible mothers.[107] The young arktoi may imitate Kallisto but they also change the sequence of events so as to avoid Kallisto's ultimate fate.

If we consider Kallisto as the key figure in the arkteia and a model for the girls' activities, we may be able to interpret the Cahn fragments. Kahil argues that the fragments illustrate a moment of the actual arkteia and interprets the bear-robed figures as participants wearing masks: the priestess disguised as a bear turns full face to confront the initiates, and the male bear represents a priest.[108] Simon, on the other hand, offers a different interpretation and one that is more convincing in light of the absence of young girls on the vase, whose presence is a regular feature of other krateriskoi from Brauron.[109] Simon sees the painting as a depiction of the Kallisto myth, specifically the moment of her transformation. If Simon is right, then we should understand the bear as the newly transformed Kallisto, who raises her hand in surprise. The male bear, then, most likely signifies her son, who is half human, half bear in the imagination of this vase painter.[110]

Contrary to Borgeaud's claim that Kallisto's transformation to a bear removes her from Artemis,[111] the metamorphosis asserts Artemis's dominance over Kallisto and firmly places her under the goddess' control. Resistant to her own sexuality, then raped by a god, Kallisto is changed from human to animal. Ironically the son that she bears is human (in all transmissions of the myth except the half-human figure on the Cahn krateriskos fragments), and although the bear was regarded as an excellent mother, Kallisto was not allowed to demonstrate this because Arkas was immediately removed from her care. Moreover, the hunter Kallisto later became the hunted prey and perished at the hands of Artemis or Arkas so that the ideal mother figure, the bear, is either killed by its own child or by its unforgiving patroness. In both instances, Kallisto offers a negative model, particularly to the young initiates at the arkteia, which stresses the importance of accepting sexual maturity and responsibility, of eschewing a lifetime in the company of Artemis the virgin.

The Calydonian Boar Hunt

Most famous of all hunts in Greek literature and most popular of all mythological hunt narratives in Greek art is the Calydonian boar hunt. Joining the heroic hunt myth motif with the myth of the followers of Artemis, the Calydonian boar hunt probes the relationship between hunting and sex, which ultimately ends in human combat and death. Both Meleager and Atalanta, who are romantically connected in the myth, experience role reversals: the hunter Meleager becomes the hunted prey (hunted by eros and eventually killed by his uncles), while Atalanta acts the part of a male ephebe, so that the female transforms into male or antifemale.[112]

The Calydonian boar hunt is one of the first recorded hunting myths in Greek literature. A common theme in Greek poetry and for visual artists from the sixth century B.C. until the end of the Roman period, the Calydonian boar hunt appears on vases, in architectural sculpture, including tomb reliefs, and later on Roman sarcophagi, which lie beyond the scope of this book.

Disentangling the literary tradition for the myth presents great difficulties. The earliest extant literary account of the Calydonian boar hunt appears in Homer (*Il.* 9.529–99), in which Phoenix relates the tale of the hunt in an effort to get Achilles to rejoin the fighting. But the structure of Homer's account reveals that an even older tradition preceded it.[113] What form the early myth took is controversial and irretrievable, but one can discern common elements to which authors add variants.[114] Some versions include the chaste huntress Atalanta, while others do not.[115] The shared elements run as follows: the ruler of Calydon made a sacrifice in which he omitted the goddess Artemis, which angered her (this hubris recalls that of Aktaion). As punishment, she sent a boar to ravage the land of Calydon in Aetolia. The king called upon his son, Meleager, to organize a hunt to kill the boar. Meleager assembled a group of huntsmen, including his ma-

FIGURE 80. Attic black-figure dinos, c. 575–550 B.C. Rome, Museo Gregoriano Etrusco Vaticano 306. Photo courtesy of the Direzione Generale, Monumenti Musei e Gallerie Pontifiche, Rome.

ternal uncles and heroes from neighboring cities, and they set out to kill the boar. The boar was killed; there was an altercation over the spoils of the hunt, the hide and head of the boar; Meleager killed his uncle or uncles; and then Meleager himself was killed.[116]

Bacchylides 5 provides the earliest written text to mention Atalanta in conjunction with the hunt, and Atalanta of Arcadia is named among the boar hunt participants listed by Apollodoros (1.8.2),[117] Ovid (*Met.* 8.299–317), and Hyginus (*Fab.* 173).[118] According to the versions that include Atalanta in the hunt, Atalanta managed to get in the first blow at the boar, but the boar was finally brought down by Meleager, who awarded the boar's hide and head to Atalanta because he had fallen in love with her. Meleager's maternal uncles objected, so Meleager killed at least one of them. In some versions, when Meleager's mother, Althaea, learned that her son had killed her brother, she tossed a wooden log onto the fire, which caused Meleager to expire.[119]

The earliest certain vase paintings of the Calydonian boar hunt date to the early sixth century and are mostly of Attic manufacture,[120] perhaps in-

FIGURE 81. Attic black-figure hydria Near the Princeton Painter, c. 550 B.C.
Florence, Museo Archeologico Etrusco 3830. Photo courtesy of the Soprintendenze
Archeologica per la Toscana-Firenze.

spired by a lost epic poem of Stesichoros.[121] Based on the surviving examples, the greatest period of production of Calydonian boar hunts in
Attic vase painting was c. 600–550; their number plummets after that,[122]
enjoying only a brief revival in Attic red-figure ware in the early fifth century, perhaps under the inspiration of monumental painting (see table 3).[123]
Typical of the Attic black-figure examples is a dinos of c. 575–550, now in
the Vatican (Museo Gregoriano Etrusco Vaticano 306; fig. 80), on which
we see the boar in the center with a hunter lying wounded or dead beneath.[124] Dogs attack the boar on its back and from the front and rear,
while hunters approach from either side. Atalanta appears at the right, distinguished by the white paint on her arms and face. She is equipped as an
archer with Scythian boots,[125] and the other hunters are armed with spears
and tridents, although a male archer appears to the left of the boar. Atalanta is shown as an archer on several other vases,[126] as on an Attic black-
figure hydria of c. 550 near the Princeton Painter, now in Florence (Museo
Archeologico Etrusco 3830; fig. 81), on which the archer Atalanta is armed
as an Amazon with helmet and short chiton.[127] An unusual example is the
François Vase of c. 570, signed by Kleitias and Ergotimos (Florence,

FIGURE 82. Attic black-figure volute krater by Kleitias and Ergotimos, c. 570 B.C. Florence, Museo Archeologico Etrusco 4209. Photo courtesy of the Soprintendenze Archeologica per la Toscana-Firenze.

Museo Archeologico Etrusco 4209; fig. 82), on which Atalanta (name inscribed) carries a spear[128] and is compositionally paired with Melanion, whose name is inscribed.

In short, the typical Attic black-figure composition shows hunters symmetrically disposed around a huge central boar (usually facing to the viewer's left, although occasionally he faces right) with dogs attacking the boar and often with a wounded or dead hunter (frequently named Ankaios) lying beneath the boar. Atalanta is usually present though not always.[129] Although Bacchylides 5 is the earliest written text to mention Atalanta in connection with the hunt, Attic vase painting representations of the Calydonian boar hunt of c. 600–550 usually include Atalanta, an indication that vase painters knew of a tradition that reckoned Atalanta among the boar hunters before the first surviving literary mentions of a century later.

Attic paintings of a boar hunt exist that do not have inscriptions or Atalanta but still bear strong resemblance to the composition of the identifiable Calydonian boar hunt images. For example, an Attic black-figure Siana cup by the Painter of Boston C. A. of c. 560, now in the J. Paul Getty Museum (86.AE.154 [Bareiss 248]; fig. 83), is decorated with the standard Attic black-figure boar hunt, yet the hunters' names are not inscribed and Ata-

FIGURE 83. Attic black-figure Siana cup by the Painter of Boston C. A., c. 560 B.C. Malibu, J. Paul Getty Museum 86.AE.154 [Barciss 248]. Photo courtesy of the J. Paul Getty Museum.

lanta is omitted.[130] One might point to the symmetrical composition as an indication of the mythological boar hunt but symmetry does not seem to be a specifically Calydonian boar hunt feature[131] because there are boar hunt paintings that are clearly Calydonian as indicated by the presence of Atalanta, such as the black-figure hydria in Florence (fig. 81), that are not symmetrical compositions. Perhaps such images depict other versions of the Calydonian boar hunt; the literary tradition of the myth is so tangled that it is difficult to talk about painters reflecting a dominant literary source, nor is it necessarily valid to do so. It seems more likely, as discussed in chapter 1, that these represent a generic boar hunt that alludes to the composition of the mythical Calydonian boar hunt in order to liken the quotidian participants to heroes.[132]

Only three certain representations of this myth occur on Attic red-figure vases, and these all date from the mid-fifth century on. They may be based on a lost wall painting of c. 460 by the Circle of Polygnotos, which Fred Kleiner reconstructs on the basis of these vase paintings (fig. 84).[133] The reconstruction depicts the hunters around the boar in a spatial arrangement

FIGURE 84. Reconstruction by Fred Kleiner of a lost wall painting by the Circle of Polygnotos, 460 B.C. Reproduced with permission from F. S. Kleiner, "The Kalydonian Hunt: A Reconstruction of a Painting from the Circle of Polygnotos," *AntK* 15 (1972): 17 fig. 6.

that suggests depth and various groundlines, and Atalanta appears at the far left, dressed as a Scythian archer with floppy cap and high boots. Exemplary is the composition on a dinos by the Agrigento Painter of c. 450, now in Athens (National Museum 1489; fig. 85), which, however, excludes Atalanta.[134] The hunters, mostly beardless and nude save for a chlamys and petasos, attack the boar from a variety of vantage points. Likewise, a Kerch pelike from Benghazi of c. 370 (St. Petersburg, State Hermitage Museum B4528) also has mostly beardless hunters, who are nude except for a chlamys, and here Atalanta is shown as a Scythian archer.[135]

Written accounts of this myth sometimes romantically link Atalanta with Meleager, and most scholars credit Euripides' *Meleager* of c. 416 with having first employed the motif of the love of Meleager for Atalanta.[136] Whether Euripides provided the inspiration or not, images of the Calydonian boar hunt drop off dramatically in the later fifth to fourth century, and vase painters instead take up the theme of post-hunt activities, which include a pronounced emphasis on the amorous association of Atalanta

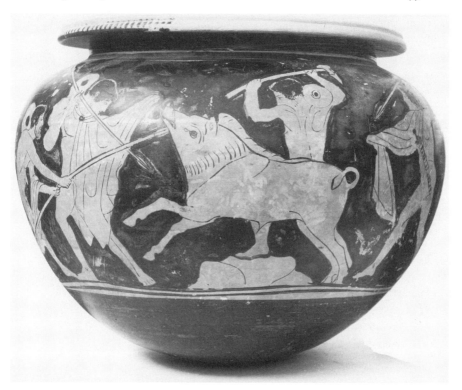

FIGURE 85. Attic red-figure dinos by the Agrigento Painter, c. 450 B.C. Athens, National Museum 1489. Photo courtesy of the National Museum and the Archaeological Receipts Fund, Athens.

and Meleager. An Attic red-figure kalyx krater by the Meleager Painter of c. 400–375 in Würzburg (Martin von Wagner Museum der Universität L522; fig. 86) bears an image of the seated figure of Atalanta lovingly touched by a standing Meleager in the center of the composition.[137] The presence of Eros and a hare,[138] a common love gift in vase painting depictions of courting couples (see chapter 2), underscores the erotic atmosphere of the painting. Even more striking is the depiction on an Apulian red-figure amphora from Canosa c. 330, now in Bari (Museo Archeologico Provinciale 872; fig. 87).[139] Atalanta, seated and dressed in Scythian garb, receives the boar's hide from Meleager, who appears beardless and nude save for a chlamys—that is, as a heroic ephebe. A winged Eros hovers between them, and Aphrodite appears behind Atalanta, holding a ἴυγξ.[140]

FIGURE 86. Attic red-figure kalyx krater by the Meleager Painter, c. 400–375 B.C. Würzburg, Martin von Wagner Museum der Universität L522. Photo by K. Oehrlein, courtesy of the Martin von Wagner Museum.

As was the case for the generic hunting images, fifth-century vase paintings of the Calydonian boar hunt portray youths beardless and nude except for a chlamys, the typical ceremonial dress for ephebes (at least as attested in the fourth century),[141] engaged in hunting.[142] Contemporary viewers may have understood the youthful hunters in the Calydonian boar hunt depictions as ephebes or preadults engaged in a hunt that exalts them to manhood. Moreover, as was also the case with the nonmythological boar and deer hunt depictions, many of the Attic red-figure Calydonian boar hunters adopt poses associated with the statue group of the Tyrannicides. While the Attic red-figure Calydonian boar hunters may simply have been copied from a lost monumental wall painting, the painting probably also employed these heroic stances, which were especially associated with Theseus,[143] one of the Calydonian boar hunt participants. So we may conclude that, like the nonmythological boar and deer hunters, the Calydonian boar hunters' attire and poses underscore their heroic status.

The Calydonian boar hunt represents a typical initiatory hunt for Meleager, and by initiatory, I do not mean a public ritual but merely a rite of

FIGURE 87. Apulian amphora, c. 330 B.C. Bari, Museo Archeologico Provinciale 872. Photo courtesy of the Soprintendenza Archeologica della Puglia, Taranto.

passage; that is, it is Meleager's first collective hunt, and he participates in the company of heroes and his maternal uncles (a youth's hunting with his maternal uncles is a typical motif of male initiatory rites).[144] Because of both the presence of numerous heroes and the dangerous quarry, the heroic nature of this hunt is unmistakable. All of the valorous aspects of hunting enumerated in chapter 1 attach to this hunt, as does the aristo-cratic patina, because mythological heroes—even Theseus, here of the Athenian democracy—are the property of aristocrats. So purely and simply, this hunt is a heroic hunt, the epitome of valor. Moreover, the myth with its hunt followed by a battle offers a mythological combination of the two aristocratic activities, whose close relationship was explored in chapter 1.

We may glean further insight into the Calydonian boar hunt paintings by again considering all images on a given vase. Battle scenes, horsemen, and occasionally heroic adventures are paired with the Calydonian boar hunt (table 3). Numerous associations link warfare and generic hunting, attaching valor and honor to both, and in addition to these aristocratic val-ues, horsemen may refer to another aspect of the aristocratic life. Generic hunting scenes are elevated when they are accompanied by heroic scenes;

when the Calydonian boar hunt is juxtaposed with another heroic scene, we seem to have a couplet of heroic themes.

Yet the Calydonian boar hunt, while heroic, is a rite of passage gone wrong. Meleager kills his uncles, and he himself dies. As a comparison, we may look at a mythological initiatory boar hunt in which everything turns out as it should, the boar hunt recounted by Homer (*Od.* 19.392–466) in which Odysseus hunts a boar with his maternal uncles: they kill the boar, return home, and celebrate, events that exalt Odysseus to manhood.[145] The wound that Odysseus receives by which he is later recognized on Ithaca signals Odysseus's manhood; it has lasting import and is a part of his identity.[146] By contrast, the Calydonian boar hunt is a civic killing or hunt, a collective enterprise that results in familial killing. The hunter, Meleager, becomes the hunted. How, then, to read the vases with paired heroic scenes, the tragic Calydonian boar hunt and a successful heroic adventure? The Attic black-figure band cup of c. 550–530 by Archikles and Glaukytes in Munich (Staatliche Antikensammlungen 2243) places Theseus slaying the Minotaur opposite the Calydonian boar hunt[147] as if to emphasize the initiatory activity of these two heroes, but, as was the case with Odysseus, Meleager presents a contrast, a negative example to Theseus.

Another peculiarity exists in this traditional heroic adventure: several versions of the myth, both literary and artistic, include a female, Atalanta, in this male initiation, which would be implausible in the real world and is therefore remarkable in the mythological realm.[148] In the Calydonian boar hunt myth, the initiatory hunt is perverted, and aspects of Atalanta's behavior place her, rather than Meleager, in the role of successful hunter as if she were the one undergoing initiation. As was the case with the model initiate Odysseus (Hom., *Od.* 19.447–48), later accounts attribute the first strike at the boar to Atalanta, and, in some versions, she receives the spoils of the hunt.[149] Moreover, Atalanta's very participation in the hunt and her appearance in visual depictions contribute to this image of male initiate. But she is also marked as alien. The only females who hunt in the Greek world are those who hunt in myth, and even these females stand outside the normal bounds of mythical society: maenads and Amazons. Not only does Atalanta hunt as do these female outsiders, but vase painters of the Calydonian boar hunt often identify Atalanta with these others by representing her as an Amazon and, less frequently, as a maenad. Maenads in vase painting commonly wear animal skins and hold leopards or snakes.

Amazons frequently appear as Scythians, Thracians (both Eastern foreigners), or archers, although they also dress as hoplites[150] and sometimes wear panther skins, like maenads (Strabo 11.51). In the Calydonian boar hunt depictions, Atalanta appears as Amazon, as maenad, and as a combination of the two: as archer,[151] often a Scythian archer (e.g., fig. 80), as armed Amazon (e.g., fig. 81), or as a non-Scythian archer with an animal skin.[152]

Such depictions of Atalanta liken her to outsiders and are intended to convey meaning about her to the viewer. The female warrior race of Amazons, like maenads, is wild, and lives apart from civilized society at the furthest reaches of the known world.[153] Maenads are known for their fearsome hunting prowess and represent an inversion of normal female behavior, a reversion to the wild nature of the female, and are enemies of order.[154] Ancient authors also mention the Amazons' hunting (e.g., Hdt. 4.114.4, 4.116.2), although this characteristic is not as prominent as their military skill, and they are, like Atalanta, devotees of Artemis (Paus. 3.25.3). The Amazons epitomized alterity for the Greeks, with their inverted society in which women behaved as men, and men either took on feminine roles or were excluded altogether,[155] and the same characteristics were attributed to maenads. Scholars have noted that the Amazons offer a negative image of what might happen if women were in control,[156] or provide a model of those who refuse marriage and, therefore, refuse culture.[157] Consequently, when Amazons invade the Greek world or fight against the Greeks, they always suffer defeat or are married or both.[158] The similarity between Amazon and maenad is highlighted by the images on an Attic red-figure alabastron from Delphi of c. 490 (Athens, National Museum 15002).[159] A maenad wearing an animal skin and Thracian boots on one side balances Penthesilea (name inscribed) dressed in Scythian garb and carrying a bow, arrows, and an ax on the other. The Amazon and maenad provide visual models for Atalanta, who dresses as they do. Such imagery is well suited to the female hunter of the Calydonian boar hunt, for she, like the maenads and Amazons, exemplifies the outsider, the ambiguous female who behaves as male, participating in the definitive male (insider) experience, and even conducts herself as if she, not Meleager, were the initiate.

Ancient written sources further explicate Atalanta in the role of male initiate and Amazon. Diodorus Siculus (3.53) states that the Amazons fight until they bear children, and François Hartog characterizes these Amazons as undergoing "the equivalent of a period of ephebeia."[160] Hartog also explains Photius's statement that the Eleans refer to the ephebes as Scythians by suggesting that the Elean ephebes wore Scythian dress as a type of uniform or that this appellation refers to the ephebes' sphere of activity, the frontier zone. Herodotos tells us that the Scythians fought as hunters, using ploys and cunning.[161] The figure of Atalanta dressed as Amazon, an initiate or ephebe according to Hartog, and as a Scythian, a term used for ephebes, engaged in a male rite of passage, the initiatory hunt, compounds the layers of meaning surrounding her. The ancient viewer would perceive Atalanta as Amazon, Scythian, outsider, and foreigner, yet performing activities and rituals of the male initiate in civilized society (though these rituals often take place physically far removed from society). Although the ephebe is not yet integrated into the adult male community, he is, in fact, already part of the insider's world for the institution of the ephebic or preadult training, whatever its form, was available only to those destined to be included among the citizens.[162]

Although we have generally confined our scope to Attic products, our interpretation of the Calydonian boar hunt and Atalanta receives confirmation and elucidation from a Caeretan hydria of c. 525–500 now in Copenhagen (Nationalmuseet 13567; fig. 88).[163] A scene of sacrifice decorates the obverse, while the reverse is ornamented with a scene of Atalanta hunting the Calydonian boar. If the two sides are read together, the sacrifice may be that performed by the king of Calydon, the action that triggered the chain of events leading to the Calydonian boar hunt.[164] Moreover, the artist may have intended the viewer to relate the two activities, sacrifice and hunting; successful hunting results in a sacrifice as a thank offering to Artemis. The painting on the reverse is extraordinary: the sole figure of Atalanta stalks the boar and she carries a shield and sword, like the nonmythological hunters.[165] In this instance, Atalanta is likened to both hoplite, which extends the metaphor that hunting is battle, and to Amazon, a foreign outsider, because Amazons sometimes carry or wear hoplite weapons and attire.[166]

Atalanta's appearance as an Amazon, while signaling her alterity and masculine attributes, also highlights the erotic nature of her relationship to Meleager because myth is replete with couples consisting of male hero and Amazon, such as Penthesilea and Achilles, Hippolyte and Theseus, and Antiope and Theseus.[167] Although no literary source prior to 416 describes a love relationship between Meleager and Atalanta, vase painting

FIGURE 88. Caeretan hydria, c. 525–500 B.C. Copenhagen, Nationalmuseet 13567. Photo courtesy of the Collection of Classical and Near Eastern Antiquities, National Museum of Denmark, Copenhagen.

may fill the written gap. Atalanta was paired with Melanion on the Cypselos Chest (known only from Paus. 5.19.2), on the François Vase, and with a male, either Meleager or Melanion (ME[. . .]), on a fragmentary dinos from the Athenian Agora (Agora Museum P334).[168] The proximity of the male to Atalanta on this dinos suggests some alliance, perhaps a romantic relationship (cf. the placement of Atalanta and Melanion on the François Vase, fig. 82). Most likely the male is Melanion but if the male on the dinos is Meleager, then perhaps we have evidence of Meleager's romantic involvement with Atalanta before Euripides' play.

Although the existence of a romantic liaison between Atalanta and another hunter prior to the evidence of Euripides remains an open question, one aspect of the sixth-century Attic vase paintings suggests an erotic reading of the myth: the shape and function of the archaic vases. Twenty-eight vases from c. 600–550 carry paintings of this myth (see table 3); one vase is connected with the women's realm or *gynaikeion*, and five are associated with the wedding—and all six include Atalanta. The myth occurs on an exaleiptron or unguent box of c. 570–560, now in Munich (Staatliche Antikensammlungen 8600), an item that was commonly employed in the gynaikeion as indicated by its use in vase painting depictions of the gynaikeion.[169] Five vases are dinoi, a shape associated with the wedding;[170] dinoi appear as wedding gifts in archaic Attic vase painting and are themselves occasionally ornamented with wedding scenes.[171] And one vase is the famous François Vase (fig. 82), which served as a wedding present because of the elaborateness and subject matter of its decoration, according to Stewart.[172] While still accepting Stewart's theory, some scholars object that the François Vase would hardly have been an auspicious gift since the wedding of Peleus and Thetis, depicted on the vase, ended badly, and their son Achilles died tragically.[173]

When we consider the version or versions of the myth that include the love affair, whether it commences with Euripides or not, the disaster that befalls Meleager can be evaluated differently. Meleager's love for Atalanta produces a role reversal. He is so enamored of Atalanta that he awards her the hide and head of the boar, thus slighting his male relatives and the attendant heroes (and also treating Atalanta as male). Meleager's presentation of the spoils of the hunt to Atalanta echoes the erastes' presentation of gifts to his beloved,[174] and one wonders if the association or simile of hunted animal with the erotic prey (erastes or eromenos) observed earlier might translate to the mythological realm. In this instance, the erotic prey is Atalanta, and the hunted animal the boar. The difficulty in capturing the Calydonian boar may serve as simile for the difficulty in capturing Meleager's erotic prey, the chaste Atalanta. The violence that erupts from Meleager's gift to his beloved does not result from Meleager's mixing of the realms of Artemis and Aphrodite but from Meleager's inappropriate and excessive fascination with, and promotion of, Atalanta and from her own excessive adherence to celibacy. Loss of self-control and perspective induces a change from hunter to hunted (by eros) for Meleager, and from female to male and thus hunted to hunter for Atalanta. Moreover, Atalanta's stringent adherence to a code of sexual abstinence is abnormal (Atalanta's footrace against potential suitors eventually ends her celibacy, and she marries) and results in a reversal of normal real-life female conduct: Atalanta hunts like a male and is honored as if she were male. Thus, hunting and the erotic sphere are combined in this myth (as they often are in real life) but the role reversals that result, which position Meleager as erotic prey and Atalanta as actual and perhaps erotic hunter (whether she actively cooperates or not), are typical of hunting myths.

The Calydonian boar hunt myth occurs on archaic vases associated with weddings and women—that is, on dinoi, an exaleiptron, and the François Vase, possibly a wedding present. Why would the boar hunt myth be appropriate for nuptial or specifically feminine vases during the archaic period? Most obviously, because, like the hunt for the male, the wedding is a rite of passage for the female, in which case these images would combine activities marking male and female maturation. But this chapter has argued that the role reversal that arises when Meleager falls prey to eros brings about his destruction. Perhaps the nuptial vases serve as cautionary examples, designed to remind bride and groom of the consequences that follow the excesses of love. But we should also bear in mind that the dinos served as an athletic prize and that such prizes were awarded to young, nude, male athletic victors, perhaps as a caution not to follow the example of Meleager, whether he is depicted as lover or as hubristic hunter who kills his family members. The connections, however, may have been made with less specificity than I have outlined; the hunt's association with heroes and marriage may have been sufficient reason to inspire the use of this myth on this shape without requiring a more elaborate correspondence.

The Calydonian boar hunt myth with its couple of Atalanta and Melanion may occur on nuptial vases to allude to heroic couples, who represent the taming of the wild by the civilized Greek male or to courting couples, particularly in the case of the later Attic red-figure examples. Atalanta's ambiguous sexual and social role also characterize Artemis, Atalanta's leader, who presides over cult and ritual designed to mark the transition between childhood and adulthood.[175] Like the myths about the other chaste devotees of Artemis, such as Kallisto, Hippolytos, and Melanion, the Calydonian boar hunt myth expresses the inappropriate excesses of chastity and the role reversals that befall those who do not acknowledge and understand the interconnected nature of hunting and sex.[176] The Calydonian boar hunt is but one of a number of masculine activities in which Atalanta participates; we can also observe her defiance of sexual norms and her adoption of masculine behaviors in other adventures.

Atalanta: From Virgin to Bride

Although all of Artemis's female followers exhibit masculine characteristics in that they hunt, Atalanta is the most masculine of all because she also adopts other masculine behaviors, observable not just in the Calydonian boar hunt but in all myths about her, where she behaves as an ephebe or male initiate; when her behavior accords with feminine standards, she exceeds the norms, thus ensuring an unfortunate fate.

Ancient authors scarcely mention Atalanta's participation in the wrestling match against Peleus at funerary games for Pelias, which took

FIGURE 89. Attic black-figure band cup, c. 540 B.C. Munich, Staatliche
Antikensammlungen 2241. Photo courtesy of the Staatliche Antikensammlungen
und Glyptothek München.

place at Argos, but it is a favorite subject of vase painters.[177] Found almost
entirely on Attic black-figure vases of the second half of the sixth century,[178]
the paintings depict Atalanta and Peleus wrestling while observed by onlookers, as on an Attic black-figure band cup of c. 540 in Munich
(Staatliche Antikensammlungen 2241; fig. 89).[179] Note that the two closest
observers wear chlamydes along their arms as if they were shields, thus emphasizing the heroic and combative qualities of the match. Athletic
prizes—dinoi and tripods—often appear in the depictions.[180] Atalanta even
strips down to a *perizoma* or girdle on some vases, leaving her nude from
the waist up.[181] Atalanta and Peleus also wrestle at the funerary games for
Pelias on a Melian relief from Attica of c. 460–450,[182] an especially fitting
subject because the Melian reliefs once adorned tombs or sarcophagi and,
in a few cases, served as grave gifts.[183]

Although much later than the vases under discussion here, the Suda
describes Atalanta as the wife of Akastos, and says she was attracted to
Peleus; Peleus eventually killed her in battle. But archaic vase paintings
already suggest this notion when features of the wrestling scenes borrow

FIGURE 90. Attic red-figure cup by Oltos, c. 510 B.C. Bologna, Museo Civico Archeologico 361. Photo courtesy of the Museo Civico Archeologico, Bologna.

ideas and images that color this mythological athletic event with erotic overtones.[184] A small feline, perhaps a leopard, decorates Atalanta's perizoma on an Attic red-figure cup by Oltos of c. 510 in Bologna (Museo Civico Archeologico 361; fig. 90).[185] The panther's appearance on Atalanta's garment, perhaps referring to the panther's ability to attract prey by its scent, may signal Atalanta's attractions and her prowess as erotic temptress. Moreover, the wrestling between Atalanta and Peleus, an activity usually confined to male combatants,[186] suggests abduction images, which depict females physically struggling against males. Peleus, in fact, was famous for his abduction of Thetis, an event that vase painting represents numerous times in similar fashion: Peleus wrestles with Thetis although Peleus usually grasps Thetis about the waist and does not confront her face to face as he does Atalanta.[187] John Boardman proposes a possible love affair between Atalanta and Peleus in his examination of an Attic red-figure cup by the Jena Painter of the early fourth century in the Cabinet des Médailles (818; fig. 91),[188] on which appear the inscribed figures of Peleus and Atalanta. Both are nude in a highly charged, sexually suggestive atmosphere as indicated by the figures' languorous poses facing each other, Atalanta's head thrown back with her free-flowing hair, and her hand just touching Peleus's right thigh. That these two figures were combatants in a wrestling contest is significant when we recall that one of the central locations of actual pederastic activity was the gymnasion; that is, the sexually charged nature of real-life athletics surely affected the ancient (particularly Attic) viewer's reading of the Jena Painter cup and the images of Peleus wrestling Atalanta.[189] The dinos, a vessel sometimes connected with weddings, also occurs in the depictions of the wrestling contest as the victor's prize.[190] Together with the Suda's testimony and the presence of the

FIGURE 91. Attic red-figure cup tondo by the Jena Painter, early fourth century B.C. Paris, Bibliothèque nationale, Cabinet des Médailles 818. Photo courtesy of the Bibliothèque nationale de France.

dual-valent dinoi in such images, the ancient viewer would have read the images and the myth as combining athletics and sex.

But both the Suda's account and the feline on Atalanta's perizoma on the Bologna cup point to a disastrous outcome for this virago. While the feline on the perizoma likens Atalanta to the odoriferous predator, it may also refer to this female hunter's ultimate outcome: transformation to a lion or leopard after having sex in a sanctuary. The Suda offers a different account of Atalanta's outcome: her death at the hand of the man with whom she is infatuated, a man who is not her husband. In both instances, Atalanta's desire leads to a loss of control, the consequence of which is death or transformation from human form to animal.

Finally, a consideration of Atalanta's famous footrace informs our picture of hunting and its connections to the erotic sphere in Greek myth. The earliest account of the footrace exists in a few fragments of Hesiod,[191] and the myth is recounted only much later by Apollodoros (3.9.2); Theocritus (3.40–42), Hyginus (*Fab.* 185), Ovid (*Met.*10.560–680), Libanius

(*Progymnasmata* 33, 34), and Servius (*In Verg. carm. comm.* 3.113). Atalanta swore off men, but finally agreed to marry the suitor who could defeat her or catch her in a footrace.[192] The race is sometimes characterized as a chase: the armed Atalanta chases an unarmed opponent; if he eludes her, he wins her, but if she catches him, he loses his head (Hyg., *Fab.* 185). The suitor, named Hippomenes or Melanion,[193] receives help from Aphrodite, who provides three golden apples,[194] which the suitor drops and Atalanta re- trieves one by one so that her progress is retarded and her athletic com- petitor and suitor overtakes her.[195] Theocritus (3.40–42) adds that Atalanta fell madly in love with Hippomenes after her defeat, and Ovid (*Met.* 10.609–37) also includes this "romantic" element of Atalanta's falling for Hippomenes though in Ovid, Atalanta begins to soften toward Hip- pomenes before the race. They were married afterward.[196]

Athletic competition to win the hand of a maiden is a common topos in Greek myth, such as the myth of Pelops and Hippodameia,[197] but in the Atalanta myth, Atalanta herself—not her father or other suitors—competes against Hippomenes or Melanion.[198] The physical pursuit of a maiden in the footrace recalls other mythological pursuits, such as Boreas pursuing Oreithyia or Peleus pursuing Thetis, and also the real-life hunter, who chases down his prey and physically confronts it.[199] Unlike the lover's metaphorical hunt, the pursuit in the Atalanta myth represents an actual tracking and capture, a real hunt.

Like the hunt itself, one can read the footrace as a metaphor for an ini- tiatory hunt, the first mature hunt for the male.[200] Furthermore, prenuptial rites, especially female rites, such as the arkteia at Brauron dedicated to Artemis and the Heraia at Olympia dedicated to Hera, goddess of mar- riage,[201] included footraces; thus we may understand Atalanta's footrace as a type of prenuptial rite, reflecting real initiatory races, because Atalanta marries after the race. Some variants of the myth name Melanion as the suitor,[202] reinforcing the reading of the footrace as initiatory since now two devotees of Artemis participate in their respective transitions to adulthood and sexual maturity: Melanion hunts (pursues), and Atalanta races in a prenuptial rite. If, as Vidal-Naquet claims, Melanion is the mythical an- cestor of the Athenian ephebe,[203] then he represents the prototypical ephebe involved in an initiatory hunt,[204] which was perhaps, in reality, part of Athenian ephebic training.

One version of the footrace myth maintains that an armed Atalanta runs after the suitor so that she hunts him down.[205] In this case, Atalanta acts as pursuer or hunter, a role usually reserved for males.[206] Mortal female pursuit of males is not normal, either in myth—for example, Phaedra—or in real life. Thus, a role reversal occurs in the footrace but, unlike role reversals in same-sex relationships, a role reversal in heterosexual relationships of the mortal sphere, with female pursuing male, violates social norms. Although the suitor weds Atalanta, the role reversal manifests trouble after their marriage: transformed to animals, Atalanta and her husband are condemned to hunt forever with Artemis.[207]

As was true for the hunt and the wrestling match, the footrace mixes erotic and athletic themes,[208] a combination expressed by the images on a white-ground lekythos of c. 500–490 by Douris in Cleveland (Museum of Art 66.114; figs. 92–93). Atalanta, whose name is inscribed, runs from an Eros, who holds a wreath, a typical athletic prize and, according to Boardman, an indication of the consummation of love.[209] The Eros also originally held a whip and not the floral ornaments, which are later additions.[210] Two other Erotes hover nearby. In this depiction, the athlete Atalanta literally races away from love and marriage,[211] an idea that is also stressed by the shape and fabric of the vase. White-ground lekythoi were most commonly associated with the funerary realm, and the Greek perception of marriage as a metaphorical death for the bride is well known.[212] Atalanta's footrace is a flight from Eros; if she is caught and marries, she undergoes a metaphorical death.

Although female, Atalanta participates in many traditional male activities and adopts masculine attributes. She carries armor; she performs in athletic contests, such as wrestling and the footrace (an armed race); she hunts; she competes with the suitors; and she exercises in the nude like an ephebe.[213] Although she partakes of the feminine sphere—she participates in a prenuptial race, which belongs to the real world—and she takes on the appearance and character of an Amazon or maenad, hers is the inverted world of the mythical transgressor against real-life norms. All of these myths and images emphasize Atalanta's liminal and inverted state. Atalanta is female yet a model ephebe in the boar hunt and in the wrestling contest, an activity of the ephebe and, in this case, possibly a struggle prior to sexual union. In the footrace, a premarital rite or initiatory hunt, Atalanta behaves as a female initiate and also a male hunter or pursuer. Atalanta wishes to remain in her girlish, virginal state forever, not attaining and accepting the responsibilities of sexual adulthood, typical of the followers of Artemis. In this way Atalanta represents everyday reality for the Greeks; she expresses a girl's reluctance to marry and become a wife and mother.[214]

Yet Atalanta finally does marry but because of her status as resister and her previous reluctance to civic norms, the outcome of her marriage is predictably dire and, once again, marked by role reversal. Although ancient authors briefly mention that Atalanta had a son Parthenopaios,[215] later Greek and Latin sources provide fuller accounts of Atalanta's aftermath.[216] According to the mythical strain that has Atalanta marry the man who defeats her in the footrace, Atalanta and her husband suffer punishment at the hands of Aphrodite, who is angered by the suitor's neglect of a thank offering after the race, yet another example of hubris (Ov., *Met.* 10.681–83; Hyg., *Fab.* 185).[217] The goddess fills the couple with lustful feelings while in a sanctuary of Zeus or Cybele; they cannot restrain themselves and consummate their love in the sanctuary,[218] breaking one of the most sacred taboos of the Greeks. Apollodoros (3.9.2) says nothing about a neglected sacrifice and instead states that while hunting, Atalanta and Melanion entered a precinct of Zeus and had intercourse there. In either case, sexual excess and loss of self-control characterize the myth. Zeus (Apollod. 3.9.2; Hyg., *Fab.* 185) or Cybele (Ov., *Met.* 10.698–707; *Myth. Vat.* 1.39) punishes Atlanta and Melanion by changing them into lions.[219] As Marcel Detienne points out, lions are animals that the ancients (at least Roman authors!) believed did not have intercourse with each other, but with a leopard (Pliny, *HN* 8.43; Serv., *In Verg. Aen.* 3.113.28–32; *Myth. Vat.* 1.39) or not at all (Hyg., *Fab.* 185), and some versions of the myth claim that once Atalanta experienced transformation into a lion, she was never permitted to have sex again.[220]

In conclusion, Atalanta exemplifies the dangers that arise from failing to gauge her sexuality and self-control correctly. Her refusal to accept her adult sexual status produces behavior typical of males, not females—a role reversal. Once she marries, she again misjudges when she fails to rein in her lust and loses her self-control in a sanctuary, which results in yet another metamorphosis, from human to animal. Because of her sexual abstention and then violation of sexual norms, Atalanta is first masculine, then animal, but in every case, she is doomed.[221]

In the mythical world, Atalanta shares several similarities with Kallisto.

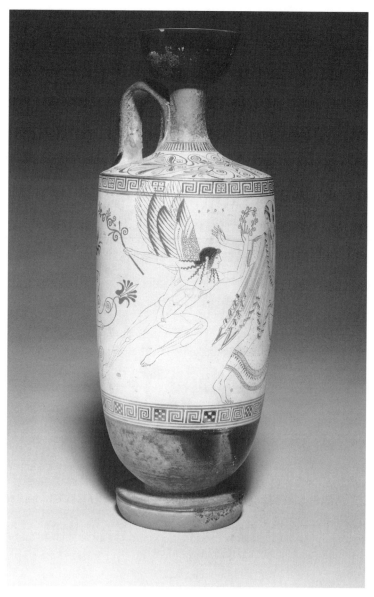

FIGURES 92–93. Attic white-ground lekythos by Douris, c. 500–490 B.C. Cleveland,
Museum of Art 66.114. Leonard C. Hanna Jr. Fund, 1966.114. Photos courtesy of
the Cleveland Museum of Art. © The Cleveland Museum of Art, 2000.

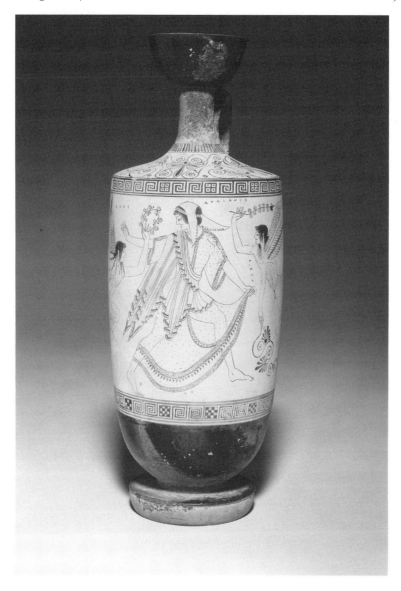

As for genealogy, both Boeotia and Arcadia have claims on Atalanta and Kallisto: both have a Boeotian or an Arcadian father,[222] and ancient authors refer to both as Nonacrian maidens and associate them with Mainalos. At the thematic level, both Kallisto and Atalanta follow the virginal example of Artemis and live and hunt in the wild with the goddess. Both are the objects of sexual desire, and such sexual power typifies the chaste followers of Artemis (e.g., Hippolytos) and the goddess herself (e.g., myth of Aktaion). Yet the activated sexuality of these virginal hunters often leads to disaster. Both Kallisto and Atalanta eventually had sex and experienced the privilege of mothering a notable son, but both suffer punishment for sexual acts. By contrast, however, Atalanta behaves as an active agent in her fate (we might also recall that Atalanta shot and killed two Centaurs, who tried to sexually attack her—see, e.g., Apollod. 3.9.2), whereas Kallisto is portrayed as the helpless victim of Zeus's lust. Scholars have recognized initiatory aspects in the myths of Kallisto and Atalanta;[223] for both females, sexual initiation severs ties to the world of Artemis with disastrous results. Kallisto unwittingly betrays her vow of chastity to Artemis and is raped by a god, and Atalanta stridently separates hunting and sex and then perverts normal sexuality by engaging in intercourse in a sanctuary.[224] Like Atalanta, Kallisto has close ties to wild animals, particularly the bear, but also indirectly to the wolf through her father and the rites of Zeus Lykaion.

Such myths demonstrate that the realms of Artemis and Aphrodite often mix, and that the rules or norms are strict and straightforward but not symmetrical: one can hunt without sex, but one can never have sex without the element of the hunt. The chaste hunter or huntress experiences either sexual conquest followed by transformation into another being or is killed. The transformation is often into a wild animal sacred to Artemis, thus ensuring that Artemis's devotee can remain with her. Artists depict both Kallisto and Aktaion in the process of metamorphosis, not still human but not yet animal. To be sure, this method of representation helps us identify them but it may also signify the marginal status of these figures, caught between the human and animal realms.[225] For the female devotees of Artemis, this transformation is especially remarkable because the Greeks regarded the female virgin as a type of wild animal, which could only be tamed through marriage. Myth demonstrates the dangers of trying to perpetuate the wild state because sexuality must be domesticated; even when they are married, Artemis's followers are not truly tamed because sexuality finds expression in inappropriate ways, and consequently these protagonists meet a bad end.

Yet the myths about Atalanta differ from those of other female hunters, such as Kallisto, in that Atalanta challenges men in a man's world. Her boldness is extraordinary, and she is therefore visually marked as an outsider; she poses a threat, but her erotic charge also subjects her to male dominance, for example, in the footrace, where she is ultimately tamed in spite of her wild ways. One can safely presume that the painters of Greek vases usually produced their wares for a male clientele, and this must certainly be the case for certain shapes, such as symposion ware; however, the wedding shapes were destined for both male and female viewers. In either case, images of Atalanta reflect the Athenian male view of women and were meant to echo, reflect, and reinforce contemporary social values in a patriarchal society.

The myths of Aktaion, Kallisto, and Atalanta thus demonstrate the inherent dangers in moderating one's sexual desire or self-control. Whether through hubris, as in the case of Aktaion, or through a violent disavowal of human sexuality, particularly the feminine role of marriage and childbearing, as is true for Kallisto and Atalanta, extreme devotion to the rubric of Artemis leads to role reversal. Contrary to scholarly claims, hunting and sex do overlap. The hunt can exist without sex (and it is worth noting that literal hunting myths are rare), such as Odysseus's boar hunt, but sex, mythological or actual, cannot exist without the hunt. An asymmetry exists between the literal and the erotic, metaphorical hunt, which explains role reversals and apparent oddities in myth. In the literal hunt, a role reversal is, by definition, a tragedy; but in the erotic hunt, role reversals are permissible under certain circumstances: males can pursue males within certain limits, as in pederastic relationships, and females can even pursue females, as Sappho demonstrates. In these sexual arenas, both real and mythological, role reversal is not only permissible and normal but even desirable. Males can pursue females, sometimes even goddesses, so long as divine male approval exists for the match (e.g., Peleus and Thetis), but mortal females, such as Phaedra or Atalanta, cannot and should not pursue males nor should males be so overcome with desire that they are hunted by eros. Myth thus reflects the social norms of real life: hunting and sex are interconnected realms, but the role reversals that occur are only tolerable within conditions that do not endanger the patriarchal order.

Table 3: Calydonian Boar Hunt and Possible Calydonian Boar Hunt
A. Attic Black-Figure

Vase	Date	Shape	Atalanta	Other Scenes
1. Rome, Museo Gregoriano Etrusco Vaticano 306 (*Heldensage*[3] 310, A3), fig. 80	c. 575–550	Dinos	X	Hoplite battle
2. Athens, Agora Museum P334 (*ABV* 23; *Addenda*[2] 7; *Heldensage*[3] 310, A2)	c. 575	Dinos	X	Sacrifice scene; silen, nymph
3. Tarquinia, Museo Nazionale Tarquiniense RC 5564 (*ABV* 84, 1; *Heldensage*[3] 311, A10)	c. 575–550	Neck amphora		Herakles and the Amazons
4. Rome, Museo del Palazzo dei Conservatori 85 (*ABV* 96, 17; *Para* 36; *Heldensage*[3] 311, A11)	c. 575–550	Tyrrhenian amphora		Horsemen
5. Philadelphia, market (*Heldensage*[3] 312, A6)	c. 575–550	Tyrrhenian amphora	?	?
6. Florence, Museo Archeologico Etrusco 4209 (*ABV* 76, 1; *Para* 29; *Addenda*[2] 21; *Heldensage*[3] 310, A1), fig. 82	c. 570	Volute krater	X	Wedding of Peleus and Thetis, Centauromachy, Ambush of Troilos, Theseus and rescue of Athenian youths and maidens, return of Hephaistos, death of Achilles, Artemis
7. Munich, Staatliche Antikensammlungen 8600 (*Heldensage*[3] 311, A15)	c. 570–560	Exaleiptron	X	0
8. Berlin, Antikensammlung F1707 (*ABV* 96, 19; *Para* 36; *Addenda*[2] 26; *Heldensage*[3] 310, A6)	c. 570	Tyrrhenian amphora		Male running between panther-cocks
9. London, British Museum B124 (*Heldensage*[3] 311, A16)	c. 570–560	Dinos	?	Boxers, wrestlers, judges
10. Bolligen, Switzerland, Blatter Collection (*Para* 42; *Addenda*[2] 28; *Heldensage*[3] 311, A16)	c. 570–560	Dinos	X	0
11. Boston, Museum of Fine Arts 34.212 (*ABV* 87, 18; *Addenda*[2] 24; *Heldensage*[3] 310, A4)	c. 560	Dinos	X	Horsemen
12. Tübingen, Eberhard-Karls-Universität, Antikensammlung des Archäologischen Instituts S/12 2452 (D2, *ABV* 96, 18; *Addenda*[2] *Addenda*[2] 25; *Heldensage*[3] 311, A7	c. 560	Tyrrhenian amphora	?	Swans between sirens
13. Malibu, J. Paul Getty Museum 86.AE.154 ([Bareiss 248], Clark, 1990 39–41), fig. 83	c. 560	Siana cup		Kaineus, horseman
14. Sardis, Manisa Museum 2137 (*Heldensage*[3] 313, A15)	c. 560	Cup	X	Battle
15. Mainz, Johannes Gutenberg Universität 72 (*Heldensage*[3] 312, A9)	c. 560	Cup		Kornos, warrior
16. Paestum, Museo Archeologico Nazionale (*ABV* 682, 69; *Heldensage*[3] 312, A11)	c. 560	Cup	?	?

Vase	Date	Shape	Atalanta	Other Scenes
17. Paris, Musée du Louvre 10698 (ABV 96, 20; Heldensage[3] 312, A7)	c. 560	Tyrrhenian amphora	?	Komast, cocks, sphinxes
18. Thessalonike (Skarlatidou 1999)	c. 560	Column krater	X	Swan between 2 boars
19. Berlin, Antikensammlung F1705 (ABV 96, 16; Addenda[2] 25; Heldensage[3] 310, A5)	c. 560–550	Tyrrhenian amphora		Horsemen
20. Germany, private collection (Güntner 1997, 28–31 no. 7)	c. 560–550	Tyrrhenian amphora		Sirens, panther, and swans, battle
21. Rouen, Musée Departmental des Antiquités 531 (9820029, ABV 88, 1; Addenda[2] 24; Heldensage[3] 311, A8	c. 560–550	Neck amphora	X	Panther between cocks
22. Germany, private collection (Heldensage[3] 313, A14)	c. 550	Cup	?	?
23. Rome, Museo del Palazzo dei Conservatori 65 (9, Heldensage[3] 313, A21)	c. 550	Hydria		Birth of Athena
24. Munich, Staatliche Antikensammlungen 2243 (ABV 163, 2; Para 68; Addenda[2] 47; Heldensage[3] 311, A14)	c. 550–530	Cup		Theseus and the Minotaur
25. Rome, Museo Nazionale Etrusco di Villa Giulia 74981, fig. 15 (Schnapp 1997, 506 no. 273)	c. 550–530	Band cup	?	Hoplite and charioteer in a chariot
26. Rhodes, Archaeological Museum 24, A1934 (Heldensage[3] 311, A12)	c. 550–525	Hydria	X	Same
27. Würzburg, Martin von Wagner Museum der Universität 442 (ABV 140, 5; Heldensage[3] 313, A23)	c. 550–525	Lekanis		Armed charioteer in quadriga
28. Florence, Museo Archeologico Etrusco 3830 (Heldensage[3] 311, A13), fig. 81	c. 550	Hydria	X	Horsemen, warrior
29. Florence, Museo Archeologico Etrusco 3890 (ABV 53, 50; Heldensage[3] 312, A10)	c. 540	Cup		Battle
30. New York, The Metropolitan Museum of Art 23.160.92 (ABV 299, 24; Heldensage[3] 313, A22)	c. 530	Fragmentary hydria	?	
31. Athens, National Museum, Acropolis 626 (Heldensage[3] 313, A27)	c. 500	Krater	?	
32. Athens, National Museum, Acropolis 782 (Heldensage[3] 313, A31)		Cup	?	
33. Cambridge, Fitzwilliam Museum 180.1910	Early 5th c.	Kotyle		Same

B. Attic Red-Figure

Vase	Date	Shape	Atalanta	Other Scenes
34. Athens, National Museum 1489 (CC1597, ARV[2] 577, 52; Heldensage[3] 314, B1), fig. 85	c. 450	Dinos		Same
35. Berlin, Antikensammlung F2538 (ARV[2] ARV[2] 1269, 5; Para 471; Addenda[2] 356; Heldensage[3] 311, B1)	c. 440	Cup		Peleus hunting stag, Themis, Aigeus
36. Perachora 3852 (Schnapp 1997 521 no. 424)	400	Bell krater frags.	Yes	Zeus, Dionysos, satyrs, maenads
37. St. Petersburg, State Hermitage Museum B4528 (Heldensage[3] 311, B2)	c. 370	Pelike	X	Two satyrs and a maenad

Chapter Four
HUNTING AND THE FUNERARY REALM

Scattered throughout the first three chapters are several instances of hunting imagery in funerary contexts, such as white-ground lekythoi and Melian reliefs. This final chapter takes a closer look at the use of hunting imagery in funerary contexts but its scope and aims differ from those of the preceding text. We begin with an examination of the Attic examples of hunting depictions in funerary contexts, mostly funerary stelai, which evidence the same connections—both metaphorical and actual—between hunting, battle, the aristocracy, and sexuality argued for in the preceding three chapters. Then, as a coda to this study, the chapter broadens its view to take in some instances of hunting in late classical funerary contexts in East Greece and Lycia, particularly the Heroon at Trysa, which differ in their ideology of hunting because of Near Eastern influence.

The idea of Near Eastern hunting as an aristocratic or royal activity had an impact in archaic Athens, but by the sixth and early fifth centuries, the time of the deer and boar hunt paintings discussed earlier, the original Near Eastern associations were muted. Instead, Athenians freely adopted and adapted the imagery of hunting wild game on horseback as a leisure activity for their own purposes;[1] the ideological image of the hunt in Athens was used not by kings or local rulers but by aristocrats within a democratic or tyrannical government. No longer a foreign exotic practice, it was truly Greek, and often used in metaphorical ways to express aristocratic ideology.

As Athens changed and the Greek world expanded in the fourth century, hunting iconography vanished in Athens. One must travel to East Greece and Lycia to find abundant hunting imagery in the late fifth and fourth century, where hunt depictions are strongly and directly shaped by local concerns and a long history of Near Eastern, particularly Persian, royal imagery that elevated local rulers to heroic and sometimes divine status. At the same time, we can detect Attic influence in East Greek and Lycian hunts of the late classical period, and Lycian rulers employed Greek mythology to further their own agendas. Such borrowings are hardly surprising, particularly since mainland Greek sculptors apparently made their way to Asia Minor as commissions became scarce at home.

Thus, in Lycia, one observes at least two traditions working to glorify deceased rulers (and possibly a third local Lycian tradition, a subject beyond the scope of this study). The Lycian tendency to combine Near Eastern royal hunting motifs with Greek myth as a means to heroize points the way to new developments in hunting imagery in the latter part of the fourth century, where hunting becomes more mythological and less metaphorical. One thinks naturally of Alexander the Great and his followers, who adopted Eastern royal traditions including royal hunting,[2] sometimes together with mythological imagery, to consciously fashion themselves as living heroes in the Eastern tradition.

Aristocrats and the Polis

White-ground lekythoi and funerary stelai offer an opportunity to examine Attic hunting ideology and imagery in funerary contexts. Only a small number of examples exist, and their numbers diminish in the fourth century, but, even so, we find confirmation and elucidation of ideas, particularly the metaphorical nature of the hunt, traced in the preceding chapters.

By the second quarter of the fifth century, white-ground lekythoi were produced exclusively for funerary use in Athens and Eretria,[3] and presumably some earlier examples were designed for this purpose as well. Several white-ground lekythoi bear hunting imagery, including two discussed earlier. On a vase of c. 470 now at Harvard University (1925.30.51; fig. 68),[4] a youth carrying dead game on a pole across his shoulder strides along; in this instance, we observe a borrowing of "returning hunter" imagery to portray an eromenos, dressed as a hunter, who returns from his hunt carrying his captured prey, a metaphor perhaps for a successful eromenos who has conquered an erastes. Hunters pursue a hare at a tomb on a lekythos of c. 440 by the Thanatos Painter (London, British Museum D60; figs. 61–62).[5] The quest for the hare may mirror a real-life amorous pursuit of the deceased eromenos. We might conjecture that the lekythoi were destined for beautiful and dead young men, caught at their prime, who were capable of capturing many an erastes (hence the returning hunter) or who were just at the age to begin chasing eromenoi themselves or were still being pursued by erastai (thus males pursuing hares around a tomb).[6] Evidence for a pederastic interpretation of the imagery comes from another white-ground lekythos of c. 450 by the Utrecht Painter (Athens, National Museum 12750), which clearly borrows from pederastic courtship compositions: an erastes, partially clad and leaning on a walking stick, extends a hare held by the ears and hind legs toward a stele as if offering the courtship gift to an eromenos, now deceased.[7]

Hunting myths decorate other white-ground lekythoi; although many are *not* ornamented with the death of Aktaion, a surprising proportion of the depictions of the death of Aktaion in Greek art *are* on white-ground lekythoi of the late sixth century. White-ground lekythoi as a group may not yet have attained their funerary associations by this time, but the myth of Aktaion's death is unmistakably funereal. If we assume that a connection exists between the decoration of the vase and its shape or function, a formula propounded elsewhere in this book, these lekythoi may have been intended for use in the funerary rites or as grave goods, and the posited dead likened to Aktaion. It is harder to discern a connection with the funerary realm in the case of the white-ground lekythos of c. 500–490 by Douris depicting Atalanta (Cleveland, Museum of Art 66.114; figs. 92–93)[8] unless one concentrates on the funerary aspects of marriage for the Greek female: when Atalanta races against and is defeated by Eros, the image on the lekythos, Atalanta will marry and therefore undergo a metaphorical death. Thus, one might construe the lekythos as destined for a deceased young bride or bride-to-be, who, like Atalanta, is captured by love.

The Melian reliefs of c. 470, which once decorated wooden sarcophagi, also employ mythological hunting imagery.[9] Exported from Melos to sites "von der Troas bis Sizilien," including Athens, the decorated sarcophagi were probably intended for a nonelite market.[10] Nearly all of the reliefs represent mythological or religious themes;[11] three of them depict the Calydonian boar hunt, and another six the death of Aktaion.[12] None was certainly found in Attica so we cannot consider them in the context of Athenian culture but one can nonetheless note the use of these two myths, which end in the death of the protagonist, in funerary contexts. One imag-

ines that wooden sarcophagi were not decorated with one but several Melian reliefs, but because none survives intact, it is difficult to speak of a unifying theme or intimate connection between decoration and the deceased. The Calydonian boar hunt and death of Aktaion end tragically but Melian reliefs also depict Odysseus or Penelope and other themes, which cannot be construed in this manner. Thus, we can say that heroic mythological themes dominate the reliefs, sometimes connected with death but sometimes not.

White-ground lekythoi are not the only Attic funerary objects to be adorned with hunting imagery. Numerous Attic marble funerary stelai or relief lekythoi are carved with hunters and hunting dogs or with imagery that refers to a metaphorical, amorous hunt. The hunters are identified by their attire and attribute—chlamys and lagobolon, for example—or by animals, such as hunting dogs and hares.[13] Unlike the case with Aktaion, hunting dogs accompany but do not attack the hunters on the stelai;[14] they represent the anti-Aktaions, hunters who do not exceed social or human norms. The earliest example is a fragmentary stele of c. 430–420 (Copenhagen, Ny Carlsberg Glyptotek 206a, inv. 2561; fig. 94) on which stands a bearded male, wearing a chlamys and chiton and holding a lagobolon raised to his left shoulder,[15] so the deceased is memorialized as a hunter.

FIGURE 95. Marble grave stele, c. 400–375 B.C. Basel, Antikenmuseum und Sammlung Ludwig BS233/S 175 + cast of Brauron, Archaeological Museum BE812. Photo courtesy of H. Rupprecht Goette.

Hunters are sometimes portrayed on horseback, such as on a stele of c. 400–375 in Budapest (Museum of Fine Arts inv. 4744), where the mounted hunter is joined by another hunter on foot, who wields a lagobolon. The portion of the stone where the prey once stood is missing, leading some scholars to suggest that the relief depicts a battle rather than a hunt.[16] Such confusion attests to the similarity of hunting and warfare iconography, a point already made about painted hunters and hoplites; only the opponent can determine the activity.

Other stelai characterize figures as hunters only by the inclusion of a hunting dog. Such is the case for a stele of c. 375–350 in Rhamnous (Museum 409), on which a nude athlete scrapes himself with a strigil while a slave boy holding a javelin stands nearby; a hunting dog jumps up on the athlete's legs.[17] Rather than choosing between the identification of hunter, suggested by the dog, or athlete, as indicated by the javelin and strigil,[18] the sculptor perhaps intended us to view this beardless youth as both hunter and athlete. The javelin on the stele may refer to both activities, because the skills learned in the gymnasion were often applicable to hunting.[19] A stele of c. 420–400 in Chalkis (Museum 2181) provides another example of a dog as the only means used to identify a hunter;[20] a hunting dog together with an athlete, indicated by a strigil and aryballos, refers to two interconnected aspects of the deceased's life. Yet another variation occurs on a stele of c. 400–375 in Athens (National Museum 2110), where a hunting dog accompanies a figure who may be a warrior;[21] the stele combines hunting and warfare, two analogous activities (see chapter 1).

Elsewhere on funerary stelai or lekythoi, hunting dogs or other features allude to the erotic hunting skill of eromenoi and erastai. The hunter Euthesion of Pallene (ΕΥΘΕΣΙΩΝ ΠΑΛΛΗΝΕΥΣ) is honored on a stele of c. 400–375 (Basel, Antikenmuseum und Sammlung Ludwig BS 233/S 175 + Brauron, Museum BE 812; fig. 95).[22] The unbearded, standing Euthesion wears a knee-length mantle draped over his left shoulder to reveal most of his upper torso. He carries a live hare by the ears in his raised right hand, while a lagobolon, held in his left hand, rests at his feet. A hunting dog stands behind him and looks up at the dangling hare. Clairmont views the hare as about to die and interprets the animal's impending death as a reflection of the unpredictability and imminence of human fate (i.e., death).[23] But because this tombstone shares iconographical features with pederastic courtship scenes, we can hypothesize alternative readings based on our findings: the attractive but unfortunate Euthesion is an eromenos, who is both hunted and a hunter of erastai, but he himself has been captured by death; or Euthesion may be an erastes, who has been successful in capturing his prey, indicated by the hare.

FIGURE 96. Fragmentary marble grave stele, c. 400 B.C. Brauron,
Archaeological Museum BE6. Photo courtesy of H. Rupprecht Goette.

Other funerary stelai, such as one from Salamis of c. 400–375,[24] honor
erastai. A partially clothed erastes, indicated by his mature physique and
perhaps traces of a beard, holding a hare—representative of his skill at
erotic hunting—leans on a walking stick, and a slave boy and a hunting
dog accompany him. Both erastai and an eromenos appear together on a
stele of c. 400 from Porto Rafti (Brauron, Museum BE 6 + New York,
Levy-White collection; fig. 96).[25] An eromenos, characterized by his nudity, a hare, and two other male figures, faces the viewer. The hare, strigil,
and aryballos signal the eromenos's desirability and youthful athleticism.

A warrior, indicated by his helmet, shield, and spear, and a mature male leaning on a walking stick flank the central figure; a hunting dog lies behind the eromenos's legs. Rather than a father and his two sons as suggested by Clairmont,[26] the iconography indicates various areas of masculine life and contest: hunting, warfare, and pederasty.

The emblematic images of the Attic funerary stelai confirm and reiterate the connections between hunting, warfare, athletics, and pederasty already observed in vase painting: that hunting and battle are not only analogous activities but are sometimes expressed in terms of one another through visual metaphor; that athletics and its attendant competitiveness are preparatory for warfare and hunting; and that pederastic courtship is a metaphorical hunt. These costly marble stelai themselves, like their carved images, are also redolent of the aristocracy.[27]

Rulers, Heroes, and Gods: Hunting in the Greek East and Beyond

While hunting imagery trickles to a few scattered examples in Attic art of the fourth century, the theme flourishes in East Greek, particularly Lycian, art of the fourth century. The sheer wealth of hunting imagery in fourth-century East Greek and Asia Minor funerary contexts is overwhelming.[28] The samples presented here are not exhaustive but demonstrate the variety of ways in which Eastern funerary art during the fifth and fourth centuries depicts hunting. One specific instance, the Heroon at Trysa, offers not only hunting in a funerary context but clear examples of hunting and mythological imagery borrowed from the Greek world and adopted for Lycian purposes. Whereas Attic hunting depictions employ metaphor to describe the hunt as battle or erotic pursuit as hunting, East Greek and Lycian hunts abandon metaphor and focus on the actual hunt *qua* hunt as a noble activity or use mythological hunting to heroize mortal men.

Funerary stelai and sarcophagi of East Greece and Asia Minor include hunting imagery whose iconography sometimes clearly shares Attic traditions; whether the same meanings can be read in the Eastern art or not is another matter. I am reluctant to describe a circle of influence but it seems possible to suggest readings based on Attic connotations in locations that were clearly Greek-populated cities. Although Greek and Eastern traditions combine or are juxtaposed in Eastern hunting imagery, teasing out which images derive from Greece and which from the Near East is a difficult (and perhaps impossible) task, one that has already been attempted by other scholars.[29]

Scholars frequently comment that the hunts depicted on Eastern stelai, sarcophagi, and especially tombs refer to or illustrate exploits of the deceased's life.[30] This may be true, but because many of the works borrow Greek myths and some were created by Greek artists, we may wonder if the combinations of images and their connotations reflect Greek cultural ideas of hunting even when depicting a real-life Eastern event. I think the answer is a provisional yes. The Eastern images that are influenced by Greek art and culture will exhibit some of the same cultural ideas about the hunt that have been argued in this book: that hunting is not merely a pastime of the deceased, as is usually conjectured, but refers to a life-style, a social class, a way of thinking of, and viewing, the world. But we should also be aware of the Near Eastern connotations of hunting, which refer to royalty and power, and why this theme was suitable for use as tomb decoration.[31] In short, these are hybrid images, and one must be cognizant of the many cultural factors at work.

Painted wooden sarcophagi produced at Clazomenae on the Asia Minor coast in the late sixth century clearly owe a debt to sixth-century Attic painting traditions.[32] Like Attic vases, some of the painted sarcophagi portray boar and deer hunts using spears with accompanying dogs.[33] A sarcophagus of c. 500 in Marburg (Philipps-Universität, no inventory number), as Cook notes, may actually depict the Calydonian boar hunt to judge from the dog on the boar's back and the figure swinging a double ax (cf. Attic red-figure examples of the Calydonian boar hunt discussed in chapter 3).[34] By contrast, some of the Clazomenian paintings have hunters in chariots, such as the deer hunters on a sarcophagus of c. 510 in Vienna (Kunsthistorisches Museum IV.1865).[35] Such a practice is unheard of for Greek hunters but forms a common motif in Near Eastern royal art as seen on cylinder seals,[36] in painting,[37] and in Assyrian reliefs from the royal palaces at Nimrud and Ninevah.[38]

Marble funerary stelai from East Greece portray actual and metaphorical hunters. Hunting dogs accompany adult or adolescent males, who lean on walking sticks[39] and sometimes wear the short tunic appropriate to hunters.[40] Dogs appear on other stelai with seated males,[41] but in these instances we would be hard pressed to read the sedentary figure with his seated dog beneath him as a hunter unless attire or weapons offer further confirmation. A boar even appears on one stele, where it is not hunted but serves as an emblematic device below the deceased male to indicate hunting prowess.[42] A reference to pederastic courtship, metaphorical hunting, occurs on a stele of c. 480 from Kos, now in the Kos Archaeological Museum.[43] A nude boy (indicated by his rolled hair and small physique) holds a cock in his right hand, while an aryballos dangles from his left forearm.[44] We are far from Athens but the cock and aryballos may indicate his athletic stature, and his nudity, age, and the cock suggest his prowess and attractiveness as an eromenos as well. Elsewhere, beardless males, sometimes nearly nude, hold hares,[45] perhaps identifying the deceased youth as an eromenos, who is both hunter of erastai and their prey.

Actual boar and bull hunting, rather than stationary hunters, adorn funerary stelai and sarcophagi, where such scenes are occasionally joined by banquet and/or battle images. The familiar combination of hunting and warfare recalls late archaic and classical Attic pottery, where literal and metaphorical hunting (battle) are juxtaposed on the same objects to create a constellation of aristocratic activities Also, the symposion offers the opportunity for the hunting of eromenoi by erastai (and vice-versa). As was the case for paintings of deer hunting on Attic vases, one sees hunters armed as hoplites on a limestone sarcophagus of the first half of the fifth century from Cyprus (New York, Metropolitan Museum of Art 74.51.2451, figs. 97–98).[46] Curiously, the hunt includes a cock, where it appears next to one of the hunters, who downs a bull; this unique instance of the cock's presence in an actual (rather than metaphorical) hunt conjures up the cock's associations with virility and combativeness. The reverse of the sarcophagus displays a funerary banquet or Totenmahl scene (either a banquet honoring the dead in this life or a banquet in the afterlife),[47] while Perseus beheading Medusa and a couple in a horse-drawn chariot adorn the short ends respectively. As was the case for Attic vase paintings, hunting and heroic deed appear together in order to heroize mortals — in this case, the deceased — by visually likening him to a hero (see chapter 1). Near Eastern tombs and funerary stelai commonly combine hunt, battle, and banquet or symposion imagery, such as a stele in Bursa (Kültürpark-Museum 8500),[48] which presents three horizontal registers: banquet, warfare, and hunting. Hunting sometimes appears only with banquet scenes. A boar hunt reminiscent of the Attic Calydonian boar hunt composition

FIGURES 97–98. Limestone sarcophagus from Cyprus, first half of the fifth century B.C. New York, Metropolitan Museum of Art 74.51.2451, Cesnola Collection. Purchase by subscription, 1874–76. Photos courtesy of the Metropolitan Museum of Art.

decorates a stele of c. 330 from near Daskyleion (Istanbul, Archaeological Museum 1502), although here the hunter closest to the boar rides on horseback unlike the Calydonian boar hunters, and a deer behind a tree flees from the hunter; a banquet scene fills the register below.[49] Hunting dogs rarely occur on the extant Attic banquet reliefs,[50] and they occasionally appear on banquet reliefs from outside Attica that decorated tombs, such as the Thasos banquet relief of c. 460 and the Paros relief of c. 500, both of which also include armor "hanging" from the background walls.[51]

The trio of themes—hunting, warfare, and banquet—occur in various combinations on the four sarcophagi from the royal necropolis at Sidon, which may have been carved, or whose execution was perhaps overseen, by

Greek sculptors.[52] Yet the sarcophagi draw on both Attic and Near Eastern royal iconography to honor their deceased occupants. The Satrap Sarcophagus of c. 420 (Istanbul, Archaeological Museum 367), usually thought to be the earliest of the group,[53] includes a panther or lioness and deer hunted by Persians, a banquet, and a Persian review of cavalry among its carved images. Here we do not see battle itself, but the cavalry review is akin to warfare. Next in time, the Lycian sarcophagus of c. 380 (Istanbul, Archaeological Museum 369; figs. 99–100) is topped by an ogival roof typical of Lycian tombs. Centauromachies reminiscent of those on the Parthenon south metopes grace the short ends of the body,[54] while pairs of griffins and sphinxes adorn the ends of the lid. The hunt scenes are on the long sides of the body: on one, hunters in chariots pursue a lion, while Greek and Persian horsemen attack a boar on the other. As noted already, lion hunting (particularly from a chariot) draws on royal imagery from Assyrian and Persian traditions, an appropriate choice here for the royal occupant of the sarcophagus.[55] The boar hunt perhaps derives from Greek art, although boar are not usually hunted on horseback in Attic vase painting, and one should note that boar hunting occasionally makes an appearance in Eastern art.[56]

Another sarcophagus from Sidon, the Mourning Women Sarcophagus for king Straton I of 367–361/358 (Istanbul, Archaeological Museum 368; figs. 101–3), also has representations of hunting but omits all references to battle.[57] The famous mourning women stand between columns around the body of the sarcophagus, while a funerary cortege processes on the long sides of the lid, and mourners sit on the short sides of the lid. The sockel frieze rings the entire sarcophagus with Persian hunters, some on foot and others on horseback, pursuing a bear, boars,[58] panthers, and stags on the long sides; returning hunters fill the short sides. On one flank, dogs, archers, and a figure wielding a sword over his head reminiscent of the Tyrannicides figures attack a boar (fig. 102). These elements suggest the Calydonian boar hunt except that the figures are all dressed in Eastern attire.[59] The range of animals and the garments of the hunters have prompted the suggestion that the hunt was a royal one, occurring in a pleasure park of the Persian king.[60]

This ensemble of themes occurs on the most famous of the Sidonian sarcophagi, the so-called Alexander Sarcophagus of c. 315 in Istanbul (Archaeological Museum 370; fig. 104), more accurately known as the sar-

FIGURES 99–100. Marble sarcophagus from Sidon, c. 380 B.C. Istanbul, Archaeological Museum 369. Photos courtesy of the Deutsches Archäologisches Institut, Istanbul, negative numbers 64/130, 71/59.

cophagus of King Abdalonymos of Sidon.[61] Macedonians fight Persians on one long side of the sarcophagus, while Alexander the Great, Macedonians, and Persians with their hunting dogs hunt a stag and a lion on the other. Some of the hunters are on horseback; one of the Persians is an archer; and two of the Persians wield double axes, recalling the Theseus figure of the Attic Calydonian boar hunt composition. The short ends of the sarcophagus pair hunt with battle: Persians hunt a panther on one end, and Persians battle Greeks on the other. As others have pointed out, the sarcophagus combines Near Eastern and Greek traditions,[62] which is not surprising; Abdalonymos, though not Greek, was from a "philhellene dynasty"[63] and installed as king by Hephaistion, Alexander the Great's confi-

dante and right-hand man. The shape and sculpted images of the sarcophagus lid, including griffins, lions, and Atargatis, a Syrian goddess, are
Near Eastern. The image and idea of the royal hunt on the sarcophagus,
perhaps the hunt that took place at Sidon in 332,[64] derive from Near Eastern traditions. Moreover, the Near East also provides the motif of lion and
panther hunting (lion hunting is associated with Eastern royalty), which
inspired Corinthian vase painters in the seventh and sixth centuries.[65] But,
as others have noted, the carving style is Greek, and the composition may
have been inspired by the Alexander Mosaic of c. 330.[66]

Near Eastern and Greek hunting imagery combine on another funerary
object, a relief squat lekythos dating to the first decades of the fourth century found in a grave in Pantikapaion (St. Petersburg, State Hermitage Museum Π 1837.2 [St. 1790 and 107]).[67] Signed by the potter Xenophantos of

FIGURES 101–103. Marble sarcophagus from Sidon, c. 367–361/358 B.C. Istanbul, Archaeological Museum 368. Photos courtesy of the Deutsches Archäologisches Institut, Istanbul, negative numbers 64/236, R13.732, R1768.

FIGURE 104. Marble sarcophagus from Sidon, c. 315 B.C. Istanbul, Archaeological Museum 370. Photo courtesy of the Deutsches Archäologisches Institut, Istanbul, negative number 8120.

Athens, the lekythos bears relief images of the Centauromachy and the Gigantomachy on the shoulder, while those on the belly depict a hunt conducted by Persians (indicated by attire, inscribed names, and hunting from a chariot) amid a setting that includes palm trees, laurel trees, and tripods atop foliate columns.[68] A smaller, better preserved version of the same vase (St. Petersburg, State Hermitage Museum 108i) with fewer figures was also created by Xenophantos and helps in the reconstruction of the larger, less well preserved squat lekythos.[69] The composition reads as follows. Hunters in two zones confront two boars, a deer, and two fantastic creatures, one a griffin and the other a lion-headed feline; eight hunters appear in relief, while others were rendered in paint. Seven of the hunters have inscribed names, of which five are clearly Persian, including Cyrus and Darius, who prepares to dispatch a deer from horseback.[70] Recalling the hunt scenes on the Sidonian sarcophagi, Tiverios refers vaguely to the lekythos's hunt as embodying afterlife symbolism, "die Jagddarstellungen auf der Lekythos des Xenophantos enthalten in ihrer allgemeinen Ikonographie möglicherweise Hinweise auf eine unterschwellige Jenseitssymbolik,"[71] but does not elaborate. I suggest that the deceased is to be identified with one of the hunters, who participates in a royal hunt (either in this life or the hereafter) suitable to his mortal status or conduct.

Lycian iconography and ideology of the fourth century also emphasize battle and hunting, those twin aristocratic Athenian activities explored in chapter 1,[72] using both mythological and nonmythological forms to heroize deceased rulers, a point sometimes made allusively and sometimes more directly. Lycian tombs present some of the most arresting combinations of Greek and Near Eastern motifs because of the size of some tombs, and because the tombs not only borrow Greek sculpting techniques (and scholars speculate that they were carved by Greeks or their local pupils)[73] but also combine clearly identifiable Greek myths with Lycian tomb shapes and Lycian and Persian artistic motifs.[74] Lycia came under Persian rule c. 550 and remained so throughout the fourth century.[75] Together with their Near Eastern features, these tombs offer an extraordinary opportunity to trace hunt imagery and its meaning in the fourth-century East.

Best known to modern students of classical archaeology is the Nereid Monument of c. 390–380 of Xanthos (fig. 105). The tall structure clearly derives its form from Lycian tombs, such as pillar tombs, while its sculptural decoration combines Greek artistic style and Greek myths with traditional Lycian funerary artistic motifs. Nereids adorn the intercolumniations,[76] and Greek mythological figures may have formed the sculpted akroteria of the heroon.[77] A nonmythological city siege[78] and battle appear in two superimposed friezes atop the base of the monument, an arrangement typical of Lycian tombs (cf. the Heroon at Trysa) but uncommon to Greek sculpture (though Greek vase painting displays stacked friezes). On friezes surrounding and inside the cella, one sees a hunt conducted on horseback against a boar and a bear;[79] a procession of figures carrying animals, spoils of the hunt; warriors; and a banqueting scene, which may refer either to a banquet enjoyed by the deceased in this life or the afterlife. Themes of city siege, hunt, and banquet have a long history in Near Eastern art,[80] and commonly decorate Lycian tombs and other Lycian funerary monuments.[81] Some of these tombs, such as the Nereid Monument, and those at Limyra[82] and Trysa are heroa, that is, the deceased, who was regarded as a hero, received offerings at the tomb. The modern interpreter reads the nonmythological sculptural decoration as depicting real achievements of the heroized deceased. In the case of the Nereid Monument, one sees the dynast portrayed as hunter, as recipient of animal offerings, as war-

FIGURE 105. Nereid Monument, restored east façade, c. 390–380 B.C. London, British Museum. Photo courtesy of the British Museum. © The British Museum.

rior, and as honoree at the banquet.[83] As for the narrative strategy of hero-ization by means of visual juxtaposition whereby an ordinary person (al-beit a dynast in this case) is likened to a hero, one struggles to see a con-nection between the dynast and Peleus, abductor of Thetis, but Peleus's fame largely depends on his son Achilles, the greatest of Achaean warriors. The Nereids, however, signal the dynast's elevation to the heroic realm be-cause Nereids possess the power to immortalize and sometimes convey the deceased to a blessed afterlife existence.[84] Although Lycian, the dynast em-

FIGURE 106. Trysa, Heroon, c. 380–370 B.C., reconstruction as seen from the northwest. Reproduced from Otto Benndorf, "Das Heroon von Gjölbaschi-Trysa," *JKSW* 9 (1889): Taf. I.

ploys Greek artists and Greek myths and mythological figures; perhaps he aspires to the ideals represented by these Greek depictions as well.

Abduction, hunt, warfare, banquet, and city siege also appear in both mythological and nonmythological form at the heroon at Gjölbaschi-Trysa of c. 380–370.[85] Discovered in 1841 by Julius August Schönborn, the monument fell into obscurity until its rediscovery by Otto Benndorf in 1881, who arranged to have its decorative friezes, its ornamented lintel, and the nearby Dereimis-Aischylos sarcophagus removed to the Kunsthistorisches Museum in Vienna, where they remain. Three monographs devoted to the heroon detail the relief sculptures decorating the temenos wall, the sarcophagus of the ruler within, and the necropolis outside the wall,[86] but none has fully engaged the iconology of the program; such a task lies beyond the scope of this study but some pertinent observations may be noted.[87] The combination of Greek mythological subjects with traditionally Near Eastern themes is cleverly orchestrated to convey the heroic nature of the deceased ruler to the viewer and worshiper. Although the Trysa reliefs have been interpreted as generally expressive of dominance over cities or the defeat of threats to the dynast's power,[88] the themes of battle,

FIGURE 107. Trysa, Heroon, c. 380–370 B.C., as seen from the south. Reproduced from Otto Benndorf, "Das Heroon von Gjölbaschi-Trysa," *JKSW* 9 (1889): Taf. III.

hunt, abduction, and banquet come together in a coherent, more specific program to heroize the now anonymous ruler.[89]

Benndorf's expedition provides drawings, notes, and engravings of the monument in the nineteenth century, when it was still in very good condition (figs. 106–107). The limestone temenos wall (21.65 x 26.54 x 22.70 x 25.50 meters) describes a polygonal area with an entrance near the middle of the south side (fig. 108). Within the temenos toward the north end was a large rectangular sarcophagus, now nearly destroyed, oriented diagonally with respect to the entry.[90] Fragments of the sarcophagus survive: enthroned and standing figures, and a dog. Nearly lifesize marble fragments of fingers from two hands suggest the presence of cult statues of the dynast and his wife honored by the heroon but the original location of the group remains unknown.[91] Sculpted reliefs adorn the exterior of the south (entrance) wall and the interior of all four walls, and a sculpted lintel and jambs articulate the entrance. The reliefs cover a range of mythological themes, clearly identifiable through their compositions and schemes, which follow standard types found elsewhere in Greece. Yet several themes appear—a city siege, battle, banqueting, and dancing—that are not clearly mythological

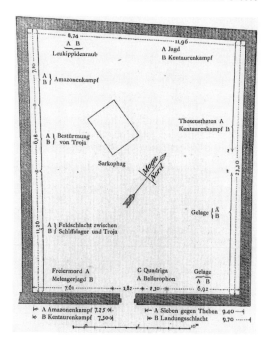

FIGURE 108. Trysa, Heroon, c. 380–370 B.C., plan. Reproduced from Otto Benndorf, "Das Heroon von Gjölbaschi-Trysa," *JKSW* 9 (1889): 55, Abb. 37.

and more closely resemble images found elsewhere on tombs in Asia Minor and the East.

Beginning at the left (west) end of the exterior south (entry) wall, the reliefs lie in two superimposed courses at the top of the temenos wall, certainly not a Greek practice,[92] and are interrupted only by the doorway. At the left of the entrance on the top frieze, one sees the Amazonomachy with the Centauromachy below; to the right of the entrance, the tale of the Seven against Thebes above with a land battle below. Inside the southern wall, reading from left (now east) to right: a male in a horse-drawn chariot and Bellerophon battling the Chimaira above and a scene of a woman's abduction below; on the other side of the doorway, Odysseus slaughters the suitors above, and the Calydonian boar hunt fills the frieze below (fig. 109). Moving along the interior western wall, three themes occupy the entire height of the two superimposed friezes that extend the length of the wall; from left (south) to right, one sees a land battle, a city siege scene, and the Amazonomachy. Along the interior north wall, ranged in two superimposed rows reading from left (west) to right, one sees the rape of the Leukippidai filling both the top and bottom friezes, then a hunt scene above the Centauromachy (fig. 110). The Centauromachy continues in this lower band around the corner to the east interior wall. Above it at the left (north) are deeds of Perseus and Theseus, then both friezes yield to themes of banqueting and dancing as the wall nears the southeast corner, where a wooden structure with two rooms, evidenced by holes in the stone blocks for wooden posts, once stood; funerary cult activities, presumably including banquets, may have occurred in this edifice.[93] The doorway at the south is adorned with four winged bull protomes on the exterior lintel separated by rosettes and a Gorgon's head in low relief (fig. 107). Beneath them are two enthroned couples, attendants, two dogs, and a goose in low relief. On the interior of the doorway, eight nude, bearded figures of the Egyptian god Bes sit, play musical instruments, and dance across the length of the lintel in low relief; lifesize dancing figures grace each jamb. No inscriptions provide the name of the ruler or person honored by the shrine, and the date can thus only be determined by stylistic comparisons for the sculpted reliefs.[94]

Scholars have traced both Greek and Asiatic influences in the style of the reliefs, and the subject matter also betrays this mixture,[95] most obviously with the appearance of images of Bes, perhaps apotropaic devices, on the interior doorway while Greek myths adorn the walls.[96] But other examples of Eastern, particularly Lycian, imagery abound at Trysa. Typical of Lycian tombs are depictions of the dynast victorious in battle and the seated royal couple,[97] the former of which occurs on the Trysa west temenos wall. The seated couple graces the dynast's sarcophagus, the exterior lintel of the entrance, and the city siege scene of the west wall, where the female holds a parasol sculpted in low relief, and a painted parasol once shaded the dynast; the parasols are an Eastern element, derived from Assyrian and Persian art (cf. Nereid Monument).[98] But, as Childs points out, the couple on the western wall does not wear Eastern dress.[99] One frequently sees the nonmythological city siege,[100] banquet, and land battle scenes in art from Asia Minor and elsewhere in the East, most notably at nearby Xanthos,[101] particularly in funerary art of prominent rulers. In fact, Jacobs argues that the art of Limyra and Trysa derives from Greek, specifically Attic themes, in an effort to express anti-Persian sentiment and to create analogies with local rulers.[102]

The subjects of some of the sculpted reliefs mirror real-life activities that occurred, both in the heroon and elsewhere. For example, the banqueting scenes of the east wall presumably reflect the activities of funerary cult participants,[103] who would have entered the temenos in a procession that led from the city on various festival days.[104] The nonmythological city siege, battle, and hunt depictions may refer to real or generic events in the life of the deceased. Among the figures on the west wall scenes of land and sea

FIGURE 109. Trysa, Heroon, interior southwest frieze: Odysseus' slaughter of the suitors (above), Calydonian boar hunt (below), c. 380–370 B.C. Photo courtesy of the Kunsthistorisches Museum, Vienna.

battles, one can recognize the Trysa ruler, who leads an attack on a coast to expand his holdings (at far left) or defends his city from attack (center), and sits and observes the fray.[105]

The heroon at Trysa stands apart from other Lycian tombs for its abundance and diversity of Greek myths.[106] Some scholars have dismissed this accumulation as nothing more than "Greek myth bought by the metre,"[107] but an alternative reading recognizes juxtapositions and parallels that reveal a clever intellect at work. As was true for the hunt paintings on Attic vases, these nonmythological reliefs heroize the ruler by means of visual analogy or juxtaposition with mythological reliefs. In the case of the Attic vase paintings, for example, generic boar hunt scenes used the same composition as the Calydonian boar hunt images to liken the everyday hunters to the mythological heroic hunters. Or hunting scenes were paired with other myths to heroize the everyday hunter. The Trysa reliefs use both kinds of heroizing tactics, repeated compositions and pairing of mythological representations, such as the deeds of Theseus and Perseus, to nonmythological scenes, to express the ruler's power and elevate him to the realm of heroes.[108]

Each nonmythological scene has a mythological counterpart (fig. 108):[109] the city siege and the Seven against Thebes; the land battle and the Amazonomachy or Centauromachy; the banquet reliefs and Odysseus

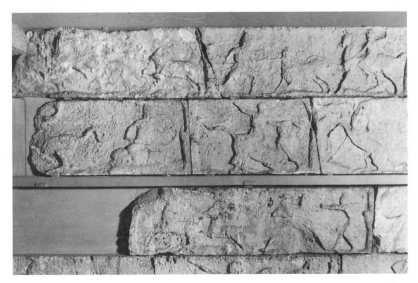

FIGURE 110. Trysa, Heroon, interior northeast frieze: hunt (above), Centauromachy (below), c. 380–370 B.C. Photo courtesy of the Kunsthistorisches Museum, Vienna.

killing the suitors, whose banqueting activities are emphasized by their reclining on klinai; the Calydonian boar hunt and the nonmythological hunt; and the rape of the Leukippidae and the abduction scene inside the entrance. In each case, a nonmythological scene is juxtaposed with a mythological scene to heroize the participants in the former. Although this may be pure intellectual play on the part of the designer, one must also question what connections the viewer might plausibly have made, and that, in part, depends on the viewer's acumen and physical orientation. As an example of meaning created by juxtaposition, the Trysa heroon places Bellerophon fighting the Chimaira next to a man, presumably the Trysa ruler, in a chariot. Scholars suggest that the mythological Bellerophon may refer to the Trysa ruler's ancestry because Bellerophon was believed to be the founder of the line of Lycian dynasts and to be buried at Tlos,[110] and he also saved Lycia from the Chimaira.[111] The theme occurs on other Lycian monuments presumably for the same purpose, such as on the Heroon of Limyra of c. 400–360, where Bellerophon fighting the Chimaira forms the south akroterion, and Perseus beheading Medusa is the northern counterpart; here and at Trysa, Perseus refers to the Persian royal family, which he founded.[112] Returning to the Trysa heroon, the abduction of a woman beneath the

Bellerophon relief may represent an episode of the family history of the
Trysa ruler.[113] Thus, we view the ruler and scenes—abduction, chariot, and
Bellerophon—that point to his origins in one easily comprehensible area
of the heroon. But one might go even further and recognize that the juxtaposition may not simply relate the hero to the ruler but actually liken the
ruler to the heroic Bellerophon.

Perseus's and Theseus's deeds on the wall opposite the nonmythological
city siege and land battle seem a plausible effort to heroize the deceased
by juxtaposition because the viewer could easily look from one side of the
temenos to the other (though it should be noted that the images are not
directly opposite each other). But Oberleitner's reading of the Seven
against Thebes as a mythological mirroring of the generic city siege scene
may be less credible because these images are physically quite distant: we
find the myth on the exterior of the south side of the temenos wall while
the city siege appears on the interior of the west wall. Would a visitor re-
ally have drawn a direct connection between the two battles? We might
posit the following scenario: either no connection between the two representations was intended, or it was intended but only a very keen viewer
would have apprehended it.[114] Perseus, however, has a more direct connection with Lycia: he worked with Lycian builders to construct edifices
in the Argolid and was an ancestor of the Achaemenid kings, who ruled
Lycia through dynasts such as the one honored at Trysa.

Oberleitner accepts the standard scholarly reading of the Amazonomachy and Centauromachy as references to the defeat of the Persians by
Greeks, but it defies credibility that the Lycians would interpret these
myths in this fashion since the Eastern Lycians would have identified with
the defeated Eastern Amazons and barbaric Centaurs.[115] A Lycian identification with the victors in these battles, the Greek men, seems much more
likely. The Amazonomachy was adjacent to the city siege on the west wall
and the Centauromachy was opposite it, thus creating credible parallels
to the nonmythological battle and city siege on the west wall.

In addition to the narrative strategies to heroize the deceased involving
juxtaposition and repeated scenes, some scholars have suggested yet another: that the seemingly nonmythological, real images of battle might actually be read as mythological. According to this reasoning, the city siege
scenes on the west wall of the heroon at Trysa might have conjured images of the sack of Troy in the viewer's mind, and the enthroned ruler

would then be read as Priam, with Hektor making a sacrifice, and Helen seated on another throne.[116] In this reversal of the usual interpretation of mythological scenes as learned references to real events, real figures are likened to mythological figures in nonmythological depictions. Likewise, Oberleitner raises the possibility that all the generic battle leaders on the Trysa friezes could be viewed as Bellerophon.[117]

Not only are the myths at Trysa themselves Greek, but their manner of depiction reflects influence from Attic sources; of special interest to us are the hunting scenes. Aspects of the Calydonian boar hunt frieze on the south wall quote from the Attic vase paintings of the theme,[118] particularly the fifth-and fourth-century red-figure examples (fig. 85). The Trysa composition revolves around a centrally placed boar, who moves to the left as do most of the boars in the Attic vase paintings. Hunters converge on the boar from all sides, wielding spears, swords, and stones, and dogs snap at the boar from front and back. Several hunters carry shields and hoplite weapons, and a figure (Theseus) behind the boar menaces the animal with a raised club.[119] Like the vases, the Trysa composition may derive from a monumental wall painting, although the figures at Trysa stand on a single groundline rather than the multiple groundlines and various planes of the vases.[120] Wounded hunters, who recall the wounded or dead hunter beneath the Calydonian boar's feet in Attic vase painting, appear but on the frieze they are transposed to the left or right side, where one hunter stands or walks with assistance, two hunters carry away a third, and a hunter drags another wounded companion away. To the left of the boar (the third figure over from the boar), a hunter holds bow and arrow poised for the strike; though the condition of the figure makes it difficult to read, the presence of breasts confirms her identity as Atalanta, and we probably can recognize the hunter closest to the boar as Meleager.[121] Most of the hunters wear girt chitons and helmets like those worn by the hunters on the Apulian amphora in Trieste of c. 350 (Museo Civico S380);[122] is it valid to interpret these warrior hunters in this Eastern context as we did in the Attic vase paintings—that is, as expressions of the analogy between hunting and warfare? This seems possible since we know of the importance of hunting and warfare for the Lycians from inscriptions but we lack the specific analogy in written sources; borrowing of meaning does not always accompany borrowing of composition.

A hunt with no mythological markers occurs on the opposite north wall of the temenos (fig. 110). Hunters on foot and horseback joined by dogs pursue goats, panthers, boars, a bear, and two unidentifiable wild beasts using spears, axes, and bow and arrow. Two of the three boar hunt vignettes share elements with the fifth-century Attic Calydonian boar hunt composition: the leftmost (west) boar vignette shows a boar flanked by hunters, the left of which swings an ax over his head, and in the third boar vignette (the rightmost) a dog attacks a boar. But Near Eastern art surely provides the source for the hunting of panthers (and other felines, usually lions or lionesses); actual panther hunting makes only an occasional appearance in Attic vase painting (as opposed to metaphorical panther or leopard hunting discussed in chapter 2) but lion hunting is ubiquitous and conventional iconography in Near Eastern, particularly Assyrian and Achaemenid, art. Stylistic and compositional similarities are close between the nonmythological hunts at Trysa and that on a sarcophagus lid from Limyra, on which hunters on foot and horseback attack a panther or lioness and a boar.[123] I propose that heroization by means of juxtaposition is operative in these two hunt friezes at Trysa in which we are meant to read the Trysa ruler among the nonmythological hunters and liken him to the great heroes of the Calydonian boar hunt. At the same time, the frieze may have conjured up a much vaguer association in the viewer's mind between the hunt's Eastern royal associations and the deceased Trysa ruler, affording the local dynast a sense of royal grandeur. The coexistence of the more specific and the more amorphous readings is credible.

Reading the hunt scenes in the context of their surrounding imagery aids our interpretation of the hunt images and the overall program of the heroon at Trysa. On both the south and north walls, the hunt is paired with an abduction scene, the rape of the Leukippidae on the north, and a large battle scene, the Centauromachy on the north, and a type of battle, Odysseus's slaughter of the suitors, on the south (fig. 108).[124] On the north wall, the placement of the numerous hunts above the Centauromachy frieze might have inspired viewers to consider these multiple combats between animals and men on the one hand, between half animals–half men and men on the other—one nonmythological, the other mythological and familiar to all. Once again, the juxtaposition of the nonmythological hunters with the heroic Greek figures battling half-animal–half-human forms seems calculated to invite comparison. This conglomeration of themes—abduction, hunt, battle, and banquet—appears repeatedly in Lycian art, but they have an older source in royal Near Eastern art and in the Greek world, the world of heroes, who provide models to which later, mere mortals could aspire.[125]

Royal Macedonian art of the last third of the fourth century continues the merging of Eastern and Greek hunting motifs. The subject itself of the lion hunt mosaic in Building I at Pella (c. 330–300) draws on Eastern art to suggest a royal hunt but this image also quotes the lunging pose and over-head gesture of the Tyrannicides statuary group, a bow to Greek heroic tradition.[126] Additionally, the hunt painting on the façade of Tomb II at Vergina of c. 336–317 betrays this mixture of Greek and Eastern elements. Macedonians, some, including Alexander the Great, dressed in Persian garb, hunt a lion, boar, and deer from horseback and on foot in a typical Eastern game park, perhaps in Babylon.[127]

At a more thematic level, Lycian heroa point the way to the bolder, more self-conscious assertion of heroic lineage by Alexander the Great and his followers. Alexander does not stop at simply honoring and emulating heroes, such as Achilles and other Homeric figures (Plut., *Alex.* 15.26), but continues the Near Eastern practice of claiming descent from heroes, particularly Homeric, and gods, such as Herakles, Perseus, and Zeus, and goes so far as to claim himself as one of them. Immediately upon embarking at Troy in 334, Alexander and Hephaistion made sacrifices to Achilles and Patroklos as if to make claim to their heroic luster. Coins issued by Alexander show Alexander in the guise of Herakles on the obverse with Zeus, Herakles' father, on the reverse.[128] Such heroic and divine self-stylization marks a continuity with Near Eastern traditions. But Alexander's choice of heroic models also plays on a nostalgic view of the Greek heroic past, where heroes performed great deeds, fought terrific battles, and hunted fierce animals, and allows the possibility of heroic status for the most noble and valorous of mortal men.

An Eastern-inspired work in a Greek context from the last quarter of the fourth century, the terminus for this study, allows us one last look at the hunt. An inscription from Delphi records the dedication of a monument, which commemorates a lion hunt by Alexander.[129] The Krateros Monument, named for one of Alexander's generals, who died in 321, was erected by Krateros's son after his father's death. Plutarch (*Alex.* 40.4) describes the bronze dedication by Lysippos and Leochares as a depiction of Alexander fighting a lion with the help of dogs, while Krateros approaches to lend aid.[130] According to Plutarch, the group represented a real event, when Alexander hunted a lion to set an example to his men lest they slacken their efforts after their defeat of the Persians.[131] The inscription refers to Alexander as the one who "hunts the bull- devouring lion,"[132] a metaphor for Alexander's conquest of the Persian king. That a Greek or Macedonian monument would employ an Eastern motif, the lion hunt, with its royal and valorous connotations to describe a military conquest is not surprising. We have repeatedly observed the borrowing of hunting motifs from the Near East, although the Greek metaphor usually likens hunting to warfare, not warfare to hunting. Homeric similes are the exception, and it is plausible to think of this work as possessing Homeric flavor since Alexander and his followers were not only familiar with Homer but emulated those heroes. It is ironic, however, that Greek artists employ the very artistic motif used by Eastern potentates to express their invincible power over their enemies in order to commemorate Alexander's conquest of the East and his killing the Persian king in retaliation for the Persian invasion of Greece nearly a century and a half before. Here, battle and hunting merge in a self-conscious gesture of Homeric valor and revenge.[133]

CONCLUSION

Hunting provides us with a tool to understand Greek culture in the archaic and classical periods, particularly in Athens, where the evidence is relatively rich. Interpreting its manifestation in material and written remains furthers our understanding of social and political developments. At its most straightforward level, hunting, particularly hunting on horseback, possesses an aristocratic character, ultimately derived from Near Eastern images of kings hunting from chariots but adapted by Greeks to simply convey elite status and social power. Hunting on horseback then, as it still can today, signaled wealth and leisure, yet hunting on foot was no less glorious because of the taxing physical and mental skills involved. How frequently or with what skill Athenian aristocrats actually hunted in the sixth through fourth century seems immaterial (and is also impossible to know). But the idea certainly appealed to their self-representation and ideology of kaloskagathos as manifested in literature and vase painting, where hunters on foot and horseback hunt boar and deer. As part of this ideology, aristocrats saw themselves as the inheritors of heroic, Homeric culture and status; thus the hunt was also imbued with heroic overtones. The likening of quotidian hunt to heroic or mythical deed finds expression on Attic vases, where everyday and mythical hunting are juxtaposed on the same vessel, inviting comparison by the viewer.

Vase paintings of the hunt increased in number as official aristocratic power waned in Athens during the precipitous changes of the late sixth and early fifth centuries that eventually resulted in a democratic government. I have argued that because aristocrats were the trendsetters and continued to set the social tone even though their political power officially diminished, we may interpret the increased numbers of hunting depictions as reflecting a greater demand for such images, by either elites or nonelites wishing to emulate their social superiors. Hunting thus provided an important venue to assert social dominance and ensure the interests of the elite class in ancient Athens. Imitation of elite behavior by nonelites may, in fact, explain the diminution of hunting imagery after c. 470. With the growing strength of the democratic government and the gradual attenuation of aristocratic dominance, the nonelite appropriation of hunting imagery (together with other aristocratic fashions) may have caused aristocrats to find it less appealing; this results in fewer vessels being produced for either type of consumer, and the substitution of some other item or activity for hunting.

Ample written evidence attests that hunting also served as a pedagogical exercise, a way of schooling men, particularly young men, to fight in battle by practicing on dangerous wild game, such as boar, before engaging with a human opponent. Maturation rites in various parts of Greece reified this concept, using hunting activities to test young men and exalt them to manhood. Firm testimony for initiatory hunting does not exist for Athens, but Attic vase painting suggests a close connection between the two activities—so close, in fact, that hunting is used as a visual metaphor for warfare. Boar and deer hunting required swiftness, steady nerves, strength, and, certainly in the case of boar, courage, and such skills found direct application on the battlefield. Hunting, which can be a heroic activity, according to aristocratic thinking, not only prepares one for warfare but *is* warfare.

Hunting can serve as a metaphor for warfare but the hunt also works in complex, myriad ways at the metaphorical level to express ideas about sexual pursuit and gender roles, for sexual pursuit, whether hetero-or homosexual, always involves a hunt. Ample written testimony likens sexual pursuit to hunting, and pederastic paintings on Attic vases also demonstrate this similarity. Borrowing artistic motifs from hunting compositions, adult male lovers pursue their younger beloved like hunters chasing their quarry. Animal gifts, often captured prey and given by erastes to eromenos, underscore the connection to hunting. The connotations attached to each animal convey desired qualities in either the giver or receiver. Pederastic courtship, like actual hunting, athletics, and warfare, was central to the ideology of Athenian aristocrats, and often took place in gymnasia, where young men trained in the nude to become great athletes and warriors, and at symposia.

Key to understanding the metaphorical use of the hunt is the role reversal that may occur in an actual hunt with a wild animal: a hunter may suddenly find himself in the position of hunted creature, defending his life against an enraged and fierce animal. In the case of warfare, to which hunting is likened, the connection is clear: the opponent is an aggressor, and the move from aggressive position to defensive position can happen rapidly and with dire consequences. As for sexual pursuit, a metaphorical hunt, role reversal is acceptable, even sometimes welcome under certain conditions. Contrary to the customary view, this study has shown that vase painting and literature attest to the acceptable, even desirable, reversibility of roles in pederastic relationships. The same is true for women sexually pursuing women. But in the case of heterosexual relations, only males should pursue females.

Grasping the rules of this metaphorical erotic hunting is profoundly important for social stability and order as evidenced in myths, which present the most complex thematic accumulations of hunting, sexual pursuit, and gender roles. Using negative and positive paradigms, hunting myths reflect societal concerns and expectations, shaped by men, about appropriate gender roles. Hunters who transgress sexually, either by overzealousness, like Aktaion, or by abstinence, such as Kallisto, or by adopting the habits of the opposite sex, as was true for Atalanta, find themselves in tragic circumstances involving a role reversal—one that places the mythological hunter in the role of hunted animal. This text addressed only Aktaion, Kallisto, and Atalanta but we could add others to this list, such as Adonis, Hippolytos, or Orion, and recognize the same patterns.

Adonis, typical of figures of Eastern origin, is feminized in the Greek imagination. Rather than playing the part of the masculine sexual aggressor, Adonis is pursued by Aphrodite and eventually dies in a hunting accident. Thus, the erotic chase that reverses appropriate gender roles for male and female (though Aphrodite is a goddess) results in a role reversal in an actual hunt where the hunter, Adonis, is killed by the boar. Phaedra's pursuit of her stepson, the perpetually chaste hunter Hippolytos, ensures his unhappy end, ensnared in the reins of his own chariot horses. Hippolytos, like Kallisto or Atalanta, fails to accept his sexual maturity; he is pursued, rather than pursuer, and meets his death in a tangled net of reins, items used to restrain animals. This image may amplify Hippolytos's own sexual self-restraint, which ultimately leads to his death. The hunter Orion, like Aktaion, expresses lust toward Artemis and is killed at the goddess's bidding. Atalanta's androgyny, her sexual resistance and gender ambiguity, represents the crystallization of social anxiety, specifically male anxiety, about the blurring of boundaries and confused gender roles. Atalanta behaves as an ephebe, rather than a female, in all her adventures, and when this devotee of Artemis marries, her conduct veers toward another extreme, sexual excess in a forbidden location. This results in a life sentence of chaste hunting in the company of Artemis.

Other types of transgression while hunting also ensure a sad end. Pentheus, like his cousin Aktaion, suffers a terrible fate for offending a god, and the Pentheus myth, like that of Aktaion, is marked by hunting reversals. But the latter is also striking for its numerous sexual inversions. Pentheus, dressed as a female maenad, is tracked down by the maenads, who themselves epitomize gender inversion in their maniacal hunting. They rip Pentheus limb from limb as if they were wild predatory animals attacking their quarry. As the townsmen hunt down the maenads at the end of Euripides' play, the men's weapons prove ineffectual while the women's draw blood. Pentheus's mother, Agave, like Atalanta, wins the trophy of the chase, the head of Pentheus (Eur., *Bacch.* 1198), and comes to a tragic end because of her blasphemy (Eur., *Bacch.* 1298). In this instance, sacrilege, the overstepping of religious rather than gender boundaries, creates the hunting disaster and role reversals: Pentheus mocks the Dionysiac rites, and the maenads are entranced by Dionysos as punishment for their slanderous remarks about Semele. The disaster that befalls those who fail to recognize their place, their appropriate social, religious, and gender roles, is the hallmark of hunting myths, which reflect the social norms established and perpetuated by a patriarchy.

Hunting also occurs in funerary contexts in Attica and elsewhere, where it appears in both straightforward and metaphorical ways. The hunting imagery of classical Attic funerary stelai and white-ground lekythoi echoes the compositions and connotations of other painted hunts, actual and metaphorical, to memorialize the deceased as aristocratic hunter or as a metaphorical amorous hunter, either an erastes or eromenos. One can trace the developmental arc of hunting imagery in the archaic and classical periods from the Athenian hunt—real, mythological, or metaphorical—to hunts depicted in East Greek and Lycian art of the late fifth and early fourth centuries. Here we are in another world, away from the classical polis and in the dynastic realms of local rulers, who joined Eastern hunting imagery with its royal connotations to Athenian iconography and Greek mythology to produce tomb decoration designed to evoke awe and veneration in the viewer. But unlike their Athenian predecessors, these hunts, both real and mythological, operate in a straightforward manner to liken Eastern rulers to the great heroes of the past. Simile, rather than subtle metaphor, is the preferred narrative strategy to convey the idea that rulers are like heroes, whether fighting, abducting, or hunting. Here again, the ruling class employs hunting with its elite connotations to attempt to control perceptions of the nonelites and assure the continuity of their own superior, heroic status even after death. Alexander the Great understood and fully exploited the heroic past to his political advantage, particularly invoking Homeric heroes, such as Achilles with his great hunting prowess, as his models. Comprehending the value of the hunt to convey social power and prestige, Alexander conducted numerous hunts on his travels to demonstrate his courage and link himself to traditions, both Near Eastern and Greek, of royal and aristocratic hunters. The hunt's ability to exalt the everyday individual to the heroic, aristocratic sphere was also not lost on later Romans, who adorned their marble sarcophagi with mythological hunts, including the famed Calydonian boar hunt, perhaps to communicate the notion to future generations that the deceased was like those great heroic hunters of the distant Greek past.

NOTES

1. On this subject, see, e.g., Hölscher 1972. Animal combats are surely meant to signify valor and ferocity, characteristics alluded to in actual human-hunting-animal scenes.

2. Cf., e.g., Neer 1995, 119, 123, 126, though I partially disagree with Neer's claim that the vase is a "closed system," asserting distance from the world. This much is true but vase paintings also refer to the real world, even when depicting mythological events, as myth is a reflection of culture.

3. See, e.g., Stansbury-O'Donnell 1999, 51–53; Steiner 1993, 207, 209–10, 211, 216–19. Steiner 2000, chap. 1, provides an excellent exposition on narrative strategies in vase painting.

4. Schnapp 1989, 81. Cf. also Stansbury-O'Donnell 1999, 124ff.; Steiner 2000, chap. 1; Koch-Harnack 1983, 82, 98, 107, 142, 166–67, 176.

5. E.g., Steiner (1993) examines the meaning created by repeated images on the same vase; Markoe (1989, 90–94, 99) describes the juxtaposition of confronted lions with struggling warriors and of a lion attacking a bull with gods defeating Giants as "pictorial similes" (90); Scheibler 1987, 99, 118; Sourvinou-Inwood 1987, 148–50; and Hoffmann 1967, 14–15, 28.

6. See Black 1981, 72–79, who discusses the "interaction view of metaphor" and how it operates.

7. Ferrari 1997, 4–5. On metaphor (and simile), see, e.g., Davidson 1978, who argues against conventional interpretations that claim that metaphor has meaning in addition to its literal sense.

8. Scheibler 1987, 57–118, esp. 70, 81–82, 87, 90–91.

9. Shapiro 1997.

10. Cf. Schnapp 1997, 11: "Mais les peintres ne se préoccupaient pas d'histoire sociale." While they may not consciously concern themselves with social history, artists surely felt the impact of social changes and sometimes reflected them in their work.

11. Schnapp (1997, 11) acknowledges the invisibility of the black hunter in Greek vase painting.

CHAPTER 1: HUNTING, WARFARE, AND ARISTOCRATS

1. See Koch-Harnack 1983, 153, who makes the same observation about homosexual courtship scenes on Greek vases.
2. Cf. Stein-Hölkeskamp 1992, 40–41; 1989.
3. On Xenophon as a written source for hunting practices, see the evaluation of Schnapp 1973.
4. Xenophon's treatise on hunting, the *Cynegeticus*, outlines many aspects of hunting, including the necessary dogs, equipment, technique, and weather conditions for hunting hares, deer, boar, lions, leopards, lynxes, and bears; the behavior of the prey; and the dangers in hunting them. On Xenophon's *Cynegeticus*, see Schnapp 1997, 56–63, and for the *Cyropaedia*, Schnapp 1997, 144–50. Schnapp (1997, 150–71) also takes up the relationship of hunt and battle in fourth-century literature.
5. Numerous scholars have discussed this issue, including Lonis 1979, 31–33.
6. Jameson (1991, 210–11) notes that both hunters and warriors were in a liminal state; hence Artemis Agrotera, who governed marginal territories, is an apt deity for their veneration. In Roman Sparta, Artemis was honored by several boys' contests connected with hunting; see Kennell 1995, 52–55. Pausanias (1.41.3) relates that after slaughtering a man-killing lion, Alcathoos, son of Pelops, married, succeeded to the kingship of Megara, and built a sanctuary to Artemis Agrotera and Apollo Agraios.
7. Aspects of this story recall that of Meleager and the Calydonian boar hunt. In both instances, a king's son organizes a hunting party to kill a boar ravaging the land, and both sons end up being killed, Atys by a misplaced spear during the hunt and Meleager either in battle after the hunt or by his mother in retaliation for his having killed her brother(s) immediately after the hunt.
8. For hunting in Herodotos, see Schnapp 1997, 63–71.
9. Meuli (1975, 699–729) discusses the credibility of these accounts and finds parallels for this dragnet operation and the integration of a hunting technique with warfare in other cultures and time periods. In her investigation of the Spartans' "beautiful death" at Thermopylae, Loraux (1995, 72) cites Herodotos's description of the desperate last stand (7.226) when Spartans fought with their hands and teeth. As Loraux notes, Aristophanes (*Lys.* 1254–61) likens these furious warriors to boars.
10. The bibliography on the krypteia is vast. See, e.g., Jeanmaire 1939, 551ff. On the problems of using Plutarch as a source for the archaic or classical *agoge*, see Kennell 1995, 31–35, and also Hodkinson 1997. Kennell also discusses the Spartan system of training boys to become warriors in initiatory terms (123–24, 135–37).
11. Kennell 1995, 132; David 1993, 407–10; Vidal-Naquet (1981b, 181–82) points out that not all Spartan males did this. Inscriptions (*IG* V¹ 274, 278, 279) from the sanctuary of Artemis Orthia in Sparta attest to a contest called καθθηρρατόριον, κασσηρατόριν, and καθθηρατόριν, a hunting contest. See Kennell 1995, 52–54, who argues for a late institution of the contest, although Brelich 1969, 175, envisages a much earlier date.
12. See, e.g., David 1993.
13. On the Spartan practice of hunting for sustenance, see David 1993, 398, 400, 405.
14. Noted also by Vidal-Naquet 1986, 118.

15. See Kennell 1995, 76–77.
16. E.g., David 1993, 405–7, 410.
17. See Kennell 1995, 126–29, 135–36.
18. Bremmer (1980, 285) states that the ox recalls both Theseus's and the Athenian ephebes' lifting of a bull.
19. Koehl (1986, 108) suggests that the cup signified that the youth was now eligible to serve as cupbearer at symposia; Bremmer (1980, 285–86) says that the cup simply indicated the youth's admission to the sphere of adult men. How far back in time this rite extended and who comprised the initiates are open to debate. Koehl (1986) speculates that the rite was practiced by the Minoans in Bronze Age Crete. For a summary of interpretations of the three gifts, see Schmitt-Pantel 1992, 79–81.
20. See Kennell 1995, 124–26; David 1993, 401, who discusses hunting and pederasty in Sparta and on Crete; Cartledge 1981; and Bremmer 1980, 282.
21. See Longo 1987, for a full exploration of "rules," both legal and cultural, for hunting. For a comparison of Plato's and Xenophon's views of the hunt, see Schnapp 1997, 162–71.
22. On the date, see Bond 1981, xxx. Bond (1981, 108–9) discusses the archer versus hoplite debate, and its appearance in other texts, and believes that the slur against archers is primarily social; hoplites armed themselves and belonged to a property class in Athens.
23. See Schnapp 1973, 311–12.
24. Schnapp 1997, 268–317; 1988; 1979a; 1979b; Schmitt and Schnapp 1982; Fittschen 1969, 60–67; Schauenburg 1969.
25. There are few nonmythological lion hunts in Attic vase painting (one black-figure, one red-figure), leaving us unable to draw any conclusions about such images. Herakles' struggle against the Nemean lion is, of course, a favorite of Attic vase painters, but because it is mythological, it will not be considered here. An Attic black-figure kyathos of c. 530–520 (Naples, Museo Archeologico Nazionale Stg. 130) bears an ambiguous scene of a man fighting a lion using a sword; like hunters of boar and deer on other contemporary vases, the hunter has a chlamys draped over his left forearm. Adriani (1950, 20) raises the possibility that the figure on the kyathos may be Herakles, but does so tentatively. On the difficulty of distinguishing generic lion hunts from heroic lion hunts, see Schauenburg 1969, 9–10.
26. See, e.g., Brommer, *Heldensage*[3], 310–15.
27. Deer hunts are relatively uncommon until the mid-sixth century, then their numbers soar in the second half of the sixth century, and they are, in fact, the most numerous of all hunting images in any fabric at any time. There are approximately three Protocorinthian, two Corinthian, three Caeretan, three Ionian, and one Boeotian vases, and a single Apulian example in addition to the Attic examples listed in the attached charts.
28. *ABV* 135, 44; *Para* 55; *Addenda*[2] 36. In his discussion of this vase, Schnapp (1997, 234) applies the Platonic distinction between different types of hunting and therefore sees these hunters as ephebes. The problems of such an anachronistic reading are well illustrated elsewhere by Schnapp (223–24), who finds discrepancies between Xenophon's views of hunting and fifth-century vase paintings of the hunt. Cf. also Munich, Staatliche Antikensammlungen 1966 of c. 510, an Attic black-figure kyathos in Schauenburg 1969, Taf. 7. Cf. an Attic amphora of c. 540 in a private

collection in Basel, where mounted hunters converge on two stags and a boar. See Schnapp 1979a, 214, fig. 14.

29. E.g., London, British Museum 88.2–8.112, illustrated in Cook 1981, pl. 106:2. It is noteworthy that the boar was one of three animals sacrificed as part of oath taking at Athens and that Pausanias (5.24.9) relates that athletic competitors at Olympia swore an oath of fair play on pieces of sacrificed boar (ἐπὶ κάπρου κατόμνυσθαι τομίων). The boar is therefore associated with honor and with males. See Cole 1996, 231, who provides the relevant ancient citations for the sacrifice in Athens.

30. New York, *ABV* 189, 5; *Addenda*² 52. London, *ABV* 190, 19; *Addenda*² 52. On the mounted hunt and typical compositions, see Schnapp 1997, 225–36.

31. *ABV* 56, 102; *Para* 23; *Addenda*² 15. See also Copenhagen, Nationalmuseet 959 (62), *ABV* 56, 103, *Addenda*² 15, whose reverse bears three mounted hunters and two panthers. On the mounted hunt, see Durand and Schnapp 1989, 63, 65.

32. Rome, *ABV* 96, 21; *Para* 37; *Addenda*² 26. Naples, *ABV* 252, 1.

33. CUPS: Hamburg, Museum für Kunst und Gewerbe 1908.255, supra n. 31; Copenhagen, Nationalmuseet 959 (62), supra n. 31; Paris, Musée du Louvre G623, *ARV*² 1294, *Addenda*² 359; New York, Metropolitan Museum of Art 41.162.9, *ARV*² 882, 39, *Addenda*² 301; Paris, Musée du Louvre G637, *ARV*² 770, 5, *Addenda*² 287.
AMPHORA: Rome, Museo del Palazzo dei Conservatori 119–39, supra n. 32.
AMPHORA LID: London, British Museum B147, *ABV* 135, 44, *Para* 55, *Addenda*² 36.
HYDRIAE: London, British Museum B304, *ABV* 266, 4, *Para* 117, *Addenda*² 69; Rome, Museo Gregoriano Etrusco Vaticano 16548, *ARV*² 179, 3, *Addenda*² 185.
ASKOI: Philadelphia, University Museum L.64.191 (1889,162), illustrated in Hoffmann 1977, pl. III:3; Bonn, Akademisches Kunstmuseum 90, *ARV*² 776, 1, *Addenda*² 288; Paris, Bibliothèque nationale, Cabinet des Médailles 853, *ARV*² 776, 2, Hoffmann 1977, 12. On the askoi, see Schnapp 1997, 404–16; and Hoffmann 1977.
LEKYTHOS: Swiss private collection, illustrated in Schnapp 1997, 307 no. 280.

34. Schnapp 1997, 487 no. 99. This directly counters Burkert 1983, 75, who claims that the hunter's quarry must be male and aggressive to serve as a father substitute so as to avoid the hunter's feeling sympathy for his prey.

35. *ABV* 190, 18.

36. *ABV* 190, 19; *Addenda*² 52. See chapter 2 for further discussion of this cup.

37. Jongkees-Vos 1971. Schnapp (1997, 257–61) interprets the Centaur Painter's hunting images as metaphors for the reversibility of hunter and prey.

38. Durand and Schnapp 1989, 65; Schmitt and Schnapp 1982, 65; Schnapp 1979b, 35. For the Oxford lekythos, supra n. 34.

39. *ABV* 530, 69; *Addenda*² 132.

40. Schnapp 1979a, 213, fig. 13.

41. *ARV*² 174, 15; *Addenda*² 184.

42. *ARV*² 179, 3; *Addenda*² 185.

43. *Para* 217; *Addenda*² 120.

44. Steiner 1993.

45. On bearded males signifying adults and unbearded signaling "ephebes," see Frontisi-Ducroux and Lissarrague 1990, 217. But contra: Castriota 1992, 159. Schnapp (1997) builds his argument around hunting and age distinctions, applying Plato's

hunting categories enunciated in *Leges* 823b–824c to Attic vase painting. According to Schnapp, archaic hunting scenes depict ephebes engaged in one aspect of paideia; such images yield to those of solitary, heroic adult hunters in the classical period. Schnapp acknowledges the difficulty of talking about ephebes before the fourth century (458–59) but does not address the problem of applying fourth-century texts to the earlier paintings.

46. *ARV*² 770, 5; *Addenda*² 287.

47. On shields, spears, swords, and occasionally rocks as typical of hoplite warfare, see Anderson 1991, 15–22; Snodgrass 1967, 48–88. Cf. also an Attic black-figure lekythos in Cracow (University 288) of c. 500–480 that shows a departure for the hunt in which the mounted hunters carry shields. See Bulas 1935, pl. 7:6a–b.

48. It should be noted that one Attic black-figure cup of c. 550–530 (Rome, Museo Nazionale Etrusco di Villa Giulia 74981; fig.15) that depicts the Calydonian boar hunt (the wounded hunter beneath the boar and the dog on the boar's back secure the identification) has a mounted hoplite and hunters carrying shields, and Calydonian boar hunters carry shields on a Paestan bell krater of c. 330–310 (London, British Museum F154). See Schnapp 1997, 303 nos. 273, 374; 521 no. 428. There is a single instance of hoplite weaponry in a nonmythological archaic hunting depiction prior to c. 520: a hunter wields a shield against a deer on an Attic black-figure cup of c. 540 by the Centaur Painter (Utrecht I.A.245). See Jongkees-Vos 1971, 13–16, pls. 7–8. For hunters with hoplite weapons on Protocorinthian vases, see Schnapp 1997, 186, 480 nos. 23, 25.

49. Schnapp 1997, 232, 492 no. 145.

50. *ARV*² 151, 52; *Addenda*² 180.

51. Assyrian reliefs also depict armed kings hunting since, "C'était l'habitude en Assyrie . . . de n'établir aucune distinction entre un exercice de poursuite du gibier et une campagne guerrière" (Ferron 1993, 179). On the mixing of hunter and warrior features, see Schnapp 1997, 243–46, who does not explore the visual metaphor and simply explains hunters armed as hoplites as references to heroes. Schnapp (1997, 245–46, 495 nos. 171–72) pairs two Attic black-figure lekythoi of c. 500 (Cracow University 288; and Basel, private collection, *ABV* 474, 16bis, *Para* 215, *Addenda*² 119) as related vessels indicating two moments of a single story: departing warriors and returning hunters.

52. *ABV* 266, 1; *Para* 117; *Addenda*² 69.

53. *ABV* 276, 3.

54. Supra n. 48.

55. Cf. Hoffmann 1997, 28 and fig. 10, a scene of pygmies battling cranes in which one pygmy wears a chlamys held out as if it were a shield as do our hunters, and another holds an actual shield.

56. *ARV*² 431, 47.

57. *ARV*² 336, 16; *Addenda*² 218.

58. Durand and Schnapp 1989, 66, fig. 96. For the identification of solitary boar hunters and heroes, see Schnapp 1997, 379–90.

59. A chlamys held as if it were a shield occurs in another mythological context and one connected to hunting: the capture of Dolon, who is disguised as a wolf on an Attic red-figure cup by the Dokimasia Painter of c. 460, now in St. Petersburg, State Hermitage Museum 653 (*ARV*² 413, 23; *Para* 512; *Addenda*² 233). Here, the "hunter"

on the right wears his chlamys in the hunting fashion. Schnapp (1997, 363, 367, 400–401) claims that the solitary deer hunts are meant to recall images of Herakles and the Keryneian hind, and acknowledges the ability of the boar hunt to heroize its quotidian hunter.

60. *ABV* 306, 39; *Addenda*² 81.

61. *ARV*² 1294; *Addenda*² 359. Cf. Paris, Musée du Louvre G22, supra n. 50.

62. *ARV*² 351, 8; *Addenda*² 221. The palm tree is puzzling here; does it indicate an Eastern location for the hunt?

63. *ABV* 182, 4; *Para* 340; *Addenda*² 186.

64. *ARV*² 126, 26; *Addenda*² 176. Cf. Würzburg, Martin von Wagner Museum der Universität 473 (*ARV*² 92, 65; *Addenda*² 171) of c. 510.

65. On the Tyrannicides group, see, e.g., Taylor 1991; Stewart 1990, 135–36, pls. 227–31; Boardman 1985, 24–25, figs. 3–9; Robertson 1975, 185–87; Brunnsåker 1971; Ridgway 1970, 79–83, figs. 115–17.

66. Taylor 1991, 36–76.

67. Taylor 1991, 36–70.

68. *ARV*² 413, 16; *Addenda*² 233.

69. Anderson (1985, 25) perceives a paucity of hunting scenes altogether after 510. Contra: Durand and Schnapp 1989, 65–66. On the existence of the cavalry in archaic Athens and its composition from the aristocracy, see Bugh 1988, 3–38. Vickers and Gill 1994, 35–37; Stein-Hölkeskamp 1989, 110ff.; and Davies 1971, xxv–xxvi also note the association of horses and horse sports with the aristocracy.

70. Durand and Schnapp 1989, 66; Schnapp 1979b, 58.

71. Schnapp 1979b, 50; Schnapp 1979a, 214.

72. Cf. Ferrari 1997, 5; Hoffmann 1997, 21.

73. On the chariot as an element situating a scene in an epic context, see Lissarrague 1990b, 98.

74. The combination of boar hunt with dog and hares on the secondary frieze recalls Protocorinthian compositions. Schnapp 1979a, 204–5.

75. Supra n. 28.

76. I thank Bettina Kreuzer for reminding me of this point.

77. *ABV* 266, 4; *Para* 117; *Addenda*² 69.

78. Supra n. 73. See also Sinos 1993, 75–78; Lissarrague 1990b, 98; and Verbanck-Piérard 1981, 15–22.

79. Cf. Burow 1989, 39, who notes that hunt depictions in the predelle of Antimenes Painter (and Circle) hydriae could be viewed together with warriors' departure scenes as references to the ideal of the wealthy aristocratic male.

80. *ARV*² 600, 17; *Addenda*² 266.

81. Hoppin and Gallatin 1926, pl. 4:13, 14.

82. Cf. Stansbury-O'Donnell 1999, 124ff., on "paradeigmatic extension."

83. Mingazzini (1971, 23) describes the youth on the interior of the Villa Giulia cup as an "efebo."

84. See also Lonis 1979, 27–36, who traces the agonistic parallels between athletics, hoplite warfare, and hunting.

85. Supra n. 63.

86. For other examples of hunting elements included in warriors' departure scenes, see, e.g., London, British Museum E448 (*ARV*² 992, 65; *Para* 437; *Addenda*² 311),

where a dog stands behind the hoplite, and Tübingen, Eberhard-Karls-Universität, Antikensammlung des Archäologischen Instituts S/10 1344 ([E104], *ARV*² 603, 35; *Addenda*² 267), on which the hoplite figure is dressed as a hunter. Both are illustrated in Lissarrague 1989, figs. 61–62.

87. Leiden, Rijksmuseum van Oudheden II 167 [PC63], the Antimenes Painter's name vase (*ABV* 266, 1; *Para* 117; *Addenda*² 69); formerly Sotheby's, London; Rome, Museo Gregoriano Etrusco Vaticano 426 (*ABV* 266, 2; *Para* 117; *Addenda*² 69); Geneva, Baron Edmond de Rothschild (*ABV* 268, 30; *Para* 118); Copenhagen, Thorvaldsens Museum H554 (*ABV* 267, 20; *Addenda*² 69); Munich, Staatliche Antikensammlungen 1694 (*ABV* 266, 5); London, British Museum B304 (*ABV* 266, 4; *Para* 117; *Addenda*² 69); Ex-Küsnacht, Hirschmann Collection G9 (*Para* 119; *Addenda*² 69); Norwich Castle Museum 72.20 (*ABV* 268, 23). See Burow 1989, 80 nos. 11, 14; 86 nos. 59, 60, 62; 91 nos. 107, 109; 98 no. U4; 99 no. U5; Taf.11–13, 16, 59, 60, 62, 105, 107, 144, 145. Cf. also Los Angeles, County Museum of Art 50.8.5 (A5933.50–11, *ABV* 277, 6; *Addenda*² 72); and London, British Museum B319 (*Para* 124; *Addenda*² 73), both Attic black-figure hydriae of c. 530 attributed to the Manner of the Antimenes Painter. Burow makes no mention of the Los Angeles vase. And see Naples, Museo Archeologico Nazionale H 2777 of c. 530–510 (*ABV* 276, 3) illustrated in Adriani 1950, Tav. 38: V3, on which boar hunting is paired with the departure of a chariot and Herakles' combat with Kyknos. An exception to the rule of the hunt in the predella is the Norwich Castle Museum hydria on which a stag hunt appears on the shoulder above the main image of Herakles wrestling the Nemean lion, and the predella is instead occupied by an animal frieze.

88. Compositional similarities of these deer hunts to those of the Centaur Painter have led Jongkees-Vos (1971, 21) to propose that some relationship existed between the two painters, either a familial one or a professional one or both.

89. Supra n. 87.

90. Supra n. 87.

91. *ABV* 282, 2; *Para* 124; *Addenda*² 74.

92. *ABV* 256, 18; *Addenda*² 66. Cf. also the Attic black-figure hydriae: Würzburg, Martin von Wagner Museum der Universität 307 (infra n. 95); Orvieto, Museo Civico, Collection Faina 69 (infra n. 95); and Princeton, University Art Museum y171 (*ABV* 260, 34).

93. Supra n. 87.

94. Simon 1983, 99. Others link the popularity of fountainhouse scenes on Attic hydriae in the last third of the sixth century to Peisistratos's construction of the Enneakrounos in the Agora c. 520. See Burow 1989, 74–75. Bettina Kreuzer suggests to me that the girls may represent *korai*, signifying the aristocratic household.

95. Noted also by Schnapp 1979b, 54–55. Schnapp (1997, 229) briefly remarks on the program of the Antimenes Painter hydriae, which he links to the world of the ephebe. Deer hunts appear together with chariot scenes and hoplites on an Attic black-figure hydria of c. 520 in Los Angeles (County Museum of Art 50.8.5; supra n. 87) and another in Würzburg (Martin von Wagner Museum der Universität 307), also assigned by Beazley to the Manner of the Antimenes Painter (*ABV* 276, 4), and with a chariot scene and hoplite battle on yet another in Orvieto (Museo Civico, Collection Faina 69, *ABV* 140, 4; *Addenda*² 38).

96. *Para* 187, 3; *Addenda*² 111; Durand and Schnapp 1989, fig. 92.

97. Würzburg, *ARV*² 92, 65; *Addenda*² 171. Paris, *ARV*² 92, 68; *Addenda*² 171. New York, *ARV*² 92, 66; Schnapp 1997, 528 no. 496.

98. Moretti 1966, n.p.

99. Cf. David 1993, 394, who makes the same observation for a relief amphora from Sparta. A different view, and one that I clearly disagree with, is offered by Lissar-rague 1989, 43, who discusses the "essential opposition" of hunting and hoplite warfare.

100. See Scheibler 1987, 86, 88–89, 92ff., for heroic scenes as models for quotidian lives. Scheibler points to Bacchylides to support her points (93). See also Steiner 1997, 162.

101. Cf. Laffineur 1983, 39, who claims that Mycenaean weapons are ornamented with hunt scenes to confer the aggressiveness and courage of the hunter on the bearer, thus ensuring success in battle.

102. *ARV*² 427, 4; *Para* 374; *Addenda*² 235; Buitron-Oliver 1995a, pl. 9.

103. See Schnapp 1997, 54–58; Lonsdale 1990; Schnapp-Gourbeillon 1981.

104. Schnapp-Gourbeillon 1981, 104–31.

105. I thank both Olga Palagia and Bettina Kreuzer for this observation.

106. See Scheibler 1987, 87–88, who argues for a link between hoplite representations on late-sixth-century vases and the contemporary social situation.

107. Forrest (1966, 183–4) speculates that while the tyranny controlled affairs in Athens proper, much of the Athenian population would still have been governed in most matters by local aristocrats. Cf. David 1993, 394–95, on hunting as an aristocratic leisure occupation in Sparta.

108. E.g., Xen, *Ath. Pol.* 1.2. Bryant 1996, 81; Hanson 1991, 5–6.

109. τοὺς δὲ βίον ἱκανὸν κεκτημένους περὶ τὴν ἱππικὴν καὶ τὰ γυμνάσια καὶ τὰ κυνηγέσια καὶ τὴν φιλοσοφίαν ἠνάγκασαν διατρίβειν. See also Ste. Croix 1981, 125, 283. Miller (1997, 252) enumerates the traditional honorific activities of the Greek elite in the archaic period: "exercise, symposia, competition in pan-Hel-lenic games, growing hair long, marrying outside the polis, making conspicuous dedications, cock-fighting, engaging in homosexual relations, raising horses, build-ing large funerary monuments." See also Stein-Hölkeskamp 1992, 41; 1989, 104ff.

110. Bryant 1996, 49–51, 153; Mitchell 1996, 91; Raaflaub 1983, 526; Cartledge 1977, 23; Snodgrass 1967, 58–59, 61, 62, 77. See Sage 1996, 26–28, 31–32, who also discusses Arist., *Pol.* 1297b16–28.

111. For a recent study that challenges the traditional view of the symposion, see Stein-Hölkeskamp 1992.

112. David (1993, 403) discusses the use of hunting to consolidate aristocratic power and political power in Sparta. See also Scheibler 1987, 109.

113. Spartan youths trained in athletics and hunting, both considered appropriate preparation for warfare. See Plut., *Lyc.* 16.5. On athletics as good training for war-fare as well as for hunting, see Bérard 1986, 196; Bažant 1981, 30. Mitchell (1996, 94) points out that "peaceful sporting competition of Greek festivals such as the Olympic Games explicitly prepared competitors for the bloody sport of Greek battle" but also cautions that "the analogy between hoplite battles and sporting contests can easily be overstressed" (95).

114. Ogden (1996, 128–29) assembles the primary evidence. But see Golden 1998,

23–28, who argues against a close identification of athletics and warfare in ancient Greece.

115. Ogden 1996, 129; Ridley 1979.

116. Whether this was Kleisthenes' intent or not is disputed. See Arnheim 1977, 139–40; Forrest 1966, 197–200. It is noteworthy that the Alkmeonidai and the Philaidai were renowned for their skill with horses (see Bugh 1988, 35), that most aristocratic of symbols, and that the greatest number of hunting scenes, many of which are conducted on horseback, at least for deer hunts, date from the period just after the Kleisthenic reforms that benefited one of these families.

117. E.g., Forrest 1966, 203, 209–10.

118. Forrest 1966, 209.

119. Arnheim 1977, 131–32; Raaflaub 1983, 519.

120. Cf. Bažant 1987, 38; and Hoffmann 1974, 210–11, who rightly states that the formerly aristocratic pursuits, including hunting, became popular with the bourgeoisie and this explains the profusion of sports and hunting imagery on vases. Raabflaub (1983, 531–32) remarks of fifth-century Athens: "Many Athenians were small, independent businessholders and craftsmen. . . . Like any other citizen who had to work hard for his living, they may have admired and aimed at imitating the aristocratic ideal of leisure . . . democracy at least partially adopted the aristocratic point of view. . . . The ideal, which was never formulated or fully realized, probably was that in democracy every citizen should be enabled to do what aristocrats had always done—namely to devote most of their energy and time to politics and public service." Raaflaub goes on to point out that "this very ideal . . . clearly refuted the political implications of the aristocratic viewpoint. For it explicitly and fully recognized all citizens . . . in their capacity as citizens." And on p. 534: "Generally speaking, values implanted themselves only if they were rooted in the lifestyle, habits, values, and characteristics of the aristocracy. The positive typology of the free man, therefore, had to be close to that of the nobleman."

121. But see Arnheim 1977, 137–38, who discusses Hdt. 5.70 as evidence for friendly relations between the tyranny and Isagoras. Certainly, political concessions were made on both sides. See Stewart 1986, 67.

122. E.g., Bowra 1964, 100–103, 148–49, 158, 394, 400.

123. Stewart (1986, 60–61, 65, 69) refers to the kouros as "the ideal of youthful kalokagathia" (61) and as a "generalized aristocratic symbol" (65). Markoe (1989, 107) discusses aristocratic Athenian families' adoption of Eastern motifs to express dynastic authority; somewhat differently, Miller (1997, 251) believes that the Athenian elite adopted Persian motifs to express their social status.

124. Scheibler (1987, 109) notes that kalokagathia competition was retained in the postarchaic period as a relic of aristocratic life. See also Stein-Hölkeskamp 1989, 139–53, on relations between the aristocracy and tyranny in Athens; and Davies 1971, xvii–xviii, who discusses the aristocrats' efforts to build goodwill, most conspicuously in their performance of liturgies, and he points out, "the influence wielded on public affairs in classical Athens by the deployment of personal wealth—in a word, property-power—cannot at any time be dismissed as negligible."

125. Stewart (1986, 69–70) rightly points out that the diminution in funerary monu-

ments and kouroi can be explained by the new democratic constitution but vase painting is a different matter altogether since it is relatively inexpensive, plentiful, and unostentatious.

126. Bažant (1987, 34) also notes a surge in the popularity of combat sports c. 500 in Attic vase painting and a subsequent decline in numbers in the fifth century. Might this be explained by the same phenomenon?

127. Supra n. 123.

128. Cf. Philipp 1968, 94–97, who argues for the independence of the Greek artist but acknowledges the restrictions of supply and demand.

129. Vickers and Gill 1994.

130. Vickers and Gill 1994, 81. They cite Vitruvius (8.6.11), who indicates a preference for ceramic rather than silver vessels because of the effect on the taste.

131. Contra: Pleket 1969, 293, who also disagrees with Vidal-Naquet's definition of the ephebe in the fifth and fourth centuries.

132. Vidal-Naquet 1986, 147. And see also Vidal-Naquet 1988b, 391, where he discusses the relationship between myth and reality with regard to the hunt as initiation.

133. Scheibler (1987, 100ff.) agrees to an early date for some form of the ephebeia and seems to accept Vidal-Naquet's arguments. She then associates Attic black-figure belly amphorae with ephebic activities, particularly the Oschophoria, which she states was instituted in the late sixth century B.C.

134. Winkler 1990, 25. Vidal-Naquet (1988b, 396) claims that the ephebes of the city were eighteen to twenty years old, while the ephebes of the phratry were sixteen to eighteen. Reinmuth (1952, 39) believes that the ephebes were sixteen to eighteen years old. See also Loraux 1975, 4–12.

135. Reinmuth (1971, 2) claimed an inscription published in 1967 (Reinmuth's no. 1, p. 1) as the earliest known ephebic inscription, dating 361/0. However, Mitchel (1975) argues that the two stones composing the inscription are from two different stelai and that the date of the portion concerning the ephebes is the mid-330s. Parker (1996, 253 n. 123) reports Reinmuth's view to be generally rejected.

136. Reinmuth 1971, 124–25. See Pélékidis 1962, 7ff., for a summary and bibliography. In c. 355, Xenophon (*Poroi* 4.51–52) suggests ways for Athens to better fund its gymnasia training for ephebes, and he notes that ephebes race, train, and do guard duty. According to Sekunda 1990, 151–52, Xenophon (4.52) refers to the Athenian ephebeia, and because of his use of *trophe* Xenophon implies that gymnasia training was not part of the ephebeia.

137. Wilamowitz 1985, 193–94.

138. E.g., Winkler 1990, 31; Vidal-Naquet 1986, 106; Rhodes 1981, 494; Moore 1975, 275; Reinmuth 1971, 138; Reinmuth 1952, who offers a summary of previous scholarship on the ephebeia on p. 34 n. 2; Lofberg 1925, 330–35; Roussel 1921. See now Parker 1996, 253.

139. Rhodes 1981, 495; Ridley 1979, 531–34; Reinmuth 1971, 128–32. Mitchel (1964, 344–45 n. 34) advocates a middle ground in terms of dating between Wilamowitz and Reinmuth. Reinmuth discusses the putative extent of Lykourgos's reforms.

140. Reinmuth 1971, 133. Reinmuth also discusses the developments in the ephebeia after the classical period.

141. Winkler 1990, 22 n.1.

142. Rhodes 1981, 503, 507. But see Winkler 1990, 32. Vidal-Naquet (1988b, 397–98)

claims that by the time Xenophon was writing in the mid-fourth century, the ephebeia was not a universal experience for all young citizens. Vidal-Naquet points to Thucydides, the Sacred Band of Thebes, and the fact that the participants in the Spartan krypteia, according to Jeanmaire, became *hippeis*. But see Winkler 1990, 34 n. 39, who cautions against using the Spartan krypteia as a comparative model to reconstruct the Athenian ephebeia. Winkler (1990, 28, 32) claims that before Lykourgos, participation in the ephebeia was a voluntary matter, and a prerogative of the wealthy.

143. The Acharnai stele was first published by Robert 1938, 296–316, and subsequently by Daux 1965; and Daux 1971. Green 1996, 239–41, provides the most recent discussion.

144. See Siewert 1977. Cole (1996, 234) discusses male oath ritual and notes that typical of oaths, including the Athenian ephebic oath, is the dependence on the success of its citizens, and the agricultural products of the ephebic oath are one way to measure this success.

145. Vidal-Naquet 1986, 97; Rhodes 1981, 494.

146. Siewert 1977. Siewert argues that certainly Thucydides 1.144.4, 2.37.3 and maybe Sophocles, *Antigone* 663–71 and Aischylos, *Persae* 956–62 allude to the ephebic oath. He suggests a date of origin for the ephebic oath approximately 100 to 120 years before hoplite warfare, perhaps even before the Solonian reforms. Cf. Moreau 1954, 341, who recognizes the ephebic oath in fragments of Aristophanes' *Horai*.

147. McCulloch and Cameron 1980.

148. Winkler 1990, 29; Lofberg 1925, 330–31. On possible peripoloi in vase painting, see Lissarrague 1990b, 203–4.

149. Ridley 1979, 533; Lofberg 1925, 330–31. As scholars have pointed out, Plutarch apparently thought that the ephebeia existed during Alcibiades' lifetime (*Alc.* 15.7).

150. Vidal-Naquet 1986, 107. The word is also used of foreigners in the service of Athens.

151. Reinmuth 1952, 36. The *OCD*³ 25, however, places Aischines' birth in c. 397, which would make his ephebic service at the age of eighteen even earlier.

152. Lofberg 1925, 333–34.

153. Lofberg 1925, 334.

154. Reinmuth 1971, 136–37.

155. Vidal-Naquet 1981a.

156. Brelich (1961, 53–59) offers a full list of sources, together with a consideration of the historical background of this legend.

157. On the myth, see Vidal-Naquet 1986, 109–11. Halliday (1926, 179) claims that if the phantom warrior in the black goatskin was seen, then Melanthos did not win by trickery, which would dissolve the connection between the myth and the Apatouria. But, as Halliday acknowledges, the earliest written sources for the story include the "trick" of a diversion and omit the vision of Dionysos Melanaigis and so the aition for the festival is secured. Diogenes Laertius (1.74) relates that Pittacus of Mytilene agreed to fight Phrynon in single combat to settle a war between Mytilene and Athens. Pittacus concealed a net beneath his shield with which he entangled and killed Phrynon, then recovered the territory.

158. Schol. to Ar., *Ach.* 146; Hesychius, s.v. *koureotis*. Brelich (1961, 58–59) discusses

the possible divinities honored by the Apatouria. See also, e.g., Lambert 1993, 143–89, who refutes Vidal-Naquet's association of the Melanthos myth with the festival (149–52); Winkler 1990, 24–25, who also discusses Parthenopaios as a mythological model for the boy at the Apatouria; Sergent 1986, 17–18; Vidal-Naquet 1986, 98–99, 108–9; Cole 1984, 233–44; Schmitt 1977; Labarbe 1953; and Deubner 1932, 232–34.

159. Vidal-Naquet 1986, 110.

160. Roussel 1941.

161. Vidal-Naquet 1986, 112–22; Roussel 1921. And see Vidal-Naquet 1988b, 392. Contra: Lonis 1979, 32–33, who argues that this is a false dichotomy; rather the contrast in types of hunting is between the formative virtues of each type of hunting. Schnapp (1979b) argues that education is based on the opposition between ephebe and hoplite, which are at opposing ends of the social code, mediated by rites of passage. But does Schnapp refer to all education or only Athenian education? Does he assume a formal ephebeia in every city? Vidal-Naquet (1988b, 396) posits that cities would have individual forms of ephebeia. Schnapp (1979b, 42) points out that Xenophon's *Cyropaedia*, written in the fourth century, seems to champion the strategies of the ephebic hunt, and Schnapp links this to contemporary historical developments, specifically the use of mercenaries, arguing that cities no longer needed to codify the hunt as preparation for warfare. See the cautionary note of Murray 1983, 199, regarding the application of evidence from Sparta and Crete to Athens.

162. But see Loraux 1995, 4: "anyone who wishes to read the Greeks, must perform mental operations that are more complex than merely verifying a table of antithetical categories again and again"; and also Ma 1994.

163. *IG* II² 3606. Contra Maxwell-Stuart 1970, but see Vidal-Naquet 1986, 124 n. 31, for a response. On the border location of ephebic service as indicative of initiatory activity, see Moreau 1992, 215.

164. Philostr., *VS* 2.550. The black chlamydes were replaced by white ones in the second century A.D. thanks to the patronage of Herodes Atticus. See Roussel 1941.

165. Vidal-Naquet 1986, 119. Ma (1994, 49–59) offers an actual, not mythological, example of a black hunter but also goes on to discuss the methodological problems of structuralism (and empiricism).

166. Boardman 1992a.

167. Roussel 1941.

168. Vidal-Naquet 1986, 114.

169. Vidal-Naquet 1981a, 156–58; Deubner 1932, 142–47.

170. Also noted by Lambert 1993, 143–89; and Winkler 1990, 35.

171. Plut., *Thes.* 23; Vidal-Naquet 1986, 114–16; Deubner 1932, 142–43.

172. Plut., *Thes.* 23; Simon 1983, 89–92; Parke 1977, 77–81.

173. On the City Dionysia, see Deubner 1932, 138–42.

174. Pickard-Cambridge 1968, 60–62. In his discussion of the inception of the City Dionysia in Athens, Parker (1996, 93–95) notes the common belief that the festival was established after Eleutherai was incorporated into Athens and cites Paus. 1.38.8 as the usually indicated source. In this passage, Pausanias remarks that Eleutherai used to be on the border of Boeotia and Attica but that after its incorporation, its image of Dionysos was taken to Athens. Parker also says that

Eleutherai claimed to be the birthplace of Dionysos and his cult. Melanaigis may have been located at Eleutherai (94). Vidal-Naquet, as indicated above, has already discussed the importance of Eleutherai's border location to the aitiological myth of the Apatouria. I wish to point it out here in connection to the ephebes' participation in the City Dionysia and to the god in particular.

175. Goldhill 1990, 99.

176. Goldhill (1990, 105–13) understands these orphans as ephebes, interprets this evidence as a demonstration of the reaffirmation of the orphans' or ephebes' ties to the city, and claims that these ties are expressed in a military way.

177. See, e.g., Schnapp 1997, 72–122.

178. Loraux 1995, 109–15, explores the association of the *brochos* (net) with betrayal and cunning in the context of female strangulation.

179. Clytemnestra's betrayal: *Ag.* 1116–17, 1187, 1233–34, 1337, 1394–95, 1402, 1446, 1545, 1643. Other hunting imagery in the trilogy: *Ag.* 129, 118–24, 360–64, 693, 1257, 1279; *Cho.* 479, 970–75, 990, 993, 994. Especially common are net images, such as *Ag.* 1116, where ἄρκυς is used to refer to Agamemnon's shroud; *Ag.* 360, where Troy is captured within a net (δουλείας γάγγαμον); and *Ag.* 1381–82, where Agamemnon is captured in a net. See Ferrari 1997, 16–17, 25–26.

180. *Cho.* 278, 335.

181. *Cho.* 924, 1054. See also Vidal-Naquet 1988a, who also discusses hunting imagery in the *Eumenides*; and Dumortier 1935, 71–87.

182. See also Pentheus's desire and attempt to hunt down the maenads (228, 231, 721–22, 1019), Dionysos's behavior toward Pentheus (804), the maenads' activities (838, 869–70, 1006, 1171, 1183, 1190, 1196, 1199, 1237–38), Pentheus's fate (847, 955, 1202, 1204–5 where Pentheus is taken by the chase, ἠγρεύσαμεν, not with nets), and Dionysos as hunter (1146, 1191). See Seaford 1996, 230, commentary to lines 1020–23 for further instances; Vidal-Naquet 1988a, 145, who points out that the *Bacchae*'s omophagy confuses hunting and sacrifice; and Segal 1982, who also discusses the hunt and sacrifice (23, 40) and states that the hunt is regarded as the key metaphor of the *Bacchae* by many scholars (32).

183. See Vidal-Naquet 1988c. Di Benedetto 1978, energetically responds to Vidal-Naquet's argument (first published in 1971).

184. Cf. Vidal-Naquet 1988b, 399–401, who also discusses the *Philoctetes* in n. 143; Schnapp 1979b, 38–40; and Zeitlin 1978, 160ff.

185. See Burnett 1986.

186. Goldhill 1990, 119–23. Vidal-Naquet (1988b, 400) also points out that Neoptolemos is elsewhere called Pyrrhos, e.g., Eur., *Andr.* 1135, schol. Pind., *Pyth.* 2.127, who was the inventor of pyrrhic, also the name of an armed dance performed by young warriors. This dance, according to Vidal-Naquet, is equivalent to the ephebic oath.

187. Contra: Goldhill 1990, 122.

188. Rhodes 1981, 508.

189. Winkler 1990, 20–62. Contra: Parker 1996, 254–55 n.127; Vidal-Naquet 1988b, 400–401.

190. Winkler 1990, 54–61. Winkler (1990, 22, 43–54) also uses visual evidence to support his argument. He believes that the Pronomos Vase of the late fifth or early fourth century (Naples, Museo Archeologico Nazionale 3240, *ARV*[2] 1336, 1; *Para*

480; *Addenda*[2] 365) depicts chorus members as ephebes, that is, full-grown but beardless, and Winkler also sees ephebes in the company of Dionysos in other vase paintings, including the Attic red-figure column krater of c. 500–490 in Basel (Antikenmuseum und Sammlung Ludwig BS 415), and on the Peiraeus relief (Athens, National Museum 1500) to support his interpretation. But we have noted that beardlessness is a common element in Attic red-figure and may not indicate age distinctions. In n. 70, Winkler responds to Vidal-Naquet's objections to the Pronomos Vase as illustrative of ephebes. For other vase paintings that display ephebic orchestral competitions, see Malagardis 1988.

191. Paris, Musée du Louvre, Éléonte 407: ABV 635, 42; Villard 1954, 99–100, pl. 113: 7, 9–10. Paris, Musée du Louvre C10422: ABV 636, 53; Villard 1954, 100, pl. 113: 8, 11. Paris, Musée du Louvre, Éléonte 14: ABV 633, 12; Villard 1954, 98–99, pl. 112:5, 8, 11. Villard refers to the interior figure as an "éphébe."

192. ABV 641, 118.

193. ARV[2] 324, 61; *Addenda*[2] 215.

194. Hunting also appears in close conjunction with drinking on one Attic red-figure cup of c. 510 by the Euergides Painter from Vulci, now in Würzburg (Martin von Wagner Museum der Universität 473; supra n. 97). On the obverse, an unarmed nude beardless youth wearing only a chlamys over his outstretched left arm looks on as a panther attacks the back of a fallen doe. Three nude youths, one with a chalmys over his left arm, cavort around a drinking vat; one carries a drinking horn, one reaches into the vat, and the chlamys-bearing figure moves as if dancing. On the interior is a beardless nude youth with chlamys over his left arm and a walking stick in his right hand. This hunting differs from the other images in that the panther is the hunter rather than the human, and while Dionysos is not specified here, we might conjecture his "presence" in the activity of drinking. Are we to understand the youth with chlamys as the same figure in all three scenes?

195. *Para* 65; *Addenda*[2] 43.

196. ABV 150, 8; *Para* 63; *Addenda*[2] 42. Another type of hunting appears in close proximity to a Dionysiac scene and athletics (wrestlng) on an aryballos attributed to the Amasis Painter in New York (Metropolitan Museum of Art 62.11.11, *Para* 66–67; *Addenda*[2] 45). Dionysos and two dancing satyrs decorate the handle; the top frieze of the body includes wrestlers and a man reining in two rearing horses surrounded by onlookers; the bottom frieze is filled by a bull being attacked by two lions, while two beardless males carrying spears and wearing only chlamydes approach the struggling animals. A draped male with spear stands behind one of the nude youths. In this case, however, the animal combat motif, a type of hunt, clearly derives from Near Eastern iconography, as demonstrated by Markoe 1989.

CHAPTER 2: EROS AND THE HUNT

1. The bibliography on pederasty and homosexuality in Athens is vast. Schnapp (1981) elegantly and succinctly summarizes the tradition of previous scholarship on homosexuality in Greece up until the time of Dover 1978 (reprinted in 1989). See also Hupperts 1988; and Patzer 1982, 11–43, who also examines the problems and limitations of the term *homosexuality* to describe Greek practices (43–67).

2. E.g., Dover 1989; Patzer 1982, 67–125; Buffière 1980, 49–61; Dover 1964, 36–38.

3. E.g., Ogden 1996; Sergent 1993; Buffière 1980, 49–61.

4. E.g., Sutton 1992, 17; Bremmer 1990, 143–45; Shapiro 1981, 142; Dover 1964, 38–39.
5. E.g., Shapiro 1992, 53; Bremmer 1990; Shapiro 1981, 140–42; Bremmer 1980.
6. E.g., Cohen 1991, 171–202.
7. E.g., Koch-Harnack 1983, 34–48.
8. Patzer 1982, 67–125.
9. E.g., Shapiro 1992, 58–63.
10. Koch-Harnack (1983, 17) opposes the use of the term *Liebesgeschenk* because of its lack of specificity. On gift giving in general and its implications and obligations, see Koch-Harnack (24–28). On hunt and the erotic sphere, see Schnapp 1997, 247–57, 325ff.
11. Koch-Harnack 1983, 25–26.
12. From the evidence of Solon's poetry, and references to Solonic legislation prohibiting slaves to engage in pederasty or to wrestle in gymnasia (Plut., *Sol.* 1), scholars have argued that pederasty was an aristocratic social institution in Athens as early as the late seventh century. See, e.g., Sergent 1993, 154; Koch-Harnack 1983, 40; and Dover 1964, 37.
13. See Koch-Harnack 1983, 27–28, for social status issues.
14. E.g., Schnap 1997, 254–55, 331, 345; Csapo 1993, 22, who doesn't speak of hunting but configures the relationship in this polar fashion; Cohen 1991, 186ff.; Dover 1989, 87–88; Detienne 1979, 34.
15. Koch-Harnack 1983, 179–80.
16. Schmitt and Schnapp 1982, 64. Ghedini (1992, 72–73) maintains this same separation and claims that the hunt makes reference to something earlier in time than the city, to a system that precedes agriculture and urbanization.
17. The late sixth and early fifth centuries also bring an increase in depictions of solitary male figures equipped for the hunt, but who are not actually hunting or setting out for the hunt. One of the best-known images of this type is that on the exquisite Attic red-figure lekythos of c. 470 by the Pan Painter (Boston, Museum of Fine Arts 13.198). See ARV² 557, 113; *Para* 387; *Addenda*² 259. Cf. Syracuse, Museo Archeologico Nazionale 15498 (ARV² 557, 118) in Beazley 1974, pl. 24:3; Leiden, Rijksmuseum van Oudheden I.1960/7.2 (ARV² 641, 98bis) of c. 470; and Karlsruhe, Badisches Landesmuseum 220 (B50; ARV² 721, 1) of c. 440 in Hafner 1951, 32, Taf. 26:5. See also Schnapp 1997, 427–30.
18. Shapiro 1981; Beazley 1947.
19. See Dover 1989, 87; Schnapp 1989, 79–80; Koch-Harnack 1983, 54–58, 80–81; Flacelière 1971, 71; and Dover 1964, 38. But see Paris, Musée du Louvre F26 (ABV 150, 5; *Para* 62; *Addenda*² 42), an amphora by the Amasis Painter, which has a painting of a nude beardless youth holding a dead hare facing a clothed bearded man holding a staff. Is this a love gift scene? Is this Beazley's type beta? See also Bristol, City Museum H803 (ABV 153, 44; *Addenda*² 44), a chous by the Amasis Painter on which a Scythian archer presents a dead hare to a bearded, draped man holding a staff. Hupperts (1988) challenges the notion of older and younger partners in the courtship images and advocates the view that the males could be coevals.
20. Beazley 1947.
21. E.g., the Attic black-figure cup of c. 540 in Bochum, Ruhr Universität, Kunstsammlungen, Funcke collection 68, illustrated in Kunisch 1972, 73 no. 68.
22. Sutton 1992, 14.

23. Koch-Harnack 1983; Schnapp 1979b, 51–54; Schauenburg 1969, 12, 16, 20. Gifts are also occasionally given in vase paintings of heterosexual courtship, and some examples are addressed later in this chapter.

24. Koch-Harnack 1983, 93.

25. Cf. Koch-Harnack 1983, 107.

26. Sutton 1992, 14; Shapiro (1981) summarizes the scholarship and explores the issue of why, in spite of the early practice of pederasty in Athens, vase painting does not reflect this until much later. Shapiro offers a political explanation for the inception of such scenes on vases and their waning at the beginning of the fifth century. Contra: Kilmer 1997, 37–38. See also Bremmer 1990, 142–44.

27. Shapiro 1992, 53; Bremmer 1990, 143; Beazley 1947. Using Beazley 1947 with addenda by Frel 1963, I count 96 Attic black-figure examples (however, Shapiro 1981, 134, comes up with a different number): 38 cups, 22 amphorae, 12 skyphoi, 9 lekythoi, 2 hydriae, 2 plates, 2 pyxides, 2 oinochoai, 1 aryballos, 1 alabastron, 1 standlet, 1 phiale, and 1 kantharos; and 13 Attic red-figure examples, including 10 cups, 1 amphora, 1 pelike, and 1 skyphos.

Add to these the following Attic black-figure examples:

TRIPOD PYXIDES: Munich, Staatliche Antikensammlungen 2290a, Schnapp 1997, 250, 496 no. 180.

AMPHORAE: Basel market, Schnapp 1997, 251, 496 no. 183; Basel market, Schnapp 1997, 496 no. 186.

LEKYTHOI: Paris, Musée du Louvre Éleonte 490, Schnapp 1997, 253, 497 no. 190.

CUPS: Bochum, Ruhr Universität, Kunstsammlungen, Funcke Coll. 68, Schnapp 1997, 254, 497 no. 193; Thessalonike I.160.36, Trakosopoulou-Salakiou 1999, 1207, fig. 13.

PLATES: Leiden, Rijksmuseum van Oudheden RO II 89, ABV 131, 1, Addenda² 35.

And these additional Attic red-figure examples:

STAMNOI: Vienna, Kunsthistorisches Museum 3729, ARV² 288, 1, Addenda² 209.

CUPS: New York, ex-Hirschmann Collection G64, fig. 37, Buitron-Oliver 1995a, pl. 59, fig. 27; Rome, Museo Gregoriano Etrusco Vaticano (no number), ARV² 375, 63, Schnapp 1997, 513 no. 347; Munich, Staatliche Antikensammlungen 2655, figs. 32–33, ARV² 471, 196, Addenda² 246; Florence, Museo Archeologico Etrusco 73750, Buitron-Oliver 1995a, pl. 38; Malibu, J. Paul Getty Museum 86.AE.290, Para 375, Addenda² 237, Buitron-Oliver 1995a, pl. 61; Madrid, Museo Arqueológico Nacional 11268, ARV² 473, 213, Addenda² 246; Berlin, Antikensammlung F2291, pl. 52, ARV² 459, 4, Addenda² 244; Vienna, Kunsthistorisches Museum 3698, ARV² 471, 193, Addenda² 246; Tarquinia, Museo Nazionale Tarquiniense 701, fig. 39, ARV² 348, 4, Addenda² 220; Adria, Museo Civico B600 + B551, cup, Riccioni 1957, tav. 12:2; Hanover, Kestner-Museum 1958.57, ARV² 356, 51, Para 363, Addenda² 221; Athens, Agora Museum P2574, Schnapp 1997, 339, 513 no. 348; New York, Metropolitan Museum of Art 96.9.36 (GR575), ARV² 341, 82, Addenda² 219; Paris, Musée du Louvre G121, ARV² 434, 78, Addenda² 238, Buitron-Oliver 1995a, pl. 76:125; once Dresden, ARV² 430, 33, Addenda² 236, Buitron-Oliver 1995a, pl. 40; Paris, Musée du Louvre G123, ARV² 435, 94, Para 375, Addenda² 238, Buitron-Oliver 1995a, pl. 82; Paris, Musée du Louvre G122, ARV² 428, 10, Addenda² 235, Buitron-Oliver 1995a, pl. 13; Paris, Musée du Louvre G276 + New York, Metropolitan Museum of Art

1973.175.1, *ARV*² 428, 11, *Addenda*² 235, Buitron-Oliver 1995a, pl. 14; Würzburg, Martin von Wagner Museum der Universität L480, *ARV*² 478, 320, *Addenda*² 247, Schnapp 1997, 329, 512 no. 332; Würzburg, Martin von Wagner Museum der Universität L482, *ARV*² 444, 239, *Addenda*² 240; Laon, Musée Archéologique Municipal 37.1056, pl. 65, *ARV*² 874, 4, *Addenda*² 300; Boston, Museum of Fine Arts 10.193, *ARV*² 1567, 12, *Para* 506, Schnapp 1997, 339, 513 no. 346; Rome, Museo Nazionale Etrusco di Villa Giulia 50384, *ARV*² 189, 75, *Addenda*² 189; Rome, Museo Gregoriano Etrusco Vaticano 16560 (H550), Koch-Harnack 1983, Abb. 9; Paris, Musée du Louvre G141, *ARV*² 465, 84, *Addenda*² 245.

AMPHORAE: Rome, Museo Nazionale Etrusco di Villa Giulia 50462, fig. 38, *ARV*² 284, 3, *Addenda*² 209, Schnapp 1997, 511 no. 327; London, University College, Follmann 1968, pl. 8:4–5.

PELIKAI: Athens, National Museum 1413, *ARV*² 285, 3, *Addenda*² 209; Boulogne, Musée Communal 134, *ARV*² 293, 47, *Addenda*² 211, Schnapp 1997, 332, 512–13 no. 340.

COLUMN KRATERS: New Haven, Yale University Art Gallery 1933.175, Schnapp 1997, 329, 511 no. 329.

28. Sutton 1992, 14.
29. *Para* 72; *Addenda*² 49.
30. Supra n. 27. Stewart (1997, 80) explains the fifth-century vase painting practice of portraying all males, even obviously mature adults, as beardless as "youthening," designed to evoke homoerotic desire in the male spectator. Cf. Bažant 1987, 34. On beards and their absence as indicators of age in homoerotic scenes, see Hupperts 1988, 257–58.
31. Koch-Harnack 1983, 63ff.
32. *ABV* 315, 3; *Para* 136; *Addenda*² 85.
33. *ABV* 297, 16; *Para* 128; *Addenda*² 78.
34. Rhomaios 1930, pl. 3:1.
35. Koch-Harnack 1983, 87–89. Dover (1989, 10) views this as a generic phrase.
36. Buitron-Oliver 1995a, pl. 59.
37. Supra n. 27.
38. Supra n. 27.
39. Supra n. 27.
40. Cf. Hanover, Kestner-Museum 1958.57, supra n. 27.
41. *ABV* 156, 80; *Para* 65, 90; *Addenda*² 46; Schnapp 1989, 78–79, fig. 108. But see the seated woman spinning wool, who receives a hare from a youth on an Attic red-figure alabastron of c. 500 in Athens (Kerameikos 2713, *Para* 331; *Addenda*² 172), while a homosexual couple embraces behind her. See Schnapp 1989, 81–82, fig. 112, who correctly identifies the woman as a hetaira. Bažant (1987, 36–37) remarks on the compositional similarity between Attic vase paintings of hetairai and their lovers and those of eromenoi and their erastai.
42. Cf. Stewart 1997, 110–16; Frontisi-Ducroux and Lissarrague 1990, 217; Dover 1973, 66.
43. *ABV* 58, 127; *Addenda*² 16.
44. On dead animals in pederastic vase paintings, see Koch-Harnack 1983, 89–97. On returning hunter iconography, see Schnapp 1997, 194–94, 218, 236–41.
45. *ABV* 181, 1; *Para* 75; *Addenda*² 50. Cf. Athens, National Museum E19167 of c. 500 by the Edinburgh Painter, *ABV* 476, 1; Schnapp 1997, 237, 493 no. 158.

46. *Para* 217; *Addenda*² 120.

47. ARV² 245, 1; *Para* 350; *Addenda*² 202.

48. E.g., Geneva, Musée d'art et d'histoire I4, ABV 150, 8, *Para* 63, *Addenda*² 42; Munich, Staatliche Antikensammlungen 8763, *Para* 65, *Addenda*² 43. The return-from-the-hunt motif is also grafted into other scenes, such as the wedding of Peleus and Thetis, where Chiron is the hunter laden with game (e.g., the Erskine dinos by Sophilos, London, British Museum 1971.11–1.1, *Para* 19, 16bis, *Addenda*² 10). Scheibler (1987, 107–9) argues that the return-from-the-hunt paintings with Dionysos that appear on belly amphorae signify the end of peripoloi training and ephebic initiation into the mysteries.

49. Cf. the fragment of an Attic red-figure cup by Douris (Munich, Staatliche Antikensammlungen 8710; ARV² 443, 219) on which a shrouded eromenos contemplates a dead fox hanging from the wall (fig. 67).

50. Lullies 1952, Taf. 140:8–9.

51. Supra n. 27.

52. Beazley 1947, 218 γ9. Cf. Boston, Museum of Fine Arts 08.330d, illustrated in Hoffmann 1974, 208, fig. 13; and a fragmentary black-figure Laconian cup from Cerveteri of c. 550–540, published by Stibbe 1976, 7–10.

53. ARV² 20; *Para* 322; *Addenda*² 153.

54. Supra n. 27.

55. ARV² 288, 1; *Addenda*² 209.

56. ABV 245, 67; *Addenda*² 63.

57. ABV 314, 6; *Addenda*² 85.

58. ABV 134, 40; *Addenda*² 36.

59. Thgn. 1335–36; Ar., *Nub.* 972–78, *Pax* 762f.; Pl., *Leg.* 1.636b–c, *Chrm.* 155c–d, *Symp.* 217b–c; Aischin., *In Tim.* 10–12; Plut., *Quaest. Rom.* 274D. Cf. Plut., *Mor.* 749F, 751F. See Ogden 1996, 128–29; Sergent 1993, 154; Bremmer 1990, 145; Lissarrague1990a, 106; Shapiro 1981, 136; and Flacelière 1971, 64–65. Cf. Hanover, Kestner-Museum 1958.57; Paris, Musée du Louvre G121; Laon, Musée Archéologique Municipal 37.1056, fig. 65; Gotha, Schlossmuseum AVa 48, fig. 49. Supra nn. 27, 53.

60. ARV² 378, 137; *Para* 366; *Addenda*² 226.

61. Sutton (1992, 14) refers to such scenes as possessing an "idealized romantic tone" in contrast to the far less common variant that offers us the pair engaging in intercrural copulation.

62. Koch-Harnack 1983, 66–71.

63. Ἔρος αὖτέ με κυανέοισιν ὑπὸ βλεφάροις τακέρῳ ὄμμασι δερκόμενος κηλήμασι παντοδαποῖς ἐς ἄπειρα δίκτυα Κύπριδος ἐσβάλλει . . ."

64. Both passages use the term δυσαλωτότεροι (hard to catch) to describe the prey. For more on Plato's hunt imagery, see Classen 1960, 27–59.

65. See Murgatroyd 1984, for citations and explication.

66. Radt 1977, frag. 932.

67. Davies 1980, 255. Cf. Stewart 1997, 19.

68. Frontisi-Ducroux (1996, 82), however, believes that the erastes is the hunter, rather than the reverse.

69. ARV² 450, 31; Shapiro 1981, 142. Kaempf-Dimitriadou (1979, 14–16) and Beazley (1947, 223) identify this composition and other similar ones as Zephyros and Hyakinthos. Shapiro (1981, 142–43 n. 71) defends his identification. Kaempf-Dimi-

triadou (1979, Taf. 7:2) illustrates the Berlin cup. On Eros as hunter, see Schnapp 1997, 417–24.

70. E.g., Attic black-figure olpe of c. 490, Rome, Museo del Palazzo dei Conservatori 66 (*Para* 288; *Addenda*[2] 138); Attic red-figure stamnos of c. 480, London, British Museum E440 (*ARV*[2] 289, 1; *Para* 355; *Addenda*[2] 210); Attic red-figure hydria of c. 450–425, London, British Museum E213 (Walters 1931, pl. 89:5); Attic red-figure pelike of c. 440–430, Vienna, Kunsthistorisches Museum 779 (*Para* 465); Attic red-figure pyxis and lid of c. 430–425, Worcester, Art Museum 1936.148 (*ARV*[2] 1250, 33; *Addenda*[2] 354).

71. See Koch-Harnack 1983, 221–27, who also associates Eros with death.

72. See Hermany, Cassimatis, and Vollkommer 1986, 878 no. 332, with other examples (878–79).

73. Texas, McCoy Collection (ex-Castle Ashby), illustrated in Boardman 1989, fig. 364.

74. See chapter 1, and Koch-Harnack 1983, 201–3.

75. Cf. Pl., *Lys.* 206a–b.

76. While birds sometimes appear, they are uncommon and will not be treated here.

77. Bremmer 1990, 142: "The gifts usually indicate the qualities expected from the eromenos." I think that the qualities refer to both erastes and eromenos.

78. Cf. Edlund 1980, 31, who tentatively suggests that the qualities of animals symbolize those of warriors.

79. Cf. Koch-Harnack 1983, 25, 157, 241, who says that the animal gifts reflect the value of the giver and recipient but in contrast to my argument, claims that specific gifts do not characterize the giver or receiver (241); rather, the gifts are used to sublimate aggression (209–10) and that vases had a pedagogic function (20). Schnapp (1989, 79), however, says that the animals symbolize sexual desire and prowess.

80. Koch-Harnack (1983, 63, 106–7) notes that there are no contemporary literary attestations for the giving of felines as love gifts. But see Ar., *Av.* 705–6 of a century later. On problems with feline identification and nomenclature, see Koch-Harnack 1983, 105–6; and on Greek felines in general, see Ashmead 1978. Lyres are also presented as courtship gifts, perhaps to indicate the pedagogic role of the erastes as he educates the eromenos in both music and sex. See Koch-Harnack 1983, 166–70.

81. Koch-Harnack (1983, 81) interprets leashed dogs as courtship gifts but Dover (1989, 92) is less certain.

82. So Koch-Harnack 1983, 119, but the limp doe on Munich, Staatliche Antikensammlungen 1468, suggests a dead animal to me (fig. 34).

83. *ABV* 243, 45; *Addenda*[2] 62.

84. Supra n. 27. See also the Attic red-figure neck amphora by the Matsch Painter of c. 490 B.C. in the Villa Giulia (50462; supra n. 27), where a bearded older man presents a beardless youth, wrapped in a himation, with a hare held with front and back legs fully extended (fig. 38); and the interior of an Attic black-figure plate of c. 520–510 (Leiden, Rijksmuseum van Oudheden RO II 89), on which a nude, bearded erastes holds an animated hare by the hindquarters and ears (supra n. 27). And also the Attic red-figure cups, Munich, Staatliche Antikensammlungen 2655 (figs. 32–33); Madrid, Museo Arqueológico Nacional 11268 (supra n. 27); Hanover, Kestner-Museum 1958.57 (supra n. 27); Copenhagen, Nationalmuseet 14268 (*ARV*[2] 1583, 2; *Para* 506; *Addenda*[2] 389); New York, Metropolitan Museum of Art 96.9.36 (GR575, supra n. 27); Paris, Musée du Louvre G121 (supra n. 27); the Attic red-fig-

ure amphorae, Rome, Museo Nazionale Etrusco di Villa Giulia 50462 (fig. 38), and London, University College; and the Attic red-figure pelike, Athens, National Museum 1413 (supra n. 27). On dead versus living animals as love gifts, see Koch-Harnack 1983, 89–97.

85. Supra n. 27.

86. *ABV* 314, 6; *Addenda*² 85. The tondo of a Laconian drinking cup of c. 550–540 from Cerveteri (Stibbe 1976, pls. 1–2) bears a striking resemblance to the homosexual courting scenes on contemporary Attic pottery, including that on the Providence amphora: two nude males with long hair stand opposite each other. One is bearded; one cannot tell whether the other is or not because that portion of his head is missing. The hands of the bearded figure are also missing but the fragments suggest that both figures held spears. Two hunting dogs run along the edge of the tondo. Although there is nothing overtly sexual about this scene, its composition seems clearly modeled on Attic pederastic courtship scenes and so may allude to the association of pederastic and hunting activities. Stibbe (1976, 8) makes the claim for a Laconian imitation of the Attic courtship composition. For Attic parallels, see, e.g., Munich, Staatliche Antikensammlungen 2290a of c. 550 (supra n. 27); Bochum, Ruhr Universität, Kunstsammlungen, Funcke Collection 68 (supra n. 27); and Paris, Musée du Louvre F85bis of c. 550–525 (fig. 48).

87. Shapiro 1992, 63; Koch-Harnack 1983, 63; Schauenburg 1965, 865. On the cock, its associations with warfare and sexuality, and cockfighting, see Csapo 1993.

88. Hoffmann 1974, 199–200; Bruneau 1965.

89. See Schneider 1912.

90. See Lucian, *Gallus* 3, in which Ares angrily transforms Ἀλεκτρυόνος into a rooster whose crest corresponds to that of Ἀλεκτρυόνος's helmet because Ἀλεκτρυόνος failed to warn Ares about Hephaistos's imminent arrival when Ares was in bed with Aphrodite; Csapo 1993, 12–14, who points out the identical nomenclature, λόφος, for helmet crest and cock's crest; and Mitchell 1996, 90. Cf. *Anth. Pal.* 7.424.

91. Hoffmann 1974, 210, 212–13, 216–17. Representations of cockfights in vase painting provide an interesting counterpoint to the discussion of hunting scenes in chapter 1. The number of cockfights in Greek vase painting decreases dramatically in the fifth century, although literary sources attest that cockfighting grew in popularity with the lower classes. Hoffmann (1974, 217–18) observes this phenomenon and suggests that perhaps the aristocratic patrons of painted vases lost interest in this activity because of its vulgarization. Chapter 1 of this book argues that changes in hunting depictions and their incorporation of martial elements can be explained by the aristocrats' desire to maintain social control or social standards. Vase paintings of hunting also decreased but did not vanish in the early fifth century. So although hunting and cockfighting were the province of the elite before the advent of democracy and both became more widely practiced after its institution, vase painting reflects differing attitudes toward each activity. Another example is the symposion, perhaps the aristocratic activity par excellence, whose depictions on Attic vases show no diminution from the late sixth to the early fifth century.

92. E.g., London, British Museum B134 (*ABV* 322, 1; *Para* 142; *Addenda*² 87) of c. 530; Copenhagen, Nationalmuseet 99 (*ABV* 403, 1; *Para* 175; *Addenda*² 105) of c. 525; New York, Metropolitan Museum of Art 07.286.80 (*ABV* 369, 114; *Para* 162; *Addenda*² 98) of the late sixth century; New York, Metropolitan Museum of

Art 07.286.79 (*ABV* 404, 6; *Para* 175; *Addenda*² 105) of c. 490; New York, Callimanopoulos coll., ex-Castle Ashby (*ABV* 408, 1; *Addenda*² 106) of c. 480; Bologna, Museo Civico Archeologico 19040 ([12], *ABV* 409, 2; *Addenda*² 106) of c. 440 to name but a few, illustrated in Beazley 1986, pls. 93:2, 94:2, 95:3, 96:2, 97:1, 4. For a recent, thorough study of Panathenaic amphorae, see Bentz 1998, who discusses the iconography of the cocks and columns and the cock's combativeness (51–53).

93. E.g., the Attic black-figure plate attributed to the Manner of Lydos, Oxford, Ashmolean Museum 1934.333 (*ABV* 115, 4; *Addenda*² 32). Cf. Bentz 1998, 52–53, who offers several examples (n. 277).

94. Noted also by Csapo 1993, 10, and Hoffmann 1974, 201. See, e.g., the Macmillan Aryballos (London, British Museum 1889.4–18.1) in Boardman 1998, fig. 176; London, British Museum E419 (*ABV* 657, 11; *Addenda*² 277); London, British Museum E154 (*ARV*² 127, 28); and Berlin, Antikensammlung F2324 (fig. 63). Cocks also adorn a Laconian aryballos, a shape typically associated with athletics and the training of young men to become warriors. See Tarquinia, Museo Nazionale Tarquiniense RC 3502 of c. 575–550 by the Naukratis Painter illustrated in Stibbe 1972, 205–7 no. 6, Taf. 3.

95. Hoffmann 1974, 203.

96. Schneider 1912, 2213–14.

97. Stansbury-O'Donnell 1999, 78–79; Markoe 1989, pl. 20; Von Bothmer 1984, 35 no. 45.

98. Samos, Archaeological Museum and Rhodes, Archaeological Museum K1189 from the Samian Heraion, illustrated in Stibbe 1972, 248–50 no. 212, Taf. 70.

99. London, British Museum, Erskine Collection, in Stibbe 1972, 251 no. 217, Taf. 72–73.

100. The last cup is Berlin, Antikensammlung 3404 from Tarquinia, in Stibbe 1972, 281 no. 218, Taf. 74.

101. Csapo 1993; Shapiro 1981, 134; Hoffmann 1974, esp. 204–7.

102. *ARV*² 660, 76; *Addenda*² 277.

103. Hoffmann 1974, 204–5, fig. 11. The reverse is painted with a satyr and another, smaller phallos bird, which ejaculates toward the satyr's backside.

104. On the phallos bird, see Boardman 1992b, who provides a catalog of images. Arguing against Hoffmann, Boardman divorces the phallos bird from the cock in the archaic and classical periods, and categorizes the phallos bird as a form of swan (234–35).

105. *ARV*² 317, 15; *Addenda*² 214; Lissarrague 1990a, fig. 26. See also Dover 1989, 133, who discusses the combination of phallos and other animals, such as a horse with a phallos-shaped head on an Attic red-figure oinochoe (Berlin, Antikensammlung 2320, *ARV*² 157, 84; *Addenda*² 181). Also noteworthy is an Attic black-figure eye cup of c. 520–510 (Jacksonville, Cummer Gallery of Art AP 66.28, *Para* 82–83, illustrated in Shapiro 1981, 162–63) on which a pederastic courtship scene on one side of the exterior is matched on the other by a youth riding a *hippalektryon*, a fantastic cock-horse creature that seems to combine aristocratic connotations of the horse with the homoerotic associations of the cock.

106. Boardman 1992b, 233–34 nos. 23–25, 27.

107. *ABV* 92; *Para* 34; *Addenda*² 25. Cf. Koch-Harnack 1983, 98–105.

108. Koch-Harnack 1983, 104, Abb. 40. Schnapp (1997, 422, 527 no. 490) notes an Attic

red-figure pyxis in Worcester (supra n. 70) on which Erotes prepare to release cocks.

109. Hoffmann (1974, 206–7) claims that the love gift of a cock relates to the aristocratic ideal of educating the eromenos and instilling fighting spirit in him. Cf. Csapo 1993, 21, who identifies cocks with aristocratic boys.

110. Dover 1964, 38.

111. See Csapo 1993, 11–15, for citations. As is evident from my argument here, I disagree with Csapo's conclusion that the cock "is the very antitype of the male homosexual. . . . Pathic homosexuality seems remote from this paradigm of martial valour and masculine fertility, upright citizen and hoplite" (16). Accepting the usual view among scholars of the empowered erastes and disempowered eromenos, Csapo (1993, 20–22) goes on to argue that the cock signifies the fact that in this courtship there will be a triumphant winner (like the cock crowing) and a humiliated loser (abased cock). Aside from perceiving a different power dynamic in the pederastic relationship, I also find that this scheme involves one too many birds for the pederatic relationships depicted in vase paintings, where either the eromenos or the erastes holds the bird but not both within the same vignette.

112. On hares as symbols of speed in vase painting, see Edlund 1980, 33–34. The hares offered as gifts are presumably wild animals and not tame pets; written texts do not, to my knowledge, talk about pet rabbits but they do describe and discuss hare hunting, a subject also documented in vase painting. In the pederastic courtship scenes, one sees both live and dead hares; presumably the latter are not dead pets! It seems likely that vase painting uses a consistent language to depict hares in pederastic courtship depictions: hares are intended to be read as wild not tame; captured, not domesticated. Schnapp (1997, 330–37, 345) perceives a shift from wild to domesticated hares corresponding to the change from black-figure to red-figure pederastic paintings. Although the Attic red-figure compositions seem more intimate with occasional interior settings, sometimes fewer participants (perhaps not due to any romanticism but to the move of pederastic scenes to cup tondi from exterior surfaces, thus restricting the available space for painting), and close embraces, the only elements that might be construed as indications of domesticated animals are animal cages and the placement of the hare on the lap of a figure or on the ground rather than being restrained by the hands. The cages and new positioning occur, however, on only a handful of vases (e.g., New York, Ex-Hirschmann Collection G64; Gotha, Schlossmuseum AVa 48; figs. 37, 49); moreover, the cages are an ambiguous feature, perhaps indicating the capture, not the domestication, of an animal, while the freer positioning of the animal is inconclusive. Schnapp (1997) also investigates the evidence for a Greek distinction between hare and rabbit and finds none.

113. Gossen 1912, 2480.

114. Foxes hunt hares, according to Xen., *Cyn.* 5.24.3 and Ael., *NA* 13.11.

115. Schnapp (1997, 57) points out that the *Shield of Herakles* 301–11 describes hare hunting as exercise for youths but here, Schnapp seems to suggest without explanation that hare hunting provides a form of military preparation.

116. There are also two bowls, one phiale, one pyxis, one amphora, one skyphos, one kyathos, one krater, one plate, and one chous.

117. Schnapp (1997) also lists five Protocorinthian examples, which date from as early

as c. 650; hare hunts are the first hunts to appear on Greek vases. There are also examples of hunters with lagobola pursuing hares where no nets are present, as on both sides of an Attic black-figure cup in Tarquinia (Museo Nazionale Tarquiniense RC7949) of c. 550–530 (Iacopi 1956, Tav. 40:6), where the composition recalls that of deer hunting. A unique hare hunt occurs on an Attic red-figure kalyx krater of c. 400–375 (Newcastle-on-Tyne, Laing Art Gallery and Museum, *ARV*² 1439, 1, *Para* 522), where four youths tree a hare. See Schnapp 1997, 321–22, 509 no. 408.

118. Smith and Pryce 1926, 6, pl. 16:2. On the hare hunt in Attic black-figure ware, see Schnapp 1997, 212–23.

119. See also the Boeotian black-figure exaleiptron tripod, Berlin, Antikensammlung F1727 of c. 570–560 from Tanagra, published in Kunisch 1971, Taf. 195, 196, 197:5–7.

120. *ABV* 689; *Addenda*² 52.

121. Schnapp 1989, 75, fig. 103; Schnapp 1979b, figs. 11–13.

122. *ARV*² 690, 9; *Addenda*² 280.

123. Tarquinia, Museo Nazionale Tarquiniense RC7949 (supra n. 117); Rome, Museo Nazionale Etrusco di Villa Giulia 74966 of c. 500, illustrated in Schnapp 1997, 216 no. 83; London, Victoria and Albert Museum 831–1884 of c. 500, illustrated in Schauenburg 1969, Taf. 8.

124. Schnapp (1997, 220–22) claims an affinity between hare and deer hunting on foot since rocks and lagobola are used in both types of scenes but such weaponry is actually quite rare for deer hunts.

Hare hunts, where hunters carry shields and spears and wear Thracian zeugmata, also ornament terracotta cima friezes of c. 540–525 from Thasos. See Daux 1967, fig. 48; Cook 1952, 39; Launey 1944, 38; and Picard 1941. The same composition minus the prey occurs on fragments of a relief pithos found in the Agora at Thasos, and Picard (1941, 68, fig. 8) likens the pithos scene to those on Clazomenian sarcophagi. Picard (1941, 66) rightly questions the peculiarity of the military weapons against the hare on the Thasian objects, and maintains that the basket-weave shields are made of reeds, which, together with theThracian zeugmata, signify Thracian cavalry, who appear as Thracian hunters (67). Picard speculates that the heroic hunting figure depicted as a Thracian cavalier refers to "un génie de l'au-delà" (92).

125. *ARV*² 1230, 37; *Addenda*² 351.

126. Noted by Friis Johansen (1942) and followed by Koch-Harnack (1983, 219); Shapiro 1981, 141; Hoffmann 1974, 218. Friis Johansen (1942, 134) also remarks on the aristocratic subject matter of the Clazomenian sarcophagi paintings. See Cook 1981, 20 no. 3, pls. 20:1, 21:1. Cf. London, British Museum 86.3–26.5–6 of c. 525–510 (Cook 1981, 15–16 no. D1, pl. 17:1), on which a youth holding two cocks stands between two enormous cocks; hunting dogs jump up on the youth's legs. Friis Johansen (1942, 134–40) discusses the cocks on the London example and notes their derivation from Attic eromenos iconography.

127. On panthers in the "Greek bestiary" and their hunting practices, see Detienne 1979, 36–40.

128. *ARV*² 293, 47; *Addenda*² 211.

129. Cf. *Paroemiogr.* 2:711 lines 8–16. Noted also by Detienne 1994, 85.

130. We should note that later physiognomic texts from the third century on offer negative assessments of the panther's physical traits. See Wotke 1949, 761–62. On Paris, Musée du Louvre A479 ([MNB 1746], figs. 40–41), Schnapp understands the panther or leopard as a reference to the prostitute pictured in the scene. See Schnapp 1984, 50. Cf. Detienne 1979, 39–40, 101–2 n. 101, who likens the panther to a female courtesan. Schnapp (1997, 263) follows this view.

131. Cf. Timotheos of Gaza 11.14.

132. Clarke 1998, fig. 9.

133. Leopards as prey: Vienna, Kunsthistorisches Museum 4690 of the end of the sixth century, and Limassol, Kakoyiannis collection of c. 550–525. See Schnapp 1997, 500 nos. 218, 220. And leopard as hunter: Munich, Staatliche Antikensammlungen 1865 (J1266) of c. 500, ABV 516, 1.

134. Aelian (NA 17.26) claims that lions (λέοντες) were used to assist hunters but Koch-Harnack (1983, 115) reads this text as referring to leopards or cheetahs, not lions.

135. New York, ARV² 92, 66; Würzburg, ARV² 92, 65, Addenda² 171; Paris, ARV² 92, 68, Addenda² 171. Schnapp (1997, 426–27) does not see the New York image or others like it as leopards assisting humans.

136. ARV² 126, 26; Addenda² 176.

137. Lissarrague 1990a, 132.

138. Schnapp 1989, 81, fig. 110; 1979b, 54, figs. 17–18; Hoffmann 1974, 210, fig. 15. Schnapp (1979b, 54–55) also notes that this collection of images often occurs on amphorae and hydriae associated with the Circle of the Antimenes Painter (see chapter 1). On the concept of kalokagathia, see Koch-Harnack 1983, 82.

139. See, e.g., Sourvinou-Inwood 1987.

140. Barringer 1995, 90–94; Sourvinou-Inwood 1987, 138–39.

141. Kaempf-Dimitriadou 1979, 22–40.

142. ARV² 115, 2; Para 332; Addenda² 174.

143. Shapiro 1981, 136, pl. 26: figs. 7–10; Beazley 1947, 220–21 α48.

144. E.g., Kaempf-Dimitriadou 1979, 105 no. 342; 107 nos. 363, 368; 108 no. 382; Taf. 27:1–2, 27:5, 30: 2, 3, 5–6.

145. E.g., Kaempf-Dimitriadou 1979, 83 no. 83; 85 nos. 104, 112; Taf. 8:1–3, 5.

146. Cf. Zeitlin 1986, 146.

147. Cf. Schnapp 1989, 84.

148. Supra n. 59.

149. Cf. Hupperts 1988, 261, who sees equality in homosexual courtship scenes on two works by The Affecter, where bearded, adult men demonstrate affection for each other.

150. ARV² 874, 4; Addenda² 300. Satyrs and maenads accompany Dionysos on the exterior of the cup.

151. Cf. Rome, Museo Nazionale Etrusco di Villa Giulia 50462 (fig. 38); Vienna, Kunsthistorisches Museum 3698 of c. 490–480; Athens, National Museum 1413; Hanover, Kestner-Museum 1958.57; New York, Metropolitan Museum of Art GR575 of c. 480; Tarquinia, Museo Nazionale Tarquiniense 701 (fig. 39); Paris, Musée du Louvre G121 by Douris, all from c. 480. Supra n. 27. There are a few exceptions where the erastes is also partially nude, e.g., Madrid, Museo Arqueológico Nacional 11268 (supra n. 27), but this is a less common variant.

152. Τίνα δηὖτε πείθω ἄψ σ᾽ ἄγην ἐς ϝὰν φιλότατα; . . . καὶ γὰρ αἰ φεύγει, ταχέως διώξει· αἰ δὲ δῶρα μὴ δέκετ᾽, ἀλλὰ δώσει. Translation by D. A. Campbell.

153. Rome, Museo Gregoriano Etrusco Vaticano H550, Koch-Harnack 1983, Abb. 9; Rome, Museo Nazionale Etrusco di Villa Giulia fragment + Florence, Museo Archeologico Etrusco fragment 12B16, ARV² 374, 62, *Addenda*² 226.

154. Kahil 1963, 11–12 no. 20, pl. 4.

155. ARV² 183, 7; *Addenda*² 186.

156. Supra n. 27.

157. Fox hunting occasionally appears in Attic vase painting, such as Glasgow, Sir William Burrell Collection 19/108, an Attic black-figure skyphos of c. 500. See Schnapp 1997, 218, 486 no. 88.

158. ARV² 302, 21; *Addenda*² 212.

159. Cf. Xen., *Mem* 1.2.24., who writes disapprovingly of Alcibiades being hunted by women on account of his beauty.

160. Cf. Koch-Harnack 1983, 220. Latin poetry also exhibits the reversal of gender and sexual roles but allows this in heterosexual relationships, as Catullus attests. See Miller 1998, 181–84, 198–99.

161. ARV 459, 4; *Para* 377; *Addenda*² 244.

162. Cohen 1991, 186–90.

163. Koch-Harnack 1983, 152–72. Schnapp (1984, 50) interprets this painting as likening the erastai to the pornoi, both of whom are sexual predators.

164. Schnapp 1984, 50.

165. ABV 134, 30; *Addenda*² 36.

166. ABV 190, 19; *Addenda*² 52.

167. Detienne (1979, 101–2 n. 101) also notes the erotic nature of the panther chasing a boy (and credits Schnapp for this) but does not take this idea to its logical conclusion, that the panther represents the erastes.

168. Dover 1989, 196; see Shapiro 1981, 135.

169. Supra n. 27.

170. Cohen 1991, 179ff., esp. 181–82.

171. E.g., Pl., *Symp.* 182d–e. See Koch-Harnack 1983, 52–53.

172. Ogden 1996, 109ff. Ogden documents the complex evidence for homosexuality in the Spartan army (117–19). On homosexual relations between males of the same age group, see Hupperts 1988.

173. Cf. Cohen 1991, 197–99.

174. Cf. Cohen 1991, 172–75.

175. E.g., Shapiro 1981, 140–41; Buffière 1980, 50, 56; Flacelière 1971, 67.

176. Ogden (1996, 111–23) enumerates other, fourth-century examples, e.g., Plut., *Pel.* 18–19, for Thebes, as well as evidence for pederasty apart from military training (113). He also discusses the possibility that the eromenos-erastes relationship continued after a man joined the army on Crete. See Patzer 1982, 70–90.

177. On the relationship between sexual aggression and warfare and its appearance in vase painting, see Koch-Harnack 1983, 206–7.

178. Cartledge 1981, 26: "The militarisation of Spartan society inevitably embraced matters erotic." Bremmer (1980, 279–90) distinguishes between pederasty as a consequence of the military way of life and as a rite of initiation and argues that Dorian

pederasty is of the latter type. I'm not sure that the two can be easily divided in Sparta and Crete, where the military was so closely bound up with rites of initiation. All the Cretan boys participated in this ritual so far as we know, and at Sparta a select (representative?) group of boys performed the krypteia.

179. Moore (1975, 97) points out a similar custom in Argos, another Dorian state, as he notes.

180. See Hawley 1998, 37–39, 50, for a recent discussion of this and other male beauty contests.

181. Ogden 1996, 111–39; Dover 1989, 191–92. But see Schnapp 1981, 112, who cautions that the military does not constitute the sole reason for homosexuality in ancient Greece. He notes that homosexuality tended to have more martial connotations in Thebes and Sparta because "ces cités sont plus militarisées qu'Athènes or les cités ioniennes." This reasoning does not seem plausible. See also Cohen 1991, 173–74 on the characteristic contradictions in Athenian attitudes toward homosexuality.

182. Cartledge 1981, 26.

183. E.g., Shapiro 1981, 140; Buffière 1980, 50.

184. E.g., Ogden 1996, 108–9.

185. Ogden 1996, 125–35.

186. Translation by Dover 1989, 124. Cf. Xen., *Cyn.* 12.20, which describes the eromenos' observation spurring the erastes to do good: "ὅταν μὲν γάρ τις ὁρᾶται ὑπὸ τοῦ ἐρωμένου, ἅπας ἑαυτοῦ ἐστι βελτίων καὶ οὔτε λέγει οὔτε ποιεῖ αἰσχρὰ οὐδὲ κακά, ἵνα μὴ ὀφθῇ ὑπ' ἐκείνου.

187. Τὸν δὲ ἀριστεύσαντά τε καὶ εὐδοκιμήσαντα οὐ πρῶτον μὲν ἐπὶ στρατιᾶς ὑπὸ τῶν συστρατευομένων μειρακίων τε καὶ παίδων ἐν μέρει ὑπὸ ἑκάστου δοκεῖ σοι χρῆναι στεφανωθῆναι ... ἐάν τίς του τύχῃ ἐρῶν ἢ ἄρρενος ἢ θηλείας προθυμότερος ἦ πρὸς τὸ τἀριστεῖα φέρειν. Translation by Sterling and Scott 1985.

188. "ἐρῶν γὰρ ἀνὴρ ὑπὸ παιδικῶν ὀφθῆναι ἢ λιπὼν τάξιν ἢ ὅπλα ἀποβαλών." Translation by Lamb 1925. Cf. Pl., *Symp.* 196c–d; *Anth. Pal.* 13.22; Plut., *Mor.* 760d. Xenophon also gives voice to the same thought when he credits Eros as the incentive for the erastes to impress the eromenos (*Cyn.* 12.20).

189. Supra n. 59, and Cartledge 1981, 27; Arieti 1975, 434–35, with primary sources.

190. What actually were the criteria for the winner of the euandria is debated; beauty, judged on the basis of size and strength, military display, or competitive dancing and singing are possibilities. See Boegehold 1996, 98–103; Crowther 1985, 288.

191. See Boegehold 1996, 97–103; Crowther 1985, 286–88.

192. *ARV*² 286, 22; *Addenda*² 209.

193. *ARV*² 155, 37; *Addenda*² 181. Koch-Harnack (1983, 156) notes that the erastes holds the helmet as if it were a hare.

194. Koch-Harnack (1983, 156–57) proposes that the helmets are prizes in a beauty contest for *paides* (boys or youths), much like the Elean practice described earlier.

195. Koch-Harnack 1983, 36–38; Cartledge 1981, 28–29. Bremmer (1990, 142) regards the gifts as symbolic of qualities expected from the eromenos and the gift giving as initiatory.

196. Koch-Harnack 1983, 37, 143ff. Cf. Bremmer 1990, 143: "pederasty became, next to sport, one of the main areas in which the competitive spirit of the aristocracy could realize itself." But I disagree with Bremmer's claim (145) that with the advent of democracy, adults lost interest in traditional education of adolescents.

Rather, as I argue in chapter 1, I believe that aristocrats would have taken even greater interest in perpetuating traditional education with its emphasis on heroes and aristocrats.

197. Cf. Cohen 1991, 184–87, 196–97; Dover 1964, 38. Yet I disagree with Cohen's argument that pederasty was widely disapproved of and that the standard for sexual relationships was heterosexuality (178–202). That the Athenians were ambivalent about pederasty, both valuing it for the erastes and disdainful of the submission of the eromenos, is indisputable, but the visual evidence makes clear in both its numbers and tenor that homoerotic courtship on the pederastic model was considered an important, if not essential, part of aristocratic society and cohesiveness in the late sixth and early fifth centuries. Cohen bases his argument largely on the writings of Plato, Xenophon, and Aristotle but does not consider the earlier writers, Pindar, Theognis, Bacchylides, and Ibycus; admittedly, none of these four is Athenian.

198. But see Cohen 1991, 181, who argues that classical Athenian hubris laws imply censure of eromenoi who capitulate and the erastai who corrupt them but then acknowledges that erastai won honor by conquering eromenoi (196–97).

199. Cf. Cohen 1991,183, 196–97; Dover 1989, 87–88; Koch-Harnack 1983, 52–53; Dover 1964, 31–32, 38. On boys as passive recipients and their consequent feminization and the attendant condemnation, see Cohen 1991, 187. Kilmer (1997) argues against the repeated claim that the eromenos is supposed to resist the attentions of the erastes.

200. See Cohen 1991, 183, with further bibliography.

201. Cartledge 1981, 28–29.

202. Cf. Stewart 1997, 10.

203. Stewart 1997, 73: "This move not only placed the homoerotic bond at the core of Athenian political freedom, but asserted that it and the manly virtues . . . of courage, boldness, and self-sacrifice that it generated were the only true guarantors of that freedom's continued existence." Unlike Stewart, however, I think that pederasty continued to be viewed as an aristocratic institution and may have inspired nonelites to imitate it.

204. Contra: Shapiro 1981, 142. Cf. Koch-Harnack 1983, 153, 245, who comes to a conclusion similar to that presented here, and sees animals as economic status symbols. Thus, according to Koch-Harnack, the display of animals strives to compensate for dwindling aristocratic power. My argument is different: aristocrats were nominally no longer in control of the government but they continued to dominate the social and political agenda after the advent of democracy. Frel (1963, 62–63) argues that Athens turned away from pederastic images because of their association with the aristocrats, but it is important to note that the number of vases does not actually fall off until c. 470, well after the beginning of democracy and the loss of official aristocratic political power. Infra. n. 212.

205. Cf. Soph. frag. 932, in Lloyd-Jones 1996.

206. Felson Rubin and Sale (1983) argue that blurring the boundaries of Artemis (hunting) and Aphrodite (sexuality) is inappropriate and therefore punished in tragedy and myth, but we have seen that hunting and sex often go together in real life. This topic will be taken up in chapter 3.

207. Sometimes love and betrayal are combined in the same literary image. As early as

Homer's *Odyssey* 8.266–366, we have Hephaistos ensnaring his wife Aphrodite and her lover Ares in nets as he catches them in flagrante delicto.

208. On Ganymede, see Sichtermann 1988; Kaempf-Dimitriadou 1979, 7–12.

209. Arafat (1997, 103) points to a fragment of an Attic white-ground bobbin (Athens, Kerameikos Museum 1961, *ARV*² 890, 176; *Addenda*² 302) decorated with a scene of Zeus abducting Ganymede and claims that it was found in the grave of a young boy in Athens, thus suggesting that the abduction was seen in a favorable light. Although the bobbin may have been in the grave of a young boy at one time, Arafat seems to have misconstrued the excavation report (Gebauer 1940, 335), which does not assign it to such a context.

210. Shapiro (1992, 63) argues that Zeus's conduct may represent a sexual fantasy of the erastes. Considering the preceding discussion, I wonder if the fantasy might not (also) belong to the eromenos. Cf. Koch-Harnack 1983, 235–38.

211. Kaempf-Dimitriadou 1979, 7ff. Shapiro (1981, 142) thinks that scenes of Zeus and Ganymede are mythological replacements for homosexual courtship scenes, which taper off in the early fifth century. Sichtermann (1959) discusses the Zeus and Ganymede vase paintings and their relationship to their nonmythological counterparts. See also Shapiro 1992, 58–63, who refers to Zeus and Ganymede as "the ideal prototype of mortal homoerotic relationships" in sixth-century lyric poetry (58). Bremmer (1980, 285) notes that the term *harpage* used by Ephoros to refer to the capture of the beloved on Crete is the same as for that of Ganymede by Zeus in Ibycus frag. 289P and Theognis 1347.

212. Shapiro 1981, 142. Frel (1963, 63–64) explains the change from actual courtship scenes to Zeus and Ganymede as a mythological expression of what is no longer permissible in reality, while Shapiro (1992, 59) notes the correspondence of this iconographical phenomenon with another: the sharp increase of interest in vase painting scenes of "loves of the gods."

213. See Shapiro 1981, 142, for citations.

214. *ARV*² 381, 182; *Addenda*² 227.

215. Sourvinou-Inwood 1985.

216. *ARV*² 409, 51; *Addenda*² 233.

217. *ARV*² 880, 12, 891, 3; *Para* 429; *Addenda*² 302.

218. E.g., Ganymede on an Attic red-figure oinochoe by the Painter of Florence 4021 (Basel, Cahn collection HC 9), *ARV*² 874, 3, *Addenda*² 300. Also noted by Shapiro 1992, 62. Cf. also Orvieto, Museo Civico, Collection Faina 2671; Paris, Musée du Louvre G175, *ARV*² 106, 124, *Para* 342, *Addenda*² 193; Oxford, Ashmolean Museum 1871.84; St. Petersburg, State Hermitage Museum B1556; Cambridge, Fitzwilliam Museum GR 37.23 (supra n. 216); Basel, Antikenmuseum und Sammlung Ludwig BS483, *ARV*² 485, 26, *Addenda*² 248; Aberdeen, University 686, *ARV*² 653, 2; Ferrara, Museo Archeologico Nazionale di Spina 9351 ([T212 B VP], supra n. 217); and Indianapolis, John Herron Art Institute 47.35, *ARV*² 1003, 21, illustrated in Sichtermann 1988, nos. 11, 12, 20, 22, 25, 28, 44, 46.

219. Schmitt Pantel 1992, 76–78; Bremmer 1990, 136–37, 139–40. On written evidence for the age of adolescent boys at the symposion, see Booth 1991, 114–17, who concludes that in Athens boys gained the right to recline at the symposion at age eighteen.

220. E.g., Munich, Staatliche Antikensammlungen 2301, *ABV* 255, 4, *Para* 113, *Ad-*

*denda*² 66, illustrated in Schmitt-Pantel 1992, fig. 19; Florence, Museo Archeo-logico Etrusco 3922, *ARV*² 432, 55, *Addenda*² 237, illustrated in Schmitt-Pantel 1992, fig. 23; Florence, Museo Archeologico Etrusco 3946, *ARV*² 792, 51, illustrated in Schmitt-Pantel 1992, fig. 24; New York, Metropolitan Museum of Art 20.246, *ARV*² 467, 118, *Para* 378, *Addenda*² 245, illustrated in Lissarrague 1990a, fig. 9.

221. London, British Museum 717; Thessalonike, Archaeological Museum 1086; Kavala Museum L424; Delphi, Archaeological Museum 7519A; Berlin, Antiken-sammlung 825, 827; Athens, Agora Museum S713; Athens, National Museum 1523, 1524, and 3872; Paros banquet relief, all illustrated in Dentzer 1982, figs. 306, 344–46, 360–61, 388, 416–17, 452, 535–39, to name but a few.

222. Laconian cups: Paris, Musée du Louvre E667 of c. 565, illustrated in Stibbe 1972, Taf. 6, and Dentzer 1982, fig. 107; Samos, Archaeological Museum K1203, illus-trated in Stibbe 1972, Taf. 58–59. Attic red-figure cups: Berlin, Antikensammlung 2298, *ARV*² 364, 52, *Para* 364, *Addenda*² 223; Paris, Musée du Louvre G469, *ARV*² 791, 32, Dentzer 1982, fig. 115.

223. Heidelberg, Ruprecht-Karls-Universität, Archäologisches Institut 104 B52 of c. 480, *ARV*² 344, 52, Schnapp 1997, no. 366; Gotha, Schlossmuseum AVa 48 (supra n. 53, fig. 49).

224. Bremmer 1990.

225. Bremmer 1990, 137, 142.

226. Bowie 1990. Theognis 993ff., for example, invites the listener to compete in song for the prize of a beautiful boy. On the symposion's relationship to warrior society, see Murray 1991.

227. Murray 1991, 96–97. Cf. Stein-Hölkeskamp 1989, 112–15.

228. Bremmer 1990, 138.

229. Bremmer 1990, 137–38. On the Apatouria, see Deubner 1932, 232–34.

230. Frontisi-Ducroux and Lissarrague 1990; Kurtz and Boardman 1986; Shapiro 1981, 139.

231. Shapiro 1981, 140, pl. 27: fig. 11. Lissarrague (1990a, 56–57) treats the Bomford Cup and cites other examples in n. 19. A symposiast uses this same type of cup on a vase of c. 510 (Lissarrague 1990a, fig. 38).

232. Sichtermann 1988, 156–57, lists nine neck amphorae, six lekythoi, four cups, four pelikai, two column kraters, two kantharoi, two oinochoai, one kyathos, one bell krater, one kalyx krater, one volute krater, one stamnos, one amphora, one hydria, one alabastron, and assorted fragments. This count excludes the paintings that show Zeus in the form of an eagle and includes only those where Zeus takes human male form.

233. Schmitt and Schnapp 1982, 60. Murray (1983, 195) claims that the pottery industry, both potting and painting, "existed primarily to serve the needs of the *symposium*, and reflected the taste of its aristocratic patrons." See also Shapiro 1992, 53; and Sutton 1992.

234. Shapiro 1981, 136.

235. Ghedini 1992, 72. E.g., Laon, Musée Archéologique Municipal 37.892 (supra n. 46, figs. 46–47); Rome, Museo Nazionale Etrusco di Villa Giulia 50372 (M442), *ARV*² 700, *Addenda*² 120, an Attic black-figure hydria of c. 520–510 in Schnapp 1997, 246 no. 173; and Munich, Staatliche Antikensammlungen 2303 (J479), *ARV*² 245, 1, *Para* 350, *Addenda*² 202, an Attic red-figure amphora of c. 490. In the case of

Munich, Staatliche Antikensammlungen 2303, Dionysos, a satyr, and a maenad appear on the opposite side of the vase.

236. E.g., Munich, Staatliche Antikensammlungen 8763, *Para* 65, *Addenda*² 43, an Attic black-figure amphora of c. 550 B.C. by the Amasis Painter; Geneva, Musée d'Art et d'Histoire I4, supra n. 48, another Attic black-figure amphora of c. 550–525 B.C. by the Amasis Painter.

237. Schmitt and Schnapp 1982, 62–63. Cf. Koch-Harnack 1983, 82, 87.

238. Cf. Miller 1997, 253–56, who also reproduces a succinct and amusing chart cre- ated by Donald Miller to indicate pottery use and hierarchical emulation in In- dian society (fig. 150). But see Bremmer 1990, 142ff., who argues that the compe- tition of gift giving and winning eromenoi substituted for warfare, which had lost its significance for aristocrats in the sixth century. Such a view, however, does not explain the acceleration of the pederastic courtship scenes c. 525–470. It's also im- portant to note that the practice of aristocratic pederasty in Athens certainly per- sisted through at least the end of the fourth century.

239. Vernant 1988, 34.

CHAPTER 3: HUNTING AND MYTH

A portion of this chapter was previously published as Barringer 1996. Aspects of Ata- lanta are addressed in this chapter, but a fuller treatment of her can be found in the aforementioned article. I should note that I have altered my views on many aspects of Atalanta since the publication of that article, and this chapter represents my cur- rent thinking.

1. Because Hippolytos has already received enormous scholarly attention, particu- larly his depiction in Euripides' tragedy, this chapter only refers to him to make comparative points. Melanion can also be included in this group of chaste hunters but he nearly always appears in conjunction with Atalanta and has no separate narratives of his own. The exception is a brief mention in Aristophanes, *Lysistrata* 785–95, which describes the misogynist Melanion, who hunts and lives in the mountains. See Boardman 1992a.

2. This chapter does not address divine hunters, such as Artemis, an enormous sub- ject best left for another occasion.

3. See, e.g., Schnapp 1997, 454–55, who notes the prohibition of mixing the hetero- sexual hunt with sex; Felson Rubin and Sale 1983.

4. E.g., Lloyd-Jones 1983, 99.

5. As many have observed, e.g., Segal 1991, 85 re: Adonis; Vernant 1991, 199–201; Zeitlin 1985, re: Hippolytos; and Detienne 1979, 26. Schnapp (1997, 37–38) ex- plains the disasters as caused by excessive zeal in hunting but misses the erotic connection. It is not, as Schnapp maintains (38ff.), the distance between men and beasts that is at stake but the distance between men and gods.

6. On suffering a reversal (rather than becoming one's opposite), see Zeitlin 1985, 106–7.

7. Zeitlin 1985, 66.

8. On the issue of the hunter becoming the hunted, see, e.g., Schnapp 1997, 430, 458–63.

9. Theseus also participates in the Calydonian boar hunt (see infra) but his addition to this list of hunters occurs late, sometime toward the end of the sixth century,

centuries after the Calydonian boar hunt myth first makes an appearance. See Arrigoni 1977, 20–21, 36–37.

10. Cf. Hor., *Carm.* 3.4.70–72, who explains that Artemis killed the hunter Orion with arrows after he tried to violate her (cf. Hyg., *Fab.* 195, *Poet. astr.* 2.34.2).

11. Pausanias 9.38.5 mentions hero worship to Aktaion at Orchomenos, where an annual sacrifice took place before a bronze likeness of Aktaion, and Plutarch, *Aristides* 11 names Aktaion (and Pan) among the figures to whom the Athenians were instructed to make sacrifices in 479 before the battle of Plataia.

12. Merkelbach and West 1990, no. 217A. Written and visual sources are collected in Guimond 1981, 454–69; and see also Burkert 1983, 111ff. Note that Janko (1984) revives and argues Lobel's suggestion that Oxyrhynchus papyrus 2509 concerns Aktaion's death and belongs to Hesiod's *Catalogus mulierem*. Contra: West (1985, 88). See also Cirio 1977, for a treatment of the sources of the Aktaion myth and their relationship to each other, particularly the names and numbers of dogs attacking Aktaion.

13. See Kossatz-Deissmann 1978, 142–65, who concludes that Aischylos's inspiration for the play derived from his participation in the battles of Plataia, Marathon, and Salamis; and Séchan 1967, 132–38. According to Kossatz-Deissmann, the earliest version of the Aktaion myth is one in which Aktaion kills a sacred deer and therefore suffers punishment (142).

14. But see Nagy 1973, who interprets ἐλάφου περιβαλεῖν δέρμα Ἀκταίωνι in Stesichoros 236P, derived from Paus. 9.2.3, to mean that Artemis simply transformed Aktaion into a stag. Cf. Ov., *Her.* 20.103–4; Hyg., *Fab.* 247, who mention Aktaion's fate but offer no explanation for the cause.

15. Cf. Schnapp 1997, 113; Reeder 1995, 315; and Kossatz-Deissmann 1978, 143–65, who also sees Dionysiac associations in the Aktaion myth. Jeanmaire (1939, 560) speculates that the myth of Aktaion reflects an orgiastic rite, similar to the Arcadian Lykaia (see infra), which took place on Mount Cithaeron.

16. Lacy 1990.

17. Already anticipated by Kossatz-Deissmann 1978, 152.

18. An Apulian volute krater attributed to the Group of the Lycurgos Painter, c. 350–300 (Naples, Museo Nazionale SA31) is adduced as evidence that Diodoros's version of the myth of Aktaion's death was known much earlier than his own time. On the vessel, Aktaion, shown with antlers, prepares to spear a stag while Hermes and Pan stand nearby, Artemis gazes on the action, and a sprightly satyr scrambles near the groundline. See Guimond 1981, 464 no. 110. Unlike other scholars who have read the vase as either an exhibition of Aktaion's hubristic claim to be a better hunter than Artemis (e.g., Cirio [1977, 57] and Séchan [1967, 136] see influence of Eur., *Bacch.* 337–42, on this painting), an impious killing of a stag sacred to Artemis (an interpretation for which no literary evidence exists), or as a depiction of Aktaion's metamorphosis already underway, Lacy sees the vase as a depiction of Aktaion's killing of a stag that will be offered to Artemis, followed by his attempt to marry her. The composition of the stag's slaughter, in fact, closely resembles sacrificial scenes on other South Italian vases. Lacy reads the spring that appears beneath the stag as the spring in which Artemis was seen bathing. We might also note the appearance of Pan and Hermes, two deities typically associated with Arcadia. Lacy explains Hermes as a prolepsis of the fate that awaits Aktaion, Pan as a signifier

of the "arrival of madness and unbridled lust," and Aktaion's antlers as a mere attribute. See Lacy 1990, 36–42.

19. Lacy 1990, 36.

20. See Guimond 1981.

21. E.g., Kossatz-Deissmann 1978, 143–65, who also sees Dionysiac associations in the
Aktaion myth; Séchan 1967, 132–38.

22. Supra n. 13.

23. *ABV* 586, 1; *Addenda*² 139.

24. Guimond 1981, 455 no. 1.

25. *ARV*² 728; *Addenda*² 282.

26. *ABV* 500, 51; *Addenda*² 124.

27. Guimond 1981, 455–56 no. 4.

28. Guimond 1981, 456 no. 5.

29. *ARV*² 550, 1; *Para* 387; *Addenda*² 256–57.

30. Hamburg: *Para* 347, 8ter; *Addenda*² 199. Paris: *ARV*² 285, 1; *Addenda*² 209. A second
example of the death of Aktaion by the Geras Painter of c. 500–475 appears on an
amphora in Copenhagen (Thorvaldsens Museum 99, *ARV*² 287, 24; *Addenda*²
209).

31. Hoffmann 1967, 17.

32. *ARV*² 552, 20; *Addenda*² 257.

33. Another example by the Pan Painter is a kalpis of c. 470, now in Certosa di Padula,
Museo 164. See Guimond 1981, 457 no. 28.

34. Guimond 1981, no. 8; Kahil 1963, 20 no. 41, pl. 11:2.

35. Guimond 1981, no. 17; Kahil 1963, 22–23 no. 46, pl. 13:2.

36. Kahil 1963, 22.

37. On Lyssa and her relationship to Pan, see Borgeaud 1988, 110.

38. *ARV*² 1045, 7; *Para* 444; *Addenda*² 320. Cf. Berlin, Antikensammlung F3239 in Guimond 1981, 462 no. 88. Neer (1995, 141–46) discusses the spatial relations between
figures on this vase, noting that Aktaion is set apart from the others because of his
three-dimensionality. He also discusses Aktaion as the "visual equivalent of Pro-
tagorean antilogic" (143), and the Lykaon Painter's vase as a self-referential play on
mimesis, here twofold (painting of a play). Neer also notes the fact that the violence shown on the vase would not have been portrayed onstage, and, therefore,
the vase does not illustrate a theatrical performance (144). But see his caution on p.
145.

39. E.g., Guimond 1981; Kossatz-Deissmann 1978, 148.

40. Guimond 1981, 462.

41. Neer 1995, 143; Robertson 1992, 207; Kossatz-Deissmann 1978, 147–48.

42. Kossatz-Deissmann 1978, 147; Séchan 1967, 133–34.

43. Cf. Borgeaud 1988, 128–29.

44. As Hoffmann (1967, 15–16) does.

45. The South Italian examples are: Taranto, Museo Archeologico Nazionale (no inventory number), Apulian volute krater of c. 400; Cambridge, Arthur M. Sackler Art
Museum 1960.367, a Lucanian nestoris of c. 330 attributed to the Painter of the
Choephoroi; Taranto, Museo Archeologico Nazionale 5163, an Apulian plate of c.
340–330; a now lost pelike; London, British Museum F176, a Lucanian nestoris of
c. 400–380 from Basilicata attributed to the Dolon Painter; Boston, Museum of

Fine Arts 03.839A and B, Italiote oinochoe fragments of c. 370–360; Naples, Museo Archeologico Nazionale SA31, an Apulian volute krater of c. 360–350 attributed to the Ilioupersis Group; Göteborg, Röhsska Konstslöjdmuseet 13–71, an Apulian bell krater of c. 350; Karlsruhe, Badisches Landesmuseum 76/106, a Paestan skyphos of c. 350–300; Taranto, Museo Archeologico Nazionale (no inventory number), Apulian oinochoe of c. 350 attributed to the Felton Painter; Bloomington, Indiana University Art Museum 70–97–1, an Apulian situla of c. 350; Paris, Bibliothèque nationale, Cabinet des Médailles 949, an Apulian stamnos of c. 350; Berlin, Antikensammlung F3239, an Apulian amphora of c. 340–330 B.C. by the Darius Painter; S. Agata de'Goti (no inventory number), a Paestan bell krater of c. 330; and two lost works, a pelike and a Campanian hydria of c. 350, formerly of the Hirsch collection. See Guimond 1981, 458–59 nos. 45, 46, 47, 48a, 49, 462 no. 83b; Kossatz-Deissmann 1978, 150–51. Aktaion is unaccompanied on the Taranto plate.

46. Kossatz-Deissmann 1978, 155.
47. Kossatz-Deissmann 1978, 156.
48. Guimond 1981, 464 no. 111; Kossatz-Deissmann 1978, 156. Cf. also Paris, Bibliothèque nationale, Cabinet des Médailles 949, Guimond 1981, 464 no. 112.
49. Séchan (1967, 138) dates this pyxis to the fourth century but Guimond (1981, 465 no. 121) gives the earlier date.
50. Naples, Museo Archeologico Nazionale CS361; Dresden, Staatliche Kunstsammlung AB1; Paris, Musée du Louvre C4447, all from South Italy; Athens, National Museum A15878 from Thasos; fragmentary relief in London, British Museum B375; Reggio, Museo Nazionale (no inventory number) from Locri. Guimond 1981, 456 no. 18a–c; 458 nos. 39, 40; Jacobsthal 1931, 31–32 nos. 24–26; 45–46 no. 60; 74–76 nos. 97–98; Taf. 13, 14, 27, 56. Guimond (1981, 461 no. 76) lists the Reggio relief as an Italiote terracotta.
51. Lloyd-Jones 1983, 99.
52. On Kallisto's name, see Jost 1985, 406–7; Arena 1979, 5–12.
53. Several of the myths about hunting and hunters take place in Arcadia, which is not surprising given Artemis's importance there, and the notoriously pastoral and backward reputation of the region in antiquity. Borgeaud (1988, x) claims that Athens viewed Arcadia as a place "symbolizing both the frontiers and the origins of civil life . . . the city could be contrasted with that which it was not." But elsewhere, Borgeaud claims that, by accepting Pan's cult in the fifth century, "the Athenians admitted that they themselves also had an 'Arcadian' aspect" (52). In fact, Athenians had incorporated Arcadian myths into their artistic repertoire a century before, so Borgeaud's claim loses force.

In addition to Atalanta and Kallisto, one could also point to Daphne as an Arcadian virgin huntress. Daphne is usually named the daughter of a river god. Like Atalanta and Kallisto, she was a virgin huntress, and was pursued by a male, this time, Leukippos. As was the case with Hippomenes and the golden apples (see infra), Leukippos attempted to trick Daphne. He adopted the disguise of a female, recalling Zeus in the Kallisto myth, and indicated his desire to hunt with her. Thinking Leukippos a female, Daphne agreed. Eventually, Leukippos's masculinity was revealed while bathing in a stream with Daphne and her companions. They killed him with their javelins and daggers (Paus. 8.20.2–4), a gender role reversal typical of the hunting myths. Another tale makes Daphne the object of Apollo's at-

tention. She attempts to outrun the god and prays to Zeus to come to her assistance. At the moment that Apollo reaches her, Daphne metamorphoses into a laurel tree. Unable to have her, Apollo adopts the laurel as his sacred tree (Ov., *Met.*
1.452–567). Because the earliest written or visual treatments of the myth do not date
until the Hellenistic period, this subject is not treated in this text. See, e.g., Dowden
1989, 174–79; Kaempf-Dimitriadou 1979, 32–33.

54. Hes. 163 M-W; Apollod. 3.8.2; Hyg., *Fab.* 155, 176, 177, 224. Schnapp (1997, 36–47)
discusses Lykaon, werewolves, and Arcadia. Written texts describe an aition of this
festival. Lykaon either sacrificed a newborn child to Zeus (*FGrH* 90 F38; Apollod.
3.98; Paus. 8.2.3) or Lykaon invited Zeus to dinner at which he served the remains
of a human sacrifice, variously named as Nyktimos or Arkas, Kallisto's son and
Lykaon's grandson (Hes. 163 M-W). As punishment, Zeus sent a thunderbolt to
Lykaon's house and then transformed Lykaon into a wolf (Hes. 163 M-W; Paus.
8.2.3; this is a strangely mutable family). Arkas was restored to life. Elsewhere, Zeus
is said to have sent a flood. As Jost (1985, 262–63) observes, Lykaon is both sacrificer
and sacrilegious (cf. Jeanmaire 1939, 562). The similarity of this myth to that of
Kallisto is striking: transgression against a god, metamorphosis as punishment, and
birth or rebirth of Arkas. For a detailed treatment of Lykaon, see Piccaluga 1968.

The rituals of the actual festival of Lykaon Zeus, the Lykaia, are known to us
from Hesiod 163 M-W. The entrails of sacrificial animals were mixed with those of
a man; participants would select their portions. Plato (*Resp.* 565d) claims that he
who ate of the human portion became a wolf. Pausanias says that at the sacrifice, a
man was simply transformed into a wolf but would change back to a man after nine
years if he abstained from human flesh in his wolf form; if not, he remained a wolf
forever (8.2.6). Not only was the rite performed secretly (Paus. 8.38.7), but entry to
the precinct was forbidden. Anyone who disregarded this interdiction would live
no longer than a year, and any creature, man or animal, within the precinct cast
no shadow; hunters and predatory animals (synonymous?) would not pursue animals that rushed into the precinct for safety (Paus. 8.38.6). See Burkert 1983, 84–90;
Henrichs 1981, 224–25; and Jeanmaire 1939, 558–60, for discussions of the myth and
ritual, and note Henrichs 1981, 195: "Most authorities on Greek religion agree that
human sacrifice occurred occasionally but existed nowhere as a regular cultic institution." Wathelet (1986) argues that Homer modeled his description of Achilles'
killing Priam on elements of the Mount Lykaon ritual, and therefore, the rites existed at least as early as Homer's time. Jost (1985, 249) indicates that the written evidence dates the cult to the Mycenaean period but that archaeology can only confirm the cult as far back as the seventh century. See also Hughes 1991, 96–107;
Dowden 1989, 185–86; and Jost 1985, 249–69, who notes that some scholars dismiss
the reality of human sacrifice on Mount Lykaon and judiciously points out that no
ancient source draws a connection between the forbidden nature of the precinct
and the human sacrifices performed there, although modern scholars have done
so repeatedly; and Immerwahr 1891, 7–10. On human sacrifice, see in addition to
Hughes 1991; Lloyd-Jones 1983, 88–89, 100–101.

55. *IG* V² 549–50; Paus. 8.2.1. Scholars, such as Burkert (1983, 90) and Jeanmaire (1939,
558–59, 565) view the Lykaon ritual with its wolf metamorphosis as an initiation
for a young man, although Jost (1985, 267) rightly states that nine years seems too
long for a rite of passage. Piccaluga and others detach the lycanthropy element

from the myth and instead view the Mount Lykaon rite as related to weather and the introduction of agriculture; that is, the rites are performed to produce rain, hence the flood sent by Zeus. But the flood seems to be a very late addition to the myth, its earliest attestation being Ovid. *Met.* 1.5.211–273. See also Apollod. 3.8.2; Serv., *Comm. ad Virgil, Bucolics* 6.5.4; Suda, s.v. Λυκάων; *Myth. Vat.* 1.189. Borgeaud (1988, 23–31) interprets the myth of Lykaon and his grandson Arkas as a description of the first appropriate sacrifices: Lykaon's actions, either human sacrifice or cannibalistic meal, indicate that Lykaon still lives the θηριώδης βίος, and Arkas's introduction of agriculture and bread marks a break from the bestial way of life and documents the "first real human being in Arcadia." He discerns two versions of the birth of Arkas myth: one that has nothing to do with Lykaon and a second classical reworking that intentionally connects Arkas to Mount Lykaon and its rites. Schnapp (1997, 41) discusses the association of incest (Arkas and Kallisto) and cannibalism and the interconnections between sexuality and the hunt. Borgeaud (1988, 33) also addresses the links between sexual coupling and hunting, using parallels from other cultures to do so. Lloyd-Jones (1983, 98) posits a female initiation at the Lykaia, which involved bears instead of wolves.

56. Most recently by McPhee 1990. See also Henrichs 1987; 1981, esp. 198–208; Sale 1965; 1962. Sale attempts to uncover the basic myth and its relationship to the cult of Artemis Kalliste at whose sanctuary in Arcadia Kallisto is said to be buried (Paus. 8.35.8). Prior to Sale, the only thorough study of the Kallisto myth was Franz 1890, which attempts to recover the Hesiodic version.

57. See Sale 1962. On the Hesiodic fragment, see West 1985, 91–93.

58. Sale (1965) recognizes an Arcadian version of the Kallisto myth, which he believes predates the Hesiodic.

59. Pherec., *FGrH* 3F157; Araithos, *FGrH* 316F2; Asios frag. 9K. See Dowden 1989, 182–83, on Nykteus and Keteus. He reports that Nykteus of Boeotia had a brother, Lykos, whose daughter, Antiope, was seduced by Zeus and bore twin boys who built the walls of Thebes. Antiope's tale sounds remarkably similar to Kallisto's.

60. Some scholars believe that Kallisto and Artemis were once one and the same; certainly by the time of Hesiod, the two were regarded as separate entities. For further discussion, see Dowden 1989, 189; Borgeaud 1988, 31, 201 n. 34; Jost 1985, 406; Bodson 1978, 138–39; Sale 1965; and Immerwahr 1891, 209.

61. Amphis as reported in Apollod. 3.8.2; Ov., *Met.* 2.425. The lion is curious because lions were not believed to have sex or to have sex only with leopards. One wonders if Kallisto may be a leopard in the metaphorical sense because she is virginal.

62. Hes. 163 M-W; Paus. 8.22.1. Arkas is also named as the son of Kallisto and Zeus in Hyg., *Fab.* 155, 224. See Trendall 1984. As Dowden (1989, 185) points out, although only Ovid (*Met.* 2.468–485) among ancient authors has Kallisto transformed before giving birth, Arkas's name clearly indicates that he was born from a bear.

63. Although only one source (Epimenides) names Pan as Kallisto's son, it is an early one (seventh or sixth century) and worth noting in relation to Pan's other qualities (I omit a detailed treatment of Pan here because he is a deity). Pan is associated most commonly with herding and shepherds, Dionysos, and sexuality, but Pan also hunts (*Hymn. Hom. Pan.* 13), is honored by hunters, and can inspire panic in battle. The Mount Lykaon *abaton* (sanctuary) also may have been sacred to Pan (Paus. 8.38.5), and a relief of the Calydonian boar hunt was found in a sanctuary to

Pan (infra n. 124). See Borgeaud 1988, 34–42, 63–65, 70–71, 98 (which also discusses Pan's relationship to battle). Depictions of Pan frequently show him with a lagobolon, the weapon used to hunt hares, which are associated with sexuality (see chapter 2). See Kahil 1991; and Jost 1985, 456–75.

64. Burkert (1979, 6–7) offers a Proppian analysis. He points out that the basic events of the Kallisto myth, which he perceives as leaving home, seclusion, rape, tribulation, and rescue, are common to other myths as well.

   I am aware that in relating the common elements of the "myth," I am creating yet another myth (and a simplified one at that), but I take this approach for the sake of brevity. I appeal to the generosity of the reader to forgive this transgression.

65. Henrichs (1987, 263) and Sale (1965, 15) think that Hera's appearance in the myth is a borrowing from the Io and Semele myths. Cf. Dowden 1989, 187–88, who reconstructs the "original myth" with the motifs: vow of virginity to Artemis, seduction by Zeus, discovery while undressing to bathe, metamorphosis into a bear by Artemis, birth of Arkas, and shooting by Artemis (189).

66. Arkas's later achievements are significant. Pausanias (8.4.1) notes that Arkas succeeded Nyktimos to rule the Pelasgians or Arcadians. Arkas made important contributions to his people, teaching them agriculture, which he had learned from Triptolemos, and how to bake bread and weave. He took the nymph Erato as his wife, with whom he had three sons, who inherited Arcadia when they came of age. Pausanias (8.9.3–4) points out the grave of Arkas near the altar of Hera at Mantinea and relates that Arkas's bones had been brought from Mainalos in accordance with a Delphic oracle (cf. Paus. 8.36.7).

67. Supra n. 54.

68. Ps. Eratosthenes, *Catast.*, in Olivieri (1907), 9–10 no. 8, lines 17–21. Presumably the precinct is that of Zeus Lykaios. Supra n. 54.

69. Although the element of catasterism is generally considered Hellenistic, Sale has argued that earlier authors knew of it and that Hesiod's *Astronomy* may have included this episode. Henrichs (1987, 260–61) rightly maintains that the matter of when the catasterism was added to the myth is not critical since it does not alter anything about the basic core of the myth.

70. McPhee 1990, 941, no. 2.

71. Scholars have seen reflections of the Acropolis dedication in Roman copies, including the Barberini suppliant of c. 430–425 in the Musée du Louvre (Svoronos, Sale) but the identification of this figure as Kallisto has generally not been accepted. See, e.g., Ridgway 1981, 112–14, figs. 86–88; Robertson 1975, 403. Other candidates for the Barberini suppliant include Danae, Alkmene, Penelope, Dido, one of the Erinyes, and Ariadne.

72. McPhee 1990, 941 no. 1. For a recent reconstruction, see Stansbury-O'Donnell 1990.

73. McPhee 1990, 941 no. 3; Borgeaud (1988, 29–30) discusses the Delphi dedication and its reliance on a version of the Arcadian myth of Arkas that aimed to connect Arkas with the traditions of Mount Lykaon.

74. See Bommelaer 1991, 104–6 no. 105.

75. McPhee 1990, 942 nos. 9, 10; Trendall 1984, 609 nos. 4, 5.

76. Jost (1985, 406) argues that this coin, together with evidence from Pausanias regarding Kallisto's tomb, enables us to understand an Arcadian tradition for the

Kallisto myth: because Artemis brings about Kallisto's death, the goddess is therefore honored at Kallisto's tomb.

77. Arkas appears on two other coins, both of the fourth-century: a stater from Pheneos and an obol, perhaps of Heraia, both of which are inscribed with Arkas's name. See Trendall 1984, 610 nos. 6, 7; Jost 1985, 407.

78. Trendall 1984, 609 nos. 1–4; 1977; McPhee 1990, 941–42 nos. 5–8.

79. On Lyssa, see Kossatz-Deissmann 1992.

80. McPhee (1990, 944) says that Lyssa indicates the vase's reliance on a tragic drama and that Kallisto may be about to commit suicide with the javelin.

81. McPhee (1990, 944) suggests that the rock on which Kallisto sits signifies her tomb. Contra: Jost 1985, 408 n. 4.

82. Trendall 1977, 101.

83. McPhee 1990, 944.

84. See Devambez 1981.

85. *ARV*[2] 604, 51; *Addenda*[2] 267.

86. Schefold 1981, 230–31. McPhee (1990, 943) refers to Schefold's suggestion as "certainly misguided."

87. Reeder 1995, 327–28 no. 100; Simon 1983, 87–88; Kahil 1977, 86–98.

88. Leto: Reeder 1995, 328; Lonsdale 1993, 188; Kahil 1977, 92. Hera: McPhee 1990, 943 no. 18.

89. Lonsdale 1993, 188. Lonsdale also points out that the dogs chasing a hare on the lower frieze of another Brauronian krateriskos (Basel, Herbert Cahn collection HC 502) echo the bear pursuing the running girls on the upper frieze, and that the girls respond to a frightening ritual (190–91). The krateriskos is well illustrated in Reeder 1995, 326–27.

90. Kahil 1977, 86, 87.

91. Simon 1983, 87–88. In her discussion of the Cahn fragments, Kahil (1977, 97) suggests that the arktoi mimic Iphigeneia. Scanlon (1990, 73–120), however, dissociates the krateriskoi from the arkteia.

92. On the arkteia, see Barringer 1996, 72; Reeder 1995, 321–28, with further references; and Deubner 1932, 204–8.

93. For the scholia, see Sale 1975.

94. Krateriskoi fragments have also been found in Pan's sanctuary at Eleusis, the only non-Artemisian use of krateriskoi. If Kallisto and Artemis are identical (supra n. 60), then one might speculate that Pan is Artemis's son. See Kahil 1965, 23, pl. 9:1.

95. Kahil 1977.

96. Henrichs 1981, 200.

97. Cf. supra n. 19.

98. Lloyd-Jones 1983, 93; Kahil 1977, 93–94. Archaeological evidence confirms Iphigeneia's association with Brauron; a shrine dedicated to her exists there, where girls made offerings.

99. See Henrichs 1981, 202. For further reading on Iphigeneia, see Dowden 1989, 9–47.

100. Henrichs 1987, 265. See also Jost 1985, 410. Dowden (1989, 190–91) proposes an Arcadian bear ritual counterpart to the arkteia; see also Arena 1979, 5–6.

101. Henrichs (1981, 202) claims that bears are interchangeable with virgins in these myths, which is true, but bears also make ideal mothers and therefore are not virgins. See infra. See also Pellizer 1982, 11–50.

102. This, like virtually everything else about the arkteia, is controversial.

103. Perlman 1989, 120, 121; Bodson (1978, 132–33) also points out the flaws of such an interpretation. The krokotos also recalls the robe worn by Iphigeneia when she was sacrificed (Aisch., *Ag.* 239); see, e.g., Arena 1979, 13.

104. E.g., Perlman 1989; Cole 1984, 241; Arena 1979, 24–25. Cf. Apollod. 3.9.2 and Ael., *VH* 13.1.19–20, who relate that Atalanta was suckled by a she-bear as a child.

105. Perlman 1989, 117.

106. Henrichs 1987, 265.

107. Cf. Dowden 1989, 190–91.

108. See Kahil 1977 followed by Lonsdale 1993, 190–91, who discounts the possibility that the painting depicts a particular moment of the ritual but accepts the general reference to the arkteia; and Jost 1985, 409–10. Contra: Bodson 1986, 307–8, who points out that the presence of a priest and priestesses at Brauron remains purely hypothetical.

109. Simon (1983, 87–88) interprets Artemis's arrow as directed against Kallisto, rather than the deer. But see Lonsdale 1993, 190, who believes the deer is the target.

110. The presence of the deer remains puzzling. The animals play a role in the Iphigeneia myth and also in the cult of Artemis Pagasitis in Thessaly (*nebreia*) in which young girls of marriageable age were identified with deer rather than bears. See Clement 1934, 401–9. Girls are likened to fawns in Archilochus frag. 196a (West). Is deer hunting a metaphor for sexual conquest?

111. Borgeaud 1988, 32–33.

112. On Atalanta's role reversals, see the brief remarks of Sourvinou-Inwood 1987, 152–53.

113. For a discussion of the possibility of a pre-Homeric version(s) and of its content, and of Homeric innovations, see Graf 1993, 64–68; Hainsworth 1993, 131–32; Bremmer 1988; Keck 1988, 153; Kakridis 1987, 11, 18–41; and March 1987, 29, 30–42. See also Felson Rubin and Sale 1984, and 1983, who argue that the story was not only pre-Homeric, but that the love of Meleager for Atalanta was part of this early tradition.

114. E.g., Stesichoros, *Suotherai* (*PMG* 221); Phrynichos, *Pleuroniae* as attested in Paus. 10.31.4; Bacchy. 5.71–154; Aisch., *Ch.* 603–12; a now lost play by Aisch. entitled *Atalanta*; a fragmentary play of Soph. entitled *Meleager* (Radt 1977, frags. 401–6); schol. at Ar., *Ran.* 1238; Euripides' fragmentary *Meleager* (Nauck 1964, frags. 515–39); Apollod. 1.8.2–3; Accius frags. 428–50; Diod. Sic. 4.34.2–5; and Ov., *Met.* 8.270–525. Barrett (1972, 1180) may be incorrect in his reading of column ii of P. Oxy. 2359 (Stesichoros, *Suotherai*) when he claims that the hunters were "taking up their positions at the nets." The Calydonian boar hunt was "conducted on a heroic scale," as Barrett acknowledges, and therefore, if we assume that later hunting ethics applied earlier, nets would have been inappropriate since they were the weapons of the immature or ephebic hunt. See Pl., *Leg.* 823e-824b and chapters 1 and 2. However, other scholars think that P.Oxy. 2359 is not part of Stesichoros's *Suotherai*, but of his *Games for Pelias*. See, e.g., Garner 1994, 29 n. 11; Lloyd-Jones 1958, 17 (Lobel had assigned 2359 to the *Suotherai*). Garner (26–38) instead proposes that P.Oxy. 3876 treats the story of Meleager and the Calydonian boar hunt and offers a reconstruction of the fragments.

115. For a full discussion of the literary sources and their relation to each other, see Arrigoni 1977, 9–47, and the summary by Woodford 1992, 414.

116. Hesiod (25 M-W, lines 12–13) states that Meleager was killed in battle by Apollo, and Pausanias (10.31.3) says that the *Eoeae* and *Minyad*, two epics, attribute Meleager's death to Apollo in the battle between the Curetes and Aetolians. Homer (*Il.* 9.566ff.) relates that Meleager killed his uncles, the Thestiadai, in a battle between the Aetolians of Calydon and the Curetes of Pleuron (cf. Bacchyl. 5.71–154), which originated in a dispute over the boar's hide; Althaea, in grief over her brother's death, cursed her son Meleager, and he subsequently withdrew from the fighting. When the Aetolians began losing badly, Meleager was approached by an embassy including family members with the hope of getting him to rejoin the fighting, but he stubbornly refused. He finally yielded to the entreaties of his wife Cleopatra, and although his fate is not explicitly stated in the *Iliad*, it can be assumed that he died in battle because 9.571 states that the Erinys heard Althaea's curse. Burkert (1983, 54) explains the battle after the hunt as a manifestation of human guilt over the killing of the boar.

   According to Phrynichus (as reported in Pausanias), Bacchylides, and the scholiast at Ar., *Ran.*1238, however, Meleager was killed when his mother Althaea placed a brand on the fire; it had been prophesied that when the brand was consumed, Meleager would die. Pausanias (10.31.4) claims that Phrynichus was repeating a story well known throughout Greece. See also n. 119 infra. Scholars suggest that Stesichoros was the inventor of the brand episode in his Συοθῆραι. See, e.g., Garner 1994, 28, 32–33; March 1987, 44–46; and Croiset 1898.

117. Apollodoros 3.9.2 also mentions Atalanta's participation in the Calydonian boar hunt.

118. For a brief discussion of the catalogs of names and the names that appear on vases, see Henrichs 1987, 252.

119. Aisch., *Cho.* 603–12; Apollod. 1.8.2–3, who recounts Meleager's love for Atalanta, but also says that he was married to Cleopatra; Accius frags. 428–50; Manilius, *Astronomica* 5.175–82; Paus. 10.31.4; Hyg., *Fab.* 174; schol. at Lucian 17.31, 30.1.17. Diod. Sic. 4.34.2–5 seems to combine several previous versions of the myth; he relates that Meleager was the first to stab the boar and tells of Meleager's love for Atalanta and that Meleager's uncles attacked Atalanta after Meleager awarded the boar's skin to her. Then Diodorus reports that Althaea responded with a curse and that the immortals paid heed to it, which recalls the Homeric version of the myth. Ovid (*Met.* 8.270–546) says that Meleager's uncles took the spoils of the hunt from Atalanta. Eustathius (*Commentarii ad Homeri Iliadem* 2.786.17–18) refers to Atalanta as Meleager's beloved and (at 2.802.3–6) says that Meleager gave the head and skin of the boar to his beloved Atalanta. Joannes Malalas (*Chronographia* 165.13–14) also states the latter. See also schol. at Hom., *Il.* 9.543; and schol. at Lucian 17.31.

   Apollodoros (1.8.2–3) offers another variant: he describes the aftermath of the hunt as recounted in *Iliad* 9 and confirms that Meleager was killed in battle, then claims that Althaea and Cleopatra killed themselves and that the women who mourned for them were transformed into birds. The metamorphoses of Althaea and Cleopatra are mentioned in the fragments of Sophocles' *Meleagros*, whose plot may have been that described in Apollodoros's second version. See Woodford 1992, 414; Radt 1977, frags. 401–6. Ovid (*Met.* 8.531–32) relates that Althaea committed suicide by driving a dagger through her heart, and both he (8.533–45) and Hyginus (*Fab.* 174) say that Meleager's sisters were transformed into birds because of their mourning for the death of Meleager. Callimachus (3.219–21) claims that the spoils of the hunt were brought to Arcadia (again, we note Arcadia's importance to hunting myths), which still possesses the boars' tusks. On the tusks, infra n. 124, and see Felson Rubin and Sale 1984, 215–17; 1983, 156–57; and Most 1983, 207.

120. Images of a boar hunt exist in earlier vase painting, but one cannot identify them with the Calydonian hunt. For example, a boar hunt appears on a Corinthian pyxis lid from Corinth of c. 600, the famous Dodwell Pyxis now in Munich (Staatliche Antikensammlungen 327; *Heldensage*³ 314, C3; Amyx 1988, 205–6, 284, 565, pl. 86). The names of the hunters are inscribed, but they do not correspond to any of the known hunters listed in the ancient literary sources. On the criteria for identifying the Calydonian boar hunt, see chapter 1; Woodford 1992, 416, 430; Keck 1988, 154–55; and Von Bothmer 1948, 44, who discounts the Corinthian vases as uncertain depictions. Cf. Schefold 1992, 197, who explains that the Corinthian vase paintings of the Calydonian boar hunt have hunters' names different from those on Attic vases because the Corinthian vases derive from a Corinthian epic; Langridge 1991; Keck 1988, 154; Schauenburg 1969, 12, who avers that in the case of the anonymous Corinthian vases, the Calydonian boar hunt is probably not intended, and that Corinthian vases with inscriptions suggest a lost myth; Daltrop 1966, 18; and Coste-Messelière 1936, 131–33. Boar hunts also appear on the interior of Laconian cups, and some of these could possibly depict the Calydonian boar hunt, e.g, Paris, Musée du Louvre E670 of c. 555–545; Basel, Antikenmuseum und Sammlung Ludwig, Moretti collection (no inventory number), illustrated in Stibbe 1972, 281 no. 220; 289 no. 350; Taf. 78:1, 127. Because of the long hair and animal skin of the leftmost hunter on Louvre E670, some have seen this figure as Atalanta, but see David 1993, 401, for a different view. The composition of the cup in Basel recalls the mythological boar hunt because of the wounded dog, which appears much like the wounded hunter Ankaios in typical Attic Calydonian boar hunt compositions.

121. Woodford 1992, 430. Keck (1988, 154) tries to demonstrate a direct link between literary text and image concerning the Calydonian boar hunt. This effort, however, is unnecessary for surely vase painters may have been influenced by oral accounts of these myths (i.e., folktales), in which details, such as the names of the participating hunters, would alter in the retelling. See also March 1987, 37–38, who tacitly assumes a strong literary influence on sixth-century vase paintings of the Calydonian boar hunt; and Minto 1960, 164.

122. Shapiro (1990, 136) explains this trend and similar ones with regard to other heroic adventures in Attic vase painting as attributable to a new interest in the deeds of individual heroes rather than in group activities. Cf. the discussion of the decline in collective hunts at the end of the fifth century in chapter 1.

123. Schnapp (1997, 286–317) traces the composition and distribution of Calydonian boar hunt paintings.

124. *Heldensage*³ 310, A3; Woodford 1992, 416 no. 8. The theme also appears on the reliefs from the heroon at Gjölbaschi-Trysa, on three Melian reliefs, on several relief

vases, in one of the pediments of the temple of Athena Alea at Tegea, on an Arcadian terracotta relief from the sanctuary of Pan Nomios in Athens, and perhaps in the metopes of the Sicyonian Treasury at Delphi. See chapter 4 for the presence of this myth in funerary contexts; Schnapp 1997, 377–79; Stewart 1977, 14–21, 60–62, 133; Coste-Messelière 1936, 120–27; and Jacobsthal 1931, 32–33 no. 27; 45 no. 59; 78–80 no. 103; 185; Taf. 15, 60, 70. It is scarcely surprising that the Calydonian boar hunt adorned the temple of Athena at Tegea because Tegea was part of the Arcadian League at the time of the creation of this pediment, and the Calydonian boar hunt features a great Arcadian figure, Atalanta. Pausanias (3.18.15, 8.46.1) draws a further connection between Tegea and the myth when he reports that the Calydonian boar's teeth were kept in the temple at Tegea and eventually transported to Rome by Augustus. Bevan (1986, 77) reports that many boars' tusks were found in the sanctuary of Athena Alea at Tegea, perhaps in connection with Atalanta. Bevan speculates that Atalanta may have had an altar in the shrine. Many boars' tusks were also found at Calydon (76).

125. On the appearance of Scythian archers, see Lissarrague 1990b, 125–49; Shapiro 1983, 111; Snodgrass 1967, 80–84; and Vos 1963, 40–52.

126. E.g., an Attic black-figure dinos of c. 560 from Greece, Boston, Museum of Fine Arts 34.212, *ABV* 87, 18; *Addenda*[2] 24; *Heldensage*[3] 310, A4.

127. *Heldensage*[3] 311, A13. On the appearance of Amazons in archaic Greek vase painting, see Shapiro 1983, 106; and Von Bothmer 1957, 6–115.

128. *ABV* 76, 1; *Para* 29; *Addenda*[2] 21; *Heldensage*[3] 310, A1. Schnapp (1979a, 197) believes that the bow designates heroic status or divinity.

129. One exception is an Attic black-figure band cup from Vulci of c. 540 signed by Archikles and Glaukytes in Munich, Staatliche Antikensammlungen 2243 (*ABV* 163, 2; *Para* 68; *Addenda*[2] 47; *Heldensage*[3] 311, A14), which bears the typical composition; the hunters are named, but Atalanta is absent. On the composition, see Keck 1988, 155–57; Kleiner 1972, 7–14; Daltrop 1966, 15–25; Von Bothmer 1948, 42–48; and Minto 1960, 36–40. Schnapp (1979a) claims that those Attic paintings that are certainly Calydonian do not include mounted hunters (204, 208). He distinguishes between mythological and nonmythological boar hunts on the basis of the inclusion of horses; the hunt on foot is, he states, narrative and diverse in its manifestations, while that on horseback is stereotypical and largely symmetrical. Schnapp, however, does not account for Munich, Staatliche Antikensammlungen 8600; Rome, Museo Gregoriano Etrusco Vaticano 306 (fig. 80); and Boston, Museum of Fine Arts 34.212, which are all clearly ornamented with the Calydonian boar hunt but include horsemen.

130. See Clark 1990, 39–41, pls. 82–84, 89:1. Clark writes that "perhaps" the scene is the Calydonian boar hunt, and the figure stabbing the boar's head may be Meleager (39). The Kaineus episode from the Centauromachy decorates the obverse, and a horseman appears on the interior.

The same composition occurs on a Corinthian krater of c. 600–575 in Toledo, Museum of Art 70.2 (*Heldensage*[3] 314, C2; Amyx 1988, 163).

131. Schnapp (1979a, 200, 204) states that the presence of any of the following in vase paintings is enough to satisfy the requirements for the Calydonian boar hunt: symmetrical placement of hunters around boar, the presence of Atalanta, a dog on the back of the boar, or Ankaios under the boar.

132. On heroizing genre scenes, see my introduction and chapter 1.

133. See Schnapp 1997, 368–76; Woodford 1992, 430; Kleiner 1972, 7–19.

134. *ARV*² 577, 52; *Addenda*² 262; *Heldensage*³ 314, B1. For the identification of this as the Calydonian boar hunt, see Kleiner 1972.

135. *Heldensage*³ 311, B2; Woodford 1992, 417 no. 25; Boardman 1984, 941 no. 9.

136. E.g., Woodford 1992, 414, 430; Most 1983, 204, 205; Séchan 1967, 423, 426; Page 1937, 179. Contra: Felson Rubin and Sale 1984, 214–15; 1983, 155; and Arrigoni 1977, 21. Page (1937, 179–80) and Séchan (1967, 423–33) offer skeletal reconstructions of the play based on the surviving fragments; and Trendall and Webster (1971, 98) claim that the play included preparations for the hunt of the boar and the events up to the death of Meleager.

137. *ARV*² 1410, 14; *Addenda*² 374.

138. On the hare, see Schnapp 1989, 82–86; Detienne 1979, 48–49.

139. *RVAp* 2, 497 no. 44.

140. On the ἴυγξ, see Shapiro 1985, 115–20; Gow 1934, 3, 5. See also Faraone 1993, 1–19; and Detienne 1994, xiii, 84–86.

141. See chapter 1 and Philostr., *VS* 2.550; Winkler 1990, 35 n. 43; Vidal-Naquet 1986, 112, 116–17; Maxwell-Stuart 1970; and Roussel 1941. Whether the cloaks were black or white matters little to this discussion of Attic red-figure vase painting, which often makes no special color distinctions. Lissarrague (1990b, 206) speaks of "la nudité éphébique" with regard to Attic red-figure depictions of warriors.

142. Two of the male hunters in the Calydonian boar hunt on a Melian relief in Berlin (Antikensammlung 5783) of c. 440 also wear only the chlamys. See Jacobsthal 1931. On male nudity and its association with ephebes and initiation in classical Greece, see Bonfante 1989, 545, 551–57.

143. Taylor 1991, 36–70.

144. Garner 1994 34; Schnapp 1992, 121 (though Schnapp [1997, 271–77] discusses Meleager and the Calydonian boar hunt and argues against an initiatory reading); Bremmer 1988, 2, 48–49. Bremmer also addresses the question of the age of the Calydonian boar hunt participants (48–49). See Vidal-Naquet 1986, 118, who refers to the Calydonian boar hunt as "the heroic prototype of the group hunt"; and Felson Rubin and Sale 1984, 213–14; 1983. Contra: Most 1983, 209–11. On the antiquity of the initiatory hunt, see Morris 1990, 151–52; Koehl 1986; and Felson Rubin and Sale 1983, 143, who also note the importance of the spear in the initiatory hunt because of its martial associations (145–46, 147).

145. Bremmer (1988, 42, 48) also compares these two myths. Felson Rubin and Sale (1983) contrast the two hunting myths and argue that Odysseus succeeds at his initiatory hunt because sexuality does not intervene at the hunt but takes place later, at its appropriate time, unlike the initiatory hunt of Meleager. Contra: Most 1983.

146. See Felson Rubin and Sale 1983, 145, 146, 147.

147. Supra n. 129.

148. Scanlon (1990, 103) claims that Atalanta as hunter is like the arktos of the arkteia, who participates in a sacred hunt as part of the initiation, and thus Atalanta, like the arktos, experiences a passage to maturity and from a wild state to a tamed state. Scanlon links Atalanta to the arktos because a bear reared Atalanta when she was a baby, and because of Artemis's association with bears.

149. Felson Rubin and Sale 1983, 154, 155. Schefold (1992, 185) proposes that the spoils

of the hunt go to Atalanta because she may be an ancient goddess as suggested by her name; therefore, her divine status would justify the gifts.

150. Hardwick 1990, 28–29; Tyrrell (1984, 2) says that the earliest vase paintings show Amazons dressed in armor with Greek weapons (49–50); Shapiro 1983, 108–9.

151. Boardman 1983, 7.

152. E.g., Attic black-figure dinos fragments of c. 570–560 in the Blatter collection in Bolligen: *Para* 42; *Addenda*[2] 28; *Heldensage*[3] 311, A16; Boeotian black-figure kantharos of c. 575–550 in Athens, National Museum 2855: *Heldensage*[3] 311, C1. Atalanta occasionally wields spears, rather than a bow and arrow, as on the François Vase (fig. 82).

153. Just 1989, 243; Lefkowitz 1986, 22; Tyrrell 1984, 55–57.

154. Just 1989, 258–59; Zeitlin 1982, 134–35.

155. See Ley 1990, 35 n. 11; Just 1989, 242; Hartog 1988, 216–24, who argues that Herodotos does not present a simple model of inversion but a more complex triangle between Greeks, Amazons, and Scythians; and Tyrrell 1984, 40–63. Cf. Detienne 1979, 32–33.

156. Just 1989, 243; Tyrrell 1984, 28; Lefkowitz 1986, 19.

157. Just 1989, 245, 249; DuBois 1982a, 38. Although see Hardwick 1990, 33–34.

158. Hardwick 1990, 18–21; Tyrrell 1984, 6, 16. Cf. Zeitlin 1978, 153.

159. *ARV*[2] 98, 2; *Addenda*[2] 172. Lissarrague 1992, 227–28; Hardwick 1990, 29. On the similarity of Amazons and maenads, see Blok 1995, 270–71, 407, 417, who also notes that in Attic black-figure, Herakles' duel with an Amazon is sometimes assimilated to an erotic image with a satyr and maenad (407). On archers as marginal figures, see Vidal-Naquet 1986, 88.

160. Hartog 1988, 217.

161. Hartog 1988, 52–54.

162. In Ovid's account of the Calydonian boar hunt (*Met.* 8.338), it is the boar who comes out of the bushes and ambushes the hunters; that is, the boar hunts like an ephebe (or the ephebe hunts like an animal).

163. *Heldensage*[3] 311, C4; Hemelrijk 1984, 29–30 no. 15; pls. 9, 16, 67–69, 131, 145–46, 152; figs. 20, 55, 61, 68, 72. Caeretan hydriae were all found in Italy (nearly all at Cerveteri) but are "Greek in character," and one bears Greek inscriptions. See Robertson 1975, 139. Hemelrijk believes that the artists of the Caeretan workshop were from East Greece and that the mythological hydriae were created for local Greeks (160).

164. Cf. Schefold 1992, 196; Friis Johansen 1962, 71. But see Hemelrijk 1984, 30, who rejects Friis Johansen's identification of Atalanta and instead reads the figure as male. Hemelrijk explains the figure's white skin as "typical of some East Greek wares" (173).

165. Atalanta appears as the ornament on a hoplite shield in literature (Eur., *Phoen.* 1108– 9; schol. at Eur., *Phoen.* 1107) but she never carries one.

166. Friis Johansen 1962, 66.

167. Ament (1993, 20) points out that the heroes associated with transvestism, Achilles and Herakles, are also associated with Amazons. I would add that these heroes take on female characteristics (i.e., role reversal) when they are smitten by love.

168. *ABV* 23; *Addenda*[2] 7; *Heldensage*[3] 310, A2; Barringer 1996, fig. 14a–b.

169. See Barringer 1996 fig. 11a–b.

170. Dinoi ornamented with the Calydonian boar hunt: Athens, Agora Museum P334; Rome, Museo Gregoriano Etrusco Vaticano 306, fig. 80; Bolligen, Switzerland, Blatter collection; Boston, Museum of Fine Arts 34.212; London, British Museum B124. See table 3.

171. Stewart (1983, 69) refers to dinoi as "wedding gifts par excellence." Dinoi decorated with wedding scenes include Sophilos's fragmentary dinos, Athens, National Museum, Acropolis 587 from the Acropolis (*ABV* 39, 15; *Addenda²* 10); the Erskine Dinos, also by Sophilos, British Museum 1971.11.1–1 (*Para* 19; *Addenda²* 10), both of which bear scenes of the wedding of Peleus and Thetis; a dinos of c. 530 in Salerno, Museo Nazionale, illustrated in Lissarrague 1992, 151, fig. 6; and perhaps the fragmentary Athens, National Museum, Acropolis 610 (*ABV* 82, 3). For dinoi used as wedding presents in Attic vase painting, see London, British Museum B197 (*ABV* 296, 1; *Para* 128; *Addenda²* 77) by the Painter of Berlin 1686 of c. 550 and Copenhagen, Nationalmuseet 9080 (*ARV²* 841, 75; *Para* 423; *Addenda²* 296) by the Sabouroff Painter of c. 460, both illustrated in Oakley and Sinos 1993, 28, 34, figs. 66, 92–95; London, British Museum 1920.12–21.1 (*ARV²* 1277, 23, *Addenda²* 357), a pyxis by the Marlay Painter of c. 430, also in Lissarrague 1992, 147–49, fig. 3; and Krauskopf 1977, 18 nos. 16–18 and 20; 20 nos. 23–24 and 28; 21, 22. Dinoi are also connected with Dionysiac reveling and occasionally appear as athletic prizes for funeral games in Attic black-figure vase painting (e.g., the games for Pelias discussed later, those for Patroklos on the François Vase).

172. Stewart 1983.

173. E.g., Haslam 1991, 45 and n.32 ("The notion that the krater was made as a wedding gift seems very attractive"); Hurwit 1985, 226–27. Contra: Shapiro 1990, 140–42. Against Stewart's claims of Stesichorean influence, see, e.g., Haslam 1991, 35–40; Schaus 1986, 119–28; and Williams 1983, 33, although Williams allows the possibility that Kleitias was aware of Stesichoros's popularity.

174. Perlman (1989, 111) points out that Artemis Καταγωγίς at Cyrene received the hide, head, and legs of an animal sacrifice. It seems likely that Atalanta is an offshoot of Artemis as is posited for Kallisto and Iphigeneia.

175. Vernant 1991, 195–243.

176. Schnapp (1989), Zeitlin (1985), Felson Rubin and Sale (1984, 218; 1983), and Detienne (1979, 26–52) discuss the prohibition against blurring the boundaries between hunting and sex, the realms of Artemis and Aphrodite but, as I've argued, I believe this to be an inaccurate view.

177. Ibyc. frag. 282A (viii) frag. 11 (5176) lines 11–14; Apollod. 3. 9. 2; Hyg., *Fab.* 273; and Tzetz., *Chil.* 12.937. In each case, writers mention Atalanta only in passing and provide no details. For a brief discussion of the names of the participants in the funerary games, see Henrichs 1987, 252–53. This episode occurred in the course of the adventures of Jason and the Argonauts among whom Atalanta is numbered.

178. Ley (1990) examines the Greek representations of this theme and reckons that fourteen vases of c. 560–475, along with a bronze relief of the mid-sixth century, depict the wrestling match. See also Boardman 1984, 945–46 nos. 62–80. Pausanias (3.19.6, 5.17.5–5.19.10) says that funeral games for Pelias also decorated the throne of Apollo at Amyklai and the Cypselos Chest and on the latter, Peleus appeared as a wrestler. See also Roller 1981, who argues that the popularity of this theme is due not only to the influence of a particular literary work, but also to the founda-

tion of three Panhellenic festivals (Pythian, Isthmian, and Nemean) in the sixth century.

179. Barringer 1996, fig. 19. See also the Attic black-figure dinos fragments of c. 560, Athens, National Museum, Acropolis 590c, illustrated in Barringer 1996, fig. 18. Other fragments of this vase (Acropolis 590a) are ornamented with the javelin throw contest at the funeral games for Pelias. See Roller 1981, 110–11, pl. 20:4, who offers a date of c. 575 for the vase.

180. E.g., Attic black-figure hydria of c. 550, Adolphseck, private collection. See Boardman 1984, 945 no. 64.

181. E.g., Attic black-figure skyphos attributed to the Krokotos Group, c. 500, London, British Museum 1925.12–17.10; Attic black-figure neck amphora from Nola by the Diosphos Painter, early fifth century, Berlin, Antikensammlung 1837 (*ABV* 509, 703; *Addenda*² 127), illustrated in Barringer 1996, figs. 20, 21. Ley (1990, 46) says that in Attic vase painting, the perizoma probably signifies the idea of "barbarian," an appropriate appellation for this female wrestler.

182. Berlin, Antikensammlung 8308, illustrated in Barringer 1996, fig. 25; Jacobsthal 1931, 61–62 no. 80, Taf. 41.

183. Jacobsthal 1931, 108–9.

184. Cf. Lefkowitz 1986, 44; Arrigoni 1985, 87, 113. Ley (1990, 55) also notes the emphasis on the sexual aspect of the palaistra in several vase paintings.

185. *ABV* 65, 113; *Addenda*² 166.

186. On female athletics, see Arrigoni 1985.

187. See Barringer 1995, 69–94.

188. *ARV*² 1512, 23; *Addenda*² 384. Roller (1981, 112) argues that the change in Atalanta's costume from chiton to perizoma suggests a new interpretation of the myth: vase painters began to associate the wrestling match less and less with the funeral games for Pelias and more and more with activities of the palaistra. In other words, Roller's argument supports the hypothesis presented here that Atalanta is regarded as an ephebe.

189. Although Atalanta appears nude and clearly female on this cup, she usually behaves as a male, and other than breasts, her physical appearance (like that of most females in late archaic and early classical Attic vase painting, e.g., Paris, Musée du Louvre A479 [MNB 1746], figs. 40–41), is usually masculine. When Atalanta wrestles Peleus, we might construe their pairing as a typical gymnasion competition, and Peleus's desire for Atalanta as almost homosexual, particularly because she has a largely masculine physique.

190. An Attic red-figure hydria by Psiax of c. 520–510 in a private collection in Tessin bears Atalanta wrestling Peleus on the body and satyrs and Dionysos on the shoulder. See Jeske and Stein 1982. Again, the two images may be complementary: the Dionysiac thiasos is typically associated with (frustrated) sexual activities and may underscore an erotic element in the wrestling match between Peleus and Atalanta. Maenads, however, are not present in this vase painting, so such a suggestion remains tentative.

191. Hes. 72–76 M-W. See also Schwartz 1960, 361–66, who discusses the fragments of Hesiod as well as the other ancient sources for this myth.

192. Either Atalanta (Apollod. 3.9.2; Ov., *Met.* 10.560–72) or her father (Hyg., *Fab.* 185) instigates the race.

193. Hippomenes: Hes. 72, 74 M-W; Euripides, according to Apollod. 3.9.2; schol. at
     Eur., *Ph.* 150; Theoc. 3.40–41; Ov., *Met.* 10.575–680; Hyg., *Fab.* 185; Lib., *Progym-
     nasmata* 33, 34; Serv., *In Verg. Aen.* 3.113.14–22; Nonnos, *Dion.* 48.180–82; Eust.,
     Il. 4.814.13–14; *Myth. Vat.* 1.39; schol. at Hom., *Il.* 23.683b1.6–7; schol. at Ap. Rhod.
     1.769–73; schol. at Theoc. 3.40–42d, 2.120b. Melanion: Hellanicus in *FGrH* frags.
     99, 162; schol. at Eur., *Phoen.* 151; Apollod. 3.9.2. Xenophon (*Cynegeticus* 1.7) re-
     ports that Meilanion [*sic*] won Atalanta, but makes no mention of the footrace.
     Cf. schol. at Eur., *Phoen.* 150; schol. at Ap. Rhod. 1.769. On Hippomenes, see
     Boardman 1990, 465–66. On Melanion, see Boardman 1992a.
194. The apples are sometimes said to be from Cyprus (Ov., *Met.* 10.644–650). Non-
     nos, (*Dion.* 48.180–82) calls them "gold-shining wedding gifts" (χρυσοφαῆ γαμήλια
     δῶρα). Cf. Nonnos *Dion.* 12.87–89. The scholiast at Theocritus 2.120b says that
     the apples were from Dionysos's wreath, and the *Mythographi Vaticani* 139 records
     that the apples came from the garden of the Hesperides.
195. Hes. 76 M-W; Theoc. 3.40–41; Apollod. 3.9.2; Ov., *Met.* 10.638–80; Hyg., *Fab.* 185;
     schol. at Theoc. 3.40–42b, which says that the apples came from the garden of the
     Hesperides. See also Eust., *Il.* 4.331.9–10.
196. Cf. Scholia to Ar., *Lys.* 785, which says that Atalanta did not flee from Meilanion
     [*sic*]. Ovid (*Ars am.* 2.185192) and Propertius (1.9–16) say that Milanion [*sic*] per-
     formed many labors (all related to hunting, according to Ovid) out of love for Ata-
     lanta, and Propertius reports that he eventually won her. Only one extant vase
     painting is firmly connected with this myth, but it only shows the preparations for
     the race: an Attic red-figure kalyx krater from Bologna of c. 420 by the Dinos
     Painter, Bologna, Museo Civico Archeologico 300; *ARV*² 1152, 7; *Para* 457; *Ad-
     denda*² 336. See Barringer 1996, 71–72. Another vase may show the race itself, but
     it is fragmentary. See Hübner 1862, 264 no. 632.
197. Ley 1990, 36; Gernet 1981, 24–25; Detienne 1979, 33–34.
198. Cf. Ley 1990, 36; Detienne 1979, xi, 34. Detienne concentrates on the Ovidian
     version of the Atalanta footrace myth, comparing Atalanta to Adonis and examin-
     ing the connections between marriage and the hunt. He does not discuss the ini-
     tiatory aspects of either activity.
199. Cf. Detienne 1979, 31.
200. Cf. Scanlon 1990, 105, 106; Brulé 1987, 58, 59. Ovid (*Met.* 10.613–15) stresses the
     youthfulness of Hippomenes.
201. On the arkteia, see earlier discussion and citations in this chapter.
202. Noted also by Detienne 1979, 41. See Ar., *Lys.* 781–96.
203. Vidal-Naquet 1986, 106–28. See chapter 1.
204. Detienne (1979, 41), however, says that "the black hunter is the net into which
     Atalanta casts herself," suggesting, if one follows later dicta, that the myth con-
     cerns hunting of the immature kind.
205. Detienne 1979, xi, 33, 34.
206. Apollodoros's description of Atalanta as an armed running athlete conjures up im-
     ages of the pyrrhic dance and ephebic contests, but a chase was not normally part
     of Greek festivals, religious or otherwise.
207. Scanlon 1990, 73–74.
208. Bérard (1988, 282) claims Atalanta as the only heroine who combines the quali-
     ties of huntress (ephebe) with those of the athlete. The apples in this myth are also

significant for their erotic and specifically nuptial associations. See Barringer 1996, 74, with further bibliography; and Reeder 1995, 363–64.

209. Boardman 1983, 4. Boardman also writes that in vase painting Eros usually wields the whip "in pursuit of boys." The highly masculine Atalanta may be a suitable substitute. On this vase, see, e.g., Buitron-Oliver 1995b; Bérard 1988, 280; Boardman 1983; Boulter 1971, 21–23, pls. 32–34, 35:1.

210. Boulter 1971, 21.

211. Cf. Boardman 1983, 18.

212. Barringer 1995, 95–109; Buitron-Oliver 1995b, 440.

213. On female nudity and dress in athletics, see Arrigoni 1977, esp. 70.

214. Cf. Calame 1977, 189.

215. Schol. at Aisch., *Sept.* 532.9–13, 533.1–4, 535.4–5, in Dindorf 1962; Soph., *OC* 1320 and schol. ad loc; Eur., *Phoen.* 150 and schol. ad loc. 1153, *Supp.* 887–89; Hecataeus in *FGrH* frag. 32; Apollod. 3.9.2; Diod. Sic. 4.65.4, 4.65.7.

216. Cf. Scanlon 1990, 106.

217. Note that this botched sacrifice mirrors Oineus's, which triggered the events leading to the Calydonian boar hunt.

218. Ov., *Met.* 10.686–695; Hyg., *Fab.* 185; Serv., *In Verg. Aen.* 3.113.22–26; *Myth. Vat.* 1.39.

219. Cf. schol. at Theoc. 3.40–42b. Nonnos, *Dionysiaca* 12.87–89 credits Artemis with changing Atalanta to a lioness, presumably as punishment for leaving her realm (cf. Kallisto). See Detienne 1979, 103 n.137. Although Apollodoros does not specify which sanctuary to Zeus is involved, Jost 1985, 256 n. 2 identifies it as a sanctuary of Zeus Lykaios and says that this myth copies another myth forbidding entry to the sanctuary of Zeus Lykaios. Supra n. 54.

220. Detienne 1979, 45–46. Note that Euripides (*Med.* 1339–43) describes Medea as a lioness and not as a woman, and Aischylos (*Ag.* 716ff.) likens Helen to a lion cub. Was this feline image reserved for strong, threatening women? Cf. DuBois 1982b, 208. DuBois (1982a, 112ff.) examines Medea as the foreigner, as the outsider who invades the Greek city, but her very femaleness makes her Other and the enemy within.

221. Detienne (1979, 46) describes Atalanta's "animal metamorphosis as a function of Atalanta's original hostility to a marital scheme whose emblem is Aphrodite qua goddess of desire and sexual union." Atalanta's son, Parthenopaios reflects her sexual ambiguity in his name, which includes *parthenos* (virgin). Parthenopaios had a distinguished history, serving as one of the leaders of the Seven against Thebes, where he fought and died bravely (Soph. *OC* 1320–22; Eur., *Phoen.* 150–54; Apollod. 3.9.2; Diod. Sic. 4.65.7) and was praised for his good character (Eur., *Supp.* 887–89).

222. According to Dowden (1989, 182) Nykteus is sometimes a Boeotian, rather than an Arcadian. Dowden (1989, 182–83) also discusses the connections between Boeotia and Arcadia, both in myth (and he cites the example of Atalanta) and in history. He explains the Arcadian-Boeotian link as a logical one based on population movements in the second millennium (183).

223. Dowden 1989, 189–91.

224. Calame (1977, 432) observes that when Zeus appears as Artemis to seduce Kallisto, Kallisto experiences sexual initiation into heterosexuality via homosexuality, that she has heterosexual sex by a seemingly same-sex seducer. Contra: Henrichs 1987, 262 n. 82.

225. Cf. Neer 1995, 142 re: Lykaon Painter depiction of Aktaion.

CHAPTER 4: HUNTING AND THE FUNERARY REALM

1. On a Persian origin for mounted hunting, see Ghedini 1992, 74.

2. Although this text has argued against the concept of a black hunter, we should note that Vidal-Naquet (1984) argues that Alexander's conduct in battle qualifies him as a black hunter.

3. Robertson (1992, 253) dates this development to the second half of the fifth century but Kurtz 1975, xix gives the earlier date. Kurtz suggests that fifth-century white-ground lekythoi developed as replacements for stone memorials that may have been prohibited by sumptuary legislation (xix–xx).

4. *ARV*² 302, 21; *Addenda*² 212.

5. *ARV*² 1230, 37; *Addenda*² 351. Cf. Bonn, Akademisches Kunstmuseum 1011 of c. 450 by the Thanatos Painter, *ARV*² 1230, 38; and New York, Metropolitan Museum of Art 06.1021.127 of c. 450 B.C. by the Tymbos Painter, *ARV*² 757, 90 for similar compositions. The painting on yet another white-ground lekythos employs the same type of hunting scene but it omits the tomb: Athens, National Museum 1973 of c. 480, *ARV*² 690, 9, *Addenda*² 280.

6. Robertson (1992, 203) interprets the hare hunting at the tomb as "life in the shadow of death," which is certainly the case but considering what we now know of the hunt and the hare, this explanation is incomplete.

7. *ARV*² 753, 2.

8. Buitron-Oliver, 1995b.

9. Jacobsthal 1931, 107–9.

10. Jacobsthal 1931, 107–9, 176. Jacobsthal, like others before him, questions the place of origin of the so-called Melian reliefs and concludes that Melos is likely (153–54).

11. Jacobsthal (1931) catalogs the reliefs and analyzes their style. A convenient listing of subjects appears on pp. 175–76 n. 1.

12. Jacobsthal 1931, 31–33 nos. 24–27; 45–46 nos. 59–60; 74–76 nos. 97–98; 78–80 no. 103; Taf. 13–15, 26, 27, 43, 56, 60. Jacobsthal thinks the reliefs were influenced by Attic vases (125ff.).

13. See Clairmont 1993, 1:225, for identification criteria. E.g., Brauron, Museum BE 66 of c. 400 (fig. 96); a marble lekythos of c. 375–350, present whereabouts unknown, in Clairmont 1993, 2:338–39 no. 2.348b; Piraeus, Archaeological Museum 5282 of c. 400–375, in Clairmont 1993, 2:695 no. 2.793; Piraeus, Archaeological Museum 4563 of c. 400–375, in Clairmont 1993, 2:696 no. 2.794; Athens, National Museum 3273 of c. 375–350, in Clairmont 1993, 2:701–702 no. 2.809; marble lekythos of c. 375–350, present whereabouts unknown in Clairmont 1993, 2:760–61 no. 2.876a; Athens, National Museum 869 (Ilissos Stele) of c. 350–300, in Clairmont 1993, 2:821–24 no. 2.950; Athens, National Museum 4016 of c. 400–375, in Clairmont 1993, 3:95–96 no. 3.232; Athens, National Museum 4015 of c. 400–375, in Clairmont 1993, 3:96 no. 3.233; Brauron, Museum BE 32 of c. 375–350, in Clairmont 1993, 3:463–67 no. 3.821; and Rhamnous, Museum 375 of c. 375–350, in Clairmont 1993, 2:701 no. 808, which perhaps portrays a hunter with a warrior. See also Clairmont 1993, 2:550 no. 2.433b; 2:747 no. 2.868, for examples of hunters with quivers or bows.

14. Dogs are an important element in hunting as evidenced by Attic vase painting and Xenophon's *Cynegeticus* of the fourth century, which was written as a manual for

aristocratic hunters. Xenophon discusses the types of dogs that should be used (3–4), the equipment for the dogs (6.1), their feeding and care (6.2), the breeding of dogs (7.1–4), the naming of hunting dogs (7.5), and training hunting dogs (7.6–12). Dogs and hunters with dogs also received sacrifices at the fourth-century Asklepieion in the Piraeus, according to *IG* II² 47 and *IG* II² 4962. Parker (1996, 182) suggests a mythological explanation for this puzzling practice: Hellenistic myth tells how Asklepios was exposed as a baby and guarded or suckled by a dog, then discovered by hunters with dogs (*FGrH* 244 F138; cf. Paus. 2.26.3–5). One might recall that the hunter Atalanta was exposed as an infant and suckled by a she-bear, then rescued by hunters. See Barringer 1996, 49, with citations.

Numerous Attic stelai or lekythoi depict dogs but many are not clearly hunting dogs, which resemble modern greyhounds, or the accompanying figure(s) (e.g., female, child) are incongruous with a hunting interpretation. On hunting dogs, see Mainoldi 1984 and Koch-Harnack 1983, 79, 81, who speculates that the dogs in pederastic courtship scenes are meant as love gifts. For hunting dogs together with Dionysos but no captured game, see Bloomington, Indiana University Art Museum 71.82, an Attic black-figure amphora by the Amasis Painter, *Para* 65, *Addenda*² 43. And on hunting dogs on Greek funerary stelai, see Zlotogorska 1997.

15. Clairmont 1993, 1:232 no. 1.030. This may also be among the earliest or the earliest of classical Attic gravestones, according to Clairmont.
16. Clairmont 1993, 2:153–54 no. 2.214a. Cf. London, British Museum 1816.6–10.384 (Stele of Aristokles) of c. 400–375, in Clairmont 1993, 2:145–46 no. 2.209a, which depicts a rider on horseback and a slave boy on foot; the figures may hold lagobola but no prey is visible on the stone. See also Cambridge, Fitzwilliam Museum Gr. 20.1865 of c. 375–350, in Clairmont 1993, 2:746–47 no. 2.867a, which shows a man, perhaps a hunter, standing near his horse.
17. Clairmont 1993, 1:478 no. 1.875. Cf. Athens, National Museum 3702 of c. 350–300, in Clairmont 1993, 1:497 no. 1.935.
18. As Clairmont 1993, 1:478.
19. See chapter 1.Some Attic stelai or funerary stone lekythoi portray the deceased holding spears without further references to either hunting or warfare. It is possible that the same type of ambiguity applies to these images—that is, the viewer was meant to understand the figure as both warrior and hunter, and also to apprehend the similarity between the two activities. See, e.g., the lekythos in Athens, National Museum (no inventory number) of c. 430–420 in Clairmont 1993, 1:507–8 no. 1.957.
20. Clairmont 1993, 1:242–43 no. 1.154.
21. Clairmont 1993, 1:443 no. 1.788.
22. Clairmont 1993, 1:296–98 no. 1.289.
23. Clairmont 1993, 1:297.
24. Clairmont 1993, 1:446–47 no. 1.796. Cf. Brauron, Museum BE 5 of c. 400–375 of which only traces of two figures, one of whom was Kallimedon as attested by an inscription, and most of a dog survives. See Clairmont 1993, 1:451–52 no. 1.820.
25. Clairmont 1993, 3:75–76 no. 3.195 and 3.200. The upper left portion of the stele is now in New York in the Levy-White Collection (it is not visible in fig. 96). I am grateful to Hans Goette and Basil Petrakos for bringing this to my attention and providing citations. See Bergemann 1997, 159 no. 45; Despinis 1991–92, who first recognized that the two slabs join; and Von Bothmer 1990, 124–26.

26. Clairmont (1993, 3:75) interprets the walking stick as indicating an elderly man but based on the evidence of chapter 2, a walking stick can simply point to an aristocrat, indeed an aristocratic erastes admiring a young man.

27. Though Ridgway (1997, 163) speculates that such monuments may represent the single large expenditure of a nonelite family.

28. Ghedini (1992, 74–75) remarks on the diffusion of hunt scenes in funerary contexts in all areas under Persian influence.

29. E.g., Ferron 1993; Jacobs 1987. For a recent discussion of the complex intermingling of Greek and Eastern characteristics on Eastern fourth-century monuments, see the brief remarks in Ridgway 1999, 53, 202, and the more extensive treatment in Ridgway 1997, 78ff.

30. E.g., Ridgway 1999, 81, 83–84; 1997, 90–91, 93, 101–2; Barringer 1995, 61; Fleischer 1983, 30–31; and Dentzer 1982, 242. Ferron (1993, 263–77) gives a summary of the traditional interpretations of various Phoenician sarcophagi but argues that the images are drawn from Near Eastern myth and religion (277–317).

31. Cf. Jacobs 1987, 57.

32. Friis Johansen 1942.

33. One may depict a hare hunt: Once Izmir, Evangelical School of c. 525–515, in Cook 1981, 10–12 no. 10, fig. 8.

34. Cook 1981, 24 no. 9, pl. 27:1–2.

35. Cook 1981, 23–24 no. 7, pl. 26. Cf. Istanbul, Archaeological Museum 1353 of c. 510, in Cook 1981, 16 no. 2, pls. 16, 17:2–3, with figures in chariots accompanied by hunting dogs but not actually hunting; and Hanover 1897.12; Istanbul, Archaeological Museum 1427 + London, British Museum 86.3–26.1 of c. 530–525; London, British Museum 96.6–15.1; and Paris, Musée du Louvre CA1024, in Cook 1981, 9–10, 31–34, pls. 6, 7, 15, 39–46, 54, with armed hoplites engaged in battle near chariots while hunting dogs run beneath the horses, a combination of battle and hunting imagery akin to those discussed in chapter 1. Princeton, University Art Museum y1990–9 (*Record of the Art Museum, Princeton University* 50:1 [1991]: 58) has a hoplite battle in one register with a boar hunt below; interestingly, a dead or wounded warrior lies between the two hoplites, a motif usually seen in the Calydonian boar hunt. For dogs in battle, see Cook 1952, who maintains that dogs are complementary motifs to horses on Clazomenian sarcophagi and not necessarily relevant to the battle shown.

36. E.g., the cylinder seal of an anonymous king of the sixth to fourth century, and another of Darius of c. 500, illustrated in Ghirshman 1964, figs. 329, 332.

37. E.g., the painting from the palace at Til Barsce from the seventh century, illustrated in Parrot 1961, fig. 345.

38. Amiet 1980, figs. 119, 600, 623; Parrot 1961, figs. 63–65. Cf. the lion hunt carved in ivory relief in Assyrian style of the end of the eighth century from Ziwiyeh, now in Teheran, and the much earlier stele of c. 3300 from Uruk, now in Baghdad, illustrated by Amiet 1980, figs. 134, 228. Ferron (1993, 189ff.) traces the history of the chariot hunt in Eastern art.

39. Pfuhl and Möbius 1977, 11–12 no. 9, Taf. 3: 9 (Athens, National Museum 40 + Komotini fragment of c. 500 from Dikaia), 12 no. 10, Taf. 4:10 (Sofia, National Museum 727 of c. 490 from Apollonia), 14 no. 13, Taf. 4:13 (Kastamonu 377 of c. 460–450 from Sinope).

40. Pfuhl and Möbius 1977, 13 no. 12, Taf. 4:12 (Naples, Museo Archeologico Nazionale 6556 of c. 480 from Lydia). Note that this figure also carries an aryballos, the attribute of an athlete.

41. E.g., Pfuhl and Möbius 1977, 25–26 no. 56, Taf. 14:56; 35–36 no. 92, Taf. 22:92.

42. Pfuhl and Möbius 1977, 11 no. 8, Taf. 3: 8 (Istanbul, Archaeological Museum 507 of c. 500).

43. Pfuhl and Möbius 1977, 17–18 no. 26, Taf. 7:26.

44. On the cock in funerary contexts, particularly standing upon a tomb, see Weicker 1905, who argues that the cock is an apparition of the deceased, and stresses its courageous and apotropaic qualities. I think Weicker is certainly right about the cock's valorous qualities, and this may be the main thrust of images of cocks standing on tombs, but I think the use of the cock also points to the bird's associations with the erotic sphere, which, as argued in chapter 2, draws on the cock's virile and combative associations. Cf. *Anth. Pal.* 7.428, which refers to the cock adorning a tomb as emblematic that the deceased was skilled in love: "που περὶ Κύπριν πρᾶτος."

45. Pfuhl and Möbius 1977, 20 no. 36, Taf. 10:36 (Rhodes, Archaeological Museum, no inventory number, of the early fourth century), 20 no. 37, Taf. 10:37 (Paris, Musée du Louvre 805 of c. 375–350 from Rhodes).

46. Dentzer 1982, 240–43, 568 no. R6, figs. 185–88; Fehr 1971, 115–16 no. 473.

47. On Totenmahl typology and iconography, see Thönges-Stringaris 1965. For the Totenmahl's heroizing connotations, see Ridgway 1970, 46. On banquets more generally (as opposed to the subcategory of Totenmahl), see Fehr 1971.

48. Jacobs 1987, 57, Taf. 13:3.

49. Nollé 1992, 27–30, Taf. 9–10; Pfuhl and Möbius 1977, 30–31 no. 73, Taf. 19:73. Ghirshman (1964, 349 fig. 442) identifies various Persian elements: the horse's trappings, the tufts of hair on the horse's head, and the "Assyro-Persian gallop" but also states that the banquet takes place in a Greek setting. A partial Greek inscription is clearly visible on the back surface of the front of the relief. See Nollé 1992, for other Daskyleion stelai with hunting images.

50. Exceptions include the votive reliefs from the Asklepieion in Athens, Athens, National Museum 1517 and 2413 (Dentzer 1982, 585 no. R147; 586 no. R160; figs. 413, 431–32); and a relief of c. 400 from Piraeus in Athens, National Museum 1501 (Thönges-Stringaris 1965, 15 no. 65).

51. Thönges-Stringaris 1965, 3–4 nos. 33, 34. Cf. Athens, National Museum 39 from Orchomenos, illustrated in Stewart 1990, pl. 254; and the combination of banquet and hunting scenes on the frieze of the temple of Athena at Assos of c. 540–520. Boardman (1978, fig. 216) speculates that the banquet on the Assos frieze may be a feast in honor of Herakles.

52. E.g., Ridgway 1997, 173–77, who also offers recent bibliography; Ridgway (1990, 44–45) considers several possibilities for authorship of the sarcophagi; Stewart 1990, 171; Robertson 1975, 404–5. Ferron (1993), however associates the Sidonian sarcophagi with local workshops.

53. Though Ridgway (1997, 173–74) reviews the controversies over the dates.

54. Boardman 1995, 215; Ridgway 1981, 150.

55. Palagia 1998, 25.

56. E.g., the boar hunt, accompanied by dogs, on a bronze belt plaque of the ninth to eighth century from Luristan, now in Paris (Musée du Louvre), illustrated by Par-

rot 1961, fig. 159. Note that the boar is not the only prey; a buck, lion, bull, fox, and antelopes are also hunted. Ghirshman (1964, 350) also points out that boars' tusks appear on the cross-straps of horses' bridles, particularly on the Persepolis reliefs, and he characterizes them as "specifically Iranian."

57. Fleischer 1983, 63, Tafs. 12–17.
58. See Fleischer 1983, Taf. 14:2. The bear and boar hunt also appear on the Nereid Monument's east architrave frieze.
59. The remains of seven dogs (greyhounds, according to Fleischer) were found together with those of the deceased in the Mourning Women Sarcophagus, and Fleischer (1983, 3, 31) posits a link between the hunting dogs of the sockel frieze and actual dogs buried in the tomb.
60. Fleischer 1983, 31. Attempts have been made to identify the deceased in the various hunting friezes but no accord has been reached on this point. See Fleischer 1983, 31–33.
61. See, e.g., Ferron 1993, pls. LX–LXVII, LXXX–LXXXIX; Ridgway 1990, 37–45, with extensive bibliography; Stewart 1990, 193–95, pls. 588–94; Robertson 1975, 481–82, pls. 151a–c.
62. E.g., Ridgway 1990, 42–45.
63. Stewart 1990, 194.
64. Stewart 1990, 194.
65. E.g., Athens, National Museum 14960 of c. 700–675, in Friis Johansen 1923, 93, pl. XXIV:1a–b; and Perachora 1570 of c. 600–575, in Schnapp 1997, 191, 480 no. 27.
66. Stewart 1990, 194–95. Robertson (1975, 482) also suggests possible influence from the now lost bronze lion hunt group at Delphi made by Lysippos and Leochares.
67. ARV^2 1407, 1; *Para* 488; Tiverios 1997; Boardman 1989, fig. 340.
68. Tiverios (1997, 272ff.) argues against Stephani's proposal that the lekythos represented a mythological hunt in the land of the Hyperboreans.
69. ARV^2 1407.
70. Tiverios (1997) thinks that the lekythos demonstrates the tone of relationships between the three key figures, Cyrus, Darius, and Abrokomas.
71. Tiverios 1997, 280.
72. Keen (1998, 52) mentions this with regard to the inscription of Erbbina from the Letoon in Lycia.
73. E.g., Ridgway 1997, 78–79; Stewart 1990, 171; Robertson 1975, 403–5.
74. Keen (1998, 182) puts their number at 1,085 including 4 heroa among which the Trysa heroon is numbered.
75. Borchhardt and Mader 1972, 15.
76. See Barringer 1995, 59–66, 233–34 no. 385, with bibliography. The traditional identification of the females in the intercolumniations as Nereids has recently been challenged, e.g., Robinson 1995, who argues that they are the Lycian water nymphs, the Eliyāna; and Keen 1998, 204–6, who proposes that they are dancing women, who represent the "Lycian female spirits of the dead," and leans toward viewing them, like Robinson, as the Eliyāna.
77. The abduction of Thetis by Peleus, seen in two stages, is the usual interpretation (see the bibliography in Barringer 1995, 62 n. 22) but Harrison (1992) proposes Herakles and Auge for London, British Museum 927, and Persephone and Hades or

Helen and Theseus for its opposite counterpart, London, British Museum 926. Ridgway (1997, 87) raises other possibilities as well.

78. On city siege scenes in Lycian art, see now Erath 1997, 172–212; and Childs 1978.

79. Robertson (1975, 404) refers to the bear as "local colour."

80. For example, an Assyrian prototype may exist for the city siege motif. See Erath 1997, 187–91; Ridgway 1997, 81; Jacobs 1987, 47ff.

81. Though Jacobs (1987, 69–70) notes that these subjects rarely appear in Persian monumental art and argues that their use in Lycian art derives from late archaic Greek art, rather than Assyrian or other Near Eastern art.

82. On the heroon at Limyra, see, e.g., Ridgway 1997, 94–99; Borchhardt and Borchhardt-Birbaumer 1992; Borchhardt 1976; and Borchhardt and Mader 1972.

83. Ghedini 1992, 74.

84. Barringer 1995, 49–66.

85. On the date, see Childs 1978, 14, who fixes it at c. 370.

86. Oberleitner 1994; Eichler 1950; Benndorf 1891; 1890; 1889. Oberleitner includes a full bibliography (68).

87. Oberleitner (1994) sees relationships between the friezes and offers some good interpretations but leaves many issues unexplored. I am presently planning a full study of the Trysa heroon's iconology.

88. Stewart 1990, 172.

89. No inscriptions survive from the Trysa heroon to aid in identifying its occupant though Thiersch (1907, 239) speculates on the basis of the iconography that the heroon honored an Athenian male married to a Lycian female of noble descent. Whether the program was devised by the ruler himself or others is not critical to our discussion though the handful of inscriptions on Lycian tombs reveals that the tombs were prepared while their intended occupants were still alive. See Keen 1998, 185.

90. The Dereimis-Aischylos Sarcophagus, which is stylistically compatible with the heroon friezes and therefore judged contemporary with them, once stood outside the temenos wall in the necropolis at the southeast and like the friezes, resides today at the Kunsthistorisches Museum in Vienna. It stands five meters high and, like many Lycian sarcophagi, consists of a wishbone-roofed central chamber standing on a stepped base. The lid is carved with reliefs: a man in a horse-drawn chariot on each of the long sides, men reclining at a banquet on both sides of the vertical roof ridge, pairs of seated men on each short side, and two lion protomes on each of the long sides. A Greek inscription bearing the names Dereimis and Aischylos, sons of Parnos, is carved on one long side, perhaps an indication of reuse in antiquity. See Oberleitner 1994, 53; Dentzer 1982, 412.

91. Borchhardt and Borchhardt-Birbaumer 1992, 100; Benndorf 1889, 37, Abb. 24.

92. Robertson 1975, 405, though Robertson thinks that the application of sculpted reliefs within the temenos wall of a heroon may have been inspired by Athenian monumental painting.

93. Dentzer (1982, 408, 410) is not certain of the funerary nature of the banquets held in this building.

94. Childs 1976. Keen (1998, 159) reports that some scholars speculate that the Trysa ruler was Mithrapata.

95. Ridgway 1997, 88ff.; Oberleitner 1994, 56–61; Stewart 1990, 171; Mackenzie 1898; Benndorf 1891; 1890; 1889.
96. Ridgway (1997, 90) believes that the interior doorway reliefs allude to "some Lykian ritual."
97. Childs 1978, 5.
98. Noted also by Childs 1978, 34. Klimowsky (1964) cites numerous examples. Parasols also appear in Attic vase painting, sculpture, and literature, and in South Italian vase painting. See, e.g., Miller 1997, 196–98.
99. Childs 1978, 34.
100. Childs 1978, 18–21, 31–36.
101. Stewart 1990, 171–72; Childs (1978) discusses the city siege scenes at Trysa, their relationship to other such scenes in Lycia, and their Eastern and Greek elements.
102. Jacobs 1987, 65–67, 70.
103. Oberleitner 1994, 51.
104. Oberleitner 1994, 54.
105. Oberleitner 1994, 33–36.
106. Childs 1978, 14.
107. Boardman 1995, 192.
108. Borchhardt and Borchhardt-Birbaumer (1992, 102) propose that Theseus's unification of Athens may have been a mythological analogy for the Lycian king Pericles' unification of Lycia but the authors concede that nothing is known of the relationship of Pericles to the dynast at Trysa.
109. Cf. Gurlitt 1894, 283–84.
110. Hom., *Il.* 6.184ff.; Quint. Smyrn. 10.161–63. See Oberleitner 1994, 28–29, 43, 55; and Borchhardt and Borchhardt-Birbaumer 1992, 101. On Bellerophon, see Lochin 1994; and on the hero's Greek origins, see Keen 1998, 211, who thinks Bellerophon may originally have been a Greek hero and not of Eastern origin.
111. Hom., *Il.* 6.168–182; Paus. 3.18.13. See also Hes., *Theog.* 325, 43 M-W.
112. See Hdt. 7.61; Hellanicos, *FGrH* 4F60; Borchhardt and Borchhardt-Birbaumer 1992, 112; Borchhardt and Mader 1972, 12–15. On Perseus, see Roccos 1994.
113. Oberleitner 1994, 28–29, 43, 55; Borchhardt and Borchhardt-Birbaumer 1992, 101.
114. Likewise, I think Oberleitner strains the limits of credibility when he views Perseus as a further elaboration of the Bellerophon story because Perseus was responsible for slaying Medusa, and Pegasos, born from Medusa's severed head, was the helper of Bellerophon. One could view these images from a single location but the connection between Bellerophon and Perseus is too remote and complex for all but the most sophisticated viewer to make. Oberleitner (1994, 55) considers what the viewer might and might not have understood: the mythological images, the heroized generic scenes, and more subtle readings would have been accessible to the most educated viewers, family members, and those participating in the funerary cult, while less sophisticated viewers, who would not have been admitted to the temenos, would have been presented with standard, simpler images of familiar themes on the exterior.
115. Ridgway (1999, 160; 1997, 107 n. 29) raises the same objection. Oberleitner (1994, 43) recognizes problems with such a reading but does not discard it. See also Stewart 1990, 172.
116. Benndorf (1889) was the first to suggest the Trojan War theme for the west wall,

whose three scenes he believed were interconnected and influenced by the *Aethiopis*, which describes the arrival of the Amazons. This view was quickly countered by Gardner (1889, 285), who thinks the west wall depicts a local Lycian battle. Noack (1893) argued further for the latter interpretation, and Childs (1978, 14) follows Noack's lead. Gurlitt (1894, 287–89) agrees with Noack on some points, whereas Borchhardt and Mader (1972, 10), Noll (1971, 42), Dentzer (1982, 410), Thiersch (1907), Mackenzie (1898), and Münsterberg (1890) follow Benndorf's interpretation. Oberleitner (1994, 42) accepts the Trojan War reading and believes that one is meant to see a local event in mythological terms. Borchhardt and Borchhardt-Birbaumer (1992, 102, 104) view the episodes as mythological but connected to local events, the Lycian kings Sarpedon and Glaukos fighting at Troy, and they identify the enthroned ruler as Priam, whereas Mackenzie (1898, 161) argued that the two primary warriors are Achilles and Agamemnon. Ridgway (1997, 92) points out difficulties with both the local battle and Trojan War interpretations.

117. Oberleitner 1994, 44.
118. See chapter 3. For the Calydonian boar hunt at Trysa, see Woodford 1992, 417 no. 29 (with illustration).
119. Cf. Schnapp 1997.
120. Cf. Schnapp 1997, 392.
121. Cf. Schnapp 1997.
122. Barringer 1996, fig. 17a–b.
123. Eichler 1950, 32–33, Abb. 14.
124. There is also a nonmythological abduction on the other side of the doorway on the south wall but I wouldn't "read" this image together with the Calydonian boar hunt.
125. Cf. Ghedini 1992, 75, who points out the Homeric overtones in Macedonian hunting and banqueting.
126. The Tyrannicides quotation appears also in the stag hunt mosaic of c. 330–300 by Gnosis at Pella. See, e.g., Pollitt 1986, fig. 35.
127. Tripoldi (1991) draws numerous Eastern parallels with the Vergina hunt painting. See Palagia 1998, for new identifications of some of the hunters.
128. E.g., Pollitt 1986, 25–26, with illustrations.
129. For the lion hunt motif exploited by Alexander and his followers, see, e.g., Palagia 1998.
130. Boardman (1995, 57) remarks that the group was a "three-dimensional version" of the Vergina hunt painting. On the present remains of the monument, see Bommelaer 1991, 225–27. Pliny mentions two other representations of Alexander hunting: a sculpture by Euthykrates at Thespiai (*HN* 34.66) and a painting by Antiphilos of Alexandria (*HN* 35.138).
131. A marble relief frieze block from Messene of the early third century (Louvre, Musée du Louvre) may reproduce the Krateros Monument. See Pollitt 1986, 38. But contra: Palagia 1998, 27–28.
132. ἄγρα . . . ταυροφόνου τοῦδε λέοντος ἔχοι. Völcker-Janssen (1993, 117–32) addresses the political implications of the monument.
133. Cf. Pollitt (1986, 38); and Plut., *De Alex. fort.* 330b–c.

REFERENCES

Adriani, A. 1950. *CVA*: Italy 20, Naples, Museo Nazionale 1. Rome.

Albizzati, C. 1925. *Vasi antichi dipinti del Vaticano*. Vol. 4. Rome.

Ament, E. J. 1993. "Aspects of Androgyny in Classical Greece." In M. DeForest, ed., *Woman's Power, Man's Game: Essays on Classical Antiquity in Honor of Joy K. King*, 1–31. Wauconda.

Amiet, P. 1980. *Art of the Ancient Near East*. New York.

Amyx, D. A. 1988. *Corinthian Vase-Painting of the Archaic Period*. Berkeley.

Anderson, J. K. 1985. *Hunting in the Ancient World*. Berkeley.

Anderson, J. K. 1991. "Hoplite Weapons and Offensive Arms." In V. D. Hanson, ed., *Hoplites: The Classical Greek Battle Experience*, 15–37. London and New York.

Arafat, K. W. 1997. "State of the Art—Art of the State: Sexual Violence and Politics in Late Archaic and Early Classical Vase-Painting." In S. Deacy and K. F. Pierce, eds., *Rape in Antiquity*, 97–121. London.

Arena, R. 1979. "Considerazioni sul mito di Callisto." *Acme* 32, 5–26.

Arias, P. E. 1963. *CVA*: Italy 37, Ferrara, Museo Nazionale 1. Rome.

Arieti, J. A. 1975. "Nudity in Greek Athletics." *CW* 68, 431–36.

Arnheim, M. T. W. 1977. *Aristocracy in Greek Society*. London.

Arrigoni, G. 1977. "Atalanta e il cinghiale bianco." *Scripta philologa* 1, 9–47.

Arrigoni, G. 1985. "Donne e sport nel mondo greco religione e società." In G. Arrigoni, ed., *La Donne in Grecia*, 55–201. Rome.

Ashmead, A. 1978. "Greek Cats." *Expedition* 20 (Spring), 38–47.

Barrett, A. A. 1972. "P. Oxy. 2359 and Stesichorus' ΣΥΟΘΗΡΑΙ." *CP* 67, 117–19.

Barringer, J. M. 1995. *Divine Escorts: Nereids in Archaic and Classical Greek Art*. Ann Arbor.

Barringer, J. M. 1996. "Atalanta as Model: The Hunter and the Hunted." *ClAnt* 15, 48–76.

Bažant J. 1981. *Studies on the Use and Decoration of Athenian Vases*. Prague.

Bažant J. 1987. "Les Vases athéniens et les réformes démocratiques." In C. Bérard, C. Bron, and A. Pomari, eds., *Images et société en Grèce ancienne: L'Iconographie comme méthode d'analyse*, 33–40. Actes du Colloque international, Lausanne, 8–11 February 1984. Lausanne.

Beazley, J. D. 1947. "Some Attic Vases in the Cyprus Museum." *ProcBritAc* 33, 195–243.

Beazley, J. D. 1971. *Paralipomena*. Oxford.

Beazley, J. D. 1974. *The Pan Painter*. Mainz.

Beazley, J. D. 1978. *Attic Black-Figure Vase-Painters*. 1956. New York.

Beazley, J. D. 1984. *Attic Red-Figure Vase-Painters*. 1963. 2d ed. New York.

Beazley, J. D. 1986. *The Development of Attic Black-Figure*. Rev. ed. Berkeley, Los Angeles, and London.

Benndorf, O. 1889. "Das Heroon von Gjölbaschi-Trysa." *JKSW* 9, 1–134.

Benndorf, O. 1890. "Das Heroon von Gjölbaschi-Trysa." *JKSW* 11, 1–52.

Benndorf, O. 1891. "Das Heroon von Gjölbaschi-Trysa." *JKSW* 12, 5–68.

Bentz, M. 1998. *Panathenäische Preisamphoren: Eine athenische Vasengattung und ihre Funktion vom 6.-4. Jahrhundert v. Chr.* Basel.

Bérard, C. 1986. "L'Impossible Femme athlete." *AdI* 8, 195–202.

Bérard, C. 1988. "La Chasseresse traquée." In M. Schmidt, ed., *Kanon: Festschrift Ernst Berger*, 280–84. Basel.

Bergemann, J. 1997. *Demos und Thanatos: Untersuchungen zum Wertsystem der Polis im Spiegel der attischen Grabreliefs des 4. Jahrhunderts v. Chr. und zur Funktion der gleichzeitigen Grabbauten*. Munich.

Bevan, E. 1986. *Representations of Animals in Sanctuaries of Artemis and Other Olympian Deities*. Vol. 1. Oxford.

Black, M. 1981. "Metaphor." In M. Johnson, ed., *Philosophical Perspectives on Metaphor*, 63–82. Minneapolis.

Blok, J. H. 1995. *The Early Amazons: Modern and Ancient Perspectives on a Persistent Myth*. Leiden, New York, and Cologne.

Boardman, J. 1978. *Greek Sculpture: The Archaic Period*. London.

Boardman, J. 1983. "Atalanta." *The Art Institute of Chicago Centennial Lectures*. Museum Studies 10. Chicago.

Boardman, J. 1984. "Atalante." *LIMC* 2:940–50. Zurich and Munich.

Boardman, J. 1985. *Greek Sculpture: The Classical Period*. London.

Boardman, J. 1989. *Athenian Red Figure Vases: The Classical Period*. London.

Boardman, J. 1990. "Hippomenes." *LIMC* 5:465–66. Zurich and Munich.

Boardman, J. 1992a. "Meilanion." *LIMC* 6:404–5. Zurich and Munich.

Boardman, J. 1992b. "The Phallos-Bird in Archaic and Classical Greek Art." *RA*, 227–42.

Boardman, J. 1995. *Greek Sculpture: The Late Classical Period*. London.

Boardman, J. 1998. *Early Greek Vase Painting*. London.

Bodson, L. 1978. *ΊΕΡΑ ΖΩΙΑ: Contribution à l'étude de la place de l'animal dans la religion grecque ancienne*. Brussels.

Bodson, L. 1986. "L'Initiation artémisiaque." In J. Ries, ed., *Les Rites d'initiation*, 299–315. Actes du colloque de Liège et de Louvain-la-Neuve, 20–21 November 1984. Louvain-la-Neuve.

Boegehold A. L. 1996. "Group and Single Competitions at the Panathenaia." In J. Neils, ed., *Worshipping Athena: Panathenaia and Parthenon*, 95–105. Madison.

Bommelaer, J.-F. 1991. *Guide de Delphes: Le site*. Paris.

Bond, G., ed. 1981. *Euripides Herakles*. Oxford.

Bonfante L. 1989. "Nudity as a Costume in Classical Art." *AJA* 93, 543–70.

Booth, A. 1991. "The Age for Reclining and Its Attendant Perils." In W. J. Slater, ed., *Dining in a Classical Context*, 105–120. Ann Arbor.

Borchhardt, J. 1976. *Die Bauskulptur des Heroons von Limyra: Das Grabmal des lykischen Königs Perikles*. Berlin.

Borchhardt, J., and B. Borchhardt-Birbaumer. 1992. "Zum Kult der Heroen, Herrscher, und Kaiser in Lykien." *AntW* 23, 99–116.

Borchhardt, J., and G. Mader. 1972. "Der triumphierende Perseus in Lykien." *AntW* 3:1, 2–16.

Borgeaud, P. 1988. *The Cult of Pan in Ancient Greece*. Trans. K. Atlass and J. Redfield. Chicago and London.

Boulter, C. G. 1971. *CVA*: United States 15, Cleveland Museum of Art. Princeton.

Bowie, E. 1990. "*Miles ludens?* The Problem of Martial Exhortation in Early Greek Elegy." In O. Murray, ed., *Sympotica: A Symposium on the Symposion*, 221–29. Oxford.

Bowra, C. M. 1964. *Pindar*. Oxford.

Brelich, A. 1961. *Guerre, agoni, e culti nella Grecia arcaica*. Bonn.

Brelich, A. 1969. *Paides e parthenoi*. Rome.

Bremmer, J. 1980. "An Enigmatic Indo-European Rite: Paederasty." *Arethusa* 13, 279–90.

Bremmer, J. 1988. "La Plasticité du mythe: Méléagre dans la poésie homerique." In C. Calame, ed., *Métamorphoses du mythe en Grèce antique*, 37–56. Paris.

Bremmer, J. 1990. "Adolescents, *Symposion*, and Pederasty." In O. Murray, ed., *Sympotica: A Symposium on the Symposion* 135–48. Oxford.

Brommer, F. 1973. *Vasenlisten zur griechischen Heldensage*. 3d ed. Marburg.

Brulé, P. 1987. *La Fille d'Athènes*. Paris.

Bruneau, P. 1965. "Le Motif des coqs affrontés dans l'imagerie attique." *BCH* 89, 90–121.

Brunnsåker, S. 1971. *The Tyrant-Slayers of Kritios and Nesiotes*. Stockholm.

Bryant, J. M. 1996. *Moral Codes and Social Structure in Ancient Greece: A Sociology of Greek Ethics from Homer to the Epicureans and Stoics*. Albany.

Buffière, F. 1980. *Eros adolescent: La Pédérastie dans la Grèce antique*. Paris.

Bugh, G. R. 1988. *The Horsemen of Athens*. Princeton.

Buitron-Oliver, D. 1995a. *Douris*. Mainz.

Buitron-Oliver, D. 1995b. "Stories from the Trojan Cycle in the Work of Douris." In J. B. Carter and S. P. Morris, eds., *The Ages of Homer: A Tribute to Emily Townsend Vermeule*, 438–40. Austin.

Bulas, K. 1935. *CVA*: Poland 2, Cracow 1. Cracow.

Burkert, W. 1979. *Structure and History in Greek Mythology and Ritual*. Berkeley, Los Angeles, and London.

Burkert, W. 1983. *Homo Necans: The Anthropology of Ancient Greek Sacrificial Ritual and Myth*. Trans. P. Bing. Berkeley, Los Angeles, and London.

Burn, L. 1991. "A Dinoid Volute-Krater by the Meleager Painter," *Greek Vases in the J. Paul Getty Museum* 5, 107–30. Malibu.

Burnett, A. P. 1986. "Hunt and Hearth in *Hippolytus*." In M. Cropp, E. Fantham, and S. E. Scully, eds., *Greek Tragedy and Its Legacy: Essays Presented to D. J. Conacher*, 167–83. Calgary.

Burow, J. 1989. *Der Antimenesmaler*. Mainz.

Calame, C. 1977. *Les Choeurs de jeunes filles en Grèce archaïque*. Rome.

Carpenter, T. H. 1989. *Beazley Addenda*. 2d ed. Oxford.

Cartledge, P. 1977. "Hoplites and Heroes: Sparta's Contribution to the Technique of Ancient Warfare." *JHS* 97, 11–27.

Cartledge, P. 1981. "The Politics of Spartan Pederasty." *PCPS*, n.s., 27, 17–36.

Castriota, D. 1992. *Myth, Ethos, and Actuality: Official Art in Fifth-Century B.C. Athens*. Madison.

Childs, W. A. P. 1976. "Prolegomena to a Lycian Chronology, II: The Heroon from Trysa." *RA* 2, 281–316.

Childs, W. A. P. 1978. *The City-Reliefs of Lycia*. Princeton.

Cirio, A. M. 1977. "Fonti litterarie ed iconografiche del mito di Atteone." *Bollettino del Comitato per la preparazione dell'edizione nazionale dei classici greci e latini* 25, 44–60.

Clairmont, C. W. 1993. *Classical Attic Tombstones*. Vols. 1–9. Kilchberg.

Clark, A. J. 1990. *CVA: United States 25, J. Paul Getty Museum 2*. Malibu.

Clarke, J. R. 1998. *Looking at Lovemaking: Constructions of Sexuality in Roman Art, 100 B.C.–A.D. 250*. Berkeley, Los Angeles, and London.

Classen, C. J. 1960. *Untersuchungen zu Platons Jagdbildern*. Berlin.

Clement, P. 1934. "New Evidence for the Origin of the Iphigeneia Legend." *AntCl* 3, 393–409.

Cohen, D. 1991. *Law, Sexuality, and Society: The Enforcement of Morals in Classical Athens*. Cambridge.

Cole, S. G. 1984. "The Social Function of Rituals of Maturation." *ZPE* 55, 233–44.

Cole, S. G. 1996. "Oath Ritual and the Male Community at Athens." In J. Ober and C. Hedrick, eds., *Demokratia: A Conversation on Democracies, Ancient and Modern*, 227–48. Princeton.

Cook, R. M. 1952. "Dogs in Battle." In T. Dohrn, ed., *Festschrift Andreas Rumpf*, 38–42. Cologne.

Cook, R. M. 1981. *Clazomenian Sarcophagi*. Mainz.

Coste-Messelière, P. de la. 1936. *Au Musée de Delphes*. Paris.

Croiset, M. 1898. "Sur les origines du récit relatif a Méléagre dans l'ode V de Bacchylide." In *Mélanges Henri Weil*, 73–80. Paris.

Crowther, N. B. 1985. "Male 'Beauty' Contests in Greece: The Euandria and Euexia." *AntCl* 54, 285–91.

Csapo, E. 1993. "Deep Ambivalence: Notes on a Greek Cockfight (Part I)." *Phoenix* 47, 1–28.

Daltrop, G. 1966. *Die kalydonische Jagd in der Antike*. Hamburg and Berlin.

Daux, G. 1965. "Deux Stèles d'Acharnes." In D. Zakythenos et al., eds., Χαριστήριον εἰς Ἀναστάσιον Κ. Ὀρλάνδον, 1:78–90. Athens.

Daux, G. 1967. *Guide de Thasos*. Paris.

Daux, G. 1971. "Le Serment des éphèbes athéniens." *RÉG* 84, 370–83.

David, E. 1993. "Hunting in Spartan Society and Consciousness." *EchCl* 37, 393–413.

Davidson, D. 1978. "What Metaphors Mean." *Critical Inquiry* 5, 31–47.

Davies, J. K. 1971. *Athenian Propertied Families, 600–300 B.C.* Oxford.

Davies, M. 1980. "The Eyes of Love and the Hunting-Net in Ibycus 287P." *Maia* 32, 255–57.

Dentzer, J.-M. 1982. *Le Motif du banquet couché dans le proche-orient et le monde grec du VIIe au IVe siècle avant J.-C.* Rome.

Despinis, G. 1991–92. "Epitembia stele apo to Porto Rafti: Apokatastase kai scholia." *Egnatia* 3, 7–24.

Detienne, M. 1979. *Dionysos Slain.* Trans. M. Muellner and L. Muellner. Baltimore and London.

Detienne, M. 1994. *The Gardens of Adonis: Spices in Greek Mythology.* 1977. Trans. J. Lloyd. Princeton.

Deubner, L. 1932. *Attische Feste.* Berlin.

Devambez, P. 1981. "Amazones." *LIMC* 1:586–653. Zurich and Munich.

Di Benedetto, V. 1978. "Il 'Filottete' e l'efebia secondo Pierre Vidal-Naquet." *Belfasor* 33, 191–207.

Dindorf, G. 1962. *Aeschylus: Tragoediae superstites et deperditarum fragmenta.* Vol. 3. Hildesheim.

Dover, K. J. 1964. "Eros and Nomos (Plato, *Symposium* 182A–185C)." *BICS* 11, 31–42.

Dover, K. J. 1973. "Classical Greek Attitudes to Sexual Behavior." *Arethusa* 6, 59–73.

Dover, K. J. 1989. *Greek Homosexuality.* Cambridge, Mass.

Dowden, K. 1989. *Death and the Maiden.* New York.

DuBois, P. 1982a. *Centaurs and Amazons: Women and the Pre-History of the Great Chain of Being.* Ann Arbor.

DuBois, P. 1982b. "On the Invention of Hierarchy." *Arethusa* 15, 203–20.

Dumortier, J. 1935. *Les Images dans la poésie d'Eschyle.* Paris.

Durand, J.-L., and A. Schnapp. 1989. "Sacrificial Slaughter and Initiatory Hunt." In C. Bérard et al., *A City of Images*, 53–70. Trans. D. Lyons. Princeton.

Edlund, I. E. M. 1980. "Meaningful or Meaningless? Animal Symbolism in Greek Vase-Painting." *Meded* 42, 31–35.

Eichler, F. 1950. *Die Reliefs des Heroon von Gjölbaschi-Trysa.* Vienna.

Erath, G. 1997. *Das Bild der Stadt in der griechischen Flächenkunst.* Frankfurt am Main.

Faraone, C. A. 1993. "The Wheel, the Whip and Other Implements of Torture: Erotic Magic in Pindar, *Pythian* 4.213–19." *CJ* 89, 1–19.

Fehr, B. 1971. *Orientalische und griechische Gelage.* Bonn.

Felson Rubin, N., and W. M. Sale. 1983. "Meleager and Odysseus: A Structural and Cultural Study of the Greek Hunting-Maturation Myth." *Arethusa* 16, 137–71.

Felson Rubin, N., and W. M. Sale. 1984. "Meleager and the Motifemic Analysis of Myth: A Response." *Arethusa* 17, 211–23.

Ferrari, G. 1997. "Figures in the Text: Metaphors and Riddles in the *Agamemnon*." *CP* 92, 1–45.

Ferron, J. 1993. *Sarcophages de Phénicie: Sarcophages à scènes en relief.* Paris.

Fittschen, K. 1969. *Untersuchungen zum Beginn der Sagendarstellungen bei den Griechen.* Berlin.

Flacelière, R. 1971. *L'Amour en Grèce.* Paris.

Fleischer, R. 1983. *Der Klagefrauensarkophag aus Sidon.* Tübingen.

Follmann, A.-B. 1968. *Der Pan-Maler.* Bonn.

Forrest, W. G. 1966. *The Emergence of Greek Democracy, 800–400 B.C.* New York and Toronto.

Franz, R. 1890. "De Callistus Fabula." *Leipziger Studien* 12:2, 235–365.

Frel, J. 1963. "Griechischer Eros." *Listy Filologikó* 86, 60–64.

Friis Johansen, K. 1923. *Les Vases sicyoniens.* Copenhagen.

Friis Johansen, K. 1942. "Attic Motives on Clazomenian Sarcophagi." *From the Collections of the Ny Carlsberg Glyptothek,* 3:123–43. Copenhagen.

Friis Johansen, K. 1962. "Eine neue Caeretaner Hydria." *OpRom* 4, 61–81.

Frontisi-Ducroux, F. 1996. "Eros, Desire, and the Gaze." In N. Kampen, ed., *Sexuality in Ancient Art,* 81–100. Cambridge.

Frontisi-Ducroux, F., and F. Lissarrague. 1990. "From Ambiguity to Ambivalence: A Dionysiac Excursion through the 'Anakreontic' Vases." In D. M. Halperin, J. J. Winkler, and F. I. Zeitlin, eds., *Before Sexuality,* 211–56. Princeton.

Gardner, P. 1889. Review of Benndorf and Niemann, *Das Heroon von Gjölbaschi-Trysa* (Vienna, 1889). *JHS* 10, 284–85.

Garner, R. 1994. "Stesichorus' Althaia: P. Oxy. LVII.3876.frr.1–36." *ZPE* 100, 26–38.

Gebauer, K. 1940. "Ausgrabungen im Kerameikos." *AA,* 307–362.

Gernet, L. 1981. *The Anthropology of Ancient Greece.* Trans. J. Hamilton and B. Nagy. Baltimore and London.

Ghedini, F. 1992. "Caccia e banchetto: Un rapporto difficile." *RdA* 16, 72–88.

Ghirshman, R. 1964. *The Arts of Ancient Iran.* Trans. S. Gilbert and J. Emmons. New York.

Giudice, F., et al. 1992. *Le Collezione archeologica del Banco di Sicilia.* Palermo.

Golden, M. 1998. *Sport and Society in Ancient Greece.* Cambridge.

Goldhill, S. 1990. "The Great Dionysia and Civic Ideology." In J. J. Winkler and F. I. Zeitlin, eds., *Nothing to Do with Dionysos?* 97–129. Princeton.

Gordon, R. L., ed. 1981. *Myth, Religion, and Society.* Cambridge.

Gossen, 1912. "Hase." *RE* 7:2:2477–86. Stuttgart.

Gow, A. S. F. 1934. "ΙΥΓΞ, ΡΟΜΒΟΣ, Rhombus, Turbo." *JHS* 54, 1–13.

Graf, F. 1993. *Greek Mythology: An Introduction.* Trans. T. Marier. Baltimore and London.

Green, P. 1996. *The Greco-Persian Wars.* Berkeley, Los Angeles, and London.

Guimond, L. 1981. "Aktaion." *LIMC* 1:454–69. Zurich and Munich.

Güntner, G., ed. 1997. *Mythen und Menschen: Griechische Vasenkunst aus einer deutschen Privatsammlung.* Munich.

Gurlitt, W. 1894. "Zum Heroon von Gjölbaschi-Trysa." *AM* 19, 283–89.

Guthrie, W. K. C., trans. 1961 "Protagoras." In E. Hamilton and H. Cairns, eds., *The Collected Dialogues of Plato.* Princeton.

Hafner, G. 1951. *CVA:* Germany 7, Karlsruhe 1. Mainz.

Hainsworth, B. 1993. *The Iliad: A Commentary.* Vol. 3, Books 9–12. Cambridge.

Halliday, W. R. 1926. "Xanthos-Melanthos and the Origins of Tragedy." *CR* 40, 179–81.

Hanson, V. D. 1991. "The Ideology of Hoplite Battle, Ancient and Modern." In V. D. Hanson, ed., *Hoplites: The Classical Greek Battle Experience,* 3–11. London and New York.

Hardwick, L. 1990. "Ancient Amazons—Heroes, Outsiders, or Women?" *GaR* 37, 14–36.

Harrison, E. B. 1992. "New Light on a Nereid Monument Akroterion." In H. Froning, T. Hölscher, and H. Mielsch, eds., *Kotinos: Festschrift für Erika Simon,* 204–10. Mainz.

Hartog, F. 1988. *The Mirror of Herodotus: The Representation of the Other in the Writing of History.* Trans. J. Lloyd. Berkeley, Los Angeles, and London.

Haslam, M. W. 1991. "Kleitias, Stesichoros, and the Jar of Dionysos." *TAPA* 121, 35–45.

Hawley, R. 1998. "The Dynamics of Beauty in Classical Greece." In D. Montserrat, ed., *Changing Bodies, Changing Meanings: Studies on the Human Body in Antiquity,* 37–54. London and New York.

Heesen, P. 1996. *The J. L. Theodor Collection of Attic Black-Figure Vases.* Amsterdam.

Hemelrijk, J. M. 1984. *Caeretan Hydriae.* Mainz.

Henrichs, A. 1981. "Human Sacrifice in Greek Religion: Three Case Studies." In O. Reverdin and B. Grange, eds., *Le Sacrifice dans l'antiquité,* 195–235. Fondation Hardt: Entretiens 27. Geneva.

Henrichs, A. 1987. "Three Approaches to Greek Mythography." In J. Bremmer, ed., *Interpretations of Greek Mythology,* 242–77. London and Sydney.

Hermany, A., H. Cassimatis, and R. Vollkommer. 1986. "Eros." *LIMC* 3:850–942. Zurich and Munich.

Hodkinson, S. 1997. Review of Nigel Kennell, *The Gymnasium of Virtue* (Chapel Hill and London, 1995). *JHS* 117, 240–42.

Hoffmann, H. 1967. "Eine neue Amphora des Eucharidesmalers." *Jahrbuch der Hamburger Kunstsammlungen* 12, 9–34.

Hoffmann, H. 1974. "Hahnenkampf in Athen: Zur Ikonologie einer attischen Bildformel." *RA,* 195–220.

Hoffmann, H. 1977. *Sexual and Asexual Pursuit: A Structuralist Approach to Greek Vase Painting.* Occasional Paper of the Royal Anthropological Institute of Great Britain and Ireland 34.

Hoffmann, H. 1997. *Sotades: Symbols of Immortality on Greek Vases.* Oxford.

Hölscher, F. 1972. *Die Bedeutung archaischer Tierkampfbilder.* Würzburg.

Hoppin, J. C., and A. Gallatin. 1926. *CVA:* United States of America 1, Hoppin Collection. Paris.

Hornblower, S., and A. Spawforth, eds., 1996. *The Oxford Classical Dictionary.* 3d ed. Oxford.

Hübner, E. 1862. *Die antiken Bildwerke in Madrid.* Berlin.

Hughes, D. D. 1991. *Human Sacrifice in Ancient Greece.* London and New York.

Hupperts, C. M. A. 1988. "Greek Love or Paederasty? Greek Love in Black-Figure Vase-Painting." In J. Christiansen and T. Melander, eds., *Proceedings of the 3rd Symposium on Ancient Greek and Related Pottery,* 256–68. Copenhagen, 31 August–4 September 1987. Copenhagen.

Hurwit, J. M. 1985. *The Art and Culture of Early Greece, 1100–480 B.C.* Ithaca and London.

Iacopi, G. 1956. *CVA:* Italy 26, Museo Nazionale Tarquiniense 2. Rome.

Immerwahr, W. 1891. *Die Kulte und Mythen Arkadiens.* Leipzig.

Jacobs, B. 1987. *Griechische und Persische Elemente in der Grabkunst Lykiens zur Zeit der Achämenidenherrschaft.* Jonsered.

Jacobsthal, P. 1931. *Die melischen Reliefs.* Berlin.

Jameson, M. H. 1991. "Sacrifice before Battle." In V. D. Hanson, ed., *Hoplites: The Classical Greek Battle Experience,* 197–227. London and New York.

Janko, R. 1984. "*P. Oxy.* 2509: Hesiod's *Catalogue* on the Death of Actaeon." *Phoenix* 38, 299– 307.

Jeanmaire, H. 1939. *Couroi et courètes: Essai sur l'éducation spartiate et sur les rites d'adolescence dans l'antiquité hellénique.* Lille.

Jeske, B., and C. Stein. 1982. "Eine frührotfigurige Hydria des Psiax." *Hefte des archäologischen Seminars der Universität Bern* 8, 5–20.

Jongkees-Vos, M. F. 1971. "The Centaur Painter." In J. H. Jongkees and M. F. Jong-kees-Vos, *Varia Archaeologica*, 13–21. Alkmaar.

Jost, M. 1985. *Sanctuaires et cultes d'Arcadie.* Paris.

Just, R. 1989. *Women in Athenian Law and Life.* London and New York.

Kaempf-Dimitriadou, S. 1979. *Die Liebe der Götter in der attischen Kunst des 5. Jahrhunderts v. Chr.* Bern.

Kahil, L. 1963. "Quelques Vases du sanctuaire d'Artémis à Brauron." *AntK* 1, 5–29.

Kahil, L. 1965. "Autour de l'Artemis attique." *AntK* 8, 20–33.

Kahil, L. 1977. "L'Artémis de Brauron: Rites et mystère." *AntK* 20, 86–98.

Kahil, L. 1991. "Artemis, Dionysos et Pan à Athènes." *Hesperia* 60, 511–23.

Kakridis, T. 1987. *Homeric Researches.* 1949. New York and London.

Keck, J. 1988. *Studien zur Rezeption fremder Einflüsse in der chalkidischen Keramik.* Frankfurt.

Keen, A. G. 1998. *Dynastic Lycia: A Political History of the Lycians and Their Relations with Foreign Powers, c. 545–362 B.C.* Leiden, Boston, and Cologne.

Kennell, N. M. 1995. *The Gynasium of Virtue: Education and Culture in Ancient Sparta.* Chapel Hill and London.

Kilmer, M. 1997. "Painters and Pederasts: Ancient Art, Sexuality, and Social History." In M. Golden and P. Toohey, eds., *Inventing Ancient Culture: Historicism, Periodization, and the Ancient World*, 36–49. London and New York.

Kleiner, F. S. 1972. "The Kalydonian Hunt: A Reconstruction of a Painting from the Circle of Polygnotos." *AntK* 15, 7–14.

Klimowsky, E. W. 1964. "Sonnenschirm und Baldachin: Zwei Sinnbilder der irdischen und himmlischen Würde, insbesondere auf antiken Münzen." *SchwMbll* 13–14, 121–34.

Koch-Harnack, G. 1983. *Knabenliebe und Tiergeschenke: Ihre Bedeutung in päderastischen Erziehungssystem Athens.* Berlin.

Koehl, R. B. 1986. "The Chieftain Cup and a Minoan Rite of Passage." *JHS* 106, 99–110.

Kossatz-Deissmann, A. 1978. *Dramen des Aischylos auf westgriechischen Vasen.* Mainz.

Kossatz-Deissmann, A. 1992. "Lyssa." *LIMC* 6:322–29. Zurich and Munich.

Kozloff, A. P., ed. 1981. *Animals in Ancient Art: From the Leo Mildenberg Collection.* Cleveland.

Krauskopf, I. 1977. "Eine attisch schwarzfigurige Hydria in Heidelberg." *AA*, 13–37.

Kunisch, N. 1971. *CVA:* Germany 33, Berlin, Antiquarium 4. Munich.

Kunisch, N. 1972. *Antiken der Sammlung Julius C. und Margot Funcke.* Bochum.

Kurtz, D. C. 1975. *Athenian White Lekythoi.* Oxford.

Kurtz, D. C., and J. Boardman. 1986. "Booners." In J. Frel and M. True, eds., *Greek Vases in the J. Paul Getty Museum*, 3:35–70. Malibu, Calif.

Labarbe, J. 1953. "L'Âge correspondant au sacrifice du κούρειον et les données historiques du sixième discours d'Isée." *Académie Royale de Belgique: Bulletin de la classe des lettres et des sciences morales et politiques*, 5th ser., 39, 358–93.

Lacy, L. R. 1990. "Aktaion and a Lost 'Bath of Artemis.'" *JHS* 110, 26–42.

Laffineur, R. 1983. "Iconographie mycénienne et symbolisme guerrier." *Art and Fact* 2, 38–49.

Lambert, S. D. 1993. *The Phratries of Attica*. Ann Arbor.

Langridge, E. 1991. "The Boar Hunt in Corinthian Pottery." *AJA* 95, 323.

Launey, M. 1944. *Le Sanctuaire et la culte d'Héraklès à Thasos*. Études Thasiennes 1. Paris.

Lefkowitz, M. R. 1986. *Women in Greek Myth*. Baltimore.

Ley, A. 1990. "Atalante—von der Athletin zur Liebhaberin." *Nikephoros* 3, 31–72.

Lissarrague, F. 1989. "The World of the Warrior." In C. Bérard et al., *A City of Images*, 38–51. Trans. D. Lyons. Princeton.

Lissarrague, F. 1990a. *The Aesthetics of the Greek Banquet: Images of Wine and Ritual*. Trans. A. Szegedy-Maszak. Princeton.

Lissarrague, F. 1990b. *L'Autre Guerrier: Archers, peltastes, cavaliers dans l'imagerie attique*. Paris and Rome.

Lissarrague, F. 1992. "Figures of Women." In P. Schmitt Pantel, ed., *A History of Women in the West*, 1:139–229. London.

Lloyd-Jones, H. 1958. Review of E. Lobel, *The Oxyrhynchus Papyri*, Part XXIII (London, 1956). *CR* 72, 16–22.

Lloyd-Jones, H. 1983. "Artemis and Iphigeneia." *JHS* 103, 87–102.

Lloyd-Jones, H. 1996. *Sophocles: Fragments*. Cambridge.

Lochin, C. 1994. "Pegasos." *LIMC* 7:214–30. Zurich and Munich.

Lofberg, J. O. 1925. "The Date of the Athenian *Ephebeia*." *CP* 20, 330–35.

Longo, O. 1987. "Le Regole della caccia nel mondo greco-romano." *Aufidus* 1, 59–92.

Lonis, R. 1979. *Guerre et religion en Grèce a l'époque classique: Recherches sur les rites, les dieux, l'idéologie de la victoire*. Paris.

Lonsdale, S. H. 1990. *Creatures of Speech: Lion, Herding, and Hunting Similes in the Iliad*. Stuttgart.

Lonsdale, S. H. 1993. *Dance and Ritual Play in Greek Religion*. Baltimore and London.

Loraux, N. 1975. "HBH et ANΔPEIA: Deux Versions de la mort du combattant athénien." *Ancient Society* 6, 4–12.

Loraux, N. 1995. *The Experiences of Teiresias: The Feminine and the Greek Man*. Trans. P. Wissing. Princeton.

Lullies, R. 1952. CVA: Germany 9, München, Museum Antiker Kleinkunst 3. Munich.

Ma, J. 1994. "Black Hunter Variations." *PCPS* 40, 49–80.

McCulloch, H. Y., and H. D. Cameron. 1980. "*Septem* 12–13 and the Athenian Ephebeia." *Illinois Classical Studies* 5, 1–14.

Mackenzie, D. 1898. "Der Westfries von Gjölbaschi." In K. Masner, ed., *Festschrift für Otto Benndorf*, 159–62. Vienna.

McPhee, I. 1990. "Kallisto." *LIMC* 5:940–44. Zurich and Munich.

Mainoldi, C. 1984. *L'Image du loup et du chien dans la Grèce ancienne d'Homère à Platon*. 1984.

Malagardis, A.-N. 1988. "Compétitions orchestiques d'éphèbes et origine de certaines idées sur l'éducation à Athènes au Ve siècle." In Πρακτικά τοῦ XII Διεθνοῦς Συνέδριου Κλασικῆς Ἀρχαιολογίας, 2:136–45. Athens, 4–10 September 1983. Athens.

Manns, O. 1988. *Über die Jagd bei den Griechen*. Kassel.

March, J. R. 1987. *The Creative Poet*. BICS, supp. 49. London.

Markoe, G. 1989. "The 'Lion Attack' in Archaic Greek Art: Heroic Triumph." *ClAnt* 8, 86–115.

Maxwell-Stuart, P. G. 1970. "Remarks on the Black Cloaks of the Ephebes." *PCPS*, n.s., 16, 113–16.

Merkelbach, R., and M. L. West, eds. 1967. *Fragmenta Hesiodea*. Oxford.

Merkelbach, R., and M. L. West, eds. 1990. *Hesiodi: Fragmenta Selecta*. 3d ed. Oxford.

Meuli, K. 1975. *Gesammelte Schriften*. Vol. 2. Basel and Stuttgart.

Miller, M. C. 1997. *Athens and Persia in the Fifth Century B.C.: A Study in Cultural Receptivity*. Cambridge.

Miller, P. A. 1998. "Catullan Consciousness, the 'Care of the Self,' and the Force of the Negative in History." In D. H. J. Larmour, P. A. Miller, and C. Platter, eds., *Rethinking Sexuality: Foucault and Classical Antiquity*, 171–203. Princeton.

Mingazzini, P. 1971. *Catalogo dei vasi della Collezione Augusto Castellani*. Vol. 2. Rome.

Minto, A. 1960. *Il Vaso François*. Florence.

Mitchel, F. W. 1964. "Derkylos of Hagnous and the Date of I. G., II², 1187." *Hesperia* 33, 337–51.

Mitchel, F. W. 1975. "The So-Called Earliest Ephebic Inscription." *ZPE* 19, 233–43.

Mitchell, S. 1996. "Hoplite Warfare in Ancient Greece." In A. B. Lloyd, ed., *Battle in Antiquity*, 87–105. London.

Moore, J. M. 1975. *Aristotle and Xenophon on Democracy and Oligarchy*. Berkeley and Los Angeles.

Moreau, A. 1992. "Initiation en Grèce antique." *Dialogues d'histoire ancienne* 18:1, 191–244.

Moreau, J. 1954. "Sur les 'Saisons' d'Aristophane." *NouvClio* 6, 327–44.

Moretti, M. 1966. *Tomba Martini Marescotti: Quaderni di Villa Giulia*. Vol. 1. Milan.

Morris, C. E. 1990. "In Pursuit of the White Tusked Boar: Aspects of Hunting in Mycenaean Society." In R. Hägg and G. C. Nordquist, eds., *Celebrations of Death and Divinity in the Bronze Age Argolid*, 149–56. Stockholm.

Most, G. W. 1983. "Of Motifemes and Megatexts: Comment on Rubin/Sale and Segal." *Arethusa* 16, 199–218.

Münsterberg, R. 1890. "Zur Helena der Gjölbaschireliefs." *AEM* 12, 84–87.

Murgatroyd, P. 1984. "Amatory Hunting, Fishing, and Fowling." *Latomus* 43, 362–68.

Murray, O. 1983. "The Symposion as Social Organisation." In R. Hägg, ed., *The Greek Renaissance of the Eighth Century B.C.: Tradition and Innovation*, 195–99. Proceedings of the Second International Symposium at the Swedish Institute, Athens, 1–5 June, 1981. Stockholm.

Murray, O. 1991. "War and the Symposium." In W. J. Slater, ed., *Dining in a Classical Context*, 83–103. Ann Arbor.

Nagy, G. 1973. "On the Death of Actaeon." *HSCP* 77, 179–80.

Nauck, A., ed., 1964. *Tragicorum Graecorum fragmenta supplementum.* Hildesheim.

Neer, R. T. 1995. "The Lion's Eye: Imitation and Uncertainty in Attic Red-Figure." *Representations* 51, 118–53.

Noack, F. 1893. "Zum Friese von Gjölbaschi." *AM* 18, 305–32.

Noll, R. 1971. "Ein fürstlicher Grabbezirk griechischer Zeit in Kleinasien." *AntW* 2:4, 40–44.

Nollé, M. 1992. *Denkmäler vom Satrapensitz Daskyleion: Studien zur graeco-persischen Kunst.* Berlin.

Oakley, J. H., W. E. D. Coulsen, and O. Palagia, eds. 1997. *Athenian Potters and Painters: The Conference Proceedings.* Oxford.

Oakley, J. H., and R. Sinos. 1993. *The Wedding in Ancient Athens.* Madison.

Oberleitner, W. 1994. *Das Heroon von Trysa: Ein lykisches Fürstengrab des 4. Jahrhunderts v. Chr.* Mainz.

Ogden, D. 1996. "Homosexuality and Warfare in Ancient Greece." In A. B. Lloyd, ed., *Battle in Antiquity,* 107–68. London.

Olivieri, A., ed., 1907. *Mythographi Graeci* 3:1.

Page, D. 1937. "A New Fragment of a Greek Tragedy." *CQ* 31, 178–81.

Palagia, O. 1998. "Alexander the Great as Lion Hunter: The Fresco of Vergina Tomb II and the Marble Frieze of Messene in the Louvre." *Minerva* 9:4, 25–28.

Parke, H. W. 1977. *Festivals of the Athenians.* Ithaca.

Parker, R. 1996. *Athenian Religion: A History.* Oxford.

Parrot, A. 1961. *The Arts of Assyria.* Trans. S. Gilbert and J. Emmons. New York.

Patzer, H. 1982. *Die griechische Knabenliebe.* Wiesbaden.

Peirce, S. 1993. "Death, Revelry, and *Thysia.*" *ClAnt* 12, 219–66.

Pélékidis, C. 1962. *Histoire de l'éphébie attique.* Paris.

Pellizer, E. 1982. *Favole d'identità, favole di paura: Storie di caccia e altri racconti della Grecia antica.* Rome.

Perlman, P. 1989. "Acting the She-Bear for Artemis." *Arethusa* 22, 111–33.

Pfuhl, E., and H. Möbius. 1977. *Die ostgriechischen Grabreliefs.* Vol. 1. Mainz.

Philipp, H. 1968. *Tektonon Daidala: Der bildende Künstler und sein Werk im vorplatonischen Schrifttum.* Berlin.

Picard, C. 1941. "Une Cimaise thasienne archaïque." *MonPiot* 38, 55–92.

Piccaluga, G. 1968. *Lykaon: un tema mitico.* Rome.

Pickard-Cambridge, A. 1968. *The Dramatic Festivals of Athens.* 2d ed. Oxford.

Plato. 1925. *Lysis, Symposium, Gorgias.* Trans. W. R. M. Lamb. Cambridge and London.

Plato. 1985. *The Republic.* Trans. R. W. Sterling and W. C. Scott. New York.

Pleket, H. W. 1969."Collegium Iuvenum Nemesiorum: A Note on Ancient Youth Organizations." *Mnemosyne* 22, 281–98.

Pollitt, J. J. 1986. *Art in the Hellenistic Age.* Cambridge.

Raaflaub, K. A. 1983. "Democracy, Oligarchy, and the Concept of the 'Free Citizen' in Late Fifth-Century Athens." *Political Theory* 11, 517–44.

Radt, S., ed. 1977. *Tragicorum Graecorum Fragmenta.* Vol. 4. Göttingen.

Reeder, E. D. 1995. *Pandora.* Baltimore.

Reinmuth, O. W. 1952. "The Genesis of the Athenian Ephebia." *TAPA* 83, 34–50.

Reinmuth, O. W. 1971. *The Ephebic Inscriptions of the Fourth Century B.C.* Leiden.

Rhodes, P. J. 1981. *A Commentary on the Aristotelian "Athenaion Politeia."* Oxford.

Rhomaios, K. A. 1930. *CVA:* Greece 1, Athens, National Museum 1. Paris.

Riccioni, G. 1957. *CVA:* Italy 28, Adria, Museo Civico 1. Rome.

Ridgway, B. S. 1970. *The Severe Style in Greek Sculpture.* Princeton.

Ridgway, B. S. 1981. *Fifth-Century Styles in Greek Sculpture.* Princeton.

Ridgway, B. S. 1990. *Hellenistic Sculpture I: The Styles of ca. 331–200 B.C.* Madison.

Ridgway, B. S. 1997. *Fourth-Century Styles in Greek Sculpture.* Madison.

Ridgway, B. S. 1999. *Prayers in Stone: Greek Architectural Sculpture, ca. 600–100 B.C.E.* Berkeley, Los Angeles, and London.

Ridley, R. T. 1979. "The Hoplite as Citizen: Athenian Military Institutions in Their Context." *AntCl* 48, 508–48.

Robert, L. 1938. *Etudes épigraphiques et philologiques.* Paris.

Robertson, M. 1975. *A History of Greek Art.* Cambridge.

Robertson, M. 1992. *The Art of Vase-Painting in Classical Athens.* Cambridge.

Robinson, T. 1995. "The Nereid Monument at Xanthos or the Eliyāna Monument at Arñna?" *OJA* 14, 355–59.

Roccos, L. J. 1994. "Perseus." *LIMC* 7:332–48. Zurich and Munich.

Roller, L. E. 1981. "Funeral Games in Greek Art." *AJA* 85, 107–19.

Roussel, P. 1921. Review of Alice Brenot, *Recherches sur l'éphébie attique et en particulier sur la date de l'institution* (Paris, 1920). *RÉG* 34, 459.

Roussel, P. 1941. "Les Chlamydes noires des éphèbes athéniens." *RÉA* 43, 163–65.

Sage, M. M. 1996. *Warfare in Ancient Greece: A Sourcebook.* London and New York.

Ste. Croix, G. E. M. de. 1981. *The Class Struggle in the Ancient Greek World.* Ithaca.

Sale, W. 1962. "The Story of Callisto in Hesiod." *RhM* 105, 122–41.

Sale, W. 1965. "Callisto and the Virginity of Artemis." *RhM* 108, 11–35.

Sale, W. 1975. "The Temple-Legends of the Arkteia." *RhM* 118, 265–84.

Scanlon, T. F. 1990. "Race or Chase at the Arkteia of Attica?" *Nikephoros* 3, 73–120.

Schauenburg, K. 1965. "Erastes und Eromenos auf einer Schale des Sokles." *AA,* 849–67.

Schauenburg, K. 1969. *Jagddarstellungen in der griechischen Vasenmalerei.* Hamburg and Berlin.

Schaus, G. 1986. "Gold or Clay: Dionysos' Amphora on the François Vase." *EchCl* 30, 119–28.

Schefold, K. 1981. *Die Göttersage in der klassischen und hellenistischen Kunst.* Munich.

Schefold, K. 1992. *Gods and Heroes in Late Archaic Greek Art.* Trans. A. Griffiths. Cambridge.

Scheibler, I. 1987. "Bild und Gefäss: Zur ikonographischen und funktionalen Bedeutung der attischen Bildfeldamphoren." *JdI* 102, 57–118.

Schmitt, P. 1977. "Athéna Apatouria et la ceinture: Les aspects féminins des Apatouries à Athènes." *AnnÉconSocCiv* 32, 1059–73.

Schmitt, P., and A. Schnapp. 1982. "Image et société en Grèce ancienne: Les Représentations de la chasse et du banquet." *RA,* 57–74.

Schmitt-Pantel, P. 1992. *La Cité au banquet: Histoire des repas publics dans les cités grecques.* Paris and Rome.

Schnapp, A. 1973. "Territoire de chasse: Représentation du territoire de guerre et du territoire de chasse dans l'oeuvre de Xénophon." In M. I. Finley, ed., *Problèmes de la terre en Grèce ancienne,* 307–21. The Hague and Paris.

Schnapp, A. 1979a. "Images et programmes: Les Figurations archaïques de la chasse au sanglier." *RA*, 195–218.

Schnapp, A. 1979b. "Pratiche e immagini di caccia nella Grecia antica." *DialArch*, n.s., 1, 36–59.

Schnapp, A. 1981. "Une Autre Image de l'homosexualité en Grèce ancienne." *Le Débat* 10, 106–17.

Schnapp, A. 1984. "Seduction and Gesture in Ancient Imagery." *History and Anthropology* 1, 49–55.

Schnapp, A. 1988. "La Chasse et la mort: L'Image du chasseur sur les stèles et sur les vases." *Annali* 10, 151–61.

Schnapp, A. 1989. "Eros the Hunter." In C. Bérard et al., *A City of Images*. 71–87. Trans. D. Lyons. Princeton.

Schnapp, A. 1992. "Heroes and Myths of Hunting in Ancient Greece." In Y. Bonnefoy, ed., *Greek and Egyptian Mythologies*, 119–21. Chicago and London.

Schnapp, A. 1997. *Le Chasseur et la cité: Chasse et érotique dans la Grèce ancienne*. Paris.

Schnapp-Gourbeillon, A. 1981. *Lions, héros, masques: Les Représentations de l'animal chez Homère*. Paris.

Schneider, K. 1912. "Hahnenkämpfe." *RE* 7:2: 2211. Stuttgart.

Schwartz, J. 1960. *Pseudo-Hesiodeia*. Paris.

Seaford, R., ed. 1996. *Euripides Bacchae*. Warminster.

Séchan, L. 1967. *Études sur la tragédie grecque dans ses rapports avec la céramique*. 2d ed. Paris.

Segal, C. 1982. *Dionysiac Poetics and Euripides' Bacchae*. Princeton.

Segal, R. A. 1991. "Adonis: A Greek Eternal Child." In D. C. Pozzi and J. M. Wickersham, eds., *Myth and the Polis*, 64–85. Ithaca and London.

Sekunda, N. V. 1990. "*I.G.* ii^2 1250: A Decree Concerning the Lampadephoroi of the Tribe Aiantis." *ZPE* 83, 149–82.

Sergent, B. 1986. *Homosexuality in Greek Myth*. Trans. A. Goldhammer. Boston.

Sergent, B. 1993. "Paederasty and Political Life in Archaic Greek Cities." *Journal of Homosexuality* 25:1–2, 147–64.

Shapiro, H. A. 1981. "Courtship Scenes in Attic Vase-Painting." *AJA* 85, 133–43.

Shapiro, H. A. 1983. "Amazons, Thracians, and Scythians." *GRBS* 24, 105–114.

Shapiro, H. A. 1985. "Greek 'Bobbins': A New Interpretation." *AncW* 11, 115–20.

Shapiro, H. A. 1990. "Old and New Heroes: Narrative, Composition, and Subject in Attic Black-Figure." *ClAnt* 9, 114–48.

Shapiro, H. A. 1992. "Eros in Love: Pederasty and Pornography in Greece." In A. Richlin, ed., *Pornography and Representation in Greece and Rome*, 53–72. Oxford.

Shapiro, H. A. 1997. "Correlating Shape and Subject: The Case of the Archaic Pelike." In J. H. Oakley, W. E. D. Coulson, and O. Palagia, eds., *Athenian Potters and Painters: The Conference Proceedings*, 63–70. Oxford.

Sichtermann, H. 1959. "Zeus und Ganymed in frühklassischer Zeit." *AntK* 2, 10–15.

Sichtermann, H. 1988. "Ganymedes." *LIMC* 4:154–69. Zurich and Munich.

Siewert, P. 1977. "The Ephebic Oath in Fifth-Century Athens." *JHS* 97, 102–111.

Simon, E. 1983. *Festivals of Attica*. Madison.

Sinos, R. H. 1993. "Divine Selection: Epiphany and Politics in Archaic Greece." In

C. Dougherty and L. Kurke, eds., *Cultural Poetics in Archaic Greece: Cult, Performance, Politics,* 73–91. Cambridge.

Skarlatidou, E. 1999. "Enas neos krateras tou Lydou apo to nekrotapheio ste Therme (Sedes) Thessalonikes." In *Ancient Macedonia* 6, Papers Read at the Sixth International Symposium, Thessalonike, October 15–19, 1996, 1031–45. Thessalonike.

Smith, A. H., and F. N. Pryce. 1926. *CVA: Great Britain 2, British Museum 2.* London.

Snodgrass, A. M. 1967. *Arms and Armour of the Greeks.* London.

Sourvinou-Inwood, C. 1985. "Altars with Palm-Trees, Palm-Trees, and *Parthenoi.*" *BICS* 32, 125–46.

Sourvinou-Inwood, C. 1987. "A Series of Erotic Pursuits: Images and Meanings." *JHS* 107, 131–53.

Stansbury-O'Donnell, M. D. 1990. "Polygnotos's *Nekyia*: A Reconstruction and Analysis." *AJA* 94, 213–35.

Stansbury-O'Donnell, M. D. 1999. *Pictorial Narrative in Ancient Greek Art.* Cambridge.

Stein-Hölkeskamp, E. 1989. *Adelskultur und Polis-gesellschaft: Studien zum griechischen Adel in archaischer und klassischer Zeit.* Stuttgart.

Stein-Hölkeskamp, E. 1992. "Lebensstil als Selbstdarstellung: Aristokraten beim Symposion." In I. Wehgartner, ed., *Euphronios und seine Zeit, Kolloquium in Berlin 19./20. April 1991,* 39–48. Berlin.

Steiner, A. 1993. "The Meaning of Repetition: Visual Redundancy on Archaic Athenian Vases." *JdI* 108, 197–219.

Steiner, A. 1997. "Illustrious Repetitions: Visual Redundancy in Exekias and His Followers." In J. H. Oakley, W. E. D. Coulson, and O. Palagia, eds., *Athenian Potters and Painters: The Conference Proceedings,* 157–69. Oxford.

Steiner, A. 2000. *The Meaning of Repetition: Redundancy on Athenian Vases.* Unpublished manuscript.

Stewart, A. 1977. *Skopas of Paros.* Park Ridge, N.J.

Stewart, A. 1983. "Stesichoros and the François Vase." In W. G. Moon, ed., *Ancient Greek Art and Iconography,* 53–74. Madison.

Stewart, A. 1986. "When Is a Kouros Not an Apollo? The Tenea 'Apollo' Revisited." In M. A. Del Chiaro, ed., *Corinthiaca: Studies in Honor of Darrell A. Amyx,* 54–70. Columbia.

Stewart, A. 1990. *Greek Sculpture: An Exploration.* New Haven and London.

Stewart, A. 1997. *Art, Desire, and the Body in Ancient Greece.* Cambridge.

Stibbe, C. M. 1972. *Lakonische Vasenmaler des sechsten Jahrhunderts v. Chr.* Amsterdam and London.

Stibbe, C. M. 1976. "Neue Fragmente lakonischer Schalen aus Cerveteri." *Meded* 38, 7–16.

Sutton, R. F., Jr. 1992. "Pornography and Persuasion on Attic Pottery." In A. Richlin, ed., *Pornography and Representation in Greece and Rome,* 3–35. Oxford.

Taylor, M. 1991. *The Tyrant Slayers: The Heroic Image in Fifth Century B.C. Athenian Art and Politics.* 2d ed. Salem, N.H.

Thiersch, H. 1907. "Gjölbaschi und lykisches Muterrecht." *JdI* 22, 235–40.

Thönges-Stringaris, R. N. 1965. "Das griechische Totenmahl." *AM* 80, 1–99.

Tiverios, M. 1997. "Die von Xenophantos Athenaios signierte grosse Lekythos aus

Pantikapaion: Alte Funde neu betrachtet." In J. H. Oakley, W. E. D. Coulson, and O. Palagia, eds., *Athenian Potters and Painters: The Conference Proceedings*, 269–84. Oxford.

Trakosopoulou-Salakiou, E. 1999. "Apo ten epeisakte Keramike tes archaikes Akanthou." In *Ancient Macedonia* 6, Papers Read at the Sixth International Symposium, Thessalonike, October 15–19, 1996, 1197–1217. Thessalonike.

Trendall, A. D. 1977. "Callisto in Apulian Vase-Painting." *AntK* 20, 99–101.

Trendall, A. D. 1984. "Arkas." *LIMC* 2:609–10. Zurich and Munich.

Trendall, A. D., and A. Cambitoglou. 1982. *The Red-Figured Vases of Apulia*. Oxford.

Trendall, A. D., and T. B. L. Webster. 1971. *Illustrations of Greek Drama*. London.

Tripodi, B. 1991. "Il Fregio della *caccia* della II Tomba reale di Vergina e le cacce funerarie d'oriente." *Dialogues d'histoire ancienne* 17:1, 143–209.

Tyrrell, W. B. 1984. *Amazons: A Study in Athenian Mythmaking*. Baltimore and London.

Verbanck-Piérard, A. 1981. "Un Cortège de l'Athènes archaïque: L'amphora à figures noires du peintre de Bucci." *Les Cahiers de Mariemont: Bulletin du Musée royal de Mariemont* 12, 5–36.

Vernant. J.-P. 1988. *Myth and Society in Ancient Greece*. Trans. J. Lloyd. New York.

Vernant. J.-P. 1991. *Mortals and Immortals*. Ed. F. I. Zeitlin. Princeton.

Vernant, J.-P., and P. Vidal-Naquet, eds. 1988. *Myth and Tragedy in Ancient Greece*. Trans. J. Lloyd. New York.

Vickers, M., and D. Gill. 1994. *Artful Crafts: Ancient Greek Silverware and Pottery*. Oxford.

Vidal-Naquet, P. 1981a. "The Black Hunter and the Origin of the Athenian Ephebeia." In R. L. Gordon, ed., *Myth, Religion, and Society*, 147–62. Cambridge.

Vidal-Naquet, P. 1981b. "Recipes for Greek Adolescence." In R. L. Gordon, ed., *Myth, Religion, and Society*, 163–85. Cambridge.

Vidal-Naquet, P. 1984. "Alessandro e i cacciatori neri." *Studi storici* 25:1, 25–33.

Vidal-Naquet, P. 1986. *The Black Hunter*. Trans. A. Szegedy-Maszak. Baltimore and London.

Vidal-Naquet, P. 1988a. "Hunting and Sacrifice in Aeschylus' *Oresteia*." In J.-P. Vernant and P. Vidal-Naquet, eds., *Myth and Tragedy in Ancient Greece*, 141–59. Trans. J. Lloyd. New York.

Vidal-Naquet, P. 1988b. "Retour au chasseur noir." In M. Marie-Madeleine and G. Évelyne, eds., *Mélanges Pierre Lévêque*, 2:387–411. Paris.

Vidal-Naquet, P. 1988c. "Sophocles' *Philoctetes* and the Ephebeia." In J.-P. Vernant and P. Vidal-Naquet, eds., *Myth and Tragedy in Ancient Greece*, 161–79. Trans. J. Lloyd. New York.

Villard, F. 1954. *CVA*: France 17, Louvre 10. Paris.

Völcker-Janssen, W. 1993. *Kunst und Gesellschaft an den Höfen Alexanders d.Gr. und seiner Nachfolger*. Munich.

Von Bothmer, D. 1948. "An Attic Black-Figured Dinos." *BMFA* 44, 42–48.

Von Bothmer, D. 1957. *Amazons in Greek Art*. Oxford.

Von Bothmer, D. 1984. "A Greek and Roman Treasury." *BMMA* 42.

Von Bothmer, D., ed. 1990. *Glories of the Past: Ancient Art from the Shelby White and Leon Levy Collection*. New York.

Vos, M. F. 1963. *Scythian Archers in Archaic Attic Vase-Painting*. Groningen.

Walters, H. B. 1931. *CVA*: Great Britain 8, British Museum 6. London.

Wathelet, P. 1986. "Homère, Lykaon, et le rituel du mont Lycée." In J. Ries, ed., *Les rites d'initiation*, 285–97. Actes du colloque de Liège et de Louvain-la-Neuve, 20–21 November 1984. Louvain-la-Neuve.

Weicker, G. 1905. "Hähne auf Grabstelen." *AM* 30, 207–212.

West, M. L. 1985. *The Hesiodic Catalogue of Women: Its Nature, Structure, and Origins*. Oxford.

Wilamowitz-Moellendorff, U. von. 1985. *Aristoteles und Athen*. 1893. 3d ed. Hildesheim.

Williams, D. 1983. "Sophilos in the British Museum." In J. Frel and S. K. Morgan, eds., *Greek Vases in the J. Paul Getty Museum* 1:9–34. Malibu, Calif.

Winkler, J. J. 1990. "The Ephebes' Song: *Tragoidia* and *Polis*." In J. J. Winkler and F. I. Zeitlin, eds., *Nothing to Do with Dionysus?* 20–62. Princeton.

Woodford, S. 1992. "Meleagros." *LIMC* 6:414–35. Zurich and Munich.

Wotke, F. 1949. "Panther." *RE* 36:2, 747–67.

Zeitlin, F. I. 1978. "The Dynamics of Misogyny: Myth and Mythmaking in the Oresteia." *Arethusa* 11, 149–83.

Zeitlin, F. I. 1982. "Cultic Models of the Female: Rites of Dionysos and Demeter." *Arethusa* 15, 129–57.

Zeitlin, F. I. 1985. "The Power of Aphrodite: Eros and the Boundaries of the Self in the *Hippolytus*." In P. Burian, ed., *Directions in Euripidean Criticism: A Collection of Essays*, 52–111. Durham.

Zeitlin, F. I. 1986. "Configurations of Rape in Greek Myth." In S. Tomaselli and R. Porter, eds., *Rape*, 122–51. Oxford.

Zlotogorska, M. 1997. *Darstellungen von Hunden auf griechischen Grabreliefs: Von der Archaik bis in die römische Kaiserzeit*. Hamburg.

INDEX OF ANCIENT CITATIONS

INDEX OF OBJECTS

GENERAL INDEX